THE LAST PAGAN EMPEROR

THE LAST PAGAN EMPEROR

Julian the Apostate and the War against Christianity

H. C. Teitler

OXFORD
UNIVERSITY PRESS

OXFORD
UNIVERSITY PRESS

Oxford University Press is a department of the University of Oxford. It furthers the University's objective of excellence in research, scholarship, and education by publishing worldwide. Oxford is a registered trade mark of Oxford University Press in the UK and certain other countries.

Published in the United States of America by Oxford University Press
198 Madison Avenue, New York, NY 10016, United States of America.

First issued as an Oxford University Press paperback, 2020

Originally published as *Julianus de Afvallige* by H.C. Teitler, Copyright © 2009
First published in 2009 by Athenaeum—Polak & Van Gennep, Amsterdam

Library of Congress Cataloging-in-Publication Data
Names: Teitler, H. C., author.
Title: The last pagan emperor : Julian the Apostate and the war against Christianity /
H. C. Teitler.
Other titles: Julianus de Afvallige. English
Description: New York : Oxford University Press, 2017. | Includes bibliographical
references and index.
Identifiers: LCCN 2016027844 | ISBN 9780190626501 (hardback) | ISBN
9780197540732 (paperback) |ISBN 9780190626525 (epub) |
ISBN 9780190626532 (online component)
Subjects: LCSH: Julian, Emperor of Rome, 331–363—Religion. | Church and state—
Rome. | Church history—Primitive and early church, ca. 30–600. | Paganism—Rome.
Classification: LCC DG317 .T4513 2017 | DDC 937/.08092 [B]—dc23 LC record
available at https://lccn.loc.gov/2016027844

1 3 5 7 9 8 6 4 2
Printed by Sheridan Books, Inc., United States of America

In memory of Rik van der Steeg

CONTENTS

Μέγα βιβλίον, μέγα κακόν
'A big book is a big misfortune'
Callimachus, *fr.* 465 Pfeiffer, trans. A. W. Bulloch

PREFACE

My interest in trying to gain an in-depth knowledge of the conflict between Christians and pagans during the reign of the Emperor Julian, and in particular of its aftermath, stems from reading Gaiffier's '"Sub Iuliano Apostata" dans le Martyrologe Romain' ('"Julian the Apostate" in the Roman Martyrology').

I came across Gaiffier's revelatory article, which appeared in 1956, at the end of the 1980s, but my acquaintance with the Apostate dates from the days when, as a student, I read Gore Vidal's novel *Julian* (1964). In the 1960s the history of Late Antiquity and its civilization were hardly taught at the University of Amsterdam. However, A. D. Leeman, my professor of Latin and a genuine *vir Ciceronianus*, advised me to read at least one book of Ammianus Marcellinus, in order to discover how ugly the style of this fourth-century historian is. Many years later, when I became a member of the Dutch team of commentators on Ammianus' *Res Gestae* (so far eleven volumes have appeared), I renewed my acquaintance with both Ammianus and Julian: Books 20 through 25 of the *Res Gestae* are mainly concerned with Julian's rise to supreme power, his brief reign as sole emperor (361–363 CE), and his untimely death during his ill-starred Persian campaign.

The literature on the apostate emperor, by scholars as well as by nonspecialists, is quite extensive. Elm's book (2012) deserves pride of place. There are also fine biographies: Bidez (1930), Browning (1976), Bowersock (1978), Bringmann (2004), and, above all, Rosen (2006). I should therefore make it clear from the outset that my book is not a biography in the proper sense, and that there are several important aspects of Julian's rule that I shall either not address at all or touch on only in passing. This book focuses on that aspect of the Apostate's reign which earned him his nickname: Julian's relationship with the Christians. In his attempt to revive paganism the emperor incurred the profound hatred of the Christians, who often, especially after his death, accused him of being a bloodthirsty persecutor. This hatred found a special expression in what the Belgian scholar Hippolyte Delehaye has called 'passions épiques,' that is, tales of sufferings that are chiefly fictitious. I shall make more use of these texts than most others have done in books about Julian.

Without my work on Ammianus this book could not have been written. I am therefore grateful to my fellow *viri Ammianei*, Jan den Boeft, Daniël den Hengst, and Jan Willem Drijvers, who are not only wonderful colleagues, but also good friends. Thanks are also due to still older friends, to Jan Bremmer, who stimulated me to make a translation of the text that originally, although in a shorter form, appeared in Dutch, and to Ines van de Wetering, who corrected my English. I thank Erika Manders for her help in numismatic matters, and Daniël den Hengst and Raphael Brendel for their corrections. To the latter I also owe many bibliographical suggestions and additions. Finally and above all, I express gratitude to my Geertje for more than thirty years of love and support.

LIST OF ABBREVIATIONS

AASS	*Acta Sanctorum,* ed. H. Rosweyde, J. Bolland et al., 68 vols., Antwerp and Brussels: 1643–1940.
Act.	*Acta Apostolorum.*
AE	*L'Année Épigraphique,* Paris: 1888–.
Ambrosiast. *Comm. II Thess.*	Ambrosiaster's Commentary to Paul's Second Letter to the Thessalonians. *Ambrosiastri qui dicitur Commentarius in Epistulas Paulinas,* ed. H. J. Vogels, V. Bulhart, and R. Hanslik (CSEL 81, pt. 1–3). Vienna: 1966.
Ambr. *Ep.*	Ambrosius, *Epistulae et acta,* ed. O. Faller (CSEL 82), Vienna: 1968.
Ambr. *Obit. Valent.*	Ambrosius, *De Obitu Valentiniani,* ed. O. Faller (CSEL 73), Vienna: 1955.
Amm.	*Ammiani Marcellini rerum gestarum libri qui supersunt,* ed. W. Seyfarth, with L. Jacob-Karau

and I. Ulmann (Bibliotheca Scriptorum
Graecorum et Romanorum Teubneriana), 2 vols.,
Leipzig: 1978; *Ammianus Marcellinus, with
an English Translation*, ed. J. C. Rolfe, 3 vols.,
Cambridge, MA, and London: 1935–1939;
Ammien Marcellin, Histoire (Collection des
Universités de France), Introduction, Texte,
Traduction, Notes, I (*Livres XIV–XVI*), ed.
E. Galletier, avec la collaboration de J. Fontaine,
Paris: 1978²; II (*Livres XVII–XIX*), ed. G. Sabbah,
Paris: 1970; III (*Livres XX–XII*), ed. J. Fontaine,
avec la collaboration de E. Frézouls et J.-D. Berger,
Paris: 1996; IV.1 and IV.2 (*Livres XXIII–XXV*),
ed. J. Fontaine, Paris: 1977; V (*Livres XXVI–
XXVIII*), ed. M.-A. Marié, Paris: 1984; VI (*Livres
XXIX–XXXI*), ed. G. Sabbah (Introduction,
Texte, et Traduction) and L. Angliviel de la
Beaumelle (Notes), Paris: 1999.

Art. pass.   *Artemii passio* (BHG 170–171c), ed. B. Kotter,
in B. Kotter, *Die Schriften des Johannes von
Damaskos V: Opera homiletica et hagiographica*
(Patristische Texte und Studien 29), Berlin and
New York: 1988, 185–245; [John the Monk],
Artemii passio (The Ordeal of Artemius,
BHG 170–71c, CPG 8082), translated by M.
Vermes, in S. N. C. Lieu and D. Montserrat,
*From Constantine to Julian. Pagan and Byzantine
Views: A Source History*, London and New York:
1996, 224–256 (with notes by S. N. C. Lieu,
256–262).

Athan. Hist. Ar.   Athanasius, *Historia Arianorum; Athanasius
Werke*, 2.1, ed. H.-G. Opitz, Berlin: 1940.

Athan. *Fest. Ind.*	Athanasius, *Index to the Festal Epistles; Histoire 'Acéphale' et Index Syriaque des Lettres Festales d'Athanase d'Alexandrie*, Introduction, texte critique, traduction, et notes, A. Martin, avec la collaboration de M. Albert (SC 317), Paris: 1985.
Athenag. *Leg.*	*Athenagoras. Legatio and De Resurrectione*, ed. W. R. Schoedel, Oxford: 1972.
August. *Civ.*	Augustinus, *De Civitate Dei*, ed. B. Dombart and A. Kalb (CCSL 47, 48), Turnhout, Belgium: 1955.
August. *Conf.*	Augustinus, *Confessiones*, ed. L. Verhijen (CCSL 27), Turnhout, Belgium: 1981.
August. *C. Ep. Parm.*	Augustinus, *Contra Epistulam Parmeniani*, ed. M. Petschenig (CSEL 51), Vienna: 1908.
August. *C. Litt. Petil.*	Augustinus, *Contra Litteras Petiliani*, ed. M. Petschenig (CSEL 52), Vienna: 1909.
August. *Doctr.*	Augustinus, *De doctrina christiana*, ed. W. M. Green (CSEL 80), Berlin: 1963.
August. *Enarr. in Ps.*	Augustinus, *Enarrationes in Psalmos*, ed. E. Dekkers et al. (CCSL 38–40), Turnhout, Belgium: 1956 (repr. 1990).
August. *Ep.*	Augustinus, *Epistulae*, ed. A. Goldbacher (CSEL 33, 44, 57), Vienna: 1895–1923.
Aur. Vict. *Caes.*	*Aurelius Victor, Livre des Césars*, texte établi et traduit par P. Dufraigne (Collection des Universités de France), Paris: 1975.
Basil. *Ep.*	Basilius Caesariensis, *Epistulae*, ed. R. J. Deferrari, *Saint Basil. The Letters* (The Loeb Classical Library), 4 vols., Cambridge, MA: 1926–1934.

Basil. pass.	*Passio s. Basilii presbyteri* (BHG 242), ed. J. Carnandet, *Acta Sanctorum Martii tomus III*, Paris: 1865, *12–*15.
BHG	*Bibliotheca Hagiographica Graeca*, ed. F. Halkin (Subsidia Hagiographica 8), Brussels: 1957[3]; *Novum Auctarium Bibliothecae Hagiographicae Graecae* (Subsidia Hagiographica 65), Brussels: 1984.
BHL	*Bibliotheca Hagiographica Latina Antiquae et Mediae Aetatis* (Subsidia Hagiographica 6), Brussels: 1898–1901; *Novum Supplementum*, ed. H. Fros (Subsidia Hagiographica 7), Brussels: 1986.
BHO	*Bibliotheca Hagiographica Orientalis* (Subsidia Hagiographica 10), Brussels: 1910.
Bon. pass.	*Passio ss. Bonosi et Maximiliani militum, de numero Herculianorum seniorum sub Iuliano imperatore et Iuliano comite eius, sub die XII kalendas Octobres* (BHL 1427), ed. Th. Ruinart, *Acta primorum martyrum sincera et selecta*, Paris: 1689, 664–668.
Cassiod. *Hist. tripart.*	Cassiodorus, *Historia tripartita*, ed. W. Jacob and R. Hanslik (CSEL 71), Vienna: 1952.
CCSL	Corpus Christianorum Scriptorum Latinorum.
Cedren.	Georgius Cedrenus, *Compendium historiarum*, ed. I. Bekker, Ioannis Scylitzae ope (CSHB), 2 vols., Bonn, Germany: 1838–1839.

Chron. Min.	Chronica Minora saec. IV.V.VI.VII, ed. Th. Mommsen (MGH Auctores Antiquissimi 13), Berlin: 1898 (repr. 1986).
Chron. Pasch.	Chronicon Paschale, ed. L. Dindorf (CSHB), Bonn: 1832; Chronicon Paschale 284–628 AD, translated with Notes and Introduction, M. Whitby and M. Whitby (Translated Texts for Historians 7), Liverpool, UK: 1989.
Chrys. Exp. in Ps.	Johannes Chrysostomus, Expositiones in Psalmos quosdam; PG 55, 39–498.
Chrys. Hom. in Mt.	Johannes Chrysostomus, Homiliae in Matthaeum; PG 57, 1857–1866.
Chrys. Jud.	Johannes Chrysostomus, Adversus Judaeos; PG 48, 843–942.
Chrys. Laud. Paul.	Johannes Chrysostomus, De Laudibus Pauli; Jean Chrysostome. Panégyrique de S. Paul, ed. A. Piedagnel (SC 300), Paris: 1982.
Chrys. Laz.	Johannes Chrysostomus, In Lazarum; PG 48, 963–1054.
Chrys. Oppugn.	Johannes Chrysostomus, Adversus oppugnatores vitae monasticae; PG 47, 319–386; A Comparison between a King and a Monk/Against the Opponents of the Monastic Life: Two Treatises by John Chrysostom, translated with an Introduction, D. G. Hunter (Studies in the Bible and Early Christianity 13), Lewiston, NY: 1988.
Chrys. Pan. Bab. 1 and Pan. Bab. 2	Johannes Chrysostomus, De sancto hieromartyre Babyla (Panegyricus in Babylam martyrem); Jean Chrysostome, Discours sur Babylas. Introduction, texte

critique, traduction, et notes, ed. M. A. Schatkin,
avec la collaboration de C. Blanc et B. Grillet,
suivi de *Homélie sur Babylas*. Introduction, texte
critique, traduction, et notes, ed. B. Grillet et J.-
N. Guinot (SC 362), Paris: 1990.

Chrys. *Pan. Juv.*   Johannes Chrysostomus, *Panegyricus in
Juventinum et Maximinum martyres;* PG 50,
571–578; *Panégyriques de martyrs* (vol. 1), 178–
211, ed. N. Rambault and P. Allen (SC 595),
Paris: 2018.

CIL   *Corpus Inscriptionum Latinarum*

Consul. Constant.   *Consularia Constantinopolitana* (see *Chronica
Minora*).

Conti 2004   S. Conti, *Die Inschriften Kaiser Julians*
(Altertumswissenschaftliches Kolloquium.
Interdisziplinäre Studien zur Antike und zu
ihrem Nachleben 10), Stuttgart: 2004.

CPG   Clavis Patrum Graecorum.

CSEL   Corpus Scriptorum Ecclesiasticorum Latinorum.

CSHB   Corpus Scriptorum Historiae Byzantinae.

CTh   *Codex Theodosianus; Theodosiani libri XVI cum
constitutionibus Sirmondianis et leges novellae
ad Theodosianum pertinentes, 1.2,* Textus cum
apparatu, ed. Th. Mommsen, Berlin: 1905
(1962³); *The Theodosian Code and Novels and
the Sirmondian Constitutions: A Translation with
Commentary, Glossary, and Bibliography,* ed.
C. Pharr, New York: 1952; *Les lois religieuses des
empereurs Romains de Constantin à Theodose II
(312–438), I, Code Théodosien Livre XVI,* Texte
Latin Th. Mommsen, Traduction J. Rougé,
Introduction et notes R. Delmaire

avec la collaboration de F. Richard (SC 497),
Paris: 2005.

Dig.   *Digesta*, ed. Th. Mommsen and P. Krueger, in
                Corpus Iuris Civilis editio stereotypa undecima,
                volumen primum, Berlin: 1908.

Domet. pass.   *Acta graeca S. Dometii martyris* (BHG 560), ed.
                [J. van den Gheyn], *Analecta Bollandiana* 19
                (1900): 285–320.

Eliph. pass.   *Passio s. Eliphii martyris* (BHL 2481), in *Acta*
                Sanctorum Octobris tomus VII, Paris: 1845, 812–815.

Ephr. cJul.   Ephraem Syrus, *Contra Iulianum; Ephrem the Syrian,*
                Hymns against Julian, Introduction
                (S. N. C. Lieu), Translation (M. M. Morgan),
                Notes (S. N. C. Lieu), in S. N. C. Lieu, *The Emperor*
                Julian: Panegyric and Polemic (Translated Texts for
                Historians, Greek Series 1), Liverpool, UK: 1986
                (1989²); *Hymnes contre les hérésies* (vol. 2): *Hymnes*
                contre les hérésies XXX–LVI, hymnes contre Julien, ed.
                E. Beck and D. Cerbelaud (SC 590), Paris: 2017.

Eugen. pass.   *La passion grecque des saints Eugène et Macaire*
                (BHG 2126), ed. F. Halkin, *Analecta Bollandiana* 78
                (1960): 41–52.

Eun. Fr.   Eunapius, *Fragmenta; The Fragmentary Classicising*
                Historians of the Later Roman Empire: Eunapius,
                Olympiodorus, Priscus and Malchus, ed. R. C.Blockley,
                2 vols. (ARCA Classical and Medieval Texts, Papers
                and Monographs 6 and 10), Liverpool, UK: 1981–1983.

Eun. VS   Eunapius, *Vitae Sophistarum; Eunapii vitae*
                sophistarum, ed. G. Giangrande, Rome: 1956;
                Eunapio di Sardi: Vitae di Filosofi e Sofisti; Testo
                greco a fronte, introduzione, traduzione, note e
                apparati, ed. M. Civiletti, Milan: 2007; *Eunapios*

	aus Sardes. Biographien über Philosophen und Sophisten. Einleitung, Übersetzung, Kommentar, M. Becker (Roma Aeterna 1), Stuttgart: 2013.
Eupsych. pass.	*La passion inédite de Saint Eupsychius* (BHG 2130), ed. F. Halkin, *Le Muséon* 97 (1984): 197–206.
Eus. *HE*	*Eusèbe de Césarée: Histoire ecclésiastique*, ed. G. Bardy, 3 vols. (SC 31, 41, 55), Paris: 1952–1958.
Eus. *VC*	*Eusebius Werke, 1.1: Über das Leben des Kaisers Konstantin*, ed. F. Winkelmann (Die Griechischen Christlichen Schriftsteller), Berlin: 1975.
Eusign. pass.	*Une recension nouvelle de la passion Grecque BHG 639 de saint Eusignios*, ed. P. Devos, *Analecta Bollandiana* 100 (1982): 209–228.
Eutr.	*Eutropii Breviarium ab urbe condita*, ed. C. Santini (Bibliotheca Scriptorum Graecorum et Romanorum Teubneriana), Leipzig: 1979; *Eutrope, Abrégé de l'histoire romaine*, ed. J. Hellegouarc'h (Collection des Universités de France), Paris: 1999; *The Breviarium ab urbe condita of Eutropius, dedicated to Lord Valens, Gothicus Maximus and Perpetual Emperor*, translated with an Introduction and Commentary by H. W. Bird (Translated Texts for Historians 14), Liverpool, UK: 1993; *Eutropio: Storia di Roma*, introduzione di F. Gasti, traduzione e note di F. Bordone. Testo latino a fronte (Grandi Classici Greci Latini), Santarcangelo di Romagna, Italy: 2014.
Evagr.	*The Ecclesiastical History of Evagrius with the Scholia*, ed. J. Bidez and L. Parmentier, London: 1898; *The Ecclesiastical History of Evagrius*

	Scholasticus, ed. M. Whitby (Translated Texts for Historians 33), Liverpool, UK: 2000.
Greg. Naz. *Or.* 4 and 5	*Grégoire de Nazianze, Discours 4–5, Contre Julien.* Introduction, texte critique, traduction, et notes, ed. J. Bernardi (SC 309), Paris: 1983; *Gregor von Nazianz, Oratio 4, Gegen Julian. Ein Kommentar,* ed. A. Kurmann (Schweizerische Beiträge zur Altertumswissenschaft 19), Basel, Switzerland: 1988; *Gregorio di Nazianzo, Contra Giuliano l'Apostata: Oratio IV,* ed. L. Lugaresi (Biblioteca Patristica 23), Florence: 1993; *Gregorio di Nazianzo, La morte di Giuliano l'Apostata: Oratio V,* ed. L. Lugaresi (Biblioteca Patristica 29), Florence: 1997.
Greg. Naz. *Or.* 18	Gregorius Nazianzenus, *Funebris oratio in patrem,* PG 35, 985–1044.
Greg. Naz. *Or.* 21	*Grégoire de Nazianze. Discours 20–23,* ed. J. Mossay (SC 270), Paris: 1980.
Greg. Naz. *Or.* 36	Gregorius Nazianzenus, *De se ipso,* PG 36, 265–279.
Greg. Nyss. *Deit.*	Gregorius Nyssenus, *De deitate Filii et Spiritus Sancti;* PG 46, 553–576.
Greg. Tur. *Mir.*	Gregorius Turonensis, *Miracula,* ed. W. Arndt and B. Krusch (MGH Scriptores rerum Merovingicarum 1), Hannover, Germany: 1885 (repr. 1969).
Hdt.	Herodotus, *Historiae.*
Hier. *Chron.*	*Die Chronik des Hieronymus,* ed. R. W. O. Helm, Berlin: 1984[3].

Hier. *Ep.*	Hieronymus, *Epistulae*, ed. I. Hilberg (CSEL 54–55), Vienna: 1910–1912.
Hier. *In Hab.*	Hieronymus, *In Habacuc prophetam,* in *Commentarii in prophetas minores,* ed. M. Adriaen (CCSL 76–76A), Turnhout, Belgium: 1964–1969.
Hier. *In Zach.*	Hieronymus, *In Zachariam prophetam,* in *Commentarii in prophetas minores,* ed. M. Adriaen (CCSL 76–76A), Turnhout, Belgium: 1964–1969.
Hil. *Lib. Const.*	Hilarius Pictaviensis, *Liber ad Constantium,* ed. A. L. Feder (CSEL 65), Vienna: 1916.
Him. *Or.*	*Himerii declamationes et orationes cum deperditarum fragmentis,* ed. A. Colonna, Rome: 1951.
Hist. *Aceph.*	*Historia Acephala; Histoire 'Acéphale' et Index Syriaque des Lettres Festales d'Athanase d'Alexandrie,* Introduction, texte critique, traduction, et notes, A. Martin, avec la collaboration de M. Albert (SC 317), Paris: 1985.
IK	*Inschriften griechischer Städte aus Kleinasien,* Bonn, Germany: 1972–.
ILAlg	*Inscriptions Latines de l'Algérie,* Paris and Algiers: 1922–1976.
ILJug	*Inscriptiones Latinae quae in Jugoslavia inter annos MCMII et MCMXL repertae et editae sunt,* Ljubljana, Slovenia: 1986.
ILS	*Inscriptiones Latinae Selectae,* ed. H. Dessau, Berlin: 1892–1916 (repr. Chicago: 1979).
Jn.	*The Gospel according to John.*
Jo. Ant.	*Fragmenta ex Historia chronica; Ioannis Antiocheni fragmenta ex Historia chronica,*

introduzione, edizione critica, e traduzione a cura
di U. Roberto (Texte und Untersuchungen zur
Geschichte der altchristlichen Literatur 154),
Berlin: 2005; *Ioannis Antiocheni fragmenta quae
supersunt omnia*, recensuit Anglice vertit indicibus
instruxit S. Mariev (Corpus Fontium Historiae
Byzantinae 47, Series Berolinensis), Berlin: 2008.

Jo. Mal. *Chronica; Ioannis Malalae Chronographia*, ed.
H. Thurn (Corpus Fontium Historiae Byzantinae
35), Berlin: 2000; *Johannes Malalas, Weltchronik*,
ed. H. Thurn and C. Drosihn (Bibliothek der
Griechischen Literatur 69), Stuttgart: 2009; *The
Chronicle of Malalas: A Translation*, by E. Jeffreys,
M. Jeffreys and R. Scott (Byzantina Australiensia 4),
Melbourne, Australia: 1986.

Jul. *Imp. Caesaris Flavii Claudii Iuliani: Epistulae Leges
Poemata Fragmenta Varia*, ed. J. Bidez and F. Cumont,
Paris: 1922; *The Works of the Emperor Julian, with
an English Translation*, ed. W. C. Wright, 3 vols.,
Cambridge, MA, and London: 1913–1923; *L'empereur
Julien: Oeuvres complètes*, ed. J. Bidez, G. Rochefort,
and Chr. Lacombrade (Collection des Universités de
France), 4 vols., Paris: 1924–1964; *Iulianus Augustus
Opera*, ed. H.-G. Nesselrath (Bibliotheca Scriptorum
Graecorum et Romanorum Teubneriana 2018),
Berlin: 2015; *Julianus de Afvallige: Afvallige contra
afvalligen: Keuze uit zijn geschriften*. Keuze, vertaling,
en inleiding K. Meiling (Grieks Proza 30), Groningen,
The Netherlands: 2016.

Jul. Caes. *Die beiden Satiren des Kaisers Julianus Apostata
(Symposion oder Caesares und Antiochikos oder
Misopogon)*. Griechisch und Deutsch, mit

	Einleitung, Anmerkungen, und Index, ed. F. L. Müller (Palingenesia 66), Stuttgart: 1998; *Giuliano Imperatore, Simposio, i Cesari.* Edizione critica, traduzione, e commento, ed. R. Sardiello (Testi e Studi 12), Galatina, Italy: 2000.
Jul. *C. Gal.*	*Giuliano Imperatore: Contra Galilaeos.* Introduzione, testo critico, e traduzione, ed. E. Masaracchia (Testi e Commenti 9), Rome: 1990; *Julian's Against the Galileans,* ed. and trans. R. J. Hoffmann, New York: 2004.
Jul. *Ep.*	*Julian. Briefe,* Griechisch-deutsch, ed. B. K. Weis (Tusculum-Bücherei), Munich: 1973; *L'Epistolario di Giuliano Imperatore.* Saggio storico, traduzione, note, e testo in appendice, ed. M. Caltabiano (Koinonia. Collana di Studi e Testi 14), Naples, Italy: 1991.
Jul. *Ep. ad Ath.*	Julianus Imperator, *Epistula ad Athenienses: Kaiser Julian, An den Senat und das Volk der Athener.* Einleitung, Übersetzung, und Kommentar, ed. S. Stöcklin-Kaldewey, *Klio* 97 (2015): 687–725.
Jul. *Ep. ad Themist.*	Julianus Imperator, *Epistula ad Themistium.*
Jul. *Misop.*	*Giuliano Imperatore, Misopogon.* Edizione critica, traduzione, e commento, ed. C. Prato and D. Micalella (Testi e Commenti 5), Rome: 1979.
Jul. *Or.* 1 (Bidez)	*La prima orazione di Giuliano a Costanzo.* Introduzione, traduzione, e commento, ed. I. Tantillo (Saggi di Storia Antica 10), Rome: 1997.

Jul. *Or.* 2 (Bidez)	*Giuliano l'Apostata, Elogio dell'imperatrice Eusebia (Orazione II)*, Introduzione, traduzione, e note, ed. S. Angiolani, Naples, Italy: 2008; *Giuliano Imperatore, Elogio dell'imperatrice Eusebia,* testo critico e commento a cura di A. Filippo Scognamillo; introduzione e indici a cura di M. Ugenti (Testi e Commenti 29), Pisa, Italy: 2016.
Jul. *Or.* 8 (Rochefort)	*Giuliano Imperatore: Alla madre degli dei e altri discorsi.* Introduzione di J. Fontaine, testo critico a cura di C. Prato, traduzione e commento di A. Marcone, Vicenza, Italy: 1987; *Giuliano Imperatore: Alla madre degli dei.* Edizione critica, traduzione e commento, ed. V. Ugenti (Testi e Studi 6), Galatina, Italy: 1992.
Jul. *Or.* 9 (Rochefort)	*Giuliano Imperatore, Contro i Cinici ignoranti.* Edizione critica, traduzione, e commento, ed. C. Prato and D. Micalella (Studi e Testi Latini e Greci 4), Lecce, Italy: 1988.
Jul. *Or.* 11 (Lacombrade)	*Giuliano l'Apostata, Discorso su Helios re.* Testo, traduzione, e commento, ed. A. Mastrocinque (Studia Classica et Mediaevalia 5), Nordhausen, Germany: 2011.
Jul. Romance	*Iulianos der Abtruennige. Syrische Erzählungen,* ed. J. G. E. Hoffmann, Leiden, The Netherlands: 1880; *Julian*

the Apostate, Now Translated for the First Time from the Syriac Original (the Only Known Ms. in the British Museum, Edited by Hoffmann of Kiel), ed. H. Gollancz, Oxford: 1928.

Lact. *Mort. pers.*   Lactantius, *De mortibus persecutorum*, ed. J. L. Creed (Oxford Early Christian Texts), Oxford: 1984.

Lc.   *The Gospel according to Luke.*

Lib. *Ep.* and *Or.*   *Libanii opera*, ed. R. Foerster, 12 vols., Leipzig: 1903–1927 (repr. Hildesheim: 1963–1985); *Libanius. Selected Works*, with an English Translation, Introduction, and Notes, ed. A. F. Norman, 2 vols. (Loeb Classical Library), Cambridge, MA, and London: 1969–1977; *Libanios, Briefe*, Griechisch-deutsch. In Auswahl herausgegeben, übersetzt und erläutert von G. Fatouros und T. Krischer (Tusculum-Bücherei), Munich: 1979; *Libanius. Autobiography and Selected Letters*, ed. and transl. A. F. Norman, 2 vols. (Loeb Classical Library), Cambridge, MA, and London: 1992; *Libanio: Sulla vendetta di Giuliano (or. 24).* Testo, introduzione, traduzione, commentario, e appendice, ed. U. Criscuolo (Koinonia, Collana di Studi e Testi 15), Naples, Italy: 1994; *Libanios, Kaiserreden.* Eingeleitet, übersetzt, und kommentiert von G. Fatouros, T. Krischer, und W. Portmann (Bibliothek der Griechischen Literatur 58), Stuttgart 2002; *Selected Letters of Libanius from the Age of Constantius and Julian.* Translated with an Introduction, ed.

	S. Bradbury (Translated Texts for Historians 41), Liverpool, UK: 2004.
Macr. *Sat.*	Macrobius, *Saturnalia*, ed. J. Willis (Bibliotheca Scriptorum Graecorum et Romanorum Teubneriana), Leipzig: 1970² (repr. 1990).
Mamert. *Grat.*	Mamertinus, *Gratiarum actio de consulatu suo Iuliano imperatori; Discours de remerciement à Julien par Claude Mamertin (1ᵉʳ juin 362)*, in *Panégyriques Latins, t. III (XI–XII)*, texte établi et traduit par E. Galletier (Collection des Universités de France), Paris: 1955, 1–44.
Marc. pass.	*La passion de S. Marc d'Aréthuse* (BHG 2248), ed. F. Halkin, *Analecta Bollandiana* 103 (1985): 217–229.
Mc.	*The Gospel according to Mark.*
MGH	Monumenta Germaniae Historica.
Mir. Art.	*Miracula Artemii* (BHG 173–173c), ed. A. Papadopulos-Kerameus, in A. Papadopulos-Kerameus, *Varia Graeca Sacra*, St Petersburg, Russia: 1909, 1–75; *The Miracles of St. Artemius. A Collection of Miracle Stories by an Anonymous Author of Seventh-Century Byzantium. Text, English Translation, and Commentary*, ed. V. S. Crisafulli and J. W. Nesbitt (The Medieval Mediterranean 13), Leiden, The Netherlands, and New York: 1997.
Mt.	*The Gospel according to Matthew.*
NASB	New American Standard Bible.
Not. Dign. Occ.	*Notitia Dignitatum Occidentalis*, ed. O. Seeck, Berlin: 1876.
Opt.	*S. Optati Milevetani libri septem*, ed. C. Ziwsa (CSEL 26), Vienna: 1893; *Optatus: Against the*

Donatists, trans. and ed. M. Edwards (Translated
Texts for Historians 27), Liverpool, UK: 1997.

Pall. *H. Laus.*   *Palladio: La storia Lausiaca/Palladius
Helenopolitanus*, introduzione di Chr.
Mohrmann, testo critico e commento a cura di
G. J. M. Bartelink, traduzione di
M. Barchiesi (Vite dei Santi 2), Milan: 1985[3].

Par.   *Parastaseis syntomoi chronikai;
Constantinople in the Early Eighth
Century: The Parastaseis Syntomoi
Chronikai*. Introduction, Translation,
and Commentary, ed. Av. Cameron
and J. Herrin (Columbia Studies in the
Classical Tradition 10), Leiden, The
Netherlands: 1984.

Paul. Med. *V. Ambr.*   *Vita sancti Ambrosii Mediolanensis Episcopi,
a Paulino eius notario ad beatum Augustinum
conscripta*, a revised Text, and Commentary,
with an Introduction and Translation
by M. S. Kaniecka (Patristic Studies 16),
Washington, DC: 1928.

[Paul.] *Sent.*   *Pauli Sententiae*, testo e interpretatio
a cura di M. Bianchi Fossati Vanzetti
(Pubblicazioni della Facoltà di
Giurisprudenza della Università di Padova
130), Padova, Italy: 1995.

PBSR   *Papers of the British School at Rome.*

PCBE II.1   *Prosopographie Chrétienne du Bas-Empire,
2.1. Prosopographie de l'Italie Chrétienne
(313–604), vol. 1, A–K*, ed. J. Desmulliez,
Paris: 1999.

PCBE III — *Prosopographie Chrétienne du Bas-Empire, 3. Prosopographie du Diocèse d'Asie (325–641)*, ed. S. Destephen, Paris: 2008.

P. Fay. — *Fayûm Towns and Their Papyri*, ed. B. P. Grenfell, A. S. Hunt, and D. G. Hogarth, London: 1900.

PG — Patrologia Graeca; J.-P. Migne, *Patrologiae cursus completus (series Graeca)*, Paris: 1857–1866.

Philost. — *Philostorgius Kirchengeschichte, mit dem Leben des Lucian von Antiochien und den Fragmenten eines Arianischen Historiographen*, ed. J. Bidez and F. Winkelmann (Die Griechischen Christlichen Schriftsteller der ersten Jahrhunderte), Berlin: 1972²; *Philostorge. Histoire ecclésiastique*, texte critique J. Bidez, traduction É. Des Places, introduction, révision de la traduction, notes et index B. Bleckmann, D. Meyer, and J.-M. Prieur (SC 564), Paris: 2013; *Philostorgios Kirchengeschichte*, ed. B. Bleckmann and M. Stein (Kleine und fragmentarische Historiker der Spätantike, E 7) 2 vols., Paderborn, Germany: 2015; *The Ecclesiastical History of Philostorgius, as epitomised by Photius, Patriarch of Constantinople*, trans. E. Walford, London: 1855.

Phot. Bibl. — *Photii Bibliotheca*, ed. I. Bekker, 2 vols., Berlin: 1824–1825.

Pimen. pass. — *Passio sancti Pimenii* (BHL 6849, 6849a), in H. Delehaye, *Étude sur le légendier romain: Les saints de Novembre et de Décembre* (Subsidia Hagiographica 23), Brussels: 1936 (repr. 1968), 259–263.

PL — Patrologia Latina; J.-P. Migne, *Patrologiae cursus completus (series Latina)*, Paris: 1841–1865.

Plin. *Nat.*   Plinius, *Naturalis Historia.*

PLRE I   *The Prosopography of the Later Roman Empire* I, A.D.
250–395, ed. A. H. M. Jones, J. R. Martindale, and J.
Morris, Cambridge, UK: 1971.

P. Meyer   *Griechische Texte aus Ägypten,* ed. P. M. Meyer,
Berlin: 1916.

PO   Patrologia Orientalis, Paris and Turnhout,
Belgium: 1907–.

P. Oxy.   *The Oxyrhynchus papyri,* London: 1898–.

Prud. *Apoth.*   Prudentius, *Apotheosis,* testo critico,
traduzione, commento, e indici, ed. G. Garuti
and P. Garuti (Collana di Studi, Accademia
Nazionale di Scienze, Lettere e Arti Modena
26), Modena, Italy: 2005.

Ps.   *Psalms.*

RAC   Th. Klauser et al. (eds.), *Reallexikon für Antike
und Christentum,* Stuttgart: 1950 ff.

RE   G. Wissowa, W. Kroll et al. (eds.),
*Paulys Real-Encyclopädie der classischen
Altertumswissenschaft,* Stuttgart: 1893 ff.

RIC 8   J. P. C. Kent, *The Roman Imperial Coinage,*
VIII. *The Family of Constantine I, A.D.
337–364,* London: 1981.

Rufin. *HE*   *Eusebii Caesariensis Historia Ecclesiastica,
Rufini continuatio,* ed. Th. Mommsen, in
Eusebios, Werke II 2 (Die Griechischen
Christlichen Schriftsteller der ersten
Jahrhunderte 9.2), Berlin: 1908, 957–1040;
*The Church History of Rufinus of Aquileia.
Books 10 and 11,* trans. Ph. R. Amidon,
New York: 1997.

Rufin. *Hist. Mon.*   Rufinus, *Historia monachorum latine uersa et retractata*, ed. E. Schulz-Flügel (Patristische Texte und Studien 34), Berlin: 1990.

s. a.   *sub anno,* 'under the year'.

SC   Sources Chrétiennes.

SEG   *Supplementum Epigraphicum Graecum*, Leiden, The Netherlands: 1923–.

Serv. *Ecl.*   Servius, *Commentarius in Vergilii Eclogas vel Bucolica,* ed. G. B. Pighi, Turin, Italy: 1976.

SIG   *Sylloge Inscriptionum Graecarum*, ed. W. Dittenberger, 4 vols., Leipzig: 1915–1924³.

Socr.   *Sokrates Kirchengeschichte*, ed. G. C. Hansen, mit Beiträgen von M. Širinjan (Die Griechischen Christlichen Schriftsteller der ersten Jahrhunderte, Neue Folge 1), Berlin: 1995; *Socrate de Constantinople, Histoire ecclésiastique*, texte grec de l'édition G. C. Hansen, traduction par P. Périchon, introduction et notes par P. Maraval, 4 vols. (SC 477, 493, 505, 506), Paris: 2004–2007; *The Ecclesiastical History of Socrates Scholasticus,* trans. A. C. Zenos, in *A Select Library of Nicene and Post-Nicene Fathers of the Christian Church,* translated into English with Prolegomena and Explanatory Notes, Second Series 2, Grand Rapids, MI: 1976, 1–178.

Soz.   *Sozomenus Kirchengeschichte*, ed. J. Bidez and G. C. Hansen (Die Griechischen Christlichen Schriftsteller der ersten Jahrhunderte, Neue Folge 4), Berlin: 1995²; *Sozomène, Histoire ecclésiastique,* texte grec de l'édition J. Bidez et G. C. Hansen (GCS), introduction et annotation G. Sabbah, traduction A.-J. Festugière et B. Grillet, 4 vols. (SC 306, 418, 495, 516), Paris: 1983–2008; *The*

Ecclesiastical History of Sozomen, Comprising a History of the Church, from A.D. 323 to A.D. 425, trans. C. D. Hartranft, in *A Select Library of Nicene and Post-Nicene Fathers of the Christian Church,* translated into English with Prolegomena and Explanatory Notes, Second Series 2, Grand Rapids, MI: 1976, 179–427.

Sulp. Sev. *Mart.*   *Sulpice Sévère, Vie de Saint Martin,* ed. J. Fontaine, 2 vols. (SC 133, 134), Paris: 1967–1968.

Tac. *Ann.*   Tacitus, *Annales*

Tert. *Apol.*   Tertullianus, *Apologeticum,* ed. C. Becker, Darmstadt, Germany: 1992⁴.

Thdt. *HE*   *Theodoret Kirchengeschichte,* ed. L. Parmentier, F. Scheidweiler, and G. C. Hansen (Die Griechischen Christlichen Schriftsteller der ersten Jahrhunderte, Neue Folge 5), Berlin: 1998³; *The Ecclesiastical History, Dialogues, and Letters of Theodoret,* trans. B. Jackson, in *A Select Library of Nicene and Post-Nicene Fathers of the Christian Church,* translated into English with Prolegomena and Explanatory Notes, Second Series 3, Grand Rapids, MI: 1976, 1–348.

Thdt. *pass.*   *La passion grecque de saint Théodoret d'Antioche* (BHG 2425), ed. F. Halkin, *Hagiologie byzantine: Textes inédits publiés en grec et traduits en français* (Subsidia Hagiographica 71), Brussels: 1986, 123–151; *Passio sancti Theodoriti martyris* (BHL 8074–8076), ed. P. Franchi de' Cavalieri, *Note agiografiche 6* (Studi e Testi 33), Rome: 1920, 89–101.

Thdt. *HR*   Theodoretus, *Historia Religiosa*; P. Canivet
and A. Leroy-Molinghen, *Théodoret de
Cyr: L'histoire des moines de Syrie*, 2 vols.
(SC 234, 257), Paris: 1977–1979.

Theophan. *Chron.*   *Theophanis Chronographia*, ed. C. de
Boor, 2 vols., Leipzig: 1883–1885 (repr.
Hildesheim: 1963); *The Chronicle of
Theophanes Confessor, Byzantine and Near Eastern
History AD 284–813*, translated with Introduction
and Commentary by C. Mango and R. Scott with the
assistance of G. Greatrex, Oxford: 1997.

V. Pach.   *Sancti Pachomii vitae Graecae*, ed. F. Halkin (Subsidia
Hagiographica 19), Brussels: 1932.

Zonar.   *Ioannis Zonarae Epitomae Historiarum Libri XVIII,
vol. 3, Libri XIII–XVIII*, ed. Th. Büttner-Wobst
(CSHB [31.2]), Bonn, Germany: 1897; *Zonaras'
Account of the Neo-Flavian Emperors. A Commentary*,
ed. M. DiMaio II, Diss. University of Missouri: 1977;
*The History of Zonaras: From Alexander Severus to
the Death of Theodosius the Great*, Translation by
Th. M. Banchich and E. N. Lane, introduction and
commentary by Th. M. Banchich (Routledge Classical
Translations), London: 2009.

Zos.   *Zosime. Histoire Nouvelle*, ed. F. Paschoud, 5 vols.
(Collection des Universités de France), Paris:
1971–1989 (vol. I: 2000^2); *Zosimus. New History*,
trans. R. T. Ridley (Byzantina Australiensia 2),
Canberra: Australia: 1984; *Zosimos. Neue Geschichte.*
Übersetzt und eingeleitet von O. Veh, durchgesehen
und erläutert von S. Rebenich (Bibliothek der
Griechischen Literatur 31), Stuttgart: 1990.

Map of the Near East in the Time of Julian

BLACK SEA

Phasis

N

DOCIA

Samosata

Edessa

Cyrrhus

Carrhae

Hierapolis

Nineveh

Antioch

Beroea

Litarba

Callinicum

Orontes

Tigris

Epiphania

Cercusium

Zaitha

Arethusa

Dura-Europus

Emesa

Heliopolis

Euphrates

Baghdad

Damascus

Caesarea Philippi

Ctesiphon

Bosra

150 MILES

150 KILOMETERS

Introduction

Flavius Claudius Iulianus, better known as Julian the Apostate, died in the night of 26–27 June 363 CE. He had governed the Roman Empire for under twenty months when he was wounded near modern Baghdad by a cavalry spear that pierced his ribs and lodged in the lower part of his liver. The young emperor, who had been born in Constantinople in 331 or 332, died a few hours later.[1]

It is practically certain that the fatal weapon had been thrown by an enemy, a cavalryman in the army of the Persian king Sapor II, against whom Julian had started a war earlier in 363. But not everyone believed this. According to the historian Ammianus Marcellinus, who took part in Julian's Persian expedition as an army officer, there were rumors that the spear came from the emperor's own ranks. Another contemporary, Libanius, professor of rhetoric and, like Ammianus, a sympathizer and admirer of Julian, goes one step further and suggests that a Christian was responsible for the death of the emperor. Though probably not true, this theory is not far fetched: Julian was hated by almost all his Christian subjects, whom he contemptuously called 'Galilaeans.' These 'Galilaeans' were unable to stomach the fact that the emperor, despite his Christian upbringing, had tried to breathe new life into the cults of the old pagan gods ever since his accession to the throne in 361. They feared that the Apostate would put a stop to the progress of Christianity, which, after the conversion of Julian's uncle Constantine in the beginning of the fourth century, had steadily gained support.[2]

There were more rumors going around about Julian's death. The 'dagger-thrust legend' of the pagan Libanius was eagerly adopted by the Christian Sozomen, albeit that this church historian, who lived in the fifth century, gave the story a twist: Sozomen is full of praise for the man who threw the spear. He does not call him a traitor or a cowardly murderer, but a brave tyrannicide. The church historian Socrates, one of Sozomen's predecessors, cites somebody from Julian's inner circle who had written an epic poem about the emperor in which Julian was killed by a demon. Others do not speak of demons, but of angels or saints—on various reliefs and paintings, artists have Julian portrayed while he is being stabbed by Saint Mercury, resembling the dragon killed by Saint Michael or Saint George (Figure 1).

Figure 1. St. Mercury killing King Oulyanos/Oleonus/Julian. Painting in the Bet Mercurius cave church in Lalibela, Ethiopia, made in 1932 by Hayla Maryarm Taddasa, with the help of Zacharias (Martin 2014a, 327). *(Credit Line: © Photograph by A. Davey, Wikimedia Commons.)*

Some Christians alleged that Julian exclaimed on his deathbed, 'You have won, Galilaean,' while collecting the blood that gushed out of his wound and throwing it heavenward. Ammianus Marcellinus and Libanius, on the other hand, both pagans, let their idolized emperor die à la the famous Athenian philosopher Socrates, talking on his deathbed with friends about the immortality of the soul.[3]

Accounts about Julian's life differ as markedly as those about his death. If we may believe the Cappadocian church father Gregory of Nazianzus, it was obvious to anyone who set eyes on Julian that he was no good. He, Gregory, at any rate, had realized that Julian was a monster the moment he saw him—that had been in Athens when both were students: Julian's bloated neck, his shaking shoulders, that jumpy look in his eyes, that nervous and uncontrolled laughter, all this (and still more; Gregory's description is longer than my paraphrase) was crafted to make anyone immediately recognize him for what he was, a fiend. The portrait Ammianus Marcellinus sketches is kinder: 'He was of middle height, his hair was smooth as if it had been combed, and he wore a bristly beard trimmed to a point. He had fine, flashing eyes, the sign of a lively intelligence, well-marked eyebrows, a straight nose, and a rather large mouth with a pendulous lower lip. His neck was thick and somewhat bent, his shoulders large and broad. From head to foot he was perfectly built, which made him strong and a good runner.'[4]

The image Gregory and Ammianus present of Julian's appearance was determined by their view on his inner self. Gregory was no friend of Julian. In two invectives the Christian bishop pulls the emperor to pieces and criticizes everything he had ever done or yearned to do. Small wonder that his description of Julian's looks is not very flattering and probably a bit of a caricature. Yet, as is to be expected from a caricature, parts of his portrayal are recognizable. Compare, for instance, the plump neck on some coins of the Apostate (of whom statues and busts have also survived). Ammianus' view of the emperor was more balanced. The historian made Julian the central figure in Books 15–25 of his *Res Gestae* (*History*) and more than once expresses his admiration for him, without glossing over his shortcomings. He himself saw in Julian the personification of the four cardinal virtues, but Ammianus also relates that others branded Julian a 'chattering mole,' 'more a goat than a man,' an 'ape in purple.' And Ammianus totally disapproved of Julian's School Edict, which forbade Christian teachers of rhetoric and literature to practice their profession unless they renounced their faith. 'This measure is cruel and should be buried under eternal silence' was his crushing comment.[5]

Soon after Julian's early death, his school law was revoked, or at least modified. His other attempts to restore the cults of the gods and to save what in his eyes was the true Hellenic civilization equally failed. This emperor's short period in office was only a small cloud that would soon pass over, according to the Alexandrian bishop Athanasius. But the indignation engendered by Julian's reign echoed long into the future. In voicing their resentment, people often played fast and loose with the facts. Julian was accused of crimes that he simply cannot have committed. For example, he allegedly tortured and killed Christians in Rome, although he never in his life visited the eternal city. While the reality was that he fought against the Persians in Mesopotamia, he supposedly ordered in Gaul the execution of a certain Elophius, who, after his decapitation, walked many kilometers with his head in his hands to what would be his final resting place. It is also reported that Julian had been made Pope by Satan, after which he secretly tried to undermine the Catholic Church. Exposed and deposed by his cardinals, he continued his destructive actions guided by Satan, until he perished by the sword of Cardinal Mercury. Needless to say, this too is pure fiction.[6]

There are few Roman emperors whose life and work are buried so densely beneath the creation of legends as Julian's, the emperor, who, in the words of one of his modern biographers, 'is without question one of antiquity's most enigmatic and compelling figures.' In this book, which focuses on one aspect of Julian's reign, I pay attention to facts as well as fiction. I try to answer the question whether under Julian the Christians were persecuted and, if so, on what scale; here one should distinguish between persecutions started by Julian himself and those that were perpetrated in his name but without his consent or knowledge. I am also interested in the impact made by the—supposed—persecutions under Julian on later generations, which, if we believe the *Passio Pimenii* ('Sufferings of Pimenius'), cost thousands and thousands of lives all over the Roman Empire.[7]

I have written this book with the use of various sources, first of all Julian's own works. No Roman emperor handed down to posterity more written works than he did. His letters especially are an invaluable source of information. These texts, written in Julian's mother tongue, Greek (but, to quote Ammianus, 'he knew Latin well enough to be able to discourse in it'), are complemented by coins, laws, and inscriptions on stone. Ammianus Marcellinus proves a fairly reliable guide, and the letters and orations of Libanius, a pagan like Ammianus, provide us with many details we would otherwise not have known.[8]

Almost without exception Christian writers were unfavorably disposed toward the Apostate. This applies to Gregory of Nazianzus as well as to his younger contemporary John Chrysostom, who became bishop of Constantinople and whose body of works is vast. It is also true of the church historians Philostorgius, Socrates, Sozomen, Theodoret, and Rufinus, all of whom followed in the footsteps of Constantine the Great's contemporary Eusebius of

Caesarea, the first author of a church history. And it applies, a fortiori, to the writers of *passiones*, which inform us about the martyrs who died, or allegedly died, during Julian's reign.[9]

How reliable all these authors are as historical sources, in particular the writers of the *passiones*, has to be examined constantly. Not an easy task, but an indispensable precondition for historical research. Implicitly or explicitly I pose throughout this book the question of the trustworthiness of the sources. Ammianus Marcellinus may be regarded by Edward Gibbon and others as an 'accurate and faithful guide'; this does not mean that he was infallible, or impartial, for that matter. Conversely, almost all Christian authors who wrote about Julian were hostile toward him, but that does not mean that their information should a priori be thrust aside.[10]

Chapter 1

Julian's Apostasy

We might well never have heard of Julian, let alone of his apostasy, for he only just evaded being murdered at the age of five or six. He barely escaped the massacre in Constantinople (modern Istanbul) among the relatives of Constantine the Great shortly after this first Christian Roman emperor died in May 337. Julian's father, brother of Constantine, was one of the victims, as was an elder brother of Julian's. Six of his cousins and an uncle met the same fate. Julian himself and his half-brother Gallus, who was his senior by some years, had a lucky escape—Gallus, we are told, because he was ill and people thought that he would soon die anyway, Julian because he was so very young.[1]

Julian later accused his cousin Constantius of having instigated the bloodbath, and he was not the only one who thought so. Both pagan and Christian writers blame Constantius II. Indeed, at first sight it seems very probable that Julian's elder cousin had pulled the strings. At any rate, this son of Constantine the Great, born in 317, clearly benefited from it. He ruled over the Roman Empire from September 9, 337, until November 3, 361, at first together with his brothers Constantinus and Constans. These three men, who all bore the title *Augustus* ('senior emperor'), gained most from the massacre of their relatives. Competition from the next of kin was not a danger for the time being—instead of fighting others, they

7

soon fought one another. Constantius turned out to be the strongest, and he was sole emperor from 350 until 361.[2]

But if Constantius and his followers had been responsible for the massacre, why on earth did they spare Gallus and Julian? In view of their youth they may not have posed an immediate threat to Constantine's sons, but that might well have changed when they grew older. A calculating murderer would have thought of this. That Julian and Gallus stayed alive and in the course of time were even appointed *Caesares* ('junior emperors') by their cousin does not plead in favor of the theory that Constantius had plotted the bloodbath. On top of accusations, moreover, there were also voices that absolved him from the charge of being the murderer of his relatives. Both the historian Eutropius and the church historian Socrates state explicitly that he had not ordered the massacre, though he had not prevented it, either—Julian himself spoke in the same vein when he did not yet dare to act against Constantius. Bishop Gregory of Nazianzus goes even further. He repudiates any responsibility on the part of Constantius, and says that it was thanks to him that his young cousins were saved from the violence of the murderous soldiers.[3]

It is possible that Constantius was less actively involved in the massacre of Constantinople in 337 than Julian and others later alleged, and Constantius may have wished to spare Gallus and Julian because they were not only his cousins, but also his brothers-in-law (Constantius' first wife was Gallus' sister, Julian's half-sister). Whatever the case may be, after the bloodbath, in which Julian's father was killed (his mother had died some months after his birth), Constantius often interfered in his cousin's life. The emperor first made sure that Julian and his half-brother Gallus were separated: Gallus was sent to Ephesus, Julian to Nicomedia.[4]

In Nicomedia in Asia Minor (modern Izmit in Turkey), Julian was left in the care of one of his relatives, the local bishop, Eusebius (not to be confused with the writer of the first ecclesiastical history and a *Life of Constantine*). Whether the young prince was brought back to Constantinople a little later when Eusebius obtained the episcopal see there is disputed, but it is certain that Julian's actual education was entrusted to a certain Mardonius, a slave who had been castrated—Julian later used to speak very appreciatively of this eunuch. To Julian's regret, Mardonius did not accompany him when the emperor Constantius, probably in 342, had him transferred to Macellum, an estate near the city of Caesarea (Kayseri) in Cappadocia (in modern-day Turkey). It is true that Julian was there reunited with his half-brother, Gallus, but he did not like his six-years-long stay on this remote estate at all. Not only was he under permanent surveillance, but he was also not allowed to receive visitors. Apart from Gallus, who was of a totally different disposition, his only companions were slaves. Young Julian sought and found consolation and comfort in reading—he had the library of George, bishop of nearby Caesarea, at his disposal.[5]

In the bishop's library Julian did not find only pious books, but also works on pagan philosophy and literature. He was already acquainted with these subjects, as was customary for upper-class boys of his age, and in Macellum he continued his literary and philosophical studies. But of course, as a cousin of the Christian emperor Constantius, born and raised in a Christian household, he first and foremost received a Christian education. It is not surprising, therefore, that Julian knew many scriptural passages by heart, went to church regularly, and honored the graves of Christian martyrs. While attending service he acted as reader. Was all this seriously meant, or a mere sham? Did Julian only pretend to be a Christian out of fear of his mighty cousin Constantius? According to the church historian Sozomen, some people did believe that Julian began to renounce Christianity during his stay in Macellum. But this is doubtless an example of reading too much into the facts. Julian himself says in a letter written in 362 that he had embraced Christianity until his twentieth year, but for twelve years now (that is, since 351) was following the right path by the grace of the gods, and there is no good reason to doubt the truthfulness of this statement.[6]

When Julian gave up Christianity in 351, his stay in Macellum lay already some years behind him. Constantius had allowed his cousin to leave this place of exile and to go, successively, to Constantinople (where Julian met his old friend and tutor Mardonius again), Nicomedia, and Pergamum (Bergama) for further education. In Constantinople and Nicomedia the young prince applied himself primarily to rhetoric, while in Pergamum, a center of Neoplatonism, he buried himself more and more in philosophy, in which he showed a lively interest. In Pergamum he heard for the first time through his teacher Aedesius (a disciple of the famous Iamblichus) and Aedesius' pupil Chrysantius of the existence of two other pupils of Aedesius, the philosophers Maximus and Priscus, whom Julian later, when he had become emperor, invited to come to the court and with whom he was on friendly terms until his dying day—it was with Maximus and Priscus that Julian on his deathbed had the talks about the immortality of the soul we already mentioned. In 351 Priscus was somewhere in Greece, while Maximus stayed in his birthplace, Ephesus, some hundred kilometers away from Pergamum. It did not take long before Julian visited him there.[7]

Like many of his Neoplatonic colleagues, the pagan Maximus of Ephesus tried to link philosophy with mysticism and theurgy (that is, 'the art or technique of compelling or persuading a god or beneficent or supernatural power to do or refrain from doing something'). He was reputedly a fortune teller and a miracle worker, who supposedly had made a stone statue of the goddess Hecate laugh. In Antiquity it was sometimes denied that he was a real philosopher, and modern scholars often regard him as no more than a charlatan. But he made an enormous impression on the twenty-year-old

Julian, who later praised Maximus as the man who had taught him to value virtue above all else and—more importantly, in view of Julian's position in world history—who had made him realize that only the pagan gods of old showed the way to the good life. Other sources, too, show that the encounter with Maximus was decisive with regard to the sudden change in Julian's religious views: from now on he was finished with Christianity.[8]

For the time being Julian wisely kept silent about his apostasy. His imperial cousin especially must not become aware of it. Only Julian's closest friends were informed. Not all of their names are known, but we may gather that Oribasius, Julian's personal physician and the author of many medical works, was among them (like Maximus and Priscus, Oribasius was present in 363 at Julian's deathbed). Julian's brother, Gallus, was not, if we may believe a letter attributed to Gallus (its authenticity is disputed). According to this letter, Gallus, who in 351 was made co-emperor with the title *Caesar* by Constantius, had heard of his brother's apostasy and was upset about it. He felt reassured, however, when a mutual acquaintance, a certain Aetius, reported to Gallus that his brother still dutifully adhered to the Christian faith. Although with regard to religion, Gallus was closer to his cousin Constantius than to Julian (we know that even without the testimony of the said letter), this was no guarantee for a good understanding between him and the emperor. Conflict was bound to ensue, and after only three years matters came to a head. In 354 Constantius ordered the *Caesar*, whom he suspected of mismanagement in the area under his jurisdiction, to come to Italy, and had him executed during his journey before it had come to a trial. Whether Gallus would have dragged Julian down with him remained a moot point.[9]

Julian was also summoned to come to Italy. In Milan he was held under house arrest for months on end, and was prevented from seeing the emperor. He was accused of having left Macellum without permission, and of secretly having met Gallus when his brother was on his way to Italy. It was not difficult for Julian to refute these allegations, but without the interference of Eusebia, Constantius' second wife, the situation would probably have ended badly. However, the empress succeeded in persuading her husband to grant Julian an audience and to permit him to devote himself again to studying, this time in Athens.[10]

Julian's stay in Athens did not last long. After only a couple of weeks Constantius called him back to Milan. The emperor was troubled by internal uprisings against his regime and attacks by barbarians from outside, and he needed the assistance of the only relative who was still alive. On November 6, 355, he appointed his cousin *Caesar* in Gaul. For Julian this came as a complete surprise: 'Some of them, as if they were in a barber's shop, cut off my beard [as a student of philosophy Julian wore a beard] and dressed me in a military cloak and transformed me into a rather laughable soldier, at least in their eyes.'[11]

On the first of December 355 Julian departed for Vienna in the province of Gallia Lugdunensis, modern Vienne in France. In Gaul this ridiculous soldier turned out to be a fine military man and a most competent administrator, to the surprise of friend and foe alike. Julian restored peace in the regions that had suffered from barbarian incursions, and he became popular with the provincials and the army. Successes against German invaders earned him the honorary epithets *Alamannicus maximus, Francicus maximus,* and *Germanicus maximus.* Ammianus is full of praise for Julian's actions in Gaul and compares him with the best of his predecessors: 'In sagacity he was reckoned to be the reincarnation of Titus, son of Vespasian, in the glorious outcome of his campaigns he was very like Trajan, he was as merciful as Antoninus [Pius], and in his striving after truth and perfection he was the equal of Marcus

Aurelius, on whom he endeavoured to model his own actions and character.' Julian's greatest triumph was the victory in the Battle of Argentoratum (Strasbourg) in 357 against a coalition of Alamannic tribes that greatly outnumbered the Roman forces. He himself was enormously proud of this achievement. 'Perhaps the fame of that battle has reached even your ears,' he wrote some years later in his *Letter to the Athenians*, and he even wrote a pamphlet (now lost) about it. The courtiers in Constantius' palace were less jubilant and ridiculed Julian for being a braggart, but Julian's soldiers loved their commander. After the fight at Strasbourg was over, the whole army hailed the *Caesar* as *Augustus*, next to, or if need be, instead of, Constantius. However, Julian reproached the soldiers for their reckless behavior. The time was not ripe yet (in the spring of 360, in Paris, Julian's troops again declared him *Augustus*, and this time he accepted the honor).[12]

As a family man Julian was less fortunate than as a general. A few days after the *Augustus* had appointed him *Caesar* in 355, he married a sister of Constantius II, Helena, in Milan. His wife, a devout Christian, went with him to Gaul and bore him a child, but the boy died as soon as he was born—according to Ammianus, the baby was murdered by a midwife at the instigation of Constantius' jealous wife, Eusebia, who was childless; this sounds like gossip, as does Ammianus' assertion that Eusebia coaxed Helena to take a drug that would cause a miscarriage every time she became pregnant. However that may be, the couple did not have children and Helena died in 360. Julian never married again. His sexual needs were minimal. Had he not been married to Helena, 'he would,' according to Libanius, 'have ended his days knowing nothing of sexual intercourse save by report. As it was, he went into mourning for his wife and never again touched another woman.' During the Persian campaign Julian gave proof of his chastity by refusing even to look at the virgins offered to him by the soldiers.[13]

During his period as *Caesar* in Gaul, Julian did not let on about his religious feelings. In letters to close friends he occasionally spoke about the gods (in the plural), and he carried out secret pagan rites together with the high priest of the Eleusinian mysteries (a religious festival, held in Eleusis near Athens, that annually attracted many initiates), but nothing of this was known to the outside world. 'To frustrate any opposition,' writes Ammianus Marcellinus when relating that Julian visited a Christian church on January 6, 360, 'and win universal good will he pretended to adhere to the Christian religion, from which he had secretly apostatized long before. Only a few were in his confidence, and knew that his heart was set on divination and augury and all the other practices followed by worshippers of the old gods. To conceal this for the time being he went to church on the holy day which the Christians celebrate in January and call Epiphany, and departed after joining in their customary worship.'[14]

Even after his soldiers had declared him *Augustus* in the spring of 360, Julian chose to be safe rather than sorry. We hear of the invocation of the goddess of war Bellona, inspection of the entrails of sacrificial animals, and augural rites to interpret the flight of birds, but all this was kept secret, as before. In his *Letter to the Athenians*, which was written in the summer of 361, he did appeal to the gods for help, but it was only after the emperor Constantius had died and Julian had triumphantly entered Constantinople on December 11, 361, that, to quote Ammianus Marcellinus again, 'he revealed the secrets of his heart and by plain and formal decrees ordered the temples to be opened, victims brought to the altars, and the worship of the gods restored.'[15]

The mask was removed. A new phase in the history of the Roman Empire had begun. Some fifty years before, on the eve of the battle of 'the Milvian Bridge' in Rome, Constantine the Great had embraced Christianity and had in so doing started a development that would make this religion at the end of the fourth century the official state religion. From 361 onward Constantine's nephew Julian tried to stop this development and, if possible, to reverse it. At the time no one could know that Julian's death in 363 would end this attempt prematurely.

Chapter 2

Constantine and the Christians

On October 28, 312, a battle was fought near Rome between the armies of Julian's uncle Constantine and Constantine's rival Maxentius. At stake was the imperial throne—it was the umpteenth civil war in the history of Rome. Constantine won the day and ascribed his victory to the power of an intriguing symbol: on the eve of the battle he is supposed to have had a dream in which he was advised to fix on the shields of his soldiers God's heavenly sign, that is, the Christogram (also called Chrismon), a X (chi) and a P (rho), the first two letters of the name of Christ in Greek, ΧΡΙΣΤΟΣ. We owe this information to a contemporary rhetorician, Lactantius, tutor to Constantine's eldest son. According to another contemporary, Bishop Eusebius of Caesarea, who inter alia wrote a *Life of Constantine*, what the emperor had seen was not a dream, but a vision in broad daylight: a sign in the shape of a cross up in the sky, with the words 'by this conquer.' Dream or vision, Christogram or cross: Constantine, whose favorite god up until then had been Apollo/Sol Invictus ('Apollo as the Invincible Sun God'), had his soldiers fix a Christian symbol on their shields and defeated his enemy.[1]

The battle of the Milvian Bridge (as it is commonly called, although the actual fighting began at a site some five kilometers away from the bridge) was an event of tremendous importance in the history of the world. In the first three centuries of the Common Era, Christianity, which of course stemmed from Judaism, was not exactly a force to be reckoned with, and the Christians had been persecuted at regular intervals. Like the Jews, they were monotheistic and unfavorably disposed toward the pagan majority of the fifty to eighty million people in the *imperium Romanum* (the estimated percentage of Christians in the beginning of Constantine's reign is 20 percent). Christian exclusivity met with opposition, more opposition than the Jews had encountered in their contacts with the Romans. Judaism was a national religion, restricted to one people, and besides, the religion of the Jews was very old. Toward such a belief the Romans showed tolerance. Conversely, Christianity could not pride itself on either of these assets. Moreover, the Christians refused to participate in the religious life of their neighbors wherever they lived, and they kept themselves aloof from them in other respects, too. That was bound to cause trouble.[2]

In 64 CE a great part of the city of Rome was destroyed by fire. The belief that the emperor Nero had deliberately started the fire in order to create a suitable setting for his lyrical drama about the fall of Troy is almost as difficult to eradicate as it is false. However, it is the case that Nero had to bear the blame for the disaster, and that he in his turn accused the Christians of having caused the inferno, thus making them scapegoats. The first persecution of Christians on a large scale was the result. 'Some of them, covered with the skins of beasts, were torn apart by dogs. Others were nailed to crosses and burnt, to serve as a nightly illumination, when daylight had gone.' Thus wrote the pagan historian Tacitus. It certainly was not the last time that Christians were persecuted. 'If the water of the Tiber rises to the quay-walls, if the water of the Nile falls off and does not irrigate the fields, if the sky is rainless, if there is an earthquake, a famine, a plague, immediately the cry arises: "the Christians to the lion!'" Thus wrote the Christian apologist Tertullian at the end of the second century.[3]

A survey of the persecutions in the Early Empire teaches us that these were local incidents, horrible incidents, to be sure, but not examples of systematic maltreatment all over the empire. The mere fact of being a Christian was regarded as a crime, but prosecution was not instigated by the government. The authorities took notice only of unambiguous accusations by private individuals. Such, at any rate, was the situation during the first two centuries of the Common Era, a relatively quiet and prosperous period in which the Pax Romana flourished. The situation changed halfway through the third century. Decius (249–251) was the first Roman emperor who ordered a general persecution throughout his realm. The demands of his time must have been the reason for this reversal of policy. The third century was a period of chaos and anarchy, of everlasting civil wars, of economical malaise, and, last but not least, of pressure on the frontiers, by German tribes on the Rhine and the Danube, for instance. In short, there was adversity everywhere. Apparently, the gods were angry. In 250 CE Decius therefore looked for a scapegoat, which he easily found in the Christians. Some of Decius' successors also organized general persecutions. The largest of these took place in the early fourth century during the reign of Diocletian. But shortly afterward things changed completely when Constantine became a Christian. The year 312 really was a turning point in the history of the world.[4]

Although the conversion of Constantine at the beginning of the fourth century was decisive with regard to the ultimate triumph of Christianity, the advance of the Christian faith had started earlier. We find in early Christianity many elements that can explain its widespread appeal. The monotheism of the Christians gave more support in times of anxiety than the traditional polytheism with its worship of Jupiter, Juno, Minerva, Apollo, and Venus, among others, and it also provided a firmer footing than the henotheism of, for example, the cults of Sol Invictus or Mithras, in which one god was worshipped but the existence of others not denied. Apart from confidence in frightening times, Christianity offered its believers a personal God and the promise of a blessed life after death. Furthermore, in contrast to pagans, Christians possessed in their Bible a holy and authoritative book, while the fact that their God had sent His only Son as the Savior to mankind in order to relieve it from sin and death was unique and inspired hope. Christian charity and the organizational structure of the Christian churches with their parishes, priests, and bishops commanded respect and admiration, as did the constancy of Christian martyrs during the persecutions—*semen est sanguis Christianorum*, Tertullian wrote, referring to the (for the pagan authorities unexpected and undesired) effects of martyrdom, 'the blood of the Christians is a seed.' However, this does not alter the fact that it was the conversion of an *emperor* that was of overriding importance for the breakthrough of Christianity.[5]

From 312 onward the Christianization of the Roman Empire proceeded at a steady pace, under emperors who, with the exception of Julian the Apostate (who reigned between 361 and 363), were Christians. Under Theodosius (379–395), Christianity became the state religion—this emperor owed his epithet 'the Great' to his attitude toward Christianity, just like Constantine, who was awarded the title by the Senate after his victory in 312. Constantine's initial attitude in the field of religion was, after all, rather ambivalent. On the one hand, he restored to the Christians the places of worship that his pagan predecessors had confiscated, he encouraged the construction of new churches, and he gave priests and bishops fiscal and juridical privileges; on the other hand he left the pagans undisturbed, as *pontifex maximus* he was in charge of the cult of the gods of the state, and on his coins he kept the symbols of the henotheistic

Sun God. However, in the course of his long reign (312–337), and especially after he had eliminated his rival Licinius in the eastern part of the empire in 324, he took the side of the Christians ever more openly. He now also became involved in their internal dissensions.[6]

The Donatist controversy in North Africa was the first problem Constantine had to tackle. The Donatists, named after their bishop Donatus, had dissociated themselves in the early fourth century from the *catholica ecclesia*, the 'universal church.' They held strict views on theology and combined a puritanical outlook with a predilection for martyrdom. In the eyes of the Catholics they were stubborn and pigheaded, obstinately convinced of being in the right, unwilling, in spite of attempts at reconciliation, to rejoin the mother church, not so much heretics as schismatics. According to the Donatists themselves, however, they, not the Catholics, were the only true Christians in Africa. To substantiate their view they appealed to history: during the 'Great Persecution' in the days of Emperor Diocletian (ca. 300), when Christianity faced one of its worst ordeals, the sheep had been separated from the goats. At that time it had become clear who were willing to die a martyr's death on behalf of their faith, and who would rather save their own skins. And not only during, but also after, the 'Great Persecution,' the difference between the two kinds of believers had become evident. Could it be tolerated that apostates and *traditores*—that is, people who had handed over (*tradiderant*) the Holy Scripture and other ecclesiastical properties to the persecutors—behaved as if nothing had happened? (The word *traditor* can also mean 'traitor.') Could such individuals go on being clerics? On this point the conflict was coming to a head.[7]

Personal and local differences contributed to the escalation of the conflict. In 312—the same year in which Constantine's victory at the Milvian Bridge fundamentally changed the situation of Christians in the Roman Empire for the better—a formal split between moderates and rigorists occurred. When the bishop of Carthage died, the legitimacy of his successor's election was challenged, because he was ordained by a neighboring bishop who was supposed to be a *traditor*. An antibishop was chosen and proclaimed by the Donatists, which meant that the schism was final. The Donatists brought the case more than once before Constantine, but the emperor did not take sides. Instead, he handed off responsibility to synods of bishops in Rome and in Arelate (Arles). Although the Donatists were turned down each time, they did not give up, thereby intensifying the quarrel. Constantine sent letters to admonish the bishops in North Africa to calm down. He urged unity, but could not end the conflict. After the emperor's death in 337, the division within the church dragged on into the next century.

While Donatists and Catholics in North Africa put up a vigorous fight against each other, an even more fundamental conflict broke out in the eastern part of the empire. It started in Egypt around the year 315 as a local dispute between the Alexandrian priest Arius and Bishop Alexander, but it triggered a controversy in which ultimately one of the central themes of the Christian doctrine was at stake—the dogma of the Holy Trinity, the unity of Father, Son, and Holy Spirit as three persons in one Godhead. Arius had argued that God alone is without beginning, unbegotten and eternal, while the Son was created and, although divine, subordinate to God. Arius' point of view found many adherents, but was rejected by Bishop Alexander, who took the priest to task and rebuked him. The bishop also exacerbated the conflict by stating that in Arius' view the Son was merely a man (something that the priest had never said). Arius stood by his opinion and refused to show his bishop obedience, defiance that in itself was regarded as heresy. Alexander then convened a synod of bishops that deposed and excommunicated Arius.

However, this did not solve the problem. In no time, 'Arianism' had found considerable support in and outside Egypt, and the conflict about Christology, that is, that part of theology which deals with the person of Christ, threatened to disturb the general peace in the Eastern Roman Empire. This threat caused the emperor to act. Constantine's first attempts at mediation were in vain, but in 325 he made a new move. He convened a general church council in Nicaea, now Iznik in Turkey, the first of the ecumenical councils (of which twenty-one have been called through the twenty-first century). He himself was present, at times took the floor, and urged unity. He wisely kept silence about Christological matters.[8]

Some 300 bishops were assembled in Nicaea. Most of them called themselves orthodox and rejected Arius' view, but they were ready to follow Constantine's appeal to look for a compromise. After long discussions the great majority accepted the following way of putting it: the Son is 'one-in-essence'—in Greek ὁμοούσιος (homoousios), in Latin *consubstantialis*—with the Father; that is, the Son was God just as the Father was. Only two of the bishops who were present in Nicaea refused to agree to this text. They were exiled, as was Arius, who, being a priest and not a bishop, had not been allowed to take part in the decision-making process.[9]

The conflict over the nature of Christ was not over yet. It continued for many years, as did the struggle between Donatists and Catholics. Arius and his followers did not admit defeat and were even able to win the backing of the emperor Constantine and his son Constantius. However, it did not take long before the 'Arians' became divided among themselves. Some of them regarded the Son in every respect dissimilar, ἀνόμοιος (anhomoios) from the Father. Others protested against the term, which was accepted by the Council of Nicaea, ὁμοούσιος (homoousios), as 'one-in-essence,' but were satisfied with an expression that comprised one more iota, ὁμοιούσιος (homoiousios), 'of similar essence.' Still others preferred the term 'the same' without further qualification, ὅμοιος (homoios).[10]

Arius' fellow townsman Athanasius, the successor of Bishop Alexander of Alexandria, was one of the fiercest opponents of Arius and his followers. The struggle was waged ferociously and persistently, but eventually, in 381, the Council of Constantinople confirmed the Nicene Declaration (often called Nicene Creed), as the only true and orthodox profession of faith—from it stems the *Credo,* which for centuries remained in force for almost all Christians. The Christological controversy affected not only clerics and educated laymen, but the common people as well, as may be concluded from an amusing anecdote told by the fourth-century Bishop Gregory of Nyssa (Nevşehir) in Cappadocia: 'If you ask about your change, the shopkeeper philosophises to you about the Begotten and the Unbegotten; if you enquire the price of a loaf, the reply is: "The Father is greater and the Son inferior," and if you say: "Is the bath ready?" the attendant affirms that the Son is of nothing.'[11]

Chapter 3

A Fleeting Cloud?

In his youth Julian must have heard of the controversy regarding the nature of Christ, an issue that greatly inflamed people's emotions in the fourth century. During his stay in the villa of Macellum in Asia Minor, the future emperor was in close touch with George, the 'Arian' bishop of nearby Caesarea, whose library, as we have seen, he was allowed to use. George's views in Christological matters would have appealed to the feelings of the young prince. At any rate, as a grown-up the Apostate did not have any sympathy for the orthodox dogma of Holy Trinity that had been accepted at the Council of Nicaea in 325: 'You are quite right to believe that he whom one holds to be a god can by no means be inserted into a woman's womb,' the emperor wrote in a letter to Photinus, bishop of Sirmium, modern Sremska Mitroviča in Serbia—the Greek original of the letter is lost, but a sixth-century Latin translation is preserved.[1]

More than once Photinus had been condemned in synods by orthodox colleagues. Julian wrote his letter to support the bishop in his polemic with a certain Diodorus, an adherent of the Nicene Creed. It was a welcome chance to stir up the discord between heretics and orthodox Christians. The emperor did not have a good word to say about Diodorus' point of view. He hoped to refute his false doctrine soon, he wrote, 'with the help of the gods and the goddesses, the Muses and the Lady Fortune' (a reference, no doubt, to his own treatise *Against the Galilaeans*), and he called Diodorus a 'charlatan priest of the Nazarene,' someone who tried to promote 'the creed of the countryfolk' (*religio agrestis*) with specious arguments—ironically, not the Christians, but precisely the pagans were in course of time associated with rusticity and backwardness. While Christianity spread especially via the cities in the Roman Empire, paganism remained popular among the people in the countryside for a long time; this explains why the word *paganus*, which originally meant 'countryman,' 'villager,' 'rustic,' came to mean 'heathen,' 'pagan.'[2]

Julian composed his treatise *Against the Galilaeans* in Syrian Antioch (now Antakya in Turkey) during the winter of 362–363. The title, with its allusion to John 7:52 ('no prophet arises from Galilee'), is revealing. The emperor wanted to stress that the worship of 'that new fangled Galilaean god,' which was propagated by 'base and ignorant theologizing fishermen,' was practiced only by a local sect from a faraway and underdeveloped part of the empire. In its original form *Against the Galilaeans* no longer exists. Supposedly, the work was banned by one of Julian's Christian successors and was then lost. However, we do have some fragments—more than enough to give us a good impression of its contents—thanks to Cyrillus, bishop of Alexandria in the first half of the fifth century, who cited large chunks of *Against the Galilaeans* in his polemical *Against Julian*, in order to show how wrong Julian's point of view was.[3]

One of Julian's aims in writing *Against the Galilaeans* was to demonstrate that there is no trace in the Old Testament of what would later become Christianity, so that according to him the Christians falsely asserted that their creed emanated from Judaism. The emperor felt a certain sympathy for the time-honored religion of the Jews, and he appreciated especially the custom of the Jews of the Old Testament to offer animal sacrifices to their god, just as the pagans did. Some Greek church historians relate that Julian encouraged the leading Jews of his day to resume their sacrifices, whereupon they answered that they could lawfully sacrifice only in the Temple in Jerusalem, which had been destroyed under Vespasian (69–79). The emperor's benevolence toward the Jews became manifest in the first months of 363, when he actually permitted the rebuilding of the Temple, which was, however, never finished. It is not quite clear why the restoration was stopped. According to Ammianus, fires near the foundations of the Temple called a halt to the enterprise. Gregory of Nazianzus and other Christian authors (who looked upon the rebuilding as an anti-Christian act of Julian's, for Jesus had said 'there shall not be left here one stone upon another, that shall not be thrown down') mention divine intervention in the form of a celestial cross appearance, storms, earth tremors and fires—from a modern perspective it does not seem unlikely that earthquakes that caused fires were the reason that the project was ended. However, despite some sympathy for the Jews, Julian was on the whole critical of Judaism. In his view the pagan gods and the Hellenic cults were by far superior to the Jewish faith: unlike the universal pagan gods the narrow-minded, jealous god of the Hebrews was merely the god of a small and unimportant nation.[4]

Julian deemed Christianity, in contrast to ancient Judaism, an arrogant modernism, and full of inconcistencies at that. How was it possible, for instance, that the Christians preached monotheism, but at the same time proclaimed that there were three gods, the Father, the Son, and the Holy Ghost? This and other such arguments had already been adduced in the third century by the Neoplatonic philosopher Porphyry of Tyre in Phoenicia (now Lebanon), a follower of the influential Plotinus, but according to Julian's sympathizer Libanius, Julian voiced them in an even more incisive way: 'As winter lengthened the nights, besides many other fine compositions, he attacked the books in which that fellow from Palestine is claimed to be a god and son of god. In a long polemic and by dint of forceful arguments, he proved such claims to be stupid, idle chatter. On the same subject he showed himself wiser than the old sage from Tyre.'[5]

Julian's aversion to Christianity went hand in hand with a deeply felt awe for the traditional gods. He ends his prose *Hymn to the Mother of the Gods*, written in March 362, with a prayer in which he begs the goddess 'to grant to the Roman people that they may cleanse themselves of the stain of impiety.' The emperor not only hoped to stop the spread of the Christian faith, which uncompromisingly and intolerantly excluded other gods and only worshipped him who, full of haughtiness, boasted, 'I am the way, the truth, and the life,' but Julian also wanted to lead the Roman people back to the pluriformity of a broad-minded paganism, which since Constantine's conversion had been oppressed, but was by no means dead.[6]

From time immemorial Graeco-Roman paganism had been receptive to new gods, and foreign deities had been identified with native gods. Accordingly, the Egyptian Ammon and the Roman Jupiter could be identified with the Greek Zeus, and Cybele, the Mother of the Gods in Asia Minor, the Egyptian Serapis, and Mithras from Persia were easily incorporated into the pantheon created by Homer, Hesiod, and other poets. The cult of the Olympian gods still flourished in imperial times, as is shown clearly by numerous inscriptions and by the fact that Constantine's predecessor Diocletian had as his agnomen *Iovius* ('dedicated to Jupiter') and founded a temple for Jupiter that faced his mausoleum in Salona near modern Split in Croatia. But besides the worship of the traditional gods, cults of oriental mystery gods like Mithras, Serapis, and Cybele were growing, cults in which participation was possible only after initiation—for example, after one had been sprinkled with the blood of a slaughtered bull. Just as in the case of Christianity (originally also an oriental mystery cult), monotheistic tendencies can be perceived in these cults, and many gods were seen as different manifestations of one central god. Julian's own *Hymn to King Helios* ('the Sun') can be adduced as evidence. In it the author's mouthpiece Apollo gives voice to this idea by saying, 'Zeus, Hades, Helios, Serapis: different names for one godhead.' There was one particularly significant difference with Christianity, though. In contrast to the exclusively monotheistic Christians, Julian and other adherents of mystery cults did not deny the existence of other gods but gave them their due. To quote Libanius in memory of his beloved emperor, 'Julian did not feast some and ignore others, but to all the gods whom the poets have handed down to us . . . he made libation and loaded the altars of every one with sheep and oxen.'[7]

In one of his letters Julian states that worship of the gods can be shown in various ways: by pious meditations and prayers, by the conservation of temples, by sacrificing on the altars of the gods, and by respectfully and reverently looking up at their images—but, he adds, these images of the gods are of course not the gods themselves, thus tackling certain misconceptions of the 'Galilaeans'; it would be equally foolish to assert that a statue or a portrait of the emperor is the emperor himself. By his own pious and modest way of life Julian hoped to be a shining example for his subjects, but he realized that more needed to be done to halt the progress of Christianity. For that reason he developed means to found a pagan church. He himself would be its leader, as *pontifex maximus*. Under him high priests would be in charge of the priests consigned to them. For priests there was a key role in store (the comparison with the organizational structure of the Christian church urges itself upon us), and Julian devised guidelines for them. Their conduct must be impeccable; banal pleasures (races, circus, theater) should be avoided. The reading of frivolous poetry was prohibited. Priests should bury themselves in philosophical works, preferably those of

Pythagoras, Plato, Aristotle, and the Stoics. Their most important duty was of course to conduct the service of the gods, but—and this was new—the care for the poor and the sick should concern them, too, for it was through poor relief and charity that the 'Galilaeans' had won many adherents.[8]

Julian's dislike of Christianity manifested itself not only in words. Deeds followed, as we shall see. However, his attempt to turn the clock back in the field of religion ended in failure. The accomplishment of the Apostate was, to quote Bishop Athanasius of Alexandria, nothing more than 'a fleeting cloud.' To be sure, Julian's reign as sole emperor did not last long, not even twenty months, a rather short period compared to the twenty-five years during which his uncle and total opposite Constantine (312–337) ruled as *Augustus*—one does wonder what would have happened if Julian had reigned as long as his uncle. Moreover, the greater part of his time in power was spent in preparing for war, first a civil war against his cousin Constantius, then a campaign against Persia. After Julian's troops had proclaimed him *Augustus* in the spring of 360, Constantius, the incumbent *Augustus*, refused to accept the declaration of Paris. It looked (in 360) as if the struggle for the throne would end in bloodshed. Constantius left the Near East, where he had tried to appease the aggression of the Persians, and moved westward at the head of his army, while Julian marched from Gaul to meet him. However, Constantius died before a battle could be fought. This was in the autumn of 361. Julian now began to prepare for a Persian expedition. His cousin's cautious, defensive strategy regarding Persia was abandoned. As a second Alexander the Great, Julian intended to defeat the enemy on his own soil. In the beginning he was rather successful, but, as we have seen already, in 363 a cavalry spear put an end to his life and his aspirations. His death meant of course also the end of his anti-Christian measures.[9]

Athanasius of Alexandria must have felt relieved when he heard that Julian had died, but he played down the danger that had threatened Christianity by comparing the Apostate's reign with 'a fleeting cloud.' Other Christians reacted less phlegmatically. According to Libanius, many of them had been afraid and had 'expected to be blinded or beheaded: rivers of blood would flow in massacres, they thought, and the new master would devise new-fangled tortures, in comparison with which the fire, sword, drowning, live burial, hacking and mutilation would seem mere child's play. Such had been the behaviour of his predecessors, and they expected his measures to be more severe still.' Nothing of this happened, but fear now turned to hatred. Julian's contemporary, Bishop Gregory of Nazianzus (whose brother, Caesarius, a famous doctor, served for a while at Julian's court), set the tone with two venomous invectives, written in Greek and finished shortly after the death of the man whom he was the first to call 'the Apostate' (he mentions Julian's real name in these diatribes only once). Another contemporary, the poet Ephraem Syrus, born near Nisibis (now Nusaybin in Turkey), shouted with joy in one of his four *Hymns against Julian*, written in Syriac: 'The king, the king of Greece, was rebuked because he provoked God to anger and . . . there, near Babel, he was judged and found guilty.' Some twenty-five years later a priest in the Syrian capital Antioch, John, later known as Chrysostom, "of golden mouth" (he became patriarch of Constantinople in 398), fulminated in his sermons against Julian as if the Apostate had still been alive. He declared again and again that Julian surpassed all other emperors in impiety, and, he added, it was by no means in the distant past that the emperor had raged like a madman against the Christians. It was only yesterday, in his and his audience's own lifetime.[10]

It is perfectly possible, that Chrysostom, like Athanasius, cherished the hope that Julian's reign had only been a fleeting cloud. But one gets the impression that he did not feel confident that the nightmare was definitely over. 'The empire might undergo a change,' he wrote in his *Against the Opponents of the Monastic Life*, prob-ably written after 379, and 'the rulers may become pagans.' From a modern perspective it may seem that the accession of the ortho-dox Christian emperor Theodosius in 379 and the laws he issued to suppress the pagan cults marked the final stage of the advance of Christianity that had begun after the conversion of Constantine in 312. But to Theodosius' contemporaries this was not so clear. Paganism was not dead yet, and it did not seem impossible that a new Julian would ascend to the throne. In 380 Bishop Gregory of Nazianzus complained that the Apostate's 'embers, although we have come safely through the flames, continue to scorch us still to this very day.' In 391 the Emperor Theodosius deemed it necessary to issue a law in which he censured apostasy, which, apparently, was a burning issue: 'If any persons should betray the holy faith and should profane holy baptism, they shall be segregated from the community of all men.' When the usurper Eugenius had taken up the reins of government in the western part of the empire in 392, pagan envoys immediately came to him and requested that he should make restitution to the pagan temples—Eugenius had been raised as a Christian, but, like Julian, he wore a (philosopher's?) beard and rumor had it that his followers would turn the basilica in Milan into a stable and enlist the clerics as soldiers.[11]

Hatred and fear continued to pursue Julian even after the fourth century had come to an end, as we shall see in the chapters to come. For the moment we return to the spring of 360, when, in Paris, *Caesar* Julian was made *Augustus*. The contemporary his-torian Eutropius says that this was done 'according to the general wish of his soldiers.' This may be true. Many of the soldiers in Gaul were reluctant to leave their homes to comply with the decision of *Augustus* Constantius, who had ordered their transfer to the East

to fight against the Persians. But whether or not it was a sponta-
neous action on the part of the troops is another matter. It is not
impossible that Julian himself had pulled the strings backstage.
However this may be, many of Julian's soldiers were of German
or Gallic descent, as is clear from what some of them did during
the coronation ceremony in Paris: they raised Julian on a shield.
Up until then the Romans had not been in the habit of doing this,
but once this feature was introduced, it was to survive until late in
Byzantine times.[12]

The news of the declaration in Paris reached Constantius while
he was busy preparing for a campaign against the Persians, who
had captured and destroyed cities in Roman territory. Julian himself informed his cousin of what had happened. He wrote a letter in
which he stated inter alia that the actions of the soldiers had been
a complete surprise for him, and that he hoped that Constantius
would accept the situation as it was. This hope (if Julian really
harbored it) proved idle. Constantius exploded as soon as Julian's
envoys had delivered their message to the *Augustus*, whom they
found in Cappadocian Caesarea. Constantius disapproved of all
that had happened and in his turn wrote a letter, informing Julian
that the power of a *Caesar* was sufficient for him. For the moment,
however, Constantius regarded the war with Persia as his main
responsibility and thus he refrained from seeking an immediate
confrontation with his cousin.[13]

Not so Julian. He was aware that his strength was inferior to
that of Constantius and felt uncertain how best to behave, but after
some hesitation he decided to attack Constantius first, because
he did not expect that his cousin would ever give in. According
to Ammianus he felt impelled to do this because prophetic signs
and dreams predicted that Constantius would soon die. Moreover,
Julian remembered very well how Constantius had eliminated
Julian's brother Gallus. But before Julian marched to the East with

his troops—remarkably, this time we do not hear the soldiers complain about leaving their homes—he first found time in the summer
of 360 for a successful expedition against the so-called Atthuarian
Franks on the other side of the Rhine, after which he spent the winter in southern Gaul. On January 6, 361 he celebrated the Christian
feast of Epiphany there, as we have already seen—the time was not
yet ripe to reveal his paganism openly.[14]

In the spring of 361, probably in the middle of April, Julian left
Gaul and began his march eastward. He divided his troops à la
Alexander the Great in three parts, sent one division ahead through
Italy, ordered another through the middle of Raetia (southern
Germany and Austria), and marched himself with the retinue to the
Danube. When he had reached the place where this river became
navigable (near present-day Ulm in Germany, presumably), 'he
embarked on boats, of which, by a fortunate chance, there was a
good supply' as Ammianus Marcellinus wrote. Zosimus does not
mention this piece of luck, but reports that Julian had these ships
built especially for this purpose, while Libanius emphatically
denies that Julian built his fleet out of hatred for Constantius, an
opinion that only strengthens the suspicion that Julian had made
arrangements in advance and had thus aided fortune. Whilst sail-
ing on the Danube Julian's army went through what is now southern Germany, northern Austria, and Hungary, until it reached
Bononia (modern Bonostar or Banoštor in Serbia), where it disem-
barked. Julian now headed for nearby Sirmium on the river Sava, a
city that not only was an imperial residence with a palace, but also
functioned as the headquarters of the military commander in the
area—the commander at the time, Lucillianus, was a supporter of
Constantius and was preparing to resist Julian, but he was taken by
surprise and had to look on as Julian took over his troops.[15]

Julian's next move was to occupy the strategically important
Succi pass, in modern Bulgaria, also known as Trajan's Gate or

Ihtiman pass. It was a crucial step. When news of this had reached Constantius, he decided to direct his forces against Julian, who for the moment retreated to Naissus (modern Niš in Serbia, the birthplace of Constantine the Great), which apparently was the place agreed upon as the destination for the other two army divisions as well. It was in Naissus that Julian heard that Constantius had died on November 3, 361. He now made haste to reach Constantinople.[16]

Chapter 4

George of Cappadocia

Julian arrived in Constantinople on December 11, 361. In this 'Second Rome,' founded by Constantine the Great on the site of ancient Byzantium, the emperor spent a couple of months, during which he was frenetically busy. He beautified the city, settled scores with supporters of his cousin and predecessor Constantius II, appointed close friends to high positions, reorganized the imperial household, attended sessions of the Senate, acted as arbiter in juridical disputes, received delegations of foreign peoples, paid his respects to his teacher Maximus of Ephesus, took care of the defense of the Danube border, promulgated laws, and all the while wrote letters and essays, especially at night.[1]

The laws issued by Julian in Constantinople provide us with a good idea of the many subjects the emperor had to deal with. They comprise decrees on the issue of military allowances, on the position of accountants 'who have learned with their clever fraud to falsify the public accounts of the municipalities,' on patronage, and on certain rights of senators. In other decrees Julian dealt with the public postal service, which had been 'prostrated by the immoderate presumption of certain persons and by the great number of post warrants' that certain officials did not cease to extend, with the position of accountants once again, and with people who concealed the property of proscribed persons. He took measures to restore public landholdings to municipalities. He took care of taxation and tax exemptions, of the duties of the members of municipal councils, of the so-called *aurum coronarium*, 'crown gold,' originally a voluntary contribution in gold presented as a thank-offering to the emperor, later a forced contribution levied upon all members of city councils. And so on and so forth.[2]

In Julian's philosophical and theological essays as well as in his letters, we sometimes find jeers directed at the first Christian emperors. In a pamphlet, written at the beginning of 362, he vehemently lashed out against Constantine the Great. He chided his uncle for not having concerned himself with the gods, and for having raised his sons so badly that after his death they massacred their relatives, were at one another's throat, followed their father's example by looting and destroying the venerable old temples, and built Christian churches in their place. Constantine is also Julian's butt in the *Symposium,* or *Kronia* (Latin *Saturnalia*), generally known as *Caesares*. In this satire Constantine is compared unfavorably to his pagan predecessors. He is depicted as a debaucher and a miserable ruler. Almost at the end of the *Caesares* the first Christian emperor seeks consolation in the arms of the goddesses Wantonness and Prodigality. With these he meets Jesus of Nazareth. Then follows a passage that brilliantly typifies Julian's way of thinking. In a parody of Matthew 11:28 ('Come to me, all you who are weary and burdened, and I will give you rest') and ridiculing the sacrament of baptism (Constantine had deliberately postponed his baptism to the very last day of his life), Julian puts these words in the mouth of Jesus: 'He that is a seducer, he that is a murderer, he that is sacrilegious and infamous, let him approach without fear! For with this water will I wash him and will straightway make him clean.'[3]

It was, of course, out of the question to criticize Constantine openly as long as Julian was on speaking terms with Constantine's son Constantius II. Indeed, when Julian acted as Constantius' *Caesar* in Gaul, he feigned friendship—'wolf's friendship,' he called it later. He even wrote panegyrics on his cousin. But Julian threw all restraint to the wind after his soldiers had raised him on a shield in Paris in 360. With bitter irony he wrote, probably in Naissus, on his way to Constantinople, 'That on the father's side I am descended from the same stock as Constantius on his father's side is well known. Our fathers were brothers, sons of the same father. And close kinsmen as we were how this most humane Emperor treated us! Six of my cousins and his, and my father who was his own uncle and also another uncle of both of us on the father's side, and my eldest brother, he put to death without a trial.' In the rest of this *Letter to the Athenians* he does not mince his words, either. Once he had arrived in Constantinople he expressed his aversion to his Christian cousin not only in writing. He also put his words into action.[4]

The burning of sacrificial victims, forbidden by Constantius and his father, was permitted again. Pagan temples, which had been closed or destroyed by order of Constantius, were reconstructed or reopened—as a result pagan admirers gave Julian the honorary title *templorum restaurator*. Landed property and real estate, which once belonged to temples and thus to the cities in the empire, but which under Constantine and Constantius had been seized by the imperial treasury or by private individuals, were restored to the cities. Privileges, granted to Christian clerics, were abolished, to the horror of those who because of their faith had backed out of the often costly obligations involved in, for instance, membership of a municipal council. Bishops and other Christians were allowed to return from exile—Constantius, who himself was a moderate 'Arian,' had banished several Christians whose views he considered heretical.[5]

One of the Christians exiled by Constantius, Aetius, was an old acquaintance of Julian's. He received a cordial letter that not only put an end to his exile but also invited him to come to the imperial court. A carriage of the imperial post was put at his disposal.

It is possible that Julian's purpose was merely to do Aetius a favor. However, it could well be that there was something more behind it. Aetius was not the only person who received an invitation to come to Constantinople. Julian also invited to the court the quarrelling bishops of this city, together with their bickering congregations. Affably he urged them to give up their mutual squabblings: everybody should be free to choose his own religion. This sounds noble, but the implicit meaning was not so generous. Julian knew perfectly well that Christological questions divided the Christians to such a degree that they would not be able to set aside promptly their differences of opinion on the emperor's order. Both pro- and anti-Julianic sources state that Julian's appeal for tolerance and the recall of exiles were meant only to stir up the flames of discord. If the Christians were divided he would have fewer problems than if they were united.[6]

The best-known bishop to return to his diocese was Athanasius of Alexandria, an indefatigable opponent of absolutely everyone who rejected the doctrine of Holy Trinity that had been accepted at the Nicene Council of 325. During Athanasius' absence, George the Cappadocian had installed himself in the episcopal see of Alexandria, with the consent of Constantius II (some years before, at the time that George was still bishop of Caesarea in Cappadocia and Julian was living nearby on the Macellum estate, Julian had borrowed books from him, as we have seen). George, who was like Constantius II a follower of Athanasius' enemy Arius, was not exactly a paragon of diplomacy. His arrogant and headstrong behavior had incurred the hatred of many Alexandrians. He often clashed with the followers of the exiled Athanasius, as well as with the traditionally turbulent pagan population. He threatened to destroy the temple of Alexandria's Patron Goddess, ridiculed the devotees of Mithras (and thus incited bloody riots), and demanded that soldiers should occupy and loot the temple of Serapis under the watchful eyes of lawful authorities represented by the military commander of Egypt—this *dux Aegypti* by the name of Flavius Artemius we shall meet in Chapter 5 as a Christian martyr, a very special Christian martyr: although he had lent a hand to the 'Arian' bishop George, he was revered by Nicene Christians after he had been executed by order of Julian.[7]

The soldiers stationed in Alexandria, to whom George more than once made a strong plea, could not save him from a horrible death. When the news of Constantius' decease (November 3, 361) and Julian's sole emperorship had reached the city, the Alexandrian populace directed its fury against the hated George and other protégés of Constantius. The bishop was put in chains and imprisoned, supposedly in anticipation of a trial. But it did not come to that. After a few weeks, on December 24, 361, George was dragged from his prison by a furious mob and severely beaten up. Subsequently he was hog-tied to a camel. Having been carried through the city he was killed and burned. His ashes were scattered at sea; the camel and some of Constantius' officials met with the same fate.[8]

The question as to who was to blame for the lynching of the 'Arian' bishop, the pagan or the Nicene Christian part of the population, became a moot point. It is to this disagreement that we owe the survival of one of Julian's letters, which would otherwise have been lost, for the church historian Socrates Scholasticus, who indignantly rejected the view that Christians were responsible for the murder, cites a letter of the emperor to prove his case. In this letter Julian rebukes the pagans in Alexandria, and expresses his disappointment with the fact that they had acted on their own authority. He acknowledges that their grievances against the 'enemy of the gods' were justified; indeed, he admits that George had deserved the death penalty, but he denounces the high-handed action of the Alexandrians and their disregard for the laws. He should really punish the city, but he would not go as far as that. A solemn reprimand would suffice, he thought, because he was confident that the Alexandrians were real 'Hellenes' and therefore wise enough to learn their lesson.[9]

Julian's lukewarm response to the events in Alexandria clearly shows where his sympathies lay. He was not favorably disposed toward the Christians in this city, as Athanasius found out to his cost. After the death of George the Cappadocian, the leader of the Nicene Christians again seized the bishop's see of Alexandria, apparently thinking that he could take advantage of Julian's offer of the opportunity to return to those Christians who had been banished by Constantius. But the new emperor did not like Athanasius' action. In letters to the Alexandrians Julian wrote that although he did permit the exiles to return to their cities, this definitely did not mean that they could return to their former churches. Athanasius had exceeded his authority, according to Julian, and had to be cut down to size. Consequently, the bishop who had been banished before by the Christian emperors Constantine and Constantius was now exiled by the pagan Julian.[10]

Thus ended the first outburst of religious violence during the reign of Julian the Apostate. It would not be the last. Julian himself, who resided in Constantinople, had not been involved at all in the disturbances in Alexandria, and he had shown his disapproval of the lynching of the 'Arian' bishop and his associates. But the mischief was done. Julian's accession to the throne had set in motion a development that would widen the gap between pagans and Christians and that would lead to outbursts of violence all over the empire, with or without Julian's say-so. The emperor personally did not instigate persecutions, but at a local level accounts were sometimes settled. This was in part because the mob that had killed George of Cappadocia had not been punished.[11]

Chapter 5

Artemius

When the son of a certain Anthimus once spent the night in the Church of John the Baptist in the Oxeia quarter of Constantinople, a miracle occurred. The young man suffered from unbearable pains in his testicles and could no longer pass water. His father, a physician, put him in a litter and had him taken to the Church of John; in the crypt of this church was a leaden sarcophagus with the mortal remains of Saint Artemius, the martyr whom we met in Chapter 4 as *dux Aegypti*. Artemius had become a saint, and possessed healing powers. He was especially good at curing diseases of the spine and the genitals, as we learn from the *Miracula Artemii*, a collection of Artemius' miracle cures that was written down in the seventh century. In the night in question the holy martyr appeared in a dream to Anthimus' son in the shape of his father. 'Undress yourself and show me what you have.' The young man obeyed, whereupon Artemius pinched his testicles so vehemently that the boy woke up and screamed aloud. He first thought that his disease had worsened, but then realized that the pain had gone and that he was cured.[1]

St. Artemius performed his miracles in Constantinople, but he died somewhere else. The *Artemii passio*, a piece of writing dating from the ninth century by an anonymous author who, in some manuscripts, is called John of Rhodes, otherwise unknown, in others John of Damascus, describes Artemius' death by the order of Julian, the tortures before he died, and the events of his life. It shows all the characteristics of 'passions épiques' (to use a term coined by Hippolyte Delehaye), that is, tales of sufferings that are largely fictitious. On the other hand, its author is familiar with the rough outlines of the political history of the time he writes about, namely, the fourth century, a familiarity that indicates that he must have consulted older sources. He himself says that he had some church historians at his disposal, one of whom was Philostorgius. This is not unlikely, although he probably did not find much about Artemius in the latter's work—only fragments of Philostorgius' church history have been passed down, so that we cannot be sure; in the remnants we have there is no mention of Artemius. The author also says that he derived some information from Eusebius of Caesarea, contemporary and biographer of Constantine the Great. This is certainly incorrect.[2]

On the authority of Eusebius it is alleged that Artemius was a senator in the time of Constantine and that he belonged to the emperor's inner circle, but no trace of him is found in Eusebius' *Ecclesiastical History* or his *Life of Constantine*. It is also alleged that Artemius was present when Constantine had his famous vision near the Milvian Bridge in 312. In that case Artemius would have been over eighty when he supposedly died a martyr's death on Julian's orders in 362, a calculation that does not tally with the information in the *passio* that he was still in active service in the time of Julian. It would seem, therefore, that the alleged quotations from Eusebius are fictitious, and are perhaps meant to provide a starker contrast between the reign of Constantine, the first Christian emperor, and that of his nephew, the 'persecutor' Julian. On the other hand, there may be some truth in the remark that Artemius and Constantine's son Constantius II were friends. At any rate, it is absolutely certain that during Constantius' reign, Artemius was military commander of Egypt for a couple of years.[3]

As we have seen in Chapter 4, in his capacity of *dux Aegypti* Artemius operated as the accomplice of Bishop George the Cappadocian. At the bishop's request he ordered his soldiers to attack and plunder the temple of Serapis in Alexandria. He also helped the 'Arian' George to hunt down Athanasius, George's orthodox predecessor, who had been exiled. We know this from sources other than the *Artemii passio*. In the *passio* nothing is said of all this, an omission that is remarkable, but not surprising. More than once the orthodox author of the *passio* makes it clear that he did not like 'Arians.' He either did not want to admit that his hero Artemius himself had supported an 'Arian' bishop or, more likely, this was no longer known in the ninth century. Presumably, this aspect of Artemius' past had been pushed into the background in the centuries between Artemius' life-time and the recording of the *passio*—for the sake of convenience I leave aside the theory that tries to solve the problem by assuming that there had been two Artemii, the 'Arianizing' commander of Egypt and an orthodox martyr executed by Julian, who at one time or another merged into one person.[4]

Although the author of the *Artemii passio* is silent about the riots in Alexandria and about Artemius' connection with Bishop George, he does refer obliquely to Artemius' stay in Egypt. He states that Artemius had a high position there, because Constantius II wanted to express his gratitude for the successful completion of an important assignment: Artemius had discovered the relics of Saint Andrew (among others) and had brought them to Constantinople. Andrew had been, according to the tradition, crucified in Patras in 62 CE on a cross afterward named after him, and Artemius had now brought his remains back to the place, where the apostle had founded the first Christian church when Constantinople was still Byzantium. The transfer (*translatio*) of Saint Andrew's relics to Constantinople is, apart from in the *Artemii passio*, mentioned in the *Chronicon Paschale* and in some other writings. However, only in the *Artemii passio* do we read something about the role Artemius played in it. It seems therefore likely that once again we are dealing with a concoction of the hagiographer.[5]

The data we have for Artemius' life are scarce and, as far as the *Artemii passio* is concerned, of doubtful historicity. With respect to his death the situation is no different. It is, for instance, not clear where he died. According to the *Artemii passio* it was in Antioch, according to the *Chronicon Paschale* in Alexandria. Ammianus Marcellinus, unfortunately, is silent on this matter, just as he is not very communicative in other respects, but at least he makes it clear that Artemius had already resigned his position as *dux Aegypti* when he was put to death after 'the Alexandrians had charged him with a mass of outrageous crimes.' Ammianus does not say what sorts of crimes Artemius was accused of, but that the execution took place at the insistence of the people of Alexandria justifies the presumption that, according to him, the main issue was that Artemius had taken the side of Bishop George. This idea is reinforced by what Ammianus goes on to say, that is, that the Alexandrians turned their wrath toward Bishop George when they heard that Artemius had paid the ultimate price. As has already been noted, Ammianus does not say where precisely Artemius was executed. However, he does say that the Alexandrians feared that Artemius would harm the many people who had injured him when he had returned with his power restored. Note the word 'returned': it is a clear indication that, according to Ammianus, Artemius was judged (and executed) not in Alexandria (as the *Chronicon Paschale* states), but elsewhere. It would seem that this time the *Artemii passio* is right, and that it was indeed in Antioch, where Julian stayed, that Artemius was court martialed.[6]

We left Julian in Chapter 4 in Constantinople in December 361. He stayed a couple of months in the city on the Bosporus, and it was here that he took his first measures to revive paganism. But the

Persian war also required his attention, and in the spring of 362 he left his native city. From Constantinople the journey went first through Asia Minor to Ancyra (Ankara). On his way the emperor deemed it opportune to deviate from the normal itinerary, in order to visit Pessinus (at a distance of some kilometers from modern Sivrihisar), where a sanctuary of the Mother of the Gods was located, for whom the emperor a little while ago in Constantinople had written a hymn. After passing through Caesarea in Cappadocia and Tarsus, the emperor and his army reached Antioch in July 362, and it was in Antioch that the confrontation took place between the emperor and Artemius, as related in the *Artemii passio*.[7]

To start with we see how the hagiographer transfers his hero from Egypt to Syria in order to acquaint him with Julian: 'Eugenius and Macarius [see for them Chapter 13] were punished atrociously and had to endure relentless tortures. While these men were being so cruelly punished and suffering the heaviest blows, the blessed and pious Artemius, as has been shown earlier, had been appointed *dux* and *Augustalis* of all Egypt by Constantius, and because of his honorable and inimitable management had also received the authority to manage the affairs of Syria. He was devoted to the Roman imperial family. On hearing that Julian had succeeded Constantius and was hastening to wage war in Persia, Artemius came to Antioch, following an invitation which bade him to come. As soon as he and his whole army had arrived, he made his way with his attendant pomp and bodyguards to the emperor and appeared precisely at the moment that the Apostate was conducting on a platform his inquisitions of the holy martyrs Eugenius and Macarius.'[8]

There he was then, the '*dux et augustalis* of all Egypt' (the title is anachronistic), all of a sudden standing with his bodyguards before the emperor, who, remarkably, was unaware that Artemius had entered the city. Julian soon discovered what kind of person Artemius was. Artemius said to him, 'O Emperor, why do you so cruelly torture men who are holy and consecrated to God, and force them to abjure their own faith? You should realize that you too are a man liable to the same suffering, with a share in the same type of physical pains, even if God has made you emperor—if in fact it is from God that you have your empire, and not the Devil, evil prince of darkness, who has sought you out against us, just as once he sought and claimed Job, and claimed you in his wickedness, so as to winnow the wheat of Christ and sow a crop of weeds. But his efforts are in vain. . . . When Julian had heard this speech by the martyr, he was totally astounded, and his anger was more aggravated, like the flame of a fire rekindled when more wood revives it. He gave a loud and piercing cry: "Who is this scoundrel and where does he come from, that has spewed forth such a torrent of oratory before me on my platform?" His troops replied "It is the Governor of Alexandria, master." "Artemius?" said the emperor, "that villain who arranged a cruel death for my brother?" "Yes," they said, "best of emperors, it is he." '[9]

Artemius accused by Julian of being the cruel murderer of his half-brother Gallus? This comes as a surprise for the reader, who remembers that in the previous chapter of the *passio* Artemius received a letter from Julian with the invitation to come to Antioch with his army and join the fight against the Persians (it is again one of the incongruities in the *Artemii passio*). 'For the murder and bloodshed of my brother, I will appoint his punishment tomorrow, gods willing,' Julian continues, 'for I shall destroy him not with one death, but with thousands and all those that murderers are subject to.' Much is then made of Artemius' sufferings. He was placed naked upon the platform and beaten with oxhide whips so that the ground became soaked with blood. He was temporarily imprisoned together with Eugenius and Macarius, deprived of bread and water, then tortured again. In between the agonies there were altercations with the emperor, who more than once was outwitted by the martyr: 'But as for your calling the sun and the moon and the stars your gods,' Artemius said, 'I am ashamed at your profession of ignorance, or rather of poor judgment. Did not Anaxagoras of Clazomenae, clearly your teacher, say that the sun was a red-hot mass and the stars were bodies of pumice-stone and entirely devoid of life and feeling? How therefore, best and most philosophic of emperors, do you yourself address as gods things that are rejected and discredited by your teachers? For I know that you belong to the Platonic school.' As a result Julian ordered other forms of torture. Artemius' flanks were pierced through with steel awls and his back was skewered with sharp spikes and split open while he was dragged along. He was crushed between rocks, so that his insides ruptured, his bones were shattered, and his eyeballs were knocked out of their sockets, but even then the martyr survived and displayed the same steadfastness as before, until finally his head was cut off, 'the date being the twentieth of October [362], the sixth day of the week, known as the "day of preparation." '[10]

Before Artemius died the soldiers of the execution squad permitted him to pray, whereupon a voice sounded from heaven saying that God answered his prayer and granted him healing powers. A pious woman, Ariste by name, a deaconess of the Church in Antioch, asked Julian for Artemius' body. The request was granted, whereupon Ariste 'made a coffin and smeared with myrrh his holy and blessed body, and anointed it with valuable scents and ointments, and laid it in the coffin, and had it carried to the prosperous city Constantinople, placing it in a conspicuous place, since she wanted to build a home worthy of the saintly and great martyr Artemius, and to create a shrine to commemorate his famous martyrdom.'[11]

This is how the former *dux Aegypti*, who had sided with the 'Arian' Bishop George against pagans and orthodox Christians in Alexandria and was executed by order of Julian in Antioch, became an Orthodox martyr in Constantinople. At the end of 361, in Constantinople, Julian took the first measures that showed clearly that a wind of change was blowing through the Roman Empire. In section 22 of the *Artemii passio* we find an outline of those measures. The words are no doubt tendentious, but in essence they agree with what we know from other sources: Julian, 'when he had taken over the Roman empire, was especially keen to reestablish paganism. So everywhere he dispatched letters and gave orders to rebuild their shrines and altars with great zeal and enthusiasm. And he took away all the revenues which Constantine the Great and his son Constantius had assigned to the churches and he consecrated these to the temples of the demons; in place of bishops, presbyters and deacons he established temple attendants and wardens, sprinklers of purifying water and sacrificial officers and carriers of holy baskets and all the titles that pagan nonsense ascribes. These acts and others Julian accomplished in Constantinople.'

Chapter 6

Pagan Temples and Christian Churches

One day in the autumn of 355, when Julian entered Vienna shortly after he had become *Caesar*, a blind old woman showed her familiarity with the revolutionary plans of the future *Augustus*. When she asked who had just entered the town—now Vienne, some thirty kilometers south of Lyon—the answer was 'Iulianus *Caesar*,' whereupon the prescient woman cried out that he would restore the temples of the gods. This no doubt apocryphal anecdote serves as a prelude to what Ammianus Marcellinus later relates more extensively in his *Res Gestae*: as soon as Julian had entered Constantinople in December 361 he decreed (as we have already seen) that 'the temples should be opened, sacrifices brought to their altars, and the worship of the old gods restored.'[1]

The statement of the historian is confirmed in other sources: literary, juridical, and, last but not least, epigraphical texts. Of these, the epigraphical texts, being concrete documents from Julian's own time, deserve to be given pride of place. There is, for instance, an inscription, found in the village of 'Anz in Syria, some hundred kilometers south of Damascus. The short Greek text, bricked in a wall above the door of a house in Umm Ir-Rammân in the region of Bosra, not far from where the inscription was found, ends with an exact date: 'the fifth day of the month Dystrus in the 256th year [of the local era],' that is, February 19, 362 CE. The preceding words read thus: 'During the reign of Imperator Augustus Flavius Claudius Iulianus the worship of the gods was restored, and the temple reconstructed and consecrated'—the Syrian followers of the Apostate had not wasted much time in implementing the emperor's decree; since Julian's entry in Constantinople, hardly two months had passed.[2]

Another inscription, this time in Latin and without a precise date, but certainly from Julian's reign, also confirms Ammianus' words. The column of limestone, little more than a meter high, on which the inscription was written, was found in 1969 near the kibbutz Ma'ayan Barukh in northern Israel. The stone is now in the Beit Ussishkin Nature Museum of the kibbutz Dan (Figure 2).

Figure 2. Inscription found in Ma'ayan Barukh, Israel, commemorating Julian inter alia as 'restorer of temples' (Conti 2004, pp. 71–72, no. 18, 2–3 *templorum [re]stauratori*). Beit Ussishkin Nature Museum, Israel. *(Credit Line: © Werner Eck, University of Cologne, Germany: 1297_EckScan.JPG.)*

The text honors Julian inter alia as *templorum restaurator,* 'restorer of temples,' words that also must have been cut into another stone with an almost identical inscription of which the top line is illegible. This stone was found in the early twentieth century in Minet-el-Hosn near modern Beirut in Lebanon, and can be seen in the Archaeological Museum of the American University of Beirut. A counterpart in Greek was discovered around 1980 during excavations under the square before the Archaeological Museum of Thessaloniki in Greece. The altar, eighty-eight centimeters high, is in the possession of the museum there. Two undated inscriptions from Samos (one of which mentions the construction of a temple of Hera), provided that they can be dated to the reign of Julian (which seems likely), may also be cited as possible evidence.[3]

These inscriptions stem from the eastern part of the Roman Empire, but epigraphical sources also attest that in the western part a wind of change was blowing. On the base of a statue in honor of Julian (the statue itself is lost), found in Casae in the province Numidia, now El Mahder in Algeria, the emperor was given the honorific title *restitutor libertatis et Romanae religionis,* 'restorer of liberty and the Roman religion,' while he was called *restitutor sacrorum,* 'restorer of sacred rites,' on the base of another, also lost, statue in Thibilis, Algerian Announa. It is of course obvious that these inscriptions were made by order of the pagan inhabitants of Casae and Thibilis. The greater part of the Christians in the province Numidia no doubt rejected Julian's religious measures. But not all Christians were equally negative toward the new emperor. In the East the Novatians, or the 'Pure' (καθαροί, katharoi), as they called themselves, had reason to be thankful to Julian because he had allowed them to rebuild their church in a suburb of Constantinople that had been destroyed by 'Arians.' The Novatians were a rigorist sect similar to the Donatists; originally followers of the third-century Roman priest and antipope Novatian, they spread out all over the Roman Empire after Novatian's death. In the West the Donatists welcomed Julian's accession to the throne.[4]

When Julian the Apostate ascended to the imperial throne, the struggle between Donatists and Catholics, which had been going on for half a century, was as vehement as ever—this nicely illustrates what, according to Ammianus, Julian knew from experience: 'that no wild beasts are such dangerous enemies to man as Christians are to one another.' Under Julian's predecessors the Catholics had won the upper hand, so that many Donatists had been driven into exile. But now the tide was turning. Early in 362 a delegation of Donatists, led by the bishops Pontius, Rogatianus, and Cassianus, applied to Julian with a request: exiles should be allowed to return; churches of which they were deprived ought to be given back. Their request was granted. Outbursts of violence were the result. For instance, a group of Donatists made a raid on Castellum Lemellefense in the province Mauretania Sitifensis, now Kherbet Zembia in Algeria, and intended to seize the church. When it appeared that the church was closed, some Donatists climbed onto the roof, made a hole in it, and pelted the Catholics, who were assembled around the altar, with roof tiles. Two deacons were killed, many others wounded. The Donatists also penetrated the coastal town Tipasa, a Catholic stronghold not far from modern Cherchel in Algeria. They behaved brutally, according to a Catholic—and probably not totally unprejudiced—contemporary, Bishop Optatus of Mileve in Numidia: they threw the communion bread and wine to the dogs, flung liturgical vessels with ointments out of the windows of the church, lacerated men, carried women off, or, when they were pregnant, cut their bellies open, raped nuns, and beat children to death. The provincial governor looked on passively, and his officials went so far as to take part in the events.[5]

In Castellum Lefellense and Tipasa in North Africa, Christians fought against Christians. We hear of course more often of conflicts between Christians and pagans. The looting of the temple of Serapis in Alexandria by soldiers of the *dux Aegypti* at the request of Bishop George of Cappadocia has already been mentioned in Chapter 4 and Chapter 5. For another example we focus on Syrian Arethusa, now Er Restan, halfway between Epiphania (Hama) and Emesa (Homs), where the local bishop, Marcus, paid dearly for the fact that he had ordered the destruction of a pagan temple and the construction of a Christian church in its place in the time of Constantius II. After Julian had become sole emperor in 361 the elderly cleric was faced with the consequences. A furious mob gave him the choice: he could either personally reconstruct the pagan temple or give money to make a restoration possible. Marcus rejected both alternatives and went into hiding. But when he saw that others were punished in his stead, he returned. He still refused, however, to give in, whereupon the mob cut off his ears, dragged him by his hair through the streets, and threw him into a cistern. He was also tossed in the air by the youths of the town and manhandled with sharp slate pencils until his body bled. Finally, rubbed with honey and fish sauce, he was put into a basket and hung in the burning sun, a prey to wasps and bees.[6]

We know about the agony of Marcus of Arethusa mainly through reports of Christian authors. One of them, the church historian Theodoret, who hailed from Antioch and became bishop of Cyrrhus (Nebi Huri in Syria), regarded it as good material for a tragedy in the manner of Aeschylus and Sophocles. Admittedly, the horrible details are dramatic indeed, but presumably our spokesmen have blown the story up. 'I rather like it here upstairs,' Marcus is supposed to have said to his tormentors, 'for I am looking down from above at you pedestrians fussing around.' Was the bishop, beaten almost to death and stung by swarms of bees and wasps, really capable of making this clever remark from his basket? It does not seem probable, but it would be naive to suppose that in this religious struggle atrocities did not take place—the history of mankind offers numerous parallels—and it would be wrong to think that the story of Marcus was totally invented by Christians. Moreover, there is the undisputable testimony of the pagan Libanius, who in one of his letters explicitly refers to the torments of the bishop of Arethusa.[7]

Libanius mentions Marcus in a letter to the governor of the province Arabia, a certain Belaeus. In this letter, written early in 362, he stands up for his Christian friend Orion. This Orion was temporarily imprisoned in Bostra (Bosra), waiting to appear before Belaeus' judgment seat. It was the third time that Libanius applied to the governor. An earlier letter of 362 and a talk with Belaeus had been unsuccessful. Orion was accused of having violated a temple and of having stolen its precious objects. Whether he was guilty or not—in the second letter Libanius seems less convinced of the innocence of his friend than in the first—it was nevertheless Belaeus' duty, according to Libanius, to make sure that Orion did not die in prison and thus become a martyr. One Marcus of Arethusa was enough: 'That fellow Marcus was racked and flogged, his beard was plucked out, and yet he endured it all bravely, and now is almost divine in prestige. Whenever he makes an appearance, people jostle to see him. And that is what our emperor knew: though he grieved for the temple, he did not execute the fellow. So take Marcus' survival as your rule: leave Orion unharmed and do not release him to be an object of admiration.'[8]

How the case of Orion ended is unknown. We do know, however, that the pagan Libanius threw himself into the breach also for other Christians who were accused of having violated pagan temples. The conflict between Christians and pagans did not have only negative sides. As to Julian, note Libanius' words: the emperor grieved for the temple in Arethusa, but did not execute the man who was responsible for its destruction. Neither did he execute Eleusius, the bishop of Cyzicus (near modern Erdek in Turkey), who, according to Socrates and Sozomen, also had destroyed temples.[9]

Chapter 7

Sacrifices to the Gods

In the autumn of 354 Julian visited the town of Ilium. On his way to the West, where in the next year he was made *Caesar* by his cousin Constantius, he came within striking distance of the place where Troy was once situated, and he did not want to miss the opportunity to visit the pagan temples of that famous location. To let sleeping dogs lie—the time that he could openly profess his faith was not yet there—he posed as a tourist (as famous men before him had done, the Persian king Xerxes, Alexander the Great, the Roman emperor Hadrian). The local bishop, a certain Pegasius, showed him around. It was a remarkable visit, Julian later stated in one of his letters, and rather surprising, too. It appeared that the Christian bishop, just like his princely guest, was sympathetic toward paganism. In Ilium people could take care of the statues of the gods and sacrifice on their altars in peace, without being disturbed, as if this were not forbidden by law since the time of Constantine the Great.[1]

Constantine the Great and his sons had reversed roles. In the first centuries of the Common Era, attempts had sometimes been made to force Christians to bring pagan sacrifices. During the reign of the emperor Decius (249–251), for instance, a pledge of loyalty in the form of a sacrifice was demanded from Christians and putative Christians. Anyone who refused was killed; whoever obeyed received a certificate that was authorized and signed by a qualified official. Some of these certified avowals written on papyrus have emerged from underneath the sands of Egypt. Here is an example: 'Aurelia Leulis from the village Euhemeria in the district Themiste to those appointed to see to the sacrifices. I have always continued to sacrifice and pay respect to the gods. Together with my underage children Palempis and T [illegible]eris I have now made libations and blood sacrifices in your presence, in accordance with the statute, and I have eaten from the sacrificial meat. I give you therefore this certificate and request you to undersign it' (then follow signatures and the date of issuance of the certificate). To the most committed of Christians this act of the Egyptian Aurelia Leulis was an abomination. 'You are to abstain from food sacrificed to idols,' reads one of the ordinances of the resolution passed by the Council in Jerusalem at the instigation of Jesus' brother James, a resolution that can be found in the *Acts of the Apostles*. James had argued that 'we do not trouble those who are turning to God from among the Gentiles, but we write to them that they abstain from things contaminated by idols and from fornication and from the meat of strangled animals and from blood.' The Christian emperors in the fourth century went much further. They were not satisfied with dissuading pagans who had converted to Christianity to eat sacrificial meat, but forbade sacrifices to the gods altogether. Since it was an essential part of their religion, this was a severe blow to those who adhered to paganism.[2]

Julian would have sadly remembered his encounter with Pegasius when, hardly one and a half years later, he had to observe that a new law against the performing of pagan sacrifices was issued also in his name. On February 19, 356, it was proclaimed in Mediolanum (Milan) that 'any person, who should be proved to devote attention to sacrifices or to worship images, should be subjected to capital punishment.' Constantius II was responsible for this resolution, but the law was, apart from by the *Augustus* himself, also subscribed by his *Caesar* Julian. The fact that Constantius deemed such an imperial proclamation necessary shows that not only in Ilium were the earlier regulations concerning the banning of sacrifices disregarded. Other sources confirm this, and even after 356 pagans ignored the law, as the example of the prefect of the city of Rome Tertullus illustrates, who in 359 publicly performed sacrifices in the temple of Castor and Pollux at Ostia when the corn ships entered the harbor.[3]

How exceptional the transgression of the law by Tertullus, Pegasius, and others was is difficult to say. Generally, Constantius and his spies did not stand for any nonsense, and not all were prepared to risk their lives for their faith. On the other hand, not one example is known of someone who was convicted on account of the laws against sacrificing, and it has been argued that the imperial laws in this respect were meant as a deterrent rather than as punitive measures. Whatever the case may be, from the end of 361, pagans who wanted to sacrifice to their gods had full scope. Constantius had died on November 3, and Julian, sole emperor now, sang a different tune. 'I sacrifice oxen in public,' Julian wrote elatedly to his friend and teacher Maximus shortly after his cousin's death, and, 'I have offered to the gods many hecatombs as thank-offerings.' After he had entered Constantinople on December 11, 361, he directed, as we have already seen, that 'the temples should be opened, sacrifices brought to their altars, and the worship of the old gods restored.' He himself used to sacrifice twice a day, in the morning and in the evening.[4]

The Greek word 'hecatomb' that Julian used in his letter to Maximus is as old as Homer. In the Iliad it refers to an offering of a hundred (ἑκατόν, hecaton) oxen. Usually, however, the number of sacrificed animals was smaller. In Julian's case we should perhaps not take the word in its literal sense, either. But this is not certain.

Maybe Ammianus exaggerates when he speaks of the offering of 'several times a hundred bulls and countless other animals, as well as white birds, for which he hunted out land and sea.' But if an otherwise totally unknown private individual could boast on a fourth-century inscription found in present-day Libya that on a certain occasion he had sacrificed fifty-one bulls and thirty-eight goats, then it seems not too far fetched to assume that the ruler of the immense Roman Empire slaughtered numbers many times larger—the meat of the sacrificed animals formed a welcome supplement to the daily diet for ordinary soldiers and civilians, which in antiquity mainly consisted of bread and other cereal products. Whatever the case, Julian was well known for his extravagant offerings. 'He in ten years offered more sacrifices than all the rest of the Greeks put together,' according to Julian's sympathizer Libanius. In this respect Julian resembled his predecessor Marcus Aurelius (161–180), whom he very much admired. On Marcus some mocking verses were composed:

> Greetings to Marcus from the oxen white.
> We're done for if you win another fight.[5]

Like Marcus, Julian was derided. People scoffed at his fancy for bloody sacrifices, his billy-goat's beard, his aversion to games in the amphitheater, and his policies in general. In Antioch, where in the winter of 362–363 the emperor prepared for his Persian expedition, he felt forced to answer his critics in an ironical open letter entitled *Antiochicus* or *Misopogon* ('Beard-Hater'). It was of no avail. Julian was ridiculed as 'sacrifice-mad,' 'butcher,' 'bullburner,' 'seller of meat.' The bull that was depicted on his coins (Figure 3) was scoffed at as a sign of his craze for sacrificing—what the emperor really wanted to express with this symbol is disputed among modern scholars.

Figure 3. Coin (maiorina) of Julian with bull and two stars. Reverse. SECVRITAS REI PVB(LICAE), 'Security of the State.' Minted in Lyons (RIC 8, p. 195, no. 236). *(Credit Line: De Agostini Picture Library/A. de Gregorio/Bridgeman Images.)*

And, as in the case of Marcus Aurelius, jokes were made about the fate of the oxen in the empire when Julian would return victorious from his expedition against the Persians.[6]

Another connection between Julian's Persian expedition and the performance of sacrifices was also found. The church historian Socrates alleges that the emperor, to cover the costs of his campaign, imposed a fine on everyone who refused to sacrifice. One may wonder if this is correct. To effectuate such a measure would have involved the citizens all over the empire in a lot of red tape, of which nothing is heard. Moreover, Socrates' words contradict what he says elsewhere in his work: that Julian wanted to encourage people to sacrifice by persuasion and by the promise of rewards. In addition, his words are also contradicted by the pagan Libanius and, more importantly, by Socrates' colleague Sozomen, who often agrees with his predecessor, but who writes about offerings, 'Although Julian was anxious to advance paganism by every means, yet he deemed it the height of imprudence to employ force or vengeance against those who refused to sacrifice.' It seems wise, therefore, to disregard Socrates' statement about a fine for not sacrificing. The church historian had a habit of inventing something to discredit dissenters. He accused pagans, for example, of cutting open babies and inspecting their entrails, and of eating the meat of children, boys and girls alike—ironically, in former days Christians had often been accused of this form of cannibalism.[7]

The emperor Julian may have rejected the enforcement of sacrifices; he nevertheless greatly deplored slackness in this respect. His own words confirm this. But what could he do about it? Perhaps, he must have thought, a financial spur might help where persuasion failed. At any rate, Julian's sympathizer Libanius does not conceal the fact that the emperor tried to incite his soldiers to sacrifice by promising pecuniary rewards. According to Christian authors, he played a mean trick in order to attain his goal. When the yearly donation to the soldiers was distributed in Antioch, he allegedly had a table with incense placed next to the table on which the gold coins were heaped up. Whoever wanted to get his money first had to throw incense into a fire. The trick worked. All the soldiers did what they were asked to do, the pagans as a matter of course, the Christians absentmindedly or oblivious of doing something wrong, but also out of greed, although sometimes they afterward regretted what they had done. All this under the watchful eye of the emperor himself—a striking detail indeed: in the Syrian capital some hundred thousand men were assembled; if one does not reject the story as fictitious on this account, one has to assume that only the elite troops were rewarded by the emperor in person.[8]

At night the donation was converted into meat and drink. Our most important spokesman in this matter, Bishop Gregory of Nazianzus, describes one of the feasts, so that we can see and hear how a Christian soldier, when raising his drinking cup, invokes Jesus Christ and makes the sign of the cross, to the surprise of a fellow soldier: 'What do you mean by that? Invoking Christ while you just a moment ago denied his existence?' 'Denied his existence? How's that?' is the answer, 'Nonsense!' 'Well, did you or did you not burn incense?' says the other, who begins to explain the implication. But the first soldier has heard enough. The scales have fallen from his eyes and from those of others. They jump to their feet and dash into the streets, fuming with anger. They swear to whoever is prepared to listen that they are still Christians, that they have not yielded to the temptation of the gold, that the emperor had cheated them. They succeed in entering the palace and, throwing the gold coins before Julian's feet, they loudly complain and request that the emperor let them die as martyrs. However, this is not to Julian's liking. Exile is his answer to the reproaches of the Christian soldiers.[9]

In the version of Sozomen, who halfway through the fifth century retold Gregory's story in brief, only the punishment is different: the soldiers are not exiled, but cashiered from the army and thrown out of the palace. In all other respects the church historian follows Gregory almost verbatim. Just like Gregory he emphasizes that Julian would not even contemplate granting the soldiers the glory of a martyr's death. On this point, essential for Julian's image, our third spokesman at first strikes a different note. I quote the end of the version of Theodoret, who, like Sozomen, wrote his church history halfway through the fifth century: (The utterances of the soldiers drove Julian out of his mind, and on the spur of the moment) 'he ordered them to be beheaded; but as they were being conducted out of the city, the mass of the people started to follow them, wondering at their fortitude and glorying in their boldness for the truth. When they had reached the spot where it was usual to execute criminals, the eldest of the soldiers besought the executioner that he would first cut off the head of the youngest, that he might not lose heart by beholding the slaughter of the rest. No sooner had he knelt down upon the ground and the headsman bared his sword, than up ran a man announcing a reprieve, and, while yet far off, shouting out to stop the execution. Then the youngest soldier was distressed at his release from death. "Ah," said he, "Romanus" (his name was Romanus) "was not worthy of being called Christ's martyr." What influenced the vile trickster in stopping the execution was his envy: he grudged the champions of the faith their glory. Their sentence was commuted to relegation beyond the city walls and to the remotest regions of the empire.'[10]

The picturesque story of Gregory and Sozomen has become even more exciting in the version of Theodoret. Is it, apart from exciting, also true? Sometimes it has been suggested that the Romanus whom Theodoret brought on stage should be identified with a namesake who became the military commander of the province of Africa. There is no proof for this identification and, even if it were correct, such an identification does not say anything about the veracity of the story as told by Theodoret. I therefore prefer to leave speculations on that subject to others, and confine myself to the observation that neither Gregory nor Sozomen nor Theodoret made the military *confessores* into martyrs, although one gets the impression that they would have liked to do so—the term *confessores* means those Christians who, although persecuted, refused steadfastly to give up their faith, but stayed alive; they are distinguished from Christian *martyres*, who suffered a martyr's death because of their faith. The conclusion must be that with respect to offerings, Julian would have liked everybody to have followed his example, but that he was not prepared to go to extremes to achieve his goal.[11]

Chapter 8

Julian's School Edict

A Form of Persecution?

Early in June 362 CE, Julian and his army left Constantinople and traveled eastward in the direction of Antioch on the Orontes, the starting point of his Persian expedition. While the emperor was still in Constantinople, or soon after his departure, he met, according to some Christian sources, the old and blind Bishop Maris of Chalcedon (Kadiköy). Maris was really blind, whereas Chalcedon was often called 'city of the blind' because its first inhabitants had chosen the eastern bank of the Bosporus to found their city instead of the much more favorably situated western shore (where shortly afterward Byzantium, later Constantinople, was built). However, Maris' handicap did not stop him from starting an argument with the emperor, whom he rebuked for his impiety, apostasy, and atheism. Julian contemptuously replied that the bishop's 'Galilaean God' would never cure him, whereupon Maris responded that he thanked the Lord for having taken away his sight, so that he could not see Julian's impious face. That reduced the emperor to silence.[1]

Maris' impertinent behavior had no immediate consequences. Julian left the bishop alone and continued on his way. Zonaras, one of the authors who mention Julian's encounter with Maris, relates the story without comment. (Although Zonaras lived in the twelfth century, he is important because he used sources for his universal history that are lost to us). The fifth-century church historian Sozomen states that Julian deliberately reacted in this way, because he thought that paganism would be better promoted by a policy of leniency vis-à-vis the Christians than by punishment. Sozomen's colleague Socrates goes into much greater detail about the emperor's behavior, and offers the following explanation. According to him, Julian overlooked Maris' boldness at the time, but had his revenge afterward: 'Julian had observed that those who died as martyrs under the reign of Diocletian were greatly honoured by the Christians, and he knew that many Christians had an urgent desire to become martyrs themselves. Refusing to grant them this pleasure he wreaked his vengeance upon them in some other way. He eschewed the excessive cruelties which had been practised under Diocletian, but did not altogether abstain from persecution—by persecution I mean any action adopted to disquiet those who put their hopes in Jesus Christ. He disturbed the Christians by issuing a law which excluded them from classical education.'[2]

Socrates' words are very interesting. The law he refers to is Julian's School Edict (whether only one law, or more than one, is disputed), subsumed by the church historian under the heading 'persecution' (διωγμός, diōgmos), a word that he uses in a rather pregnant sense, as he himself evidently realized (this is shown by his deeming it necessary to clarify his terminology: 'by persecution I mean any action adopted to disquiet those who put their hopes in Jesus Christ'). Elsewhere in the first three books of his work the term mostly has the connotation of 'bloody persecution' and refers to the way in which emperors like Decius and Diocletian had acted. The law in question, issued on June 17, 362, probably in Ancyra, happens to be partly preserved. We find it in the *Theodosian Code*, a collection of laws of former emperors assembled and published in 438 by order of Theodosius II. When reading the text of the law, one wonders why its content was ever interpreted as an example of persecution. It opens thus: 'Masters of studies and teachers must excel first in character, then in eloquence.' Is that really shocking? The rest of the text is not very spectacular, either: since Julian himself could not be present in person in all the municipalities, he demanded that if any man wished to teach, he should not suddenly rush into this job, but should be approved by the judgment of the municipal senate and should obtain a certificate from the municipal senators that proved that he had met all legal demands. Julian further wanted this certificate to be referred back to him, the emperor, for consideration, in order that such teachers might enter upon their pursuits in the municipalities with more honor because of the emperor's judgment. That is all. Note that Christians are not even mentioned.[3]

Indeed, if we did not have more information at our disposal, the commotion about this law would be quite incomprehensible. There is of course a snag in the phrase 'excellence of character,' which is a notion open to interpretation. Who decides what its precise meaning is? Without the information found in another text, which perhaps refers to another law but at any rate can serve as a sort of explanatory statement to the one issued on June 17, 362, one probably would not have understood why the law created such a general outcry. This other piece of writing, found among Julian's letters, makes perfectly clear what Julian meant. In his eyes conduct and religious persuasion were inextricably bound up with each other. A Christian teacher who despised the pagan gods, he argues, could never correctly explain to his pupils the works of Homer, Hesiod, Demosthenes, Herodotus, Thucydides, Isocrates, and Lysias (Julian lists them all). Whoever tried to do this was a hypocrite. 'When a man thinks one thing and teaches his pupils another, he fails in my opinion not only in his educational task, but is also a dishonest person.' Such individuals should 'betake themselves to the churches of the Galilaeans to expound Matthew and Luke.'[4]

A clear statement. Julian wanted to forbid Christian teachers from teaching the classics, unless they were willing to renounce their faith. It would not be the last attempt to target dissenters through measures in the field of education. Modern parallels, like the university purges in Nazi Germany, spring to mind. Understandably, Julian's School Edict gave rise to many emotions. It does not come as a surprise that the Christians especially were very upset. Admittedly, a classical education was not valued by all Christians in Antiquity. In the second century the Greek-speaking philosopher Tatian from Mesopotamia fulminated against it, as did, in the sixth century, the Latin-speaking Caesarius of Arles. Others were less negative. Basil of Caesarea and Augustine of Hippo, to name but two, argued in favor of a selective use of the classics, while Socrates Scholasticus was plainly in favor of a traditional curriculum. At any rate, there were Christians who taught the classics in the fourth century, and we hear that some of them, Prohaeresius in Athens and Marius Victorinus in Rome, preferred to abandon their profession rather than their faith. But Christians were not the only ones who were upset. The pagan historian Ammianus Marcellinus, for instance, a great admirer of Julian, was highly indignant, and rebuked the emperor twice in his *Res Gestae* in no uncertain terms for issuing the law.[5]

In the previous section I quoted the passage of Socrates about the emperor's encounter with Bishop Maris of Chalcedon. I want to draw attention to two points in this passage. In the first place, when one compares the text of Julian's school law, including its explanatory statement, with Socrates' words, it becomes immediately clear that the church historian distorts Julian's words. The School Edict did not, as Socrates alleges, exclude Christians altogether from classical education, but merely tried to prohibit Christian teachers from teaching the classics. The same interpretation of the content of the law is found elsewhere in Socrates' work, and also in the works of other church historians, Sozomen, Rufinus, and Theodoret. It is simply not true. One could object that Julian's ban to teach the classics was only the first part of an attempt to target the Christians in the field of education, and that other, stricter measures were to follow. Maybe so, but nobody knows what Julian kept in store. According to Theodoret, the emperor planned 'a war on Christianity after the fighting with the Persians was over.' With all due respect to the church historian, this is pure speculation. Julian's reign was too short to say anything meaningful in this regard.[6]

For my second point I once again refer to the remark of Socrates about Julian's persecution. Is there a better witness for the defense? The Christian church historian admits that Julian never ordered a bloody persecution. Granted, the emperor was not keen to make life more agreeable for Christians. Apart from the school law there is, for instance, Julian's decree of March 13, 362, which reversed some measures that his Christian predecessors had taken: from now on Christians—that is, Christian clergymen—would again be subject to the financial burdens that members of municipal councils had to bear. And there is Julian's funeral decree of February 12, 363, which, among other things, stipulated that funerals should be carried out only between sunset and sunrise (and not, therefore, in broad daylight, as was customary among Christians). In personnel matters he favored pagans above Christians. The emperor also gave preferential treatment to cities where pagans were in the majority, and neglected cities where Christians had the upper hand; the latter he never visited, and he refused to receive their embassies or listen to their complaints, while pagan cities had only to breathe the word to be showered with benefactions. This, at least, was the opinion of the Christian Sozomen. The pagan Libanius depicts the emperor's policy less negatively: if cities had temples that were still standing, Julian considered them deserving of the greatest kindness, while he called cities that had destroyed pagan shrines polluted; nevertheless, in spite of this, he offered the inhabitants of such cities a share in the benefits he dispensed, for the reason that they too were his subjects.[7]

I shall not go into the question as to whether Sozomen or Libanius is right about Julian's policy with respect to the cities. I confine myself to the remark that one might conceivably accuse Julian of discrimination, but not of launching a bloody persecution. The relevant sources and modern scholarly literature sometimes suggest otherwise. The church historian Philostorgius speaks of a persecution under Julian 'which was past all endurance.' In his commentary on the prophet Habakkuk, Jerome states bluntly that Julian was actually guilty of the shedding of Christian blood, and that he should be put on a par with the persecutors Maximianus, Valerian, Decius, Domitian, and Nero. In his continuation of Eusebius' *Chronicle,* Jerome states that Julian vowed to offer the blood of the Christians to the gods after his victory over the Persians. However, the same Jerome formulates his criticism of Julian far more cautiously in another passage of the *Chronicle.* He does use the word persecution (*persecutio*) there, but qualifies the term (as did Socrates with respect to Julian's διωγμός/diōgmos). Rufinus argues in the same vein, as do other authors, pagan and Christian alike. Rufinus calls Julian 'smarter than others as a persecutor,' because he tried to win the Christians over to his side 'not by force and torture, but by gifts, honours, flattery, and persuasion.' According to Eutropius, Julian did 'persecute the Christian religion,' but, the pagan historian adds, 'yet so that he abstained from shedding blood.' Libanius also states that the emperor refused to use force against Christians. I already referred to Sozomen's comment on Julian's encounter with Bishop Maris ('Julian thought that paganism would be better promoted by a policy of leniency vis-à-vis the Christians than by punishment'). Even the Christian bishop

Gregory of Nazianzus, who hated the 'Apostate' like poison and called him a persecutor, had to admit that Julian did not treat the Christians as cruelly as some of his predecessors had done.[8]

All this should prompt us to take Julian's own utterances on this subject very seriously. It would be wrong to dismiss them as mere propaganda or as a whitewash, 'a mask of moderation,' as Theodoret of Cyrrhus put it. The final words of the text that can serve as an elucidation to Julian's school law form, so to speak, the emperor's credo: 'one ought to teach the silly Christians rather than punish them.'[9]

Chapter 9

Basil of Ancyra

After his encounter with Bishop Maris of Chalcedon early in June 362, Julian moved eastward. He went past Libyssa (Gebze), Nicomedia, and Nicaea, and then marched through Asia Minor to Ancyra at the head of his army. The story of the priest Basil is set in Ancyra.[1]

In this city, according to an interesting chapter in Sozomen's church history, a presbyter of the local church called Basil died a martyr's death during the reign of Julian. Sozomen relates that Basil was already well known because of certain activities of his under Julian's cousin and predecessor Constantius II: he had turned against Christians whose views he considered heterodox, whereupon supporters of Bishop Eudoxius stopped him from holding divine services. When Julian had become sole emperor, Basil urged his fellow Christians to stick to their faith and to keep their distance from pagan rituals. One day he vehemently protested when he saw some pagans offering sacrifice, wailed aloud, and, to the indignation of the pagans, uttered the wish that no Christian would follow their example. Basil was seized, conveyed to the provincial governor, tortured, and put to death.[2]

Sozomen's reference to the martyrdom of Basil of Ancyra is remarkable, because he alone of the church historians devotes attention to it. It does not come as a surprise that the incident in Ancyra is not mentioned in the most important pro-Julianic pagan sources for Julian's reign—Libanius, Eunapius, Ammianus Marcellinus, and Zosimus—but one would at least have expected Socrates Scholasticus to refer to this event, given the close relationship between Socrates' ecclesiastical history and that of Sozomen. However, neither Socrates nor his colleagues Rufinus, Theodoret, and Philostorgius report anything about the priest of Ancyra. One also looks in vain for his name in the writings of Christian authors such as Gregory of Nazianzus and John Chrysostom, who occasionally provide us with additional information about ecclesiastical affairs during the short reign of the Apostate. But for Sozomen, therefore, Basil's name would not have appeared in the list of those said in historical sources to have been martyred under Julian. There is, to be sure, another text that tells the story of Basil's sufferings in great detail. Unfortunately, the date of composition of this *Passio sancti Basilii presbyteri*, written in Greek, is unknown (the oldest manuscript dates from the tenth or eleventh century) and its authenticity is open to doubt. In the seventeenth century the Bollandists—philologists and historians named after Jean Bolland, originally all Jesuits, who have studied (and still study) hagiography—regarded the *passio* as a genuine report written by eyewitnesses, and some modern scholars are of the same opinion. Others are more sceptical and consider the work a concoction fabricated by an anonymous Late Antique or Byzantine author who deemed Sozomen's sober report as too scant.[3]

The *passio* has several suspicious features. We are told in sections 13 and 14 that Basil was led before the emperor Julian and that an altercation between them took place—this in itself is worthy of note, since in Sozomen's version of Basil's martyrdom Julian is not mentioned at all (we did see, however, that Julian visited Ancyra in 362, so that theoretically an encounter cannot be ruled out).

During their dispute the emperor was angered by the priest's frankness to such an extent that he ordered him to be flayed by daily stripping seven pieces of skin from his body. This is a most interesting piece of information, but in the very chapter in which he tells us about Basil's torment and death, Sozomen states that, although the actions of some of Julian's officials against Christians were cruel, these cruelties were perpetrated contrary to the will of the emperor himself. Moreover, Sozomen says elsewhere that Julian, though anxious to advance paganism by every means, deemed it the height of imprudence to employ force or vengeance against those who refused to make a sacrifice. And this emperor is supposed to have flayed a living human being?[4]

Sozomen is not the only author who denies that Julian used violence against Christians. In Chapter 8, we referred to similar utterances on this subject of pagan authors such as Eutropius and Libanius, not to mention Julian himself, and of the Christians Rufinus, Socrates Scholasticus, and Gregory of Nazianzus—Gregory could not resist remarking that it was not out of benevolence that Julian refrained from violence, but because he knew that persecution would only make the Christians stronger and he begrudged the Christians the glory of martyrdom. Anyhow, it should be clear that in his attitude toward Christians, the Julian as depicted in sections 13–14 of the *passio* differs rather strikingly from the one we encounter in Sozomen and the other pagan and Christian sources mentioned above.[5]

In sections 15–18 of the *Passio Basilii* the rest of the confrontation between Julian and the priest is related. While being flayed by one of the imperial officers, a certain Frumentinus (or Frumentius), *comes scutariorum* ('count of the guards bearing shields'), Basil suddenly asked for an interview with the emperor. His request was gladly granted, because it was considered to be a sign of weakness. But instead of giving in, the priest persisted in his defiant attitude and reproached Julian for believing in deaf and blind idols. Finally, abusing the emperor and praising God, he took one of the pieces cut out of his own body and threw it into Julian's face—not a very common event, one might say, but certainly one that provokes curiosity as to Julian's reaction. Alas, the author of the *passio* is conspicuously silent. All Julian did in response to Basil's behavior is expressed in no more than one sentence: he became annoyed with Frumentinus and left for Antioch.[6]

Julian's departure was not the end of Basil's story. Before the priest was allowed to die, the following episode occurred. First, there were new torments, worse than before. Of course, Basil did not yield and continued to praise the Lord (section 17). The next day he was once again made to choose between sacrificing and death. Needless to say that this time he also stood firm. Note his answer to Frumentinus: 'You foolish and impious wretch, don't you remember how many strips you cut out of my back yesterday? All those who saw your illegal punishment felt sorry for me and moaned. But look at me now, you spawn of the Devil, you cruel and inhuman brute: Christ has willed that I stand here before you safe and sound' (section 18).

Basil's miraculous recovery conforms with a well-known pattern of hagiography. Miracles, as Father Delehaye has reminded us in his epoch-making *Passions des Martyrs*, are among the most significant characteristics of nonhistorical martyrologies ('passions épiques'). He continues that the most simple and frequent of those miracles is the one that makes the martyr totally insensible to pain. In this respect section 18 of the *Passio Basilii* can be put at the side of more than fifty examples taken by Delehaye from various *passiones* both in Latin and in Greek. But there is more to come. The *passio* presents many other details that Delehaye has shown up as of doubtful reliability, such as when in section 18 Basil called Frumentinus foolish, impious, and cruel. Quoting an anthology of abusive words gathered from many martyrologies, including the *passio* of Basil of Ancyra, Delehaye observes, 'often words are put into the mouth of a martyr which fit in badly with a victim who resigns himself to his fate.' Another characteristic feature can be detected in section 17, already cited, when Basil, threatened with new torments, praises the Lord. 'It is more or less the rule that when the examining magistrate orders new torments, the accused answers by invoking God.' This is by no means all. Consider that Basil is interrogated not only by the provincial governor Saturninus (sections 5–6 and 12), but also by a certain Felix (section 8), the apostate Pegasius (section 10), the emperor Julian (sections 13–16), and the *comes scutariorum* Frumentinus (sections 16–19) while in between interrogations he is imprisoned, and compare this with the findings of Delehaye, who has observed that frequent and repeated interrogations and imprisonments are the order of the day in 'epic' martyrologies.[7]

One could further point to the excessive length of the martyr's answers (for instance, in section 10), and to the fact that the dialogues (section 5) and the composition in general are stereotyped. But this is unnecessary, I think. It will be clear by now that the *Passio sancti Basilii presbyteri* belongs to the category of fictitious martyrologies, and that the early Bollandists and their followers have not assessed its character accurately. Admittedly, it contains some historical elements. Julian did pass through Ancyra on his march from Constantinople to Antioch. Also, the *passio* does mention some individuals whose names are identical, or practically identical, with known historical figures. But this carries little weight when compared with the many features that plead against its reliability. Besides, the main events of the Apostate's reign remained common knowledge long after the emperor had died. Any reader of Sozomen would have been familiar with them and would have known that in the spring of 362 Julian traveled through Asia Minor and stayed in Ancyra for a while. As to the names of Basil's torturers (Felix and Pegasius are also attested elsewhere), once again it pays to heed the lessons taught by experts in hagiography: the tossing about of historical names is a common characteristic of nonhistorical martyrologies.[8]

Although evidently not a reliable historical source, the *Passio sancti Basilii presbyteri* is nevertheless an interesting text. It is a good example of what a French scholar has dubbed '*Julianisation*,' the tendency of Christian authors to ascribe to Julian the Apostate all sorts of heinous deeds, whether he committed them or not. In the case of the *Passio Basilii* the author seized the opportunity to blacken the reputation of the hated emperor by writing a stereotyped martyrology based on a short passage of Sozomen, in which he alleged, unlike Sozomen, that Julian was personally involved in the torture of one of his subjects.[9]

Chapter 10

Idols and Psalm Singing

It says in the Scriptures, 'And a woman who had been suffering from a hemorrhage for twelve years, came up behind Him and touched the fringe of His cloak; for she was saying to herself, "If I only touch His garment, I will get well." But Jesus turning and seeing her said, "Daughter, take courage; your faith has made you well." At once the woman was made well.'[1]

According to Eusebius of Caesarea the woman hailed from Paneas, called Caesarea Philippi by the Romans (the modern name of this town in the north of Israel is Bāniyās). Out of gratitude she erected two bronze statues on a stone pedestal near the entrance of her house. One statue was of a kneeling woman, who stretched out her hands in an imploring gesture; the other, on the opposite side, was of Jesus, represented in full length and extending a hand toward the woman. He himself had seen it with his own eyes, Eusebius writes, adding that it actually was a pagan habit to put up statues of benefactors. Philostorgius, who wrote a sequel to Eusebius' ecclesiastical history around the year 400 and who, like his predecessor, says that he had personally seen the Jesus of Paneas, also refers to the pagan background of such statues. Philostorgius emphasizes that, of course, the Christian faithful did not really worship the statue, which had meanwhile been placed in the local church, but only held it in the highest regard. He further explains that in his time only the statue's head was left, because during the reign of Julian the inhabitants of Paneas had pulled it from its pedestal, bound a rope around its feet, and dragged it through the streets of the town. Sozomen holds Julian personally responsible for this iconoclasm. The emperor, he says, had destroyed the statue of Jesus in order to replace it with a statue of himself. But God punishes quickly. Julian's statue was hit by lightning and knocked down; that of Jesus was restored and put up again in the church.[2]

One should take the information of the church historians about the Jesus of Paneas cum grano salis, if only because, according to a parallel tradition, the statue had disappeared long before the reign of Julian, with the involvement of the emperor Maximinus Daia (305–313). Sozomen goes too far especially when he depicts Julian as an iconoclast, even though the emperor never visited Paneas. Similar stories occur quite frequently. It was alleged, for example, that Julian once buried a statue of the patron goddess of Constantinople in a deep pit, because Constantine the Great had supposedly put a cross on its head. It was said that in Nicomedia Julian fooled Christians by claiming that the statues of Apollo and Artemis that he had erected in their city were images of himself and his late wife, so that the citizens, when ordered to worship these statues, adored idols instead of the emperor and the empress. This is not to say that it is unthinkable that after Julian's accession to the throne pagans violated Christian churches and symbols, just as, conversely, in the course of the fourth century Christians plundered and destroyed pagan temples. Christians also tried to stop the worship of what, in their eyes, were idols. Ironically, Julian himself contributed somewhat to this, for on February 19, 356, the following law was issued in Milan: 'If any person should be proved to devote his attention to sacrifices or to worship images, We command that he shall be subjected to capital punishment.' This was thought up by the emperor Constantius II, but, as we have already seen, the law was also subscribed to by Julian, who shortly before had been made co-emperor.[3]

Between 361 and 363 this law was no longer valid. The worship of pagan images was again permitted, or rather, was propagated by Julian, to the chagrin of many Christians. Their spokesmen cried out against it. They reported, for instance, that in Emesa in the province of Phoenice, present-day Homs in Syria, the Christians had to endure the transformation of their newly built church into a temple of Dionysus, in which a 'ridiculous, effeminate effigy' of this god was placed. Something similar occurred some forty kilometers north of Emesa in Epiphania (Hama). Pagans there forced their way into the Christian church and brought an idol inside, accompanied by the sounds of flutes and tambourines. The local bishop, Eustathius, a pious and dutiful man, died the moment he heard what was going on—thus his prayer, not to have to watch the desecration of his church, was fulfilled. Pagans in Heliopolis, now Baalbek in Lebanon, took revenge on the deacon Cyrillus, because, in the time of Constantine the Great, the deacon had destroyed the images of their gods: they cut Cyrillus open and tasted his organs. However, his liver disagreed with the man who ate it. The latter suffered excruciating pains, his tongue began to rot and fell out of his mouth, his teeth crumbled, his eyes ulcerated, and he lost his sight before he finally died.[4]

Christians did not always look on passively when pagans became active. When the images of the gods had been cleaned up and polished in the newly reopened temple of the town of Merus in the province of Phrygia Secunda, three inhabitants of this town (near modern Şuhut in Turkey) entered the sanctuary at night and smashed everything to pieces. Amachius, the provincial governor, was furious and immediately had three men, chosen at random from among the Christian citizens, arrested, whereupon Macedonius, Theodulus, and Tatianus revealed that they were the perpetrators, not the accused. The governor then gave the threesome the choice: either death or, if they showed remorse and offered a sacrifice, mercy. Socrates and Sozomen describe, full of admiration, the reaction of their fellow believers. The three men did not hesitate for a moment, and preferred to die rather than make a sacrifice to the gods. The consequence of their steadfastness was that they were tortured and then burned at the stake. Still Macedonius and his friends did not falter. 'If you wish to eat broiled flesh, Amachius, turn us on the other side, lest we should appear but half cooked to your taste.'[5]

The most famous statue that became a cause of tension between pagans and Christians was the one in the temple of Apollo in Daphne, modern Harbiye in Turkey, a lovely village some seven or eight kilometers southwest of Antioch. The Apollo of Daphne was a work of the sculptor Bryaxis, who lived in the fourth century BCE. It had the same dimensions as the Zeus of Phidias in Olympia—one of the seven Wonders of the World—and it was so big that it only just fit in the temple. In the night of October 22, 362, the ancient statue and part of the Apollo temple were burned to ashes. Opinions differed greatly about the cause and the circumstances of the fire. Ammianus Marcellinus, who himself hailed from Antioch, does not rule out the possibility that the fire started by accident. Perhaps, Ammianus says, the carelessness of Asclepiades was to blame for it. This philosopher had lit some candles at the feet of the god's statue before he left the temple, an act that had perhaps resulted in short-circuiting sparks setting the statue and the temple ablaze. John Chrysostom, also an Antiochene, and other Christian authors thought that the fire had been caused by a bolt of lightning, as a punishment from God. Not surprisingly, the emperor in his turn was of a totally different opinion—Julian assumed that Christians had set fire to the temple of Apollo, and ordered a thorough investigation (which in the end was inconclusive). While awaiting the outcome he closed the Great Church in Antioch.[6]

Much as Chrysostom and Julian disagreed about the fire in Daphne, about one thing the emperor and the cleric had the same opinion: the case had a previous history, which had begun with the death of Babylas more than a hundred years before the reign of Julian. This Antiochene bishop had died after having been persecuted because of his faith during the reign of the emperor Decius. For a century Babylas' bones had rested in a cemetery just outside Antioch, but Gallus *Caesar*, Julian's Christian half-brother, had brought the relics over to Daphne to be buried in the grounds of the temple of Apollo. The oracle of the god had been silent ever since. This made Julian furious, because he, like his Christian adversaries, saw a connection between the two events—Christians believed that the bones or the ashes of martyrs had a special power, and that the transfer of their relics to a certain place would make that place holy; pagans believed that everything that had to do with death defiled a place. Finally, when Apollo remained silent, the emperor ordered the excavation of the bones of Babylas and other bodies, and the desecrated temple area was ritually purified. Thereupon Christian citizens transported Babylas' mortal remains to another resting place, where later a church arose, but their hearts were not in it. By way of protest they sang psalms and repeated again and again the verses 'let all those be ashamed who serve graven images, who boast themselves of idols.'[7]

Julian was certainly not ashamed. On the contrary, he must have been infuriated. According to a Christian contemporary, Rufinus, author of a sequel in Latin to Eusebius' ecclesiastical history, he was so enraged that he ordered the imprisonment and torture of Christians all over the empire—a very striking measure, but the question arises whether Rufinus is perhaps exaggerating: had he forgotten that in one of the previous chapters he had argued that Julian, smarter than the persecutors who had preceded him, always tried to win Christians over to his side by persuasion and never by force, let alone torture? In any case, the church historian writes that Julian's praetorian prefect Secundus, entrusted with the implementation of the emperor's order, arrested the first Christian who came along and tortured him from early morning until late at night. However, the victim, a certain Theodorus, did not flinch, and even during the most horrible torments continued to sing the psalm that the day before had been sung by the whole congregation. Thereupon the prefect dissuaded Julian from continuing the torture: it would be to no avail and might even be counterproductive. Rufinus then ends his chapter about Theodorus with a nice final chord: later, in Antioch, he himself had heard Theodorus say that, when taken off the rack, he felt sad, because at this very moment the angel disappeared, as quickly as he had come during the torment to wipe the sweat from his body and to give him a sip of cold water so that he felt hardly any pain.[8]

Rufinus' story about Theodorus the *confessor* was later passed on by Greek church historians. One of them, Theodoret of Cyrrhus, relates in addition a similar event, which also took place in Antioch during the reign of Julian. The main part in it was played by a certain Publia, a distinguished lady, well known in the city because of her benefactions, and the mother of a priest. She spent her days in singing God's praise in the company of women who had taken the vow of chastity. One day Julian passed by her house. The choir of maidens sang more loudly than they normally did, thus deriding and ridiculing the despised emperor. This time, too, psalms were used as weapons: 'The idols of the nations are but silver and gold, The work of man's hands,' and, 'Those who make them will be like them, Yes, everyone who trusts in them.' Julian was not amused. He ordered the women to be silent, but was ignored. On another occasion the emperor was treated once more to psalm singing that was meant to hurt him: 'Let God arise, let His enemies be scattered, And let those who hate Him flee before Him.' Julian could no longer restrain his anger. He had Publia brought before him (Figure 4) and despite her venerable age had her ears cuffed, so that blood poured down her cheeks.

Figure 4. Publia the Confessor before Julian in Antioch. Miniature painting in the *Menologium Basilii*, an illuminated service book compiled for the Byzantine emperor Basil II (976–1025). Codex Vaticanus Graecus 1613. *(Credit Line: © Vatican Apostolic Library.)*

Needless to say, the woman carried on with her actions against the emperor.[9]

Theodoret, in contrast to his colleague Rufinus in his story about Theodorus, did not bother to find a connection between Publia's deed and the transfer of Babylas' relics to Antioch. Theodoret's female *confessor* Publia acted spontaneously. She harassed the emperor with psalms without an immediate cause, a narrative that does not seem very likely. However, one can only speculate about the veracity of the story about Publia. I have my doubts, as in the case of the *confessor* Theodorus, who in his distress was aided by an angel, but strictly speaking we have no proof. At any rate, it is clear that neither Rufinus nor Theodoret in an undeniable attempt to blacken the emperor's name ventured to allege that it was Julian who had killed their heroes. Both

Theodorus and Publia stayed alive, while the inquiry into the fire of the temple of Apollo in Daphne also did not result in convictions, let alone capital punishments. This confirms what I have observed before: persecutions on a grand scale, instigated by the emperor himself, did not occur.

Chapter 11

Julian and His Uncle Julianus

As we saw in Chapter 10, an ancient statue of Apollo was destroyed by fire in Antioch's suburb Daphne in October 362. Part of the temple in which the statue stood was also burned to ashes. As was to be expected, the emperor Julian was very angry, but Julian was not the only person who was infuriated. His uncle and namesake, a brother of his mother, was furious as well. This Julianus, who, as the highest civil official in the diocese of *Oriens* ('the East'), bore the title *comes Orientis*, and who resided in Antioch, rode the very same night at full speed to the scene of the calamity to size up the situation. When he saw the heap of ashes, left from the statue of the god—of the 'so-called god,' to cite our spokesman Theodoret correctly—he immediately had the guards who were in charge of the temple whipped. *Comes* Julianus suspected, like his nephew, that Christians had started the fire. However, the temple guards did not confirm his suspicion. In spite of being tortured they stuck to their assertion that the fire had started 'not from below but from above,' while, as Theodoret adds, 'some of the neighboring rustics came forward and asserted that they had seen the thunderbolt come rushing down from heaven.'[1]

The destruction of the temple of Apollo in Daphne must have come as a shock to the *comes Orientis*, not only because he was a pagan (*comes* Julianus was an apostate, like his nephew), but also because he had gone to great lengths to restore the temple. In a letter, which the emperor Julian had written on his way to Antioch in the spring of 362, he had urged his uncle to concern himself above all with the decayed temple in Daphne: he must bring back the marble pillars that were taken away to be set up elsewhere, or, if there were not enough of these left, replace them with cheaper ones of baked brick covered with a coat of stucco made with marble dust. The *comes* no doubt acquitted himself satisfactorily of this task, just as he had earned the approval of the emperor in other respects. Christian authors were less happy about him. Theodoret relates that Julian's uncle broke into the Great Church in Antioch with some of his soulmates after the Christians had been barred from it, stole its precious objects, urinated against the main altar, and boxed the ears of Bishop Euzoius when that bishop tried to stop him.[2]

Immediately after this—we still follow Theodoret—*comes* Julianus and the other wrongdoers fell ill. Julianus' intestines began to rot. His excrements were no longer discharged in the normal way, but came out of his mouth, the same foul, stinking mouth through which he had earlier poured out blasphemous language. To make things worse, he was taken to task by his wife, a pious Christian. He had better praise Jesus Christ, she said, and thank the Lord for the lesson He had taught him, for without His interference, Julianus would never have realized how great the Savior's power was. As a result of these words and because of his sufferings, *comes* Julianus repented, and at the very last moment tried to mend his ways: he begged the emperor to give the Great Church back to the Christians. However, Julian's uncle died before his nephew had time to consider his plea. According to Philostorgius, Julianus died after an illness lasting forty days, which tallies well with the date of the *comes'* dying day, which can be worked out on the basis of other data: after December 6, 362, and before the end of January 363.[3]

Apart from Philostorgius and Theodoret there are other Christian authors who refer to Julianus' death, in order to demonstrate that God punishes his enemies relentlessly, but the unsavory details of the ordeals that the *comes Orientis* had to suffer during his last days vary. According to some authors, maggots appeared in his underbelly, with which even experienced doctors did not know how to cope. Their attempt to lure the worms to come outside by putting meat of newly butchered fat pigeons on the rotting parts of the body failed. The maggots scorned the pigeons and continued to devour Julianus' intestines until he died. One of the authors who report this is Sozomen of Gaza. It is worthwhile to compare his version with that of Theodoret.[4]

What strikes one most is that Sozomen's Julianus is an even more fanatical pagan than the one we find in Theodoret's history. According to Sozomen, the *comes Orientis* was not only filled with an extraordinary hatred toward the Christians, but also persecuted them in a bloodthirsty way with all his energy, contrary to the wishes of the emperor Julian—an interesting piece of information. Sozomen, like Theodoret, relates Julianus' misbehavior in a church in Antioch and the looting of its precious objects and also refers to his urinating in the church, adding that immediately afterward Julianus' penis and the rest of his underbelly began to rot. However, Sozomen is silent about a cuff on the ears of Bishop Euzoius. Instead, Sozomen reports that all clerics but one fled from the city. Only the priest Theodoretus (not to be confused with his namesake, the ecclesiastical historian) stayed, with the intention to protect the church against sacrilege. It turned out quite differently. The priest was arrested on the order of *comes* Julianus, cruelly tortured, and finally decapitated.[5]

Surprisingly, the church historian Theodoret, who himself hailed from Antioch, completely ignores his namesake's sufferings and death in the city on the Orontes. Scholars have tried to gloss over the discrepancy between his narrative and that of Sozomen by assuming that Bishop Euzoius was earcuffed in the Great Church, whereas the priest Theodoretus was arrested in another church in Antioch. Not a very satisfying solution, if only because in that case one has to suppose that *comes* Julianus urinated in two churches, but that God punished him only after the second time. More attractive is the assumption that the passage concerning the martyr was originally not found in Sozomen's church history, but was a later interpolation. However this may be (the hypothesis cannot be proved), it is a fact that Euzoius' earcuffs, if he got any, impressed later generations less than the supposed martyr's death of Theodoretus. A *passio* devoted to this priest is known, both in a Greek and in a Latin version.[6]

Out of the twelve sections of the *Passio Theodoreti*, I choose sections 9 and 10 for some comments. The priest happened to have been decapitated shortly before, after he had suffered the most atrocious torments lasting for days, torments that, to the annoyance of *comes* Julianus, he survived splendidly. In between the torture sessions he even calmly answered the questions that his interrogator imposed. The various versions of the *passio* and the hagiographical literature dependent on it are at considerable odds regarding the day of death of the martyr (and, accordingly, that of *comes* Julianus shortly afterward): March 2, 3, 4, 23, and 29 are mentioned, but April 10, May 6, 12, 17, and 18, and October 23 as well. None of these tallies with the date on which the historical *comes* Julianus died, which was, as we saw, after December 6, 362, and before the end of January 363—proof, for those who need proof, of the fictitious character of the *Passio Theodoreti*.[7]

The author of the *passio* says that *comes* Julianus hastily went to the emperor on the morning of the execution. Julian's uncle had slept fitfully (his severe intestinal pains that would cause his death are revealed only later in the *passio*): 'Greetings, mighty emperor,' he said, handing over to his nephew a list of all the precious objects that were stolen from the church in Antioch. 'All your wishes have been fulfilled splendidly. And I vigorously tortured that villain, the priest Theodoretus, before I had him decapitated by the sword.' If Julian's uncle had expected to be praised, he must have been greatly disappointed by the emperor's reaction. 'You did precisely the opposite of what I have always advocated, uncle,' he was told. 'I have always tried to oppose the doctrine of the Galilaeans purely through arguments. I declined violence, I never put anyone to death. Your conduct was absolutely wrong. You played into the Galilaeans' hands. Be assured that they shall now blacken my name in their writings, for that is precisely what they did in the case of my predecessors. When these had executed some criminal, the Galilaeans said that a martyr had died. So, from now on Christians shall not be killed anymore, either by you nor by your subordinates.'[8]

So much for the story of the *comes Orientis* Julianus and the priest Theodoretus. Whoever wants to believe that a priest called Theodoretus was tortured and put to death in Antioch during the reign of Julian can appeal to Sozomen and the *Passio Theodoreti*. He or she then takes for granted that the church historian Theodoret does not say a word about this event. In my view this is an insurmountable obstacle. Consequently, I do not believe in the historicity of Theodoretus' death as a martyr; but one thing is clear: if the priest Theodoretus actually died as a martyr, then the *comes Orientis* Julianus, Julian's uncle, is responsible for it. Both Sozomen and the author of the *Passio Theodoreti* make unambiguously clear that the emperor himself had nothing to do with it.

Chapter 12

Caesarea and Gaza

In July 362 Julian arrived in the Syrian capital Antioch on the Orontes, the domicile of Babylas, Publia, Theodorus, and the priest Theodoretus, who have been mentioned in previous chapters. On his way through Asia Minor the emperor visited for a stopover among other places Ancyra, the capital of the province of Galatia, where, as we have seen, he supposedly brought about the martyr's death of the priest Basil. A certain Busiris also narrowly escaped the same fate in Ancyra during Julian's reign, if we can believe the church historian Sozomen. The narrative of Sozomen—our only source—makes clear as well that the emperor himself was not a witness of Busiris' sufferings.[1]

Busiris belonged to the sect of the Encratites, or 'Self-Controlled,' an extremely ascetic Christian sect that recommended abstinence from wine and meat, and spurned marriage as a lifestyle. Arrested because he had insulted pagans, he was openly taken to a torture post in Ancyra by the governor of Galatia, where Busiris was tied up in order to be tortured and hanged. But before the governor's command could be carried out, Busiris raised both hands and bared the upper part of his body. The hangman's servants need not lift him up onto the rack and help him down afterwards, he said to the governor. That was unnecessary trouble. As far as he was concerned they could torture him without tying him up, for as long as the governor wanted. The governor was stupefied. He had never seen such behavior. His surprise increased when he saw what happened next. Although meat hooks were hammered into his rib cage, Busiris did not falter. Quietly and willingly he endured the torture with his hands raised, until the governor had had enough of it and had him imprisoned. Busiris was released when the news came that Julian had been killed in battle—that was approximately a year after the emperor had left Ancyra.

The sufferings of Busiris of Ancyra ended happily: he gloriously bore the torments inflicted upon him, and lived happily ever after. Sozomen joyfully reports that the *confessor* died many years later, in the time of the emperor Theodosius (379–395), after he had renounced Encratism and had joined the Nicene church (to which the church historian himself also belonged).

The Cappadocian Eupsychius fared differently. Sozomen relates the death of this martyr after Busiris' story. Eupsychius hailed from Caesarea, a city also visited by Julian on his march to Antioch in 362. The march from Ancyra through Cappadocia was a mixed blessing for the emperor. In a letter to the philosopher Aristoxenus, Julian complains that he hardly had met a 'genuine Hellene' in this province, someone who worshiped the traditional gods. Instead he had encountered only people who refused to sacrifice or, if at times they were keen, lacked the know-how. In Caesarea, formerly known as Mazaca, the emperor clashed with the locals—Julian knew the city from the days he had spent as a youth in the nearby villa of Macellum. The quarrel escalated to such an extent that the emperor felt obliged to punish Caesarea by taking away its city status and by altering its name. From now on the city was a village and its name was Mazaca again—it had received the honorific name Caesarea in the beginning of the Common Era (precisely when is disputed). The mere fact that the modern name is Kayseri proves that the imperial order was soon repealed.[2]

Under Julian's Christian predecessors, temples of Zeus and Apollo had been destroyed in Caesarea. For that reason, as Sozomen tells us, Julian took a dislike to the citizens of this Cappadocian city. His dislike increased further, when during his own reign the temple of Tyche (Fortuna) was demolished—the emperor was the more indignant because the pagans in the city had not lifted a finger to prevent the destruction. Not only did he take Caesarea's name and privileges away, so that the citizens had to pay more taxes, but he also forced the Christian churches in and near the city to hand over their precious objects and other possessions, imposed a fine of three hundred pounds of gold, and enlisted all the clerics as soldiers into the troops of the provincial governor. In addition he demanded the restoration of the destroyed temples. If the people procrastinated, he would take more punitive measures and would not hesitate 'to kill those Galilaeans.' There cannot be any doubt, as Sozomen says at the end of his report, that Julian would have carried out his threats, had he not died in battle shortly afterward.[3]

There is no mention at all of Eupsychius in Sozomen's chapter about Julian's stay in Caesarea. It is only later in his work that Sozomen relates that this scion of a distinguished Cappadocian family ended his life as a martyr while he was on his honeymoon. 'I surmise,' the church historian adds, 'that Eupsychius was put to death because of the temple of Tyche.' Note that Sozomen does not know for certain what caused Eupsychius' death, but only expresses an educated guess. 'I already reported,' Sozomen continues, 'about that destruction, which aroused the anger of the emperor against all the inhabitants of Caesarea.' The attentive reader will agree. But Sozomen's next remark comes as a surprise to those who remember what the church historian had said earlier. 'The men who had demolished the temple were all punished, some with death, others with exile.' Punished with death? Was it not the same Sozomen who shortly before had written that Julian's death prevented the Galilaeans in Caesarea from being killed?[4]

Sozomen may be right when he reports that a certain Eupsychius ended his life by martyrdom in Caesarea, but in view of the inconsistencies in his story it seems very doubtful that it was the emperor Julian who ordered Eupsychius' execution. Such an action, which is, other than Sozomen, mentioned only in medieval martyrologia based on Sozomen, does not befit the Julian whom we have met thus far. It is telling that Gregory of Nazianzus, who does relate that Julian punished the city of Caesarea, does not refer to Eupsychius' fate in this connection. The only document that deals extensively with the martyr's agonizing death, the *Passio Eupsychii*, and which is preserved in an eleventh-century manuscript, should be regarded as a 'passion épique.' Significantly, in this text it is not Julian, but his second-century predecessor Hadrian who condemns Eupsychius.[5]

Admittedly, in a letter of Gregory of Nazianzus and in some letters of Basil of Caesarea, mention is made of a martyr by the name of Eupsychius, in whose honor a yearly feast was held in Caesarea. It was celebrated on September 7. Basil further relates that not only Eupsychius, but also Damas (of whom nothing further is known) and other martyrs were commemorated on that day. However, neither Gregory nor Basil reports that the martyrs whose commemoration day was September 7 died during the reign of Julian, so it is by no means certain that they are referring to Sozomen's newlywed noble. There might well have been another, earlier martyr named Eupsychius who inspired Sozomen's opinion. Moreover, the date of the celebration festival in Caesarea militates against this identification. On September 7, 362, Julian was not in Caesarea, but in Antioch (he arrived, as we have already seen, in the Syrian capital in July of that year). As I do not wish to be hypercritical I do not rule out the possibility that there is a kernel of truth in Sozomen's story, but, even if there was a martyr by the name of Eupsychius during Julian's reign, the emperor himself cannot be blamed for his death.[6]

Neither do I want to call into question the historicity of the violent deaths of Eusebius, Nestabus, and Zeno, three brothers from the province of Palaestina Prima—in this case, too, Sozomen is our only source. The story of these brothers is set in the town of Gaza. The emperor Julian never visited Gaza, but during his reign, or rather, during the fourth century in general, paganism was the dominant religion there. Interestingly, the example of Gaza's seaport, which was originally called Maiuma, shows that the religious character of one place could differ from that of another. Constantine the Great had made the seaport independent of Gaza as a reward for Maiuma's embrace of Christianity, granted it privileges, and changed its name to Constantia after his sister, or, according to another source, after one of his sons. But as soon as Julian had become emperor, Constantine's measure was reversed. The citizens of Gaza successfully appealed to the new emperor, who once again punished a Christian city because of its religious preference. As in the case of Cappadocian Caesarea/Mazaca, so now in Palaestina the name of a city was struck from the records. Apart from its name, Constantia also lost its independence: the seaport became a district of pagan Gaza.[7]

We hear that in pagan Gaza and in nearby Ascalon some Christian priests and women who had taken vows of chastity were murdered by the cities' inhabitants during Julian's reign, and that their bodies were violated: they were thrown before pigs after their bellies had been disemboweled and filled with barleycorn. We find this information in Theodoret's ecclesiastical history and in the *Chronicon paschale*, which was written in the seventh century. A shocking story. Is it true? Certainly not totally. It is perfectly possible that such atrocities were committed. But apparently Theodoret and the Byzantine chronicle had read their source, which was presumably Gregory of Nazianzus, less than carefully. Gregory sets the incident not in Gaza and Ascalon in the southern part of the province Palaestina Prima, but more to the north, in Heliopolis near Mount Lebanon. Sozomen does the same, which is decisive, because we may assume that Sozomen knew the history of Gaza too well to confuse Heliopolis and Gaza. His own grandfather, who was the first of his family to embrace Christianity, hailed from a village near Gaza, from where he fled during the reign of Julian. Sozomen himself tells us that in his youth he had been able to talk with his grandfather and other refugees from Gaza about the history of their native region.[8]

The priests and the virgins who were fed to pigs lived in Heliopolis, whereas Eusebius, Nestabus, and Zeno died in Gaza. We can accept this on the authority of Sozomen. Here follows the tale of their sufferings and death, as told by the church historian: 'The inhabitants of Gaza, being inflamed with rage against them, dragged them from the house, in which they had concealed themselves, and cast them into prison, and beat them. They then assembled in the theater, and cried out loudly against them, declaring that they had committed sacrilege in their temple, and had used the previous time to denigrate and insult paganism. Shouting thus and instigating one another to murder the brethren, they were filled with fury; and when they had reached fever pitch, which tends to happen when a crowd revolts, they rushed to the prison. They treated the men very cruelly; sometimes on their bellies and sometimes on their backs the victims were dragged along, and then were dashed to pieces on the pavement. I have been told that even women quit their distaffs and pierced them with the weaving-spindles, and that the cooks in the markets snatched from their stands the boiling pots foaming with hot water and poured them over the victims, or perforated them with spits. When they had torn the flesh off them and crushed their skulls, so that the brains ran out on the ground, their bodies were dragged out of the city and flung on the spot generally used as a receptacle for the carcasses of animals; then a large fire was lit, and the bodies were burnt; the remains of the bones not consumed by the fire were mixed with those of camels and asses, that they might not be found easily. But they were not long concealed; for a Christian woman, who was an inhabitant, though not a native of Gaza, collected the bones at night, directed by God. She put them in an earthen pot and gave them to Zeno, their cousin, to keep, for thus God had informed her in a dream, and He had also indicated to the woman where the man lived: and before she saw him, God showed him to her, for she was previously unacquainted with Zeno; and when the persecution started he had found a hiding-place. He was within an inch of being seized by the people of Gaza and of being put to death; but he had managed to escape while the people were occupied with the murder of his cousins, and had fled to Anthedon, a maritime city, about twenty stadia from Gaza and similarly favorable to paganism and devoted to idolatry. When the inhabitants of this city discovered that he was a Christian, they beat him fiercely on the back with rods and drove him out of the city. He then fled to the harbor of Gaza and concealed himself; and there the woman found him and gave him the remains. He kept them carefully in his house until the reign of Theodosius, when he was ordained bishop; and he erected a house of prayer beyond the walls of the city, placed an altar there, and deposited the bones of the martyrs near those of Nestor, the *confessor.* Nestor had been a very close friend of his cousins, and was seized together with them by the people of Gaza, then imprisoned and scourged. But those who dragged him through the city were struck by his personal beauty; and filled with compassion, they cast him, when he was not quite dead, out of the city. Some people found him, and carried him to the house of Zeno, where he died whilst his cuts and wounds were being dressed.'[9]

So much for Sozomen's story about the death of Eusebius, Nestabus, and Zeno, with that of the *confessor* Nestor as a bonus. The fifth-century church historian probably based his report for the greater part on oral tradition, although there exists already a succinct account of the disturbances in Gaza in the work of Julian's contemporary Gregory of Nazianzus (but without mention of any names). We have seen that Sozomen, through his grandfather, had contacts with former inhabitants of Gaza and its surroundings. He explicitly relates later in his work that he had known Zeno, the cousin of the murdered brothers, who himself also became almost a victim of the killing. The core of his story therefore deserves to be believed, although one may ask oneself whether all the details are true.[10]

The emperor Julian has only indirectly come up in what is stated above. This changes, however, at the end of Sozomen's narrative about the martyrs of Gaza. There the church historian scornfully remarks that the emperor did not deign to take the pagan inhabitants of Gaza to task, and did not even write a letter—as he had done in the case of the Alexandrians after the killing of Bishop George. Worse still, when the governor of the province of Palaestina Prima started an investigation and, pending the verdict, imprisoned the instigators of the riots, he incurred Julian's displeasure. The governor was removed from office and only just escaped execution. 'What right had he,' asked the emperor in Sozomen's version, 'to arrest the citizens who were merely taking revenge on a few Galilaeans for the injuries that had been inflicted on them and their gods?'[11]

It is doubtful whether Julian really spoke the words put into his mouth by Sozomen with respect to Gaza. Sozomen probably borrowed the anecdote and the quotation from Gregory of Nazianzus, but Gregory can hardly be called an objective informant. The emperor himself and other non-Christian sources are silent about the whole affair. As for Julian's letter to the Alexandrians, in this letter the emperor made clear that he disapproved of the lynching of Bishop George and his followers. There are no indications that he had changed his mind. No doubt the pagan–Christian quarrels in Gaza created victims, but it is not likely that the emperor approved of the killing.

Chapter 13

Eugenius and Macarius

In the summer of 362 Julian marched from Caesarea in Cappadocia via Tarsus in Cilicia to Antioch in Syria. When the news of his arrival reached the city, the inhabitants came pouring out to meet the emperor. 'He was received with public prayers as if he were some deity.' Thus writes Ammianus Marcellinus, a witness of the event. Ammianus further observes that the emperor was surprised to hear so many shouts of welcome. 'A lucky star has risen over the East' was but one of the tributes. But when Julian entered the gates of his Syrian residence he heard other, less jubilant sounds. His arrival concurred with the yearly day of remembrance of the death of Adonis, the lover of Aphrodite, who, according to the myth, was killed by a boar during a hunting party. Everywhere in the city wailing and cries of grief were heard. That did not bode well.[1]

Julian's stay in Antioch lasted about half a year. In the Syrian capital he became consul for the fourth time on January 1, 363, together with his good friend Flavius Sallustius—Julian had already obtained the consulship in 356, 357, and 360 (the consulate was in the Late Empire still the most prestigious function for any Roman citizen, including the emperor), in each case together with his cousin Constantius. Libanius states in an address to the emperor on this occasion that many other speakers were prepared to celebrate the festival of the First of January (*Kalendae Ianuariae*) with their speeches, too. Feelings in the city were far from ecstatic, however. Julian's stay in Antioch turned out to be very unpleasant. Especially the Christian part of the population criticized him severely, but the Christians were not the only ones. Almost everybody thought that Julian's animal sacrifices were ridiculous and over the top. It was generally resented that the philosopher and bookworm, in contrast to his cousin and predecessor Constantius, could not work up any interest for public entertainment in theater and arena. It was felt as a great burden that Julian's soldiers were billeted in the city, and most people found his method of solving the problem of food shortage inadequate. When on March 5, 363, Julian departed from the city on the Orontes to start his Persian campaign, nothing was left of the initial enthusiasm for the young emperor. Julian himself felt deeply aggrieved. To the Antiochenes who saw him off he gave to understand that he would never set foot in their city again, and that on his way back from Persia he would go directly to Tarsus. Prophetic words: shortly after Julian had died in Mesopotamia his mortal remains were buried in a suburb of Tarsus.[2]

During his stay in Antioch, Julian felt the need to vent his indignation in an open letter—a unique occurrence in the history of the Roman Empire. This piece of writing, full of sarcasm and irony, is officially called *Antiochicus*, but its common name is *Misopogon* ('Beardhater'), an allusion to Julian's philosopher's beard, which more than anything else provoked ridicule among the Antiochenes. In this pamphlet he contrasts the serious and modest Celts he had met in Gaul with the frivolous inhabitants of the city on the Orontes, 'in which there are numerous dancers and flute players and more actors than ordinary citizens, and no respect at all for those who govern.' Indeed, he continues, 'fellows like you it befits to begin your revels at dawn, to spend your nights in pleasure, and to show not only by your words but by your deeds also that you despise the laws.' As stated by Libanius, it was this letter that Julian used as a weapon in his conflict with the citizens of Antioch, and, so the rhetor stresses, the *Misopogon* was his only weapon in his conflict with hostile critics. The gentle emperor scorned the use of torture, not to mention executions, to keep the turbulent citizens in line. In every respect Julian's behavior was exceptionally moderate in Libanius' eyes. For example, he left people who had plotted an attack on his life alone—even Julian's admirer Libanius, though, could not deny that the emperor did have some enemies, who hated him so much that they wanted to kill him.[3]

We saw earlier that other, anti-Julianic sources actually made mention of unpleasant punitive measures against citizens of Antioch. Recall the fate of Theodorus, who, despite ghastly torture, cheerfully continued to sing psalms, and that of the venerable lady Publia, who was so severely hit in her face that blood streamed over her cheeks. I further refer to the case of young Romanus, the soldier who was not executed, as the emperor had first ordered, but banished to the farthest borders of the empire. The stories of these Christian *confessores* are told by Christian authors, and their veracity is dubious. But the pagan Ammianus Marcellinus, well disposed toward Julian, also sketches a Julian different from Libanius' Julian. According to this historian, the emperor banished two officers of his bodyguard during his stay in Antioch, and executed three men: a high official, the son of a general, and the former military commander of Egypt, Flavius Artemius.[4]

There is no reason to doubt Ammianus' statement. Although Julian compares favorably with most other Roman emperors as regards clemency, his punishments were severe in the few cases in which he deemed this necessary. Did he deliberately persecute Christians in these cases? I do not think so. At any rate, the arguments adduced in the previous chapters to prove such a persecution do not appear cogent. As to the victims Ammianus mentions in his chapter about Antioch, there is in my opinion no sufficient proof in their cases, either. Two of them can be disregarded, anyway. Nobody ever saw a link between the death of the general's son and that of the high official on the one hand, and a persecution of Christians, if there was one, on the other. The exile of the two officers of Julian's bodyguard is a different matter. It has sometimes been argued that these officers, Romanus and Vincentius, were punished on account of their religion, on the assumption that Romanus is identical with the soldier of that name whom we met in Chapter 7. This identification, however, cannot be proved, and about Romanus' colleague, Vincentius, nothing further is known. Therefore, I prefer to leave speculations about this identification to others, and return to the partly apocryphal story of Flavius Artemius, the former military commander of Egypt.[5]

We have already met this *dux Aegypti* in Chapters 4 and 5. He sided with George, the 'Arian' bishop of Alexandria, lynched in 361, and was later venerated by orthodox Christians as a martyr who had healing gifts. We have also seen that the data concerning Artemius' life and death are scarce, and that our most extensive source, the *Artemii passio*, is of dubious historicity. What follows in the next sections is part of the 'history' of Artemius, derived from the same muddled source. The former commander himself plays only a supporting role in this drama, which in its turn is no doubt fictitious. The main characters are two priests of the church of Antioch, Eugenius and Macarius, for whom Artemius is said to have stepped into the breach when they were brought before Julian's bench as recalcitrant Christians. I summarize the relevant chapters of the *Artemii passio*.[6]

As soon as the emperor, who came from Tarsus, had arrived in Antioch, Eugenius and Macarius were brought before him. Things did not look good for the two priests, for Julian had shortly before in anger threatened to sweep all Christians from the face of the earth.

An altercation ensued, first between the emperor and Eugenius, whom the author of the *passio*, ahead of events, already calls 'martyr,' then between the emperor and Macarius. Eugenius was not impressed by his imperial judge. He simply laughed with a note of pity at Julian's attempt to put Jesus Christ, risen from the dead, on a par with Hermes Trismegistus ('Thrice-Greatest,' the title of Toth, the Egyptian Hermes) and the mysterious philosopher and mathematician Pythagoras, who introduced the doctrine of reincarnation into Greece and whose soul, it was said, once lodged in the body of an Egyptian sailor and in that of the Trojan hero Euphorbus. Actually, Eugenius did not want to respond to such nonsense, but because he saw that many citizens of Antioch, a city that was for the most part Christian, were assembled around the emperor's bench, he talked back.[7]

Eugenius spoke in glowing terms about the Incarnation of the Son of God, his Crucifixion, his Resurrection after three days, his Ascension. He talked about the work of the Apostles, who, inspired by the Holy Ghost, had been able to speak in tongues, bring dead people back to life, and heal lepers. They were simple fishermen, who could not read or write. What a difference with the supposed sages Julian had mentioned! Take Pythagoras. When in Olympia in his presence a bull that was being slaughtered began to bellow, he shouted: 'Stop! My best friend's soul is lodged in that bull. The bellowing reminds me of the poor man's voice,' but that was about the most important feat Pythagoras ever accomplished. And so Eugenius carried on. He praised Jesus Christ, and wiped the floor with Julian's arguments. After a while the emperor became annoyed. He handed Eugenius over to the assistants of the bench and ordered them to flog the priest 500 times. Without a whimper the priest endured the merciless torture.[8]

Now it was Macarius' turn. The emperor gave him a piercing look and asked, 'What have you got to say for yourself, you miserable good-for-nothing?' 'Look at yourself,' was the answer. 'Of all people you are the greatest scum, you dirty scoundrel. My name is Macarius. That means "blessed," and blessed I am, or rather thrice blessed, for I worship Jesus Christ, the Son of God.' Whereupon Julian said, 'I know that you are eager to die, and that you try to make me so angry that I shall execute you soon. But you shall not get off so easily, you wicked rascal.' And he posed some questions to Macarius, who made the following riposte: 'Apparently you did not listen to the wise lessons Eugenius just gave you, you nasty fellow, for you ask for the sake of asking. But okay, I shall once again explain it to you.' By way of explanation Macarius cited some scriptural passages, such as Jeremiah 10:11 ('The gods that did not make the heavens and the earth will perish from the earth and from under the heavens'), and then referred to Julian's uncle Constantine the Great, who, as a believer in Jesus Christ, destroyed pagan temples and forbade sacrificing.[9]

Of course, the name of Constantine set Julian off. Constantine had been dazzled by illusions, he said, and was misled by the Galilaeans. Not his uncle, but he himself represented the true Graeco-Roman civilization, well versed as he was in the teachings of Hermes Trismegistus, Orpheus, and Plato. He also knew the scriptures of the Jews with their hairsplitting subtleties, but that was exactly the reason that he rejected their stupid innovations and held on to the time-honored traditional worship of the gods. 'But come on, let us no longer wait. Take the man's clothes off and let him feel the whip. That will teach him willy-nilly to obey our laws.'

Then Artemius appeared on the scene. He set himself up as defender of Eugenius and Macarius, with the result that he himself was also tortured for a long time. Finally, Artemius was sent to prison, together with the two priests. On their way the threesome sang and prayed to God. The next day Julian decided thereafter to deal exclusively with Artemius. He exiled Eugenius and Macarius and sent them to Oasis, an inhospitable place in Arabia. There, on the emperor's order, they were decapitated after forty days, on December 20. On the spot where they died a miracle occurred. Until then there had been no water, but now a medicinal spring welled up. The name of the spring keeps the memory of both martyrs alive down to the present day.[10]

And so the story of Eugenius and Macarius in the *Artemii passio* ends surprisingly: the emperor Julian had the priests taken from Antioch to Arabia, and had them executed there—a rather laborious procedure. Elsewhere it is related that Eugenius and Macarius were exiled to Mauretania, modern Morocco, and that they died a natural death. We find this version in the *Passio Eugenii et Macarii*, a martyrology written in Greek that cannot be dated accurately. Although its content is rather different from that of the *Artemii passio*, it belongs firmly, just like that piece of writing, to the genre of 'passions épiques.' In this version, Eugenius and Macarius were not priests, but brothers. There was not a word in it about Antioch. Both heroes were interrogated by Julian, but the dialogues are totally different. The torture that Eugenius and Macarius had to endure also differed from that in the *Artemii passio*. The Christian brothers were first hanged upside down above a fire, and then forced to stand for hours on a red-hot stove. When, with the help of God, they had undergone these torments unscathed, the emperor tried to lure them into apostasy by promising heaps of gold and silver, through a courtier. In vain, of course. The snakes, which were set on them, turned against Julian himself: terrified, he fled away from his throne, whereupon the snakes peacefully settled down at the feet of Eugenius and Macarius. Now the emperor was at a loss. 'But don't imagine that I will do what you like best,' he exclaimed twice, when Macarius asked if the emperor had at last understood that their belief in God was steadfast, and they gladly wanted to die for Him.[11]

The satisfaction of a martyr's death was not granted to Eugenius and Macarius. Instead, the emperor exiled them to Dindona in Mauretania, where the brothers discovered that the local population had never heard of Jesus Christ, but was receptive to missionary work, the more so after the brothers succeeded, with the help of God, in beating a fire-breathing dragon. More miracles occurred. A shooting star announced the death of the emperor Julian, and a heavenly fire split a rock in two, which had blocked a well. After four months the forced but salutary stay of Eugenius and Macarius in Mauretania ended. On February 22 they passed away calmly and peacefully, with a prayer on their lips.[12]

It is time to say goodbye to Eugenius and Macarius. We followed them from Antioch to Oasis in Arabia and subsequently to Dindona in Mauretania, where they were decapitated on December 20 and peacefully passed away on February 22, respectively. I shall not attempt to reconcile the differences between the *Passio Artemii* and the *Passio Eugenii et Macarii*. That makes no sense, given the character of both *passiones*, which are fictional for the greater part. The author of the *Passio Eugenii et Macarii* ends his story with a pious 'amen.' That seems an appropriate end for my chapter, too. Let us return to Antioch, or rather, let us go via Antioch once again to Caesarea in Cappadocia.[13]

Chapter 14

The Banner of the Cross

It was in Cappadocian Caesarea that a certain Eusignius, a former soldier of the Roman army, was beheaded on the order of Julian. The two had met in Antioch in Syria, but Eusignius was taken to Caesarea to be put on trial there. At least, this is related in the *Eusignii passio*, a martyrology written in Greek that presumably dates back to the seventh century. Now, as we have seen in Chapter 12, Julian had already visited Caesarea before he arrived in Antioch (during this visit he downgraded Caesarea from a city to a village and stripped it of its name), but apparently the author of the *Eusignii passio* was unaware of this fact. Nor did he know Caesarea's exact location, for he let Julian start his Persian campaign by marching in the wrong direction. Instead of heading from Antioch eastward toward the Euphrates, the emperor, according to the *passio*, advanced to Caesarea, which lies more than 450 kilometers north of Antioch—a detail that speaks volumes about the historical accuracy of the *Eusignii passio*.[1]

I shall present the main points of this *passio*, not because they contribute anything toward understanding Julian as a historical figure—the martyrology belongs firmly to the genre of *passions épiques*, of which we have already seen some examples—but because the text gives a good impression of how later generations regarded

Julian, and because it contains several quirks worth noting. Firstly, a good deal of attention is given to Julian's uncle Constantine the Great, who, when it came to religion, was his total opposite, specifically to his conversion after he had witnessed a cross in heaven. Secondly, in contrast to other martyrologies, out of the twelve paragraphs of the *passio,* only one directly describes the torture of Eusignius. Thirdly, it states that Julian forbade Eusignius' examination under torture from being written down by stenographers (stenography had been invented in the first century BCE by Cicero's freedman Tiro), supposedly because acts of martyrdom would only reinforce the Christian faith. Luckily for us, Eusignius asked a relative, the deacon Eustochius, to arrange for a stenographer to report in secret, so I can now relate his findings in summarized form.[2]

After the death of his predecessor, Julian resided primarily in the imperial palace in Antioch, and it was from this palace that he hunted down followers of Jesus Christ. A certain Eusignius also lived in Antioch, a retired soldier, 113 years of age, a pious and god-fearing man, who used to spend many days and nights in prayer at the local church. One day a pair of quarreling 'Hellenes' (that is to say, pagans) asked him to be the arbiter in one of their disputes. After Eusignius had agreed, the one whose appeal was turned down promptly produced a letter to the emperor, complaining that the old man was a Galilaean, a follower of Christ, that he mocked the gods and, to add insult to injury, presented himself as a competent judge in the emperor's stead; moreover, he discouraged the practice of sacrifices to the gods.[3]

Julian summoned Eusignius, abused him verbally, and threatened to have him hanged. Eusignius for his part protested loudly: a veteran of sixty years of exemplary military service in the armies of both Constantine the Great and Constantine's father Constantius Chlorus should not die in this way. He also brought up his age of 113.

What had he done to deserve death without any form of trial? The emperor took Eusignius' protests as a sign of fear, and fully expected that he would soon be able to persuade the old man to abandon his faith. He released him for the time being and left for Caesarea, to start his Persian campaign with the troops he had summoned to gather there. Eusignius was ordered to follow the emperor to Cappadocia.[4]

In Caesarea the trial was resumed with the entire army in attendance. Torture devices had been constructed beforehand. After Eusignius rebuked Julian's attempts to get him to renounce his faith in Jesus, the torturers went to work. Sometime later, the emperor tried once more to change the old man's mind. Again, his efforts were in vain. 'Are you not ashamed, you atheist,' Eusignius snapped, 'for having deserted the Lord Jesus Christ, whereas the emperor Constantine, hark you, the son of a whore, acknowledged him as the only true God?' 'Nonsense, you scoundrel,' Julian exclaimed, apparently offended—an interesting detail: as we have seen, the historical Julian had spoken very negatively about his uncle—'don't you dare call the great emperor Constantine the son of a whore.' 'But he certainly was, sir,' Eusignius answered. 'It would be my pleasure to explain this to you, if you order me to do it.' 'Go ahead,' Julian said, 'but woe betide you if you are only babbling.'[5]

Eusignius then started to tell his story: one day his commander, the tribune Constantius Chlorus, on the way back from a campaign against the Sarmatians, met a girl named Helena in a public house, fell in love with her, slept with her, and the next morning gave her a purple tunica as remuneration; on his arrival in Rome the tribune was made emperor; Constantius married, and had a son who was mentally deficient; upset by this misfortune he ordered some officers of the imperial guard to look for a well-formed, healthy boy whom he could adopt and make his heir—he did not know that divine providence had already given him a son; one day the guards found themselves in the tavern where Helena lived with her son, now twelve years old; while the soldiers were feasting, young Constantine mounted one of their horses, which cost him a cuff on the ears from its owner; crying aloud he made a complaint to his mother. 'Do not hit that boy again, my friend,' Helena shouted. 'He is the son of the emperor'; as proof she showed the purple garment she had obtained from Constantius; without delay the soldiers rode back to Rome, reported to the emperor what had happened, and presented him with his son; a delighted Constantius gave Constantine a high rank in the army and made him commander of a few units, among which was that of Eusignius—the fact that Constantine was only twelve years old apparently was no problem.[6]

It is disputed in which year the historical Constantine reached the age of twelve. According to most scholars his year of birth was 272, but 276 and 288 are also put forward. His birthplace was Naissus. It is certain that Helena and Constantius Chlorus were his parents, but the answer to the question, whether his mother was Constantius' legal first wife or merely a concubine, is in doubt. It is, however, undisputed that Helena was of very humble origin, and that Constantine's father, Constantius, later married Theodora, stepdaughter of the emperor Maximianus. In 293 Constantius was made co-emperor by Diocletian, and from that year onward four emperors ruled the Roman Empire, two *Augusti* and two *Caesares*— modern scholars speak of the Tetrarchy. After Constantius Chlorus' death in 306 the Tetrarchy became obsolete. It was again each for himself, and Constantine did his part: in 312 he eliminated his rival Maxentius in the battle of the Milvian Bridge before the gates of Rome. As we already saw in Chapter 2, according to one source he had a dream on the eve of the battle in which he was advised to fix God's heavenly sign on the shields of his soldiers; according to another he had a vision in broad daylight: a sign in the shape of a cross up in the sky, with the words 'by this conquer.' Relying on this sign he also defeated his last rival, Licinius, and thus became sole emperor of the Roman Empire in the year 324.[7]

There is no trace of Maxentius or the Milvian Bridge in the *Eusignii passio*. Miraculous signs, however, are duly mentioned. Constantine, it is reported, saw a cross up in the sky in a battle against the 'Byzantines'—presumably, Licinius and his troops are meant— and because of that sign won the fight. On the spot where he was victorious, in the center of Byzantium (from now on Constantinople), a huge cross was erected. Incidentally, Constantine at first did not understand the purport of this symbol. He grasped its meaning only seven years later, when, after his father's death, he was waging a war against barbarians from the north side of the Danube. One night he saw a shining cross in the sky, and with it the words 'Conquer by this sign.' He thereupon had his soldiers march to the battlefield behind a cross. After he had won the war, he asked some pagan priests to which god this attribute belonged, but he did not obtain a satisfying answer until some Christian soldiers, called Nazaraeans, informed him. Then Constantine embraced the Christian faith.[8]

The greater part of what the author of the *Eusignii passio* had to say has now been told. There follows a short sequel, about Helena visiting Jerusalem and Constantine's miraculous escape from imprisonment in Persia, but then the time has come to let Eusignius die. It took only a few words. At the end of his story the old man once again pointed to the contrast between Constantine and Julian, an observation that greatly annoyed Julian, because Eusignius' words were approved by the soldiers who were assembled around the emperor's bench. Subsequently, the order was given to carry Eusignius away and decapitate him. He was buried by Bishop Basil.[9]

So much for the *Eusignii passio.* We let the martyr rest in peace in his grave in Caesarea and return to Antioch. It was in the Syrian capital that, according to the *Passio sanctorum Bonosi et Maximiliani* ('Sufferings of the Holy Bonosus and Maximilian') the imperial banner (Figure 5), the so-called *labarum,* had become a point of contention. This standard, according to Eusebius of Caesarea, introduced by Constantine after his conversion, consisted of a long pole and a crosspiece. On top was the Christogram. Fixed to the crosspiece was a banner, originally with the portraits of Constantine and his sons, and, later, with the Christogram or words like these: *in nomine XPI vincas semper* (in the name of Christ, may you always conquer). A showpiece of the *labarum,* full of gold and jewels, was protected by a special guard of at least fifty men, whilst the various army units each had a replica.

Figure 5. Coin of Constantine the Great with a depiction of the *labarum* spearing a serpent. Reverse. SPES PVBLIC(A), 'Hope of the People.' Minted in Constantinople (RIC 7, p. 572, no. 19). The British Museum, London. *(Credit Line © bpk, Berlin/Reinhard Saczewski/Art Resource/NY.)*

That is, until Julian decided otherwise. 'Ultimately he even dared to grapple with the banner of the cross, which, proudly held up high, used to be carried in front of the army,' Gregory of Nazianzus grumbles in one of his invectives against Julian. Sozomen adds that Julian not only replaced the *labarum* with the standard that had been used in former times, but that he had depicted on it, apart from the portrait of the emperor, icons of Jupiter, Mars, and Mercury, in order that the soldiers, when they greeted the standard, would show deference to these gods at the same time.[10]

What is the reliability of Gregory and Sozomen in this respect? The information of the Christian authors is not confirmed in the other sources that are normally tapped whenever Julian's deeds are concerned, but the abolition of the typically Christian symbol of the banner of the cross neatly fits in with the anti-Christian policy of the emperor. So there may be a kernel of truth in their stories. By means of analogy we can point to Julian's coinage. Christian symbols like the *labarum*, the christogram, or the cross had repeatedly been depicted on coins of Constantius. We even sometimes find Constantius holding a standard with Chi-Rho on the banner on coins of Iulianus *Caesar*, no doubt to Julian's regret. Such Christian symbols disappeared from Julian's coins after he became *Augustus* (although, interestingly, this did not occur immediately). Under Julian's successor Jovian, the *labarum* returned. But is it correct to say that it was only after Julian had come to Antioch that the emperor decided to get rid of the banner of the cross? And is it true that in the Syrian capital two standard-bearers had to pay with their lives for refusing to remove the sign of Christ from their *labarum*? This is what we read in the *Passio sanctorum Bonosi et Maximiliani*, a text, written in Latin, that some scholars regard as a reliable historical source. However, no other source relates that the two standard-bearers died as martyrs, and to me the story of their sufferings seems of dubious historicity.[11]

The *passio* comes straight to the point. 'Count [*comes*] Julianus said to Bonosus and Maximilianus, "our lord the emperor has ordered that you must remove the sign that you have on your *labarum*." ' No introductory words, no clue about the place where the encounter took place, no details about the dramatis personae. Information concerning Bonosus and Maximilianus has to be deduced from the title of the *passio*. According to this title both men were soldiers, ostensibly standard-bearers, who belonged to a squad of the Herculiani—there was indeed among Julian's forces a legion of that name—unless we must assume that only one of the men belonged to the Herculiani and the other to the Ioviani (the legion that often is mentioned in one breath with the Herculiani), for the author of the *passio* twice writes 'Iovianus and Hercolianus' instead of Bonosus and Maximilianus. As to *comes* Julianus, it seems more than likely that Julian's uncle and namesake, whom we met before, is meant. As *comes Orientis* he resided in Antioch, and Antioch was apparently the scene of the action. *Comes* Julianus was, like his nephew, an apostate. Christian authors evidently regarded him as a bad character, as we saw in Chapter 11.[12]

Count Julianus' command to remove the sign of Christ from the standard-bearers' *labarum* was in vain. Bonosus and Maximilianus were not willing to worship the pagan gods, either. 'We cannot adore gods who are made by human hands,' they answered the *comes*. Threats of torture did not impress them, nor did the actual torments change their minds. More than three hundred blows with the cat-o'-nine-tails, the rack, the immersion in red-hot pitch: they endured all these ordeals without flinching. Jews and pagans, who had come flocking in, hoping to feast their eyes on the death of the soldiers, started to shout when they saw what happened, 'Those men must be magicians and wizards.' When the prefect Secundus (whom we also met before) heard this, he came running. He was stunned and wanted to see if pagan priests were as capable as the

Christian standard-bearers to undergo such sufferings. But alas, the priests who were thrown into a barrel with red-hot pitch did not stand the test.[13]

Perhaps those scholars who believe in the historicity of what the *passio* relates are becoming a little suspicious now. Torture as part of legal proceedings was quite common in Late Antiquity, but it certainly was unusual that the accused left the rack as fresh as a daisy and was immune to immersion in red-hot pitch. The fact that a *comes Orientis*, a civil official, led the inquiry against soldiers is unusual, too. This alone provides food for thought. However, it is as nothing compared to the assertion that a praetorian prefect by way of a test had some men, notably priests and pagans (he himself was a pagan), burnt alive in boiling pitch. This is not only quite unusual; it is totally incredible as well. A reader of the rest of the *passio* discovers more oddities. It is full of content that one normally finds in fictional martyrologies rather than in reliable historical sources.[14]

Bonosus and Maximilianus were locked in a dungeon for seven days and seven nights without food or drink while awaiting new torments. When a loaf of bread was offered to them, they scorned it, because Count Julianus had stamped pagan symbols on its surface with his signet ring. In the meantime a new torment was devised. Quicklime was poured out over their bodies. However, to the surprise of Count Julianus and his companions they passed this test also with flying colors, for the lime had no effect whatsoever and the bodies remained intact. Subsequently, the soldiers were imprisoned once more, this time for twelve days and twelve nights. Again they refused to eat the food presented to them, this time because it had been part of pagan sacrifices. Count Julianus was very much put out because of all this, and his anger increased when he heard that the Persian prince Hormisdas, a general in the Roman imperial army and a Christian, had visited the prisoners and had asked them to pray for his spiritual welfare. Count Julianus had the soldiers brought before him, and threatened to inflict still worse tortures. Then there was a surprising turn of events. Not only Christian bystanders loudly expressed their support for the martyrs, but the pagan prefect Secundus also turned against *comes* Julianus. He wanted the torture to be stopped and said, appealing to one of the standard-bearers, 'By God, I beseech you, Bonosus, my holy lord, remember me in your prayers.'[15]

Count Julianus now wanted to settle the matter once and for all. He said to 'Iovianus and Hercolianus,' 'I still wonder why you so stubbornly defend that sign of the Christians, but anyhow, remove it from your *labarum*, and replace it with the sign of the gods.' The standard-bearers refused, replying that on his dying day (that is, in 337, some twenty-five years before) they had promised Constantine the Great to do nothing that would run counter to the interests of the Church. That did finish them. They were brought to the place of their execution, accompanied by Bishop Meletius and other clerics, and were beheaded. According to the *passio*'s title, this was on September 20 [362]. A few days later Count Julianus died. As is also related elsewhere, he died a horrible death, heralded by a great quantity of maggots creeping out of his mouth. Terrified, he wanted his wife to go to the church and implore the Christians to pray for him, in order that God would stop his plague. However, his wife refused to do so. She said that he himself was to blame for God's punishment. Julianus now began to moan wordlessly. Shortly afterward he died, with a prayer to the God of the Christians on his lips, lips that were crawling with maggots.[16]

The *comes* Julianus of the *Passio sanctorum Bonosi et Maximiliani* died at the end of September 362, whereas the historical *comes Orientis* of that name breathed his last some months later, in December 362 or in the beginning of 363. Those scholars who believe that there is a kernel of truth in the *passio* do not worry about this discrepancy, or try to argue the problem away. In my view, however, this chronological irregularity is all the more reason that one should regard the martyrology of the standard-bearers as fictional. I further point to the fact, mentioned in Chapter 11, that according to other sources, the *comes Orientis* Julianus died after he had caused the martyr's death of the priest Theodoretus. In any case, one thing is certain. It was his uncle and namesake, not the emperor Julian himself, who in the *passio* ordered the standard-bearers Bonosus and Maximilianus to be tortured and executed.[17]

Chapter 15

Chrysostom and Julian

To the vast body of work of John Chrysostom belongs a sermon that he delivered in his native city of Antioch in honor of Bishop Babylas, the fellow citizen, who, as we have seen, died as a martyr during the persecution under the emperor Decius (249–251). In this sermon Chrysostom discusses the events in Antioch during Julian's stay there, as he had done in an earlier piece of writing, also dedicated to Babylas' memory. In 362, as we have already seen, the emperor had brought the remains of the martyr from the temple of Apollo in Daphne to another resting place, a move that had provoked the anger of the eloquent 'Golden Mouth.' Chrysostom's sermon is therefore not so much a hymn on Babylas as an invective against Julian.[1]

In another sermon, delivered not long after the one concerning Babylas, Chrysostom again heaps numerous reproaches on the Apostate, who had died some twenty-five years before. He points inter alia to the emperor's cunning and deceitful way of going about things. According to Chrysostom, Julian did not grant Christians the glory of martyrdom, aware as he was of the fact that this might greatly boost their cause. Instead, he ordered Christian physicians, soldiers, sophists, and rhetoricians to give up their jobs or renounce their faith. Those who under his Christian predecessors had destroyed pagan altars or temples were summoned to appear in court. The emperor did not bother with conclusive evidence: an accusation sufficed to condemn people to death. Julian even invented crimes, and used any pretext to execute Christians without awarding them the martyr's crown. Chrysostom examines in more detail one case in particular: the condemnation of two soldiers, whose names, Juventinus and Maximinus, do not occur in the sermon itself, but are mentioned in the title, which was given to this sermon at a later date.[2]

The two martyrs, as Chrysostom, anticipating events, calls them, once took part in a banquet with fellow soldiers in Antioch. As tends to happen on such occasions, all partygoers drank heavily and talked a lot. Our couple complained loudly about the current troubles and spoke highly of the good old days. 'Does life make any sense nowadays?' they openly wondered. 'All things holy are despoiled. Our faith in the Lord of Creation is treated with contempt and disgrace. Wherever one is, one inhales the ugly smell of animal fat and sacrificial meat. Nowhere can one find any fresh air.' These words did not remain unnoticed. One of their fellow soldiers reported what had been said to the emperor, who had waited for just such an opportunity. He had Juventinus and Maximinus put in jail and confiscated all their belongings on a charge of high treason, because, although they would die for their faith, he did not want to make martyrs out of them (Chrysostom repeats this theme a number of times). Soon afterward—January 29 [363] is the traditional date—the two soldiers were executed, in the middle of the night. Again, Julian did not want their deaths to get any attention. If this really was the emperor's aim, his purpose failed, for at least two other Christian authors in antiquity, Theodoret and John Malalas, kept the memory of Juventinus and Maximinus alive (there is no reference to them in the works of Gregory of Nazianzus, Rufinus, Socrates, and Sozomen).[3]

In his *Ecclesiastical History* Theodoret devotes half a page to Juventinus and Maximinus. Whereas Chrsystom only speaks of 'soldiers,' Theodoret states that they belonged to Julian's bodyguard.

Theodoret's account differs from that of Chrysostom in one other respect (he lets Julian himself interrogate the two men), but for the rest both authors agree (they either had a common source or Theodoret copied Chrysostom). Theodoret, too, speaks of a party with heavy drinking, criticism of Julian, an informer who reports to the emperor, and the death penalty on a charge of high treason because Julian did not want to give the martyr's crown to his victims. These details are missing in the version of the sixth-century John Malalas, who was probably also born in Antioch, and whose *Chronicle* shows a great familiarity with the history of this city. Malalas' account of the background of the event is less extensive than that of Theodoret and Chrysostom. He merely relates that the Christians Juventinus and 'Maximianus' (he uses this name instead of Maximinus) belonged to the imperial bodyguard, quit their job, blended into the crowd, and stirred the people up against Julian, an activity that cost them their lives.[4]

No pagan author mentions the names of Juventinus and Maximinus, but it is often assumed, though not by everyone, that Libanius, the rhetor of Antioch, refers to their case when he speaks about a conspiracy of soldiers, which came to light when the conspirators divulged the truth when they were drunk. It should be noted, however, that, if this assumption is correct, Libanius tells a story that is completely different from the one we find in the Christian authors. According to Libanius, the soldiers had treasonable intentions and wanted to murder Julian. The Antiochene rhetor is silent about a possible religious motive and—the most important difference—does not mention the execution of the conspirators. On the contrary, he repeatedly argues that Julian did not execute individuals who had made an attempt on his life. This is confirmed by Ammianus Marcellinus, who often speaks highly of Julian's clemency. 'It is common knowledge,' according to the historian, 'that in dealing with some outspoken enemies, who conspired against him, he was so merciful that he allowed his innate leniency to mitigate the severity of the law's demand.' It is possible that Julian himself refers to this case in one of his letters. After he had left Antioch and was on his way to Persia, the emperor wrote to Libanius that he looked back with pleasure at a court-martial in which he showed in his decision 'the utmost clemency and justice.'[5]

When reading these passages one almost forgets that the emperor actually did sentence some people to death. Julian's admirer Ammianus reports these cases. The emperor not only exiled two officers of his bodyguard, Romanus and Vincentius, during his stay in Antioch, because they nursed 'designs above their stations,' but he also (as we have already seen) condemned three men to death, a high official, the son of a general, and the former military commander of Egypt, Flavius Artemius. However, Ammianus is completely silent about the execution of Juventinus and Maximinus. Did he deliberately omit to mention their deaths, because he did not want to besmirch the memory of his beloved emperor?[6]

It has indeed been argued by a distinguished scholar that Ammianus intentionally kept quiet: although Christian sources name several dozen martyrs under Julian, the Antiochene historian faithfully reflected the emperor's official propaganda, which claimed that there were no Christian martyrs at all during Julian's reign. This view is open to objections. In the first place, not only Ammianus is silent about Juventinus and Maximinus. Gregory of Nazianzus, contemporary of Ammianus, Libanius, and Julian, does not mention them, either. Nor do we find these martyrs mentioned in the church histories of Socrates and Sozomen, authors whom no one accuses of knowingly withholding information that could compromise Julian. Secondly, in the previous chapters I hope to have shown that of the many martyrs named in Christian sources, some may have been victims of violence unleashed by pagans, but not a single person was executed because of his faith by Julian himself. And would this be different in the case of Juventinus and Maximinus? Instead of assuming that Ammianus (and Libanius) disguised the real facts in order to whitewash Julian, one can just as reasonably put forward that John Chrysostom, and in his wake Theodoret, pinned something on Julian in order to blacken his reputation. It would not be the first time that Chrysostom—the same holds good, mutatis mutandis, for Theodoret and Malalas—stretches the truth or at least is guilty of exaggeration. Does not Chrysostom in his sermon about Juventinus and Maximinus allege that soldiers had to give up their jobs or renounce their faith? And that Julian carried out death sentences without any form of justice when a temple was desecrated? These are unfounded accusations, for which there is no evidence in serious sources.[7]

According to Leopold von Ranke, the task of a historian is not 'to judge the past,' but only to demonstrate 'how it essentially was.' If I were to stick to this rule, I would end this chapter now. The witnesses are heard; the facts, as far as they are retrievable, have been laid on the table. But this is not yet the end. I cannot resist the temptation to act as a judge in the case of John Chrysostom, Theodoret, and John Malalas versus Julian the Apostate. I recapitulate briefly.[8]

The indictment consisted, as we have seen, of three parts. In the first place, it was alleged that Julian ordered the execution of two soldiers of his bodyguard. This is not confirmed by Libanius or Julian, or by Ammianus Marcellinus. Admittedly, Ammianus speaks of the conviction of two members of the imperial bodyguard, but their names were Romanus and Vincentius, not Juventinus and Maximinus, and Romanus and Vincentius were exiled, not executed. Ammianus does not deny that Julian sentenced some people to death in Antioch, and it is possible that the three victims he mentions are referred to only by way of example, so that actually more men were executed. In that case, however, one would expect

Gregory of Nazianzus and the church historians Socrates and Sozomen to mention the names of Juventinus and Maximinus. After all, Chrysostom and Theodoret not only alleged that Julian put two soldiers to death, but also stated as Julian's motive that these soldiers were Christians—the second point of the accusation. Nothing of this is found in the works of Gregory and the two church historians. The allegations of Chrysostom and his followers meet with a deafening silence on the part of our other witnesses, both pagan and Christian. Of course, in itself this argumentum ex silentio does not prove the opposite, but it does provoke thought. And there is more. Both Chrysostom and Theodoret claim that Juventinus and Maximinus were indicted for high treason (the third point of accusation), because the emperor begrudged them the martyr's crown. It follows that both authors had to admit that public persecution under Julian did not take place. For Chrysostom this meant that he had to look for other points to attack the hated emperor in his sermons.

Chrysostom was not lacking in ingenuity and he possessed a talent to manipulate the data he had. The sermons about Babylas as well as about Juventinus and Maximinus, which were both delivered in Antioch about the year 387, make this abundantly clear. In these sermons Chrysostom deals with the recent history of his native city. He reminds his listeners of the emperor Julian's visit to Antioch in 362–363, when he himself was a teenager, or even younger, but presumably old enough to remember later that Julian's stay in the Syrian capital had caused a great deal of controversy. Elderly fellow townsmen would have informed Chrysostom about this sojourn, and he probably read the Julianic speeches of Libanius, whose pupil he had been, and Julian's *Misopogon,* or 'Beardhater.' But of course, the Christian Chrysostom interpreted the information he had thus gathered in his own way. Whereas Julian in his *Misopogon* was of the opinion that arson had caused the temple of Apollo in Daphne to burn down, and blamed the Christians for it, Chrysostom in his sermon about Babylas attributed the fire to lightning, which he saw as God's punishment for the godless behavior of the apostate emperor. In the sermon about Juventinus and Maximinus we find a similar example of Christian reinterpretation. The account of his teacher Libanius about a conspiracy of soldiers plotting to murder Julian was seized by Chrysostom as an opportunity to accuse the emperor of murder in an underhanded way, since he could not charge Julian with openly persecuting the Christians.[9]

Apart from the *Misopogon* and Libanius' Julianic speeches, Chrysostom possibly used other sources when he prepared his sermons. 'When reading the panegyric on the holy Juventinus and Maximinus . . . one can't get away from the impression that St. John Chrysostom remembered what he had read in martyrs' acts or chronicles,' the Bollandist Hippolyte Delehaye writes. In this, Pio Franchi de' Cavalieri, like Delehaye a great master of hagiography, only hesitatingly follows his colleague (he is more inclined to think that Chrysostom consulted eyewitnesses), but he does argue that the passage concerning Juventinus and Maximinus in Theodoret's ecclesiastical history stems from a lost *passio*. These suppositions cannot be proven, but even if we assume that Delehaye and De' Cavalieri are right, this says nothing about the reliability of the story of Chrysostom and Theodoret. We have seen too many examples of fictional martyrologies to accept uncritically that a hypothetical *Passio Juventini et Maximini* can be trusted.[10]

So much for my closing arguments. It remains only to pronounce the verdict, which is as follows. Having heard the diametrically opposing statements of Julian's sympathizers and Julian's opponents, I have the opinion that the charge of the Christian authors against the emperor should be rejected. There is insufficient evidence to prove the alleged judicial murder of Juventinus and Maximinus.

Chapter 16

To the End and Beyond

On March 5, 363, Julian left Antioch at the head of his army to start his Persian campaign. For the emperor the campaign was not merely one of his notable exploits, but a grand and much-needed expedition to solve the problems on the eastern borders once and for all. He aimed, according to Ammianus, at nothing less than the annihilation of Persian power. 'We expected,' Libanius wrote after the campaign had ended disastrously, 'the whole empire of Persia to form part of that of Rome, to be subject to our laws.' Not everyone had been as optimistic as Libanius, but attempts to dissuade the emperor from the enterprise did not prevail. Unlucky omens were ignored. A stern letter in which a highly esteemed friend of Julian's, the prefect of Gaul Sallustius, pleaded postponement of the project was disregarded. And, admittedly, at first all went well.[1]

We know the exact route through Syria that Julian took during the first days of his expedition: via Litarba and Beroea, modern Aleppo, to Hierapolis, which is now called Membidj. He did not go via Cyrrhus, some seventy kilometers north of Beroea, nowadays Nebi Huri, even though this is alleged by the Christian chronicler John Malalas (Malalas' short and highly inventive account is expanded and embellished with still more implausible details by later hagiographers). Malalas relates that the emperor, on his way to Persia, saw a big crowd standing near the cave of the holy Dometius in the vicinity of Cyrrhus. When he asked what the matter was, he heard that the people had assembled there in order to invoke the blessing of the monk in hopes that he would cure them. The emperor then sent a Christian official with a message to Dometius: 'You entered this cave to please that god of yours. Stop therefore your attempts to please the people outside. A solitary life suits you better.' Dometius replied, 'I indeed locked myself in this cave long ago, in order to dedicate myself body and soul to God. But I cannot turn down people who, trusting in God, come to me.' Julian reacted promptly. He had the entrance to the cave barricaded with huge boulders, so that the pious Dometius could no longer leave. And so the holy man died.[2]

Just like the historical Julian, we leave Cyrrhus and Dometius' cave behind, and follow the imperial army on its way from Hierapolis to Carrhae (Altinbasak), and from there to Callinicum (Al Raqqah). The emperor stayed in Carrhae for several days and, among other things, offered sacrifices according to the native customs to the Moon Goddess, who was worshipped in that region. We owe this information to Ammianus Marcellinus. In Theodoret's version the emperor offered a very special sacrifice: in order to learn about the outcome of his war against Persia, he cut open the belly of a woman, inspected her liver, and afterwards hanged her in the temple by her hair—inspection of the liver of slaughtered animals was a well-known, originally Etruscan form of divination in Antiquity, but to sacrifice a human being for this purpose was not, which makes Theodoret's story rather suspect.[3]

In Callinicum Julian celebrated the rites for the Mother of the Gods on March 27, 363. He left the city on the following day and then marched speedily southward along the high bank of the Euphrates, to arrive in Cercusium, the present-day village of Busaira at the confluence of the Euphrates and the Khabur, at the beginning of April. Here he stayed some days, to wait for a fleet with supplies— it was probably at Cercusium that Ammianus Marcellinus joined Julian's army. From Cercusium Julian went to the neighborhood of Dura-Europos on the Euphrates (Qal'at es-Salihiye). During the journey toward Dura two striking and ominous incidents occurred: the presentation of a slain lion to Julian, and the death of a soldier who was struck by a bolt of lightning—of the latter event Ammianus gives the precise date, April 7.[4]

From Dura the army marched in the direction of Ctesiphon on the Tigris. On its way it set Persian fortresses on fire and captured and destroyed cities. With the capture of Ctesiphon, the capital of the Persian Empire, about thirty-five kilometers south of modern Baghdad, Julian would have crowned his expedition, which had so far been successful. But instead of laying siege to the city, he gave the signal for retreat. The reasons for his decision, on June 16, 363, remain unexplained. Ten days later the emperor was fatally wounded in a skirmish near modern Baghdad. He died within a few hours.[5]

The reactions of people who heard of Julian's death varied. In Carrhae the bearer of the bad news was stoned by the deeply distressed inhabitants. In Antioch Libanius wrote in a letter to a friend, 'from the day I heard the news I have been practically dumb and I have given up writing.' In Gaul a bloody mutiny broke out, when a former paymaster of the army, who alleged that Julian was still alive and that his successor, Jovian, was merely a rebel, was believed by the troops (on the day after Julian's death the leading officeholders deliberated whom to appoint as successor, but were unable to reach a conclusion; their momentary indecision was used by a group of supporters of Jovian, a thirty-one-year-old Christian army officer, to cause a disturbance, which resulted in his surprise election as emperor). In many cities of the empire, admirers of Julian placed his image in the temples of the gods, paid the deceased divine respects, and supplicated the new god for help—not without success, according to our spokesman, Libanius, for some prayers were answered. Not surprisingly, the reactions of Christian contemporaries were different. In Antioch the citizens spontaneously went out into the

streets to celebrate. People danced in the churches and shrines of martyrs. In the theaters the victory of the cross was proclaimed. Julian's friend and teacher Maximus, the philosopher and theurgist, who was supposed to be able to foretell the future and who had been with the emperor in his last hours, was ridiculed. 'Maximus, you fool, where are your oracles now? The Lord and the Lord's Anointed have won!' There was rejoicing and festivity elsewhere, too, but there was no official *damnatio memoriae* ('condemnation of one's memory').[6]

The news of Julian's death spread quickly. In Alexandria in the very same night, the theologian Didymus the Blind saw a vision that announced the death of the emperor. On Mount Sinai, nearer to the scene of the calamity, but nevertheless more than a twenty days' journey away, the hermit Julianus Sabas had the same experience. In faraway Dindona in Mauretania, a falling star informed the holy Eugenius and Macarius of what had happened. And in Cappadocian Caesarea, Bishop Basil saw in the night of June 26–27, 363, in a dream how the heavens split open and Christ the Savior, sitting on a throne, cried out to Saint Mercury, 'Go and kill Emperor Julian, the enemy of the Christians.' Mercury, who at this very moment stood before the Lord, wearing a shining cuirass, immediately disappeared. Some moments later he was back and shouted, 'Julian is slain, My Lord, as you ordered.'[7]

The story of Saint Mercury's apparition before Basil (who in reality became bishop of Caesarea many years after Julian's death) is told by John Malalas and is also found in a passage of the *Chronicon Paschale,* which is based on Malalas. A similar story is reported in the so-called *Julian Romance,* a text written in Syriac, which presumably goes back to a Greek original of the fourth century. However, in this document it is not Bishop Basil of Caesarea, but the Emperor Jovian, Julian's successor, who is told in a dream that Mercury would kill Julian.[8]

The author of the *Julian Romance* has given his imagination free rein, and not only with respect to Julian's death. Right at the beginning of his book he states that Julian unleashed a persecution of the Christians in Rome (a city that the emperor in reality never visited). In a long-drawn-out argument he narrates how Julian tried to turn Bishop Eusebius, 97 years old, and his fellow Christians away from God, first by persuasion, then, when this was to no avail, by force— to the delight of Rome's pagan and Jewish inhabitants (the *Julian Romance* has a strong anti-Jewish bias). Ridiculed and humiliated and with a garland on his head, the gray-haired bishop was going to be burned alive on an altar in honor of Zeus and Apollo. However, not Eusebius, but the thirty-two pagan priests who had brought him to the altar were destroyed by the flames. The executioner, who subsequently had to end the bishop's life with the sword, himself dropped dead before the altar. The sword of a second executioner melted away in his hands, and even the most horrible torments did not succeed in slaying the bishop of Rome, so that Julian, at a complete loss as to what to do, stopped the persecution and left the Eternal City. The triumphant Eusebius lived to see the hated emperor die during his campaign against Persia.[9]

Rome was seldom visited by emperors in Late Antiquity. However, the prestige of the Eternal City remained as great as ever. It does not come as a surprise, therefore, that many stories about Julian's supposed persecution are situated in Rome, although the Apostate never went to the city. It is alleged, for example, that it was his fault that the senator Apollonius and his daughter Apollonia, both of whom had been converted to Christianity, were put to death. The senator and his daughter were denounced as Christians by Dina, wife of Apollonius and mother of Apollonia (whose name, before her conversion, was also Dina). The senator was killed with a few quick strokes. He died by the sword before the eyes of the emperor. His daughter first had to endure all sorts of torments before Julian stabbed her with his own hands. Put on the rack, she was flayed alive, her tongue was pulled out, her teeth and molars were knocked out of her mouth—a significant detail, and an indication of the origin of the story: another, more famous Apollonia is said to have undergone the same ordeal in Alexandria during the reign of Philip the Arab (244–249); in many churches teeth and molars of this Apollonia are venerated as relics. Apollonia's father, Apollonius, was also modeled on an earlier martyr: a namesake, also a senator, was decapitated under Commodus (180–192).[10]

We find such derivations with a certain regularity. For example, the answer that the blind Bishop Maris of Chalcedon gave to Julian in June 362 ('I thank the Lord for having taken away my sight, so that I cannot see your impious face') is, in more or less the same words, put into the mouth of the Roman priest Pimenius (or Pigmenius) by the author of the *Passio sancti Pimenii*. Pimenius had baptized Julian and had initiated him in the Christian doctrine, but fled to Persia after Julian had become emperor and had started his persecutions. In Persia Pimenius lost the sight of his eyes. After a while he returned to Rome by order of Jesus, who had appeared to him in a dream. Julian, wrapped in a golden garment, saw him coming and recognized him immediately. He had him brought before him and said, 'Glory to the gods and goddesses whom I worship! I am delighted to see you again.' Pimenius answered, 'Glory to the Lord whom I worship, Jesus Christ, the Nazarene, the Crucified! I am delighted that it is impossible for me to see you,' whereupon he was thrown into the Tiber by the enraged emperor and drowned.[11]

According to the *Passio Pimenii*, 'many thousands of Christians' lost their lives as a result of Julian's persecutions. Among the victims in the city of Rome were the clerics Priscus and Priscillianus, the pious Benedicta, and, together with his wife, Dafrosa, and their daughters Demetria and Bibiana (also known as Viviana), the former city prefect Flavianus, who had been converted to Christianity. Flavianus was branded before he died; his wife was to die of starvation, unless she sacrificed to the gods and married the pagan Faustus. Dafrosa, of course, did not offer sacrifices and even succeeded in converting Faustus to Christianity, whereupon both were put to death, followed shortly afterward by Demetria and Bibiana—a drawing of Pietro da Cortona (Figure 6) depicts Bibiana and Dafrosa before Julian.

Figure 6. St. Bibiana and St. Dafrosa before Julian. Drawing by Pietro da Cortona (1596–1669). Grand Palais, Paris. (*Credit Line © Photograph by Thierry Le Mage, RMN-Grand Palais/Art Resource, NY.*)

The author of the *Passio Pimenii* refers further to the decapitation of two eunuchs, Johannes and Paulus, former chamberlains of the imperial court. Elsewhere we read that these men died as martyrs in their own house on Mount Caelius, because they were held responsible for the conversion to Christianity of the pagan Gallicanus, general of Constantine the Great and engaged to Constantine's daughter. Gallicanus too died as a martyr under Julian, and his friend Hilarinus as well, Hilarinus in Ostia, Gallicanus in Alexandria—dedicated to Gallicanus is a drama, written in Latin by Hrotsvitha of Gandersheim in the tenth century; Lorenzo de' Medici published in 1489 a short play entitled *La Rappresentazione di San Giovanni e Paolo,* in which the story of the martyr's death of Johannes and Paulus is combined with that of Julian's by the hand of St. Mercury.[12]

This book would have been twice as big if I had reviewed separately all the dubious stories of *confessores* and martyrs who are said to have been persecuted in and outside Rome during Julian's short reign. We find them in every corner of the Roman Empire. Some of them are historical personages, others entirely mythical figures. In Caesarodunum, now Tours in France, Saint Martin had to appear before Julian's judgment seat. In Antioch the future emperor Valentinian was exiled to a fortress in the desert for defending his faith before Julian. In Durostorum, modern Silistra in Bulgaria, Aemilianus was thrown into an oven. In Jerusalem, according to the *Judas Cyriacus Legend*, Cyriacus died as a martyr, a Jew, also known as Judas, who converted to Christianity and became bishop of Jerusalem after helping Constantine's mother, Helena, discover the True Cross. In Phoenician Tyrus, Dorotheus was killed, 107 years old, a priest who had already been persecuted under Diocletian (284–306), but who only under Julian obtained the martyr's crown. In Chalcedon,

Manuel, Sabel, and Ismael died, ambassadors of the Persian king Sapor II. In Bythinian Prusa (Bursa in Turkey) the local bishop, Timotheus, was killed. And so it went. About them and many others I intend to be silent. It is only to Elophius or Eliphius that I dedicate another chapter.[13]

Chapter 17

Elophius

When traveling southward through France on the A31, the *Autoroute du Soleil*, one can, soon after passing Nancy, leave the highway at Toul and take the N74 in the direction of Neufchâteau. Some forty kilometers south of Toul (Tullum Leucorum in Antiquity) and six kilometers north of Neufchâteau (formerly Noviomagus) is the village of Saint-Élophe, one of the four villages that together form the municipality of Soulosse-sous-Saint-Élophe. There, from time immemorial, the memory is kept alive of a martyr, a certain Elophius or Eliphius, who was supposedly executed on the orders of the emperor Julian the Apostate. Every year on the third Monday of October, Roman Catholic priests and pilgrims gather there in honor of this saint, who, after he had been decapitated on October 16, 362, walked a few hundred meters with his head under his arm to the spot where he was to find his resting place. On this spot a little church stands, containing a marble statue of the martyr lying down, his head in his hands. Next to the church there is a statue of Elophius, seven meters high, which was originally meant to be placed on top of the church.[1]

In Antiquity Elophius is not mentioned in any of the sources. His name appears for the first time in the tenth century, when Bishop Gerardus of Toul gave almost all the bones of the martyr as a religious relic to his colleague Bruno, the powerful archbishop of

Cologne, a brother of the emperor Otto the First. In the eleventh century a *Passio Sancti Eliphii martyris* was devoted to the memory of the cephalophorous martyr, while in the twelfth century an adaptation of this work by Rupertus of Deutz made the name of Elophius or Eliphius more familiar—some four hundred kilometers west of Saint-Élophe, not far from Chartres, lies another village named after the martyr, this time called Saint-Éliph. And not only Elophius/Eliphius became better known. Relatives of the martyr also attracted attention. Eucharius, Libaria, Susanne, and Menne, as well as Ode and Gontrude, were, just like their brother, represented as victims of Julian's persecution. No villages were named after them, but in the (former) diocese of Toul churches were dedicated to four of Elophius' sisters, to Libaria in Grand (a stained glass window in the church depicts her decapitation), to Menne in Poussay, to Gontrude in Hagnéville, and to Ode in Saint-Ouen-lès-Parey. None of these churches lies at a distance of more than forty kilometers from Saint-Élophe. One has to travel a little farther to visit a church dedicated to Elophius' brother, Eucharius, that is, to Liverdun, northeast of Toul, fifty-six kilometers from Saint-Élophe. There lies Eucharius, immortalized in marble. Showing solidarity with his brother, he carries his head in his hands.[2]

The author of the *Passio Sancti Eliphii martyris* begins his story in the village of Grand, twenty kilometers west of Saint-Élophe. Through the agency of 'perfidious Jews,' Eliphius had been imprisoned there, together with thirty-three other Christians. One night they managed to escape from their dungeon with the help of divine providence. Eliphius went to Toul in order to bury his recently deceased mother, and afterward came back to Grand, where Julian happened to be at the time (in reality the emperor was in Antioch in the second half of 362). Eliphius spent his days in doing works of mercy and preaching the gospel. He converted and baptized

226 people ('not counting women and children,' the author of the *passio* adds for the sake of completeness). This caused trouble for him from the local Jews, who despised the words of Christ and implored the Devil and his cronies to help them stop Eliphius' preaching. Nevertheless, the man of God succeeded in winning for Christ another 620 men (again it is explicitly stated that there are no women among this number).[3]

The Devil, disguised as an informer, passed along this information to the emperor, who, inflamed with anger, went to look for Eliphius. He found him on the bank of the river Vair. After a fierce altercation Julian pulled his sword and prepared to kill Eliphius with his own hands. But before the emperor could stab his victim, Eliphius begged for a respite of one hour, so that he could pray to God. This wish was graciously granted. The emperor also permitted Eliphius to choose his own burial place, whereupon Eliphius pointed to the hill, a few hundred meters away, where now the village of Saint-Élophe is situated. Julian then made a final attempt to placate Eliphius with tempting promises but, when he achieved nothing, he ordered Eliphius' decapitation. Subsequently, Eliphius walked with his severed head in his hands to the place which he had pointed out before—a visitor of modern Soulosse-sous-Saint-Élophe (where remains of antique Solimariaca have been found) can follow the route which the martyr took: it starts on the bank of the Vair where the executioner had decapitated Eliphius with his sword and where nowadays a chapel stands, dedicated to Sainte-Épéotte (presumably, the name of this saint, who is not otherwise known, is a corruption of the French word *épée*, 'sword'); via the fountain where the martyr washed his head and the cave where he hid for a while, the visitor comes to the place where Eliphius surrendered his spirit and found his final resting place (Figure 7).[4]

Figure 7. St. Elophius or Eliphius with his head in his hands. Sculpture in a niche of the local church in Soulosse-sous-Saint-Élophe. *(Credit Line © Photograph by Sarah Ozolins, Wikimedia Commons.)*

It goes without saying that the martyrology of Elophius/ Eliphius belongs to the genre of 'passions épiques,' but the fact that we here have to do with a cephalophorous martyr makes it different from all other fictitious accounts that depict Julian as an evil genius. This is one reason that the *Passio sancti Eliphii* deserves some attention. There is another difference. Whereas in other martyrologies the authors usually indulge in describing various kinds of torture, the author of the *Passio sancti Eliphii* is silent about this aspect of the persecution. Vergil's dictum *ab uno disce omnes* ('from one example judge the rest'), therefore, is only partly applicable. Within the genre of the 'passions épiques,' variety is possible. However, the tendency to ascribe to Julian all sorts of crimes and to depict him as a harsh and cruel persecutor of the Christians ('*Julianisation*') is found in all these pieces of writing, in the *Passio Eliphii* no less than in others. It is this tendency, already in existence shortly after Julian's death, that has shaped the emperor's image for a long time—erroneously.[5]

Chapter 18

Praise and Blame

Among the Christian authors, who in Antiquity expressed their opinion on the Apostate, Prudentius occupies a special place. The Spanish poet, born in 348, criticized Julian, but he also praised him. Halfway through his *Apotheosis*, an epic poem of more than a thousand verses about the divinity of Christ, he looks back at the reign of the man 'who worshipped 300,000 gods'—Prudentius could not bring himself to mention Julian's name anywhere in his work. The poet had personal memories of the period when this emperor was in power, as he says himself, although he was only a boy at the time. The emperor was, admittedly, a brave general, but he had foolishly abolished the veneration of the banner of the cross, a custom that for a long time had been kept up by his predecessors. The man was an excellent lawgiver and an outstanding defender of the interests of his country, but alas, he did not care for the true religion. 'He betrayed God, although he did not forsake his duty to the empire.'[1]

Prudentius does not speak of a persecution of the Christians. His Julian may be blinded, but he is not the intolerant fanatic others see in him, particularly Gregory of Nazianzus. This bishop depicted the emperor, as we have seen, not only as a monster, but also as a cunning and sly politician who did not allow his victims to obtain the crown of martyrdom—a modern historian compared the Apostate with fanatical revolutionaries such as Lenin and

Mao, in that he went to any lengths to reach his goals. Admirers of Julian like Libanius and Ammianus paint a totally different picture. Ammianus saw in him 'a man of heroic stature, conspicuous for his glorious deeds and his innate majesty,' the personification of the four cardinal virtues (prudence, justice, temperance, and courage). According to Libanius, he was more prudent than Hippolytus (the hero in Euripides' play of the same name), as just as Rhadamanthys (one of the judges of the dead in the Underworld), more intelligent than (the Athenian statesman) Themistocles, braver than (the Spartan general) Brasidas, in short, 'a hater of wrong, kindly to the just, foe to the wicked, friend to all good men.'[2]

When one examines Julian's own writings, one encounters passages that point to tolerance rather than to fanaticism. To Atarbius, governor of the province Euphratensis, the emperor wrote, 'I affirm by the gods, that I do not wish the Galilaeans to be either put to death or unjustly beaten, or to suffer any other injury.' Julian's letter to Hecebolius, who, presumably, was governor of the province of Osrhoene (now a border region between Syria and Turkey), opens with the words 'I have behaved to all the Galilaeans with such kindness and benevolence that none of them has suffered violence anywhere or been dragged into a temple or threatened into anything else of the sort against his own will.' In his letter to the citizens of Bostra (modern Bosra in Syria) we read inter alia, 'It is by reason that we ought to persuade and instruct men, not by blows, or insults, or bodily violence. Wherefore, again and often I admonish those who are zealous for the true religion not to injure the communities of the Galilaeans or attack or insult them. Nay, we ought to pity rather than hate men who in matters of the greatest importance are in such an evil predicament.'[3]

With the letter last mentioned, written in Antioch on August 1, 362, Julian intervened in the religious conflict that had broken out in Bostra. In plain terms he took the side of the pagans against

Bishop Titus and other clerics in the town, where Christians and pagans had equal numerical strength. He accused the 'leaders of the Galilaeans' of having incited the populace to disorder, and of having disobeyed the imperial edicts, humane though these were. He would have expected more gratitude! Under his Christian predecessor Constantius II, numerous bishops had been exiled, persecuted, and thrown into prison. So-called heretics had actually been butchered. In Samosata (its ruins near Samsat in Turkey are now under water, due to the building of a flood-control dam), in Cyzicus (Baliz near Erdek, also in Turkey), in Paphlagonia (a region in Turkey, east of Bithynia), in Bithynia, in Galatia (in central Anatolia), and in other regions, many villages inhabited by Christians had been sacked and completely devastated. During Julian's own reign nothing of the sort had happened. On the contrary, exiles had been recalled and confiscated property had been returned. And now this! The emperor advised the Christians of Bostra to chase their bishop away and to refrain from hostile actions against pagans, just as he, conversely, wanted the pagans to leave their Christian fellow citizens in peace.

Julian did not conceal his sympathy for the pagan citizens of Bostra—elsewhere he writes, 'I do assert absolutely that the god-fearing must be preferred to the Galilaeans.' One can therefore not rule out that his accusations against Bishop Titus and the other clerics of Bostra were incorrect and that not the Christians but the pagans had started the disturbances there. Whatever the case may be, the emperor strictly rejected violence. It is not known whether there were victims to be deplored in Bostra because of the riots. In view of the vehemence with which religious conflicts were usually settled, it seems quite likely that this was the case. It is also likely that elsewhere in the Roman Empire during Julian's reign, blood was shed, whenever we hear of clashes between pagans and Christians. Reliable numbers are not available, but the statement in the *Passio Pimenii* about many thousands of victims is completely unfounded. Likewise unfounded is the allegation that those victims were cruelly tortured by order of the emperor. Riots because of religious disputes did occasionally occur, but for a general persecution under Julian, let alone for a persecution ordered by Julian, there is absolutely no evidence in reliable sources.[4]

The youthful Julian the Apostate (he was just over thirty when he died) reigned as sole emperor for only a short time, barely twenty months. Unlike his uncle Constantine the Great he did not change the course of world history. The progress of Christianity, which had started in the first three centuries of the Common Era, continued to advance and increased its pace in the fourth century after it had gathered even more momentum because of Constantine's conversion in 312. Julian's attempts to stop this development were all in vain. Christianity, which originated in classical Antiquity and became the official religion of the Roman Empire in the time of Theodosius the Great (379–395), profoundly marked the history of the Middle Ages and later times. In the perspective of world history, Julian's reign was really no more than a 'passing cloud' (Athanasius). However, the short reign of the Apostate made an indelible impression on contemporaries and later generations. Julian is abused and criticized by some, honored and glorified by others. There were plenty of legends about his life and work, legends in which the emperor invariably comes off badly, worse than he deserves.

Such fictional stories testify to the remarkably productive afterlife of the Apostate. About his actual life we are also rather well informed, although the literary sources are not unbiased, either. Both Julian's detractors, Gregory of Nazianzus and John Chrysostom, as well as the church historians on the one hand, and his admirers, notably Libanius and Ammianus Marcellinus, shed much light on Julian's life. They make his reign to be a fascinating period in the history of mankind, however brief it was. Coins, laws, inscriptions, and, last but not least, the writings of Julian himself help to complete the overall picture—no other king or emperor in the history of the world was such a prolific writer as the last pagan Roman emperor. Quite understandably, the life and times of this intriguing personality, a genuine intellectual, well versed in rhetoric and philosophy, captivated not only numerous historians, but philosophers (Voltaire), poets (Cavafy), playwrights (Ibsen), novelists (Gore Vidal) and the general public as well.[5]

CHRONOLOGICAL OUTLINE

64	Great fire of Rome. Nero persecutes the Christians
250	Decius organizes the first general persecution of the Christians throughout the empire
312	Julian's uncle Constantine defeats Maxentius in 'the Battle of the Milvian Bridge' and 'converts' to Christianity
331 or 332	Birth of Flavius Claudius Iulianus in Constantinople
337	Constantine the Great dies; his sons Constantinus (337–340), Constantius (337–361), and Constans (337–350) succeed him; massacre in Constantinople of Constantine's relatives; Julian and his half-brother Gallus spared
337–351	Julian stays in Nicomedia, Constantinople, Macellum, Constantinople, Nicomedia, Pergamum, and Ephesus, in that order
350	Julian's cousin Constantius II sole emperor (*Augustus*)
351	Julian secretly turns away from Christianity
354	Julian's half-brother Gallus executed by order of Constantius II
Autumn 354	Julian visits Troy and meets Bishop Pegasius
Summer 355	Julian in Athens
November 6, 355	Julian appointed co-emperor (*Caesar*) by Constantius II
355–361	Julian in Gaul
February 19, 356	Law of Constantius: 'any person, proven to have devoted attention to sacrifices or to have worshipped images, should be subjected to capital punishment'
Spring 360	Julian raised on a shield by his soldiers and proclaimed *Augustus*

Summer 360	Julian's expedition against the Atthuarian Franks
January 6, 361	Julian celebrates in Vienna the Christian feast of Epiphany
Spring 361 (April)	Julian leaves Gaul and begins his march eastward
November 3, 361	Death of Constantius II; Julian sole emperor
December 11, 361	Julian arrives in Constantinople
December 24, 361	Bishop George lynched in Alexandria
February 19, 362	Inscription in Syria: 'the worship of the gods restored, and the temple reconstructed and consecrated'
Early 362	Donatists apply to Julian with a request
March 13, 362	Law of Julian: Christian clergymen no longer exempt from the financial burdens that members of municipal councils had to bear
Early June 362	Julian leaves Constantinople, heading for Antioch; encounter with Bishop Maris of Chalcedon
June 362	Julian in Ancyra
June 17, 362	Julian's School Edict issued
June or July 362	Julian in Caesarea
July 362	Julian arrives in Antioch, where he stays until March 5, 363
October 22, 362	Fire in the temple of Apollo in Daphne
Between December 6, 362 and the end of January 363	Death of Julian's uncle and namesake
January 363	Julian publishes his *Misopogon* ('Beardhater')
February 12, 363	Law of Julian: funerals allowed only between sunset and sunrise
March 5, 363	Julian leaves Antioch for his campaign against Persia
June 26–27, 363	Julian dies not far from modern Baghdad

NOTES

Introduction

1. SOME BOOKS ABOUT JULIAN: Rode 1877, Geffcken 1914, Bidez 1930, Browning 1976, Head 1976, Bowersock 1978, Pack 1986, Athanassiadi-Fowden 1981, Marcone 1994, Smith 1995, Renucci 2000, Tantillo 2001, Giebel 2002, Murdoch 2003, Bringmann 2004, Rosen 2006, Tougher 2007, Hepperle 2010, Wedemeyer 2011, Ramos 2012, Th. Nesselrath 2013, Stöcklin-Kaldewey 2014, Spinelli 2015, Ross 2016; also valuable are Borries' article in *RE* 10 (Borries 1919) and that of Lippold in *RAC* 19 (Lippold 2001); cf. further Hunt 1998b (*Cambridge Ancient History*) and Rohrbacher 2002, 237–273; important collections of articles include Klein 1978, Schäfer 2008, Baker-Brian and Tougher 2012, Marcone 2015, Rebenich and Wiemer 2020; relevant are also special issues of journals, such as *Rudiae* 10 (1998 [2000]) and *Antiquité Tardive* 17 (2009). CONSTANTINOPLE JULIAN'S BIRTHPLACE: Jul. *Ep.* 59, 443b Bidez (= 48 Wright = 52 Weis): '(Constantinople) is the place of my birth and more closely connected with me than with the late Emperor. For though he loved the place as a sister I love it as my mother,' trans. Wright. YEAR OF BIRTH: Radinger 1891, Neumann 1891, Gilliard 1971, Bowersock 1977, 203–204, Bringmann 2004, 205, Ehling 2005–2006. DEATH: Büttner-Wobst 1892, I. Hahn 1960, Straub 1962, Conduché 1965, Selem 1973, Frend 1986, Azarnoush 1991, Richter 1998, Arand 2001, 233–236, Lagacherie 2002, Pfeil 2012, Martin 2014a, 314–316, Woods 2015.

2. DEATH: e.g., Eutr. 10.16.2 *hostili manu interfectus est* (Bonamente 1986, 105–110; for an introduction to Eutropius see Rohrbacher 2002, 49–56),

Amm. 25.3.6, 25.6.6 (introductions to Ammianus are Rohrbacher 2002, 14–41 and Treadgold 2010, 47–78; the most important studies are Sabbah 1978, Matthews 1989, Barnes 1998, and Kelly 2008); Zos. 3.29.1 (with Paschoud 1979 n. 84 ad loc., inter alia about the fact that Zosimus has Julian killed not by a spear, but by a sword; for an introduction to Zosimus: Treadgold 2010, 107–114), Lib. *Or.* 18.274–275, 24.6 (the date of Lib. *Or.* 18 is disputed; Wiemer 1995, 260–268, and Felgentreu 2004 opt for 365, but Van Nuffelen 2006 argues for a date after October 11, 368; for a critical introduction to Libanius see Van Hoof 2014). GALILAEANS: Jul. *Ep.* 46, 404b–c (Bidez), *Ep.* 83, 376c–d, *Ep.* 84, 430d (see for this letter Van Nuffelen 2002, which rejects, and Bouffartigue 2005 and Aceto 2008, which defend its authenticity), *Ep.* 88, 450c, *Ep.* 89b, 305b–c, *Ep.* 110, 398d, *Ep.* 114, 435d, *Ep.* 115, 424c; cf., e.g., Greg. Naz. *Or.* 4.74, 4.76 and see Karpp 1954, 1131, Scicolone 1982, Mimouni 1999, Malosse 2010, Malosse 2011, 219–220; see for Gregory above all Elm 2012. For other pejorative terms used by Julian to denote the Christians see Dorival 2008, 28–34. PAGAN: this term, of Jewish-Christian origin and biased, is used by me for want of a better one; cf., e.g., Chuvin 1991, 15–20, Leppin 2004, 62–64, Remus 2004 and Al. Cameron 2011, 14–32, esp. 24–25, where the author argues that the word developed as a 'neutral, nonspecific term' to use in polite company. APOSTATE (ἀποστάτης): Greg. Naz. *Or.* 4.1 (with Kurmann 1988 ad loc.; for other terms of abuse used by Gregory see Schmitz 1993), 18.32, 36.5, Socr. 3.12.1 (see for introductions to the work of Socrates, Rohrbacher 2002, 108–116, and Treadgold 2010, 134–145; see further Ch. 8 n. 8, this volume), Soz. 5.4.8 (for Sozomen see Rohrbacher 2002, 117–125, Treadgold 2010, 145–155 and the literature cited in Ch. 8 n. 8); cf. παραβάτης in Philost. 7.15 (for an introduction to Philostorgius: Treadgold 2010, 126–134), Jo. Mal. 13.18 (for Malalas, who wrote a chronicle in Antioch during the first half of the sixth century, see Treadgold 2010, 235–256), *Chron. Pasch.* s. a. 361 (for an introduction to the *Chronicon Paschale* of ca. 630, see Treadgold 2010, 340–349), in Latin *apostata* (e.g., Hier. *Chron.* s. a. 363; August. *Civ.* 5.21, *C. Ep. Parm.* 1.12.19, *C. Litt. Petil.* 2.92.203, *Enarr. in Ps.* 124.7, *Ep.* 93.4.12, 105.2.10; *Consul. Constant.* s. a. 363) and *praevaricator* (e.g., Ambr. *Ep.* 74.21). Cf. Andrei 2015 and in general about apostasy in Antiquity: S. G. Wilson 2004.

3. Soz. 6.2.1, Socr. 3.21.14–16 (cf. for the demon in Socrates' passage Lunn-Rockliffe 2015, 126). SAINT MERCURY AND JULIAN: see for the iconography of Mercury's legend Curta 1995a, which inter alia notes, 'The image of St. Mercury on horseback, piercing Julian with a lance . . . first appeared in an illuminated manuscript of St. Gregory of Nazianzus's *Orations* from the Bibliothèque Nationale at Paris,' and '[it was] the favorite image of the saint in Coptic Egypt and Christian Nubia' (p. 116). For a picture of Gregory's manuscript from the 9th century (B. N. Ms. grec 510 f° 409 v) see Cohen 1978,

pl. 10, and Martin 2014a, 322, for Egypt and Nubia/Ethiopia Martin 2014a; for a picture of St. Mercury and Julian on a relief in Seminara see Cohen 1978, pl. 14–15; cf. further for Mercury below, Ch. 16 nn. 7 and 8, this volume. YOU HAVE WON, GALILAEAN (νενίκηκας Γαλιλαῖε): Thdt. *HE* 3.25.7 (see for Theodoret, Rohrbacher 2002, 126–134, and Treadgold 2010, 155–164; see further Ch. 8 n. 8, this volume). DEATHBED: Amm. 25.3.15–20, Lib. *Or.* 18.272; see Scheda 1966, Gärtner 1989, Teitler 2000, and cf. Taisne 1992, Malosse 1998, Huttner 2009, Martin 2014a.

4. Greg. Naz. *Or.* 5.23, Amm. 25.4.22 (trans. Hamilton); cf. Asmus 1906, 410–415 ('Das Julianporträt bei Gregor von Nazianz'), Elm 2012, 459–460. BEARD: Guidetti 2015 discusses the various kinds of beards Julian wears on his coins, as Babelon 1903 has already done and, summarily, Gilliard 1964, 135–137. Caputo 1971–1974 identifies a bearded man on a graffito of the theater in Leptis Magna with Julian, but see Tantillo 2010, 180 ('interpretato in modo inverosimile come l'imperatore Giuliano').

5. VIEW ON INNER SELF: for physiognomic interpretations, that is, what one's physique reveals about his character, see, in the case of Amm., Sabbah 1978, 424–429 and De Biasi 1990; see in general, e.g., Evans 1969, Swain 2007, and cf. Brown 1992, 59: 'Physiognomics were a serious business in the later empire.' INVECTIVES: Greg. Naz. *Or.* 4 and *Or.* 5; cf. Asmus 1910, Moreschini 1975, Bernardi 1978, Criscuolo 1987, Lugaresi 1998, Molac 2001, Elm 2010, and above all Elm 2012, passim, esp. 336–377; see for Gregory also McGuckin 2001 and Daley 2006, and in general for Late Roman invectives Flower 2013. COINS: Babelon 1903, Kent 1959, Gilliard 1964, Cohen 1978, 220–222, Kent 1981, Arce 1972–1974, Arce 1975, Arce 1984; cf. also Somville 2003, Royo Martínez 2009, López Sanchez 2012, Sánchez Vendramini 2013, Woods 2014, Brendel 2016; apart from these studies there are quite a few articles on Julian's bull coinage, see Ch. 7 n. 6, this volume. STATUES AND BUSTS: Jonas 1946, Lévêque 1963, Alföldi 1972, Cohen 1978, 213–219, Heintze 1986, Fleck 2008, Varner 2012; cf. further Jonas 1971, R. R. R. Smith 2001, and, for an unorthodox view, Fittschen 1997. CARDINAL VIRTUES: Amm. 25.4.1, cf. Ch. 18 n. 2, this volume. CHATTERING MOLE (*loquax talpa*), etc. (*capella, non homo; purpurata simia*): Amm. 17.11.1. SCHOOL EDICT: see Ch. 8, this volume. AMMIANUS' COMMENT: *illud autem erat inclemens obruendum perenni silentio, quod arcebat docere magistros rhetoricos et grammaticos ritus Christiani cultores* (22.10.7), cf. 25.4.20.

6. SCHOOL EDICT REVOKED OR MODIFIED: *CTh* 13.3.6 (but see Germino 2004, Ch. 6); whether Jovian issued this law (thus, e.g., Rosen 2006, 273), or Valentinian and Valens (Pergami 1993, 6) is disputed. HELLENIC CIVILIZATION: for Julian's concept of Hellenism see Huart 1978, Athanassiadi-Fowden 1981, 1–12, Fouquet 1981, Criscuolo 1986, Bowersock 1990, 6–13, Bouffartigue 1991, Al. Cameron 1993, Curta 2002, Hepperle

2010, Elm 2012, 387–395; cf. further Stenger 2009, 22–34. ATHANASIUS: quoted by Rufin. *HE* 10.35 (see, for an introduction to Rufinus, Rohrbacher 2002, 93–107), Socr. 3.14.1, Soz. 5.15.3. PERSECUTION IN ROME: BHL 6849. ELOPHIUS: BHL 2481–2482 (see Ch. 17, this volume). POPE: Thomas 1934.

7. LEGENDS: Gaiffier 1956, Braun-Richer 1978, Richer and Braun 1981; cf. Gaddis 2005, 97: 'For decades and even centuries after Julian's death, legends about that emperor's ferocious persecutions, and the spirited resistance of the martyrs, grew more and more elaborate.' See for Julian's reputation also Ziegler 1971. MODERN BIOGRAPHER: Bowersock 1978, xi. THOUSANDS OF VICTIMS: *Pass. Pimen.* 2.

8. JULIAN AS A WRITER: Bouffartigue 1992, Baker-Brian and Tougher, 2012, Célérier 2013. LETTERS: Eitrem 1957, Caltabiano 1991, Malosse 2007, Luchner 2008, Dorival 2008, Trapp 2012. KNOWLEDGE OF LATIN: Jul. *Or.* 3 Bidez (= 2 Wright), 77d–78a, Amm. 16.5.7, trans. Hamilton, Eutr. 10.16.3, Lib. *Or.* 12.92 and 18.21, cf. Thompson 1944, Rochefort 1962, Bouffartigue 1992, 500–501, Rochette 2010. LAWS AND LAWMAKING: Ensslin 1923, Andreotti 1930, Sargenti 1979, Arina 1985, Carrié 2009, Germino 2009, Harries 2012, Brendel 2013. INSCRIPTIONS: There is in the first place Conti 2004; cf. further Arce 1975a, Arce 1984, Oikonomides 1987, Ruggeri 1999, Salway 2012 (mentioning inter alia 'five examples of texts in which Julian certainly features,' which 'have appeared in the decade since Conti's text was finalized,' p. 137 with nn. 3–7 on p. 152), Greenwood 2014b, Agosti 2015; cf. also Ch. 1 n. 12, this volume. AMMIANUS AND JULIAN: Fontaine 1978, Matthews 1989, 81–179, Den Boeft 2008, Brodka 2009, 54–105, and Ross 2016. LIBANIUS AND JULIAN: Petit 1978, Criscuolo 1982, Wiemer 1995, Malosse 1995a and Malosse 1995b, Wiemer 1996 ('Wiemer [1996] argues persuasively, largely on prosopographical grounds, that the Julian addressed in *ep.* 13/B23 is in fact the future emperor,' Bradbury 2004, 52), Criscuolo 1998, Malosse 1998, Wintjes 2005, 119–133, Sandwell, 2007, 216–225 ('scholars now generally accept that Libanius' relationship with Julian was far from straightforward,' p. 221), H.-G. Nesselrath 2012, 74–94, Watts 2014, 48–55, Pellizzari 2015; cf. further the literature cited in Malosse 2009. For convenient introductions to Libanius' letters and orations see Cabouret 2014 and Malosse 2014, respectively (esp. Malosse 83–84 about the so-called Julianic orations).

9. EXCEPTIONS: As we shall see in Ch. 18, this volume, the Spanish poet Prudentius criticized Julian, but he also praised him; Hilary of Poitiers, sent into exile in Asia Minor in 356 (Barnes 1992b, cf. Williams 1991 and Beckwith 2005; cf. further Just 2003, 112–118), called Julian *dominum meum religiosum* (Hil. *Lib. Const.* 2.2), but that was before Julian's 'coming out'; Ambrose of Milan called Julian a *praevaricator* (Ambr. *Ep.* 74.21), but

admitted that the provincials praised him because he had cut down taxes (*Obit. Valent.* 21). CHURCH HISTORIANS AND JULIAN: Leppin 1996, 72–85; cf. further Ch. 8 n. 8, this volume. MARTYRS: For the importance of the image of martyrdom in Late Antiquity see, e.g., Grig 2004, Gaddis 2005, esp. 68–102, and Drake 2011, 193–206 ('Inadvertently, Julian contributed to a significant re-definition of the criteria for martyrdom that emerged in the second half of the fourth century,' p. 205); see in general for martyrdom and Rome, Bowersock 1995, Barnes 2010.

10. GIBBON ON AMMIANUS: 'It is not without the most sincere regret that I must now take leave of an accurate and faithful guide, who has composed the history of his own times without indulging the prejudices and passions which usually affect the mind of a contemporary' (Gibbon 1994, II, xxvi, 1073). GIBBON AND AMMIANUS: Matthews 1997, Kelly 2009; cf. for Gibbon and Julian, e.g., Ziegler 1974 ('measured by contemporary standards, his opinion of Julian was decidedly ungenerous,' p. 136), Bowersock 1977 ('overall the treatment of Julian in the *Decline and Fall*, in spite of its incon-sistencies, may be justly admired,' p. 203), Womersley 2002, 127–141 (about Gibbon's chapters on Julian and Athanasius), and Lach 2015. AMMIANUS' (UN)RELIABILITY: e.g., Seeck 1906, Austin 1983, Paschoud 1989, Paschoud 1992, Szidat 1992, Barnes 1998, passim, Bleckmann 2007, Teitler 2007a, Fournier 2010, Weisweiler 2015.

Chapter 1

1. MASSACRE OF CONSTANTINOPLE: Olivetti 1915, Lucien-Brun 1973, Leedom 1978, Klein 1979, Del Tredici 1982, DiMaio and Arnold 1992, Novikov and Mudd 1996, Burgess 2008, Maraval 2013, 24–27. DATE (337 or 338) is disputed: Barnes 1980, 160, Piétri 1989, 122–123. GALLUS AND JULIAN SPARED: Lib. *Or.* 18.10, Socr. 3.1.8, Soz. 5.2.9.

2. CONSTANTIUS MURDERER: Jul. *Ep. ad Ath.* 270c–271a (see for this letter Caltabiano 1974, Stenger 2006, and Humphries 2012, who notes on p. 75 that 'the text has generally received only scant attention from schol-ars'), 281b, Eun. *VS* 7.1.5 (see for introductions to the sophist and historian Eunapius, born at Sardes ca. 345, Rohrbacher 2002, 64–72, and Treadgold 2010, 81–89), Amm. 21.16.8 (cf. 14.11.7), Athan. *Hist. Ar.* 69.1, Thdt. *HE* 3.2, Zos. 2.40.1–3; cf. Greg. Naz. *Or.* 21.26. CONSTANTIUS IN GENERAL: PLRE I, Constantius 8, Klein 1977, Kienast 1996², 314–317, Hunt 1998a, 1–39, Barceló 2004, Laconi 2004. CONSTANTIUS AND HIS BROTHERS: Frakes 2006, Maraval 2013.

3. NOT ORDERED, BUT NEITHER HINDERED: Jul. *Or.* 1, 17a, Eutr. 10.9.1, Socr. 2.25.3; cf. Greg. Naz. *Or.* 4.22. SAVED BY CONSTANTIUS:

Greg. Naz. *Or.* 4.3, 4.21, cf. 4.91 (about the involvement of Bishop Marc of Arethusa in saving Julian).

4. CONSTANTIUS' FIRST WIFE: PLRE I, Anonyma 1. JULIAN'S MOTHER: PLRE I, Basilina; according to Zonar. 13.10.2 it was said that Julian appeared in a dream to her when she was pregnant and that she thought that she bore Achilles; cf. Weber 2000, 163–164, and see for Zonaras Ch. 8 n. 2, this volume. GALLUS IN EPHESUS: Socr. 3.1.9.

5. JULIAN IN NICOMEDIA: Amm. 22.9.4, Zonar. 13.10.4, cf. Den Boeft et al. 1995, 159. JULIAN AND MARDONIUS: Jul. *Ep. ad Ath.* 274d, *Misop.* 351a–353b, *Or.* 9 Rochefort (= 6 Wright), 198a–b, *Or.* 4 Bidez (= 8 Wright), 241c. LOCATION OF MACELLUM: Hadjinicolaou 1951. STAY IN MACELLUM: Jul. *Ep. ad Ath.* 271b–d, Soz. 5.2.9, Amm. 15.2.7, cf. Festugière 1957. DATE: Bowersock 1977, 205, Bouffartigue 1992, 29–39, cf. Csízy 2004. JULIAN AND GALLUS: Malosse 2004. APPETITE FOR READING AND LIBRARY OF GEORGE: Jul. *Ep.* 106 (= 38 Wright = 38 Weis), 411 c and 107 (= 23 Wright = 37 Weis), 378 a–c, cf. Volkoff 1980. IN GENERAL ON STAY IN ASIA MINOR: Sanz 1993. JULIAN'S EDUCATION: Koch 1899, Baynes 1925, Schemmel 1927, Richtsteig 1931, and above all Bouffartigue 1992, 13–49.

6. MAINLY (BUT NOT EXCLUSIVELY) CHRISTIAN EDUCATION: Eun. *VS* 7.1.7, Greg. Naz. *Or.* 4.23, 4.97, Soz. 5.2.10–11, Thdt. *HE* 3.2; from the fact that Julian acted as reader it may be inferred that he had been baptized, cf. Greg. Naz. *Or.* 4.52, D. F. Wright 2006. APOSTASY ALREADY IN MACELLUM: Soz. 5.2.14, Greg. Naz. *Or.* 4.24–29 (cf. Amm. 21.2.4 and 22.5.1; Amm. does not mention Macellum, but assumes that Julian was still very young when he nourished pagan sympathies). APOSTASY WHEN TWENTY: Jul. *Ep.* 111 (= 47 Wright = 61 Weis), 434d; thus, e.g., Bowersock 1978, 29, DiMaio 1989, 101, Bringmann 2004, 36, Bringmann 2008a, 90–91 n. 9. Rosen 1997 (cf. Rosen 2006, 99–101, 229–233) rejects this view ('Nicht das Ephesos des Maximus, nicht das Paris der aufrühre-rischen gallischen Truppen, sondern Naïssus, die Wiege seines Geschlechts, wurde Julians Damaskus,' 2006, 229), as does Th. Nesselrath 2013, 24–28; cf. further the literature cited in n. 8. Braun 1978, 159–166 does not express a belief in a real conversion ('nous pensons que les convictions chrétiennes de Julien n'ont jamais été très profondes et que le christianisme n'a jamais touché la partie vivante de son âme,' p. 161) and contends that 'sa rencontre avec les théurges, et notamment Maxime d'Éphèse, son initiation à la philosophie néoplatonicienne ont été déterminantes; mais elles n'ont fait que préciser, en l'orientant vers un paganisme mystique et des pratiques théosophiques, un choix qui s'était déjà clairement accompli depuis quelques temps dans l'esprit de Julien' (p. 166). Cf. further Tanaseanu-Döbler 2008, 61–65 ('Forschungsstand zur Konversion Julians').

7. CONSTANTIUS ALLOWS JULIAN TO LEAVE MACELLUM: Eun. *VS* 7.1.8–9. IN CONSTANTINOPLE: Lib. *Or.* 15.27, *Or.* 18.12–13, Socr. 3.1.10–12, Soz. 5.2.15. IN NICOMEDIA: Lib. *Or.* 13.10–11, *Or.* 18.13, Socr. 3.1.13–15, Soz. 5.2.15; Libanius was also in Nicomedia at the time. Pace Simmons 2000, 1251, Julian did not attend his lectures (Lib. *Or.* 18.13–15), but 'the two men probably got to know each other at least indirectly' (Van Hoof 2014, 7); Wiemer 1995, 14–17, Wintjes 2005, 119–120, Tougher 2007, 25–26; H.-G. Nesselrath 2014, 254–255; according to Eun. *VS* 16.2.6 Julian admired Libanius very much. IN PERGAMUM: Eun. *VS* 7.1.9–2.12, cf. Greg. Naz. *Or.* 4.31; for Julian and philosophy see R. Smith 1995, Riedweg 1999, Bringmann 2008a, Tanaseanu-Döbler 2008; cf. also Ch. 13 n. 2, this volume. AEDESIUS: PLRE I, Aedesius 2. IAMBLICHUS: see Ch.3 n. 7, this volume. TO EPHESUS: Eun. *VS* 7.2.12. IN GENERAL FOR THE PERIOD BETWEEN MACELLUM AND MILAN (348–355): Henck 1999–2000.

8. THEURGY: The definition quoted I found in *Merriam Webster's Collegiate Dictionary* (1997[10]). Tanaseanu-Döbler 2013, 9 says this: 'Theurgy is commonly taken to denote a complex of rites which are based on the so-called *Chaldaean Oracles*, a collection of oracles in hexameters, which were probably composed during the late second century AD'; cf. further Dodds 1947, Luck 1989, R. Smith 1995, 91–113. MAXIMUS (PLRE I, Maximus 21): Eun. *VS* 7.2.6, Socr. 3.1.16, Thdt. *HE* 3.28.2, cf. Amm. 29.1.42 (and Brown 1982, 89: 'Maximus was not everybody's cup of tea'), Criscuolo 2006. CHARLATAN: Koch 1926, 183, cf. Browning 1976, 56, but Bouffartigue 1992, 43 is less negative. MAXIMUS AND JULIAN'S APOSTASY: Jul. *Or.* 7, 235b, Lib. *Or.* 12.33–34, 13.11–12 (n.b. *Or.* 13 was written in 362, *Or.* 12 in 363), Socr. 3.1.18, Soz. 5.2.16, cf. Lib. *Or.* 18.18 and 18.156; Bidez 1925, Cook 2000, 277–284. JULIAN'S RELIGIOUS DEVELOPMENT AND CONVERSION: n. 6 and Bidez 1914, Koch 1926, Gauthier 1987, R. Smith 1995, 179–189, Criscuolo 2001, Bouffartigue 2004, Coppola 2007, Tanaseanu-Döbler 2008, 61–65 and Tanaseanu-Döbler 2013, 136–148, Barceló 2013, 101–109.

9. APOSTASY KEPT SECRET: Amm. 22.5.1, Lib. *Or.* 18.19, Socr. 3.1.19–20. CLOSEST FRIENDS: Jul. *Ep. ad Ath.* 277 b, Amm. 21.2.4, Eun. *VS* 7.3.8; cf. Lib. *Or.* 13.13–14, 14.42. ORIBASIUS: PLRE I, Oribasius; Baldwin 1975, Faro 1987, Sabbah 2013, 691–697, Olszaniec 2013, 302–307. Pfeil 2012, 78–79 claims that 'der Bericht des Oreibasios [sc. about a Saracen who wounded Julian in his last battle] bei dem arianischen Kirchenhistoriker Philostorgios enthalten [ist], so dass die Sicht des kaiserlichen Leibarztes auf die letzten Stunden Julians erhalten blieb," but he fails to furnish evidence for this theory. GALLUS AS *CAESAR*: Blockley 1972, Bleckmann 2003. LETTER OF GALLUS: [Jul.] *Ep.* 82 Wright, cf. Den Boer 1962, 182–186 and, differently, Malosse 2004, 190 n. 47; cf. also Malosse 2010. GALLUS' RELIGIOSITY: Greg. Naz. *Or.* 4.24, Soz. 3.15.8, Thdt. *HE* 3.3.1.

IN GENERAL ABOUT GALLUS: PLRE I, Gallus 4, cf. Thompson 1947, 56–71, Den Boer 1949, Traenkle 1976, Barceló 1999, Guzmán Armario 2004, Bleckmann 2011, Leppin 2011. AETIUS: Prieur 2005, Fatti 2009, 27–47, Sabbah 2013, 700–703.

10. JULIAN IN MILAN: Amm. 15.2.7–8, Jul. *Ep. ad Ath.* 272d –274a, Lib. *Or.* 18.25, Socr. 3.1.22–23. INTERCESSION OF EUSEBIA: Amm. 15.2.8, Jul. *Ep. ad Ath.* 273a–274b, Jul. *Or.* 2, 118a–c, Lib. *Or.* 18.27, Socr. 3.1.24, Soz. 5.2.19, Zos. 3.1.2–3.2.1. IN GENERAL ABOUT EUSEBIA: PLRE I, Eusebia; Tougher 1998a; Tougher 1998b; Wieber-Scariot 1998; Tougher 2000; García Ruiz 2008; cf. Vatsend 2000; Wieber-Scariot 2010; James 2012; Girotti 2016.

11. NOVEMBER 6, 355: Amm. 15.8.17. TRANSFORMED INTO A SOLDIER: Jul. *Ep. ad Ath.* 274c, trans. Wright.

12. DECEMBER 1, 355: Amm. 15.8.18. ARRIVAL IN VIENNA: Amm. 15.8.21. TRAVEL TO GAUL: Cerri 1972. JULIAN IN GAUL: Blockley 1972, 445–450; Browning 1976, 79–104; Bowersock 1978, 33–45; Caltabiano 1979; Barceló 1981, 34–49, Pack 1986, 62–103, Bringmann 2004, 52–66; Rosen 2006, 122–177, García Ruiz 2013 (2014), Szidat 2015, 120–130. ALAMANNICUS MAXIMUS and FRANCICUS MAXIMUS: AE 1973.544 (= Conti 2004, no. 13), AE 1907.191 (= Conti 2004, no. 17), AE 1969–1970.631 (= Conti 2004, no. 18), ILS 751 n. 2 (= Conti 2004, no. 34; cf. Bringmann 2008a, 89 n. 7), CIL 3.12333 (= Conti 2004, no. 58), AE 1992.1510 (= Conti 2004, no. 59), ILJug 1460 (= Conti 2004, no. 60), ILJug 1461 (= Conti 2004, no. 61). GERMANICUS MAXIMUS: AE 1973.544 (= Conti 2004, no. 13), CIL 3.12333 (= Conti 2004, no. 58), AE 1992.1510 (= Conti 2004, no.59), ILJug 1460 (= Conti 2004, no. 60), ILJug 1461 (= Conti 2004, no. 61); on some of the inscriptions just cited (Conti 2004, nos. 13, 17, 18, 34, 58, 59) we also find the epitheton *Sarmaticus*; see for this Bowersock 2006, 705, which states that 'in the present state of our knowledge we have no information about any encounter of Julian with the Sarmatians,' but adds, pointing to Lib. *Or.* 17.30, that Julian 'must have achieved or claimed a military victory over them on his way to the East after the episode in Paris.' See for *Sarmaticus* most recently Kovács 2016, 175–178. In Conti 2004, nos. 17 and 18, just cited, we also find the expression *barbarorum extinctor* (cf. Conti 2004, no. 54, where Julian is called δεσπότης καὶ νικητὴς παντὸς ἔθνους βαρβαρικοῦ): 'Credo che tali formule non si limitassero a ricordare le vittorie sui Germani, ma volessero propiziare quelle future sui Persiani, visti come barbari,' Conti 2006–2007, 33, referring to Bowersock 1978, 123–124 and Dietz 2000, 821–822. For an interesting inscription from the time that Julian was Caesar in Gaul, see Rothenhöfer and Hollaender 2012; its text begins with *D(ominus) n(oster) Fl(avius) Cl(audius) Iulianus n(obilissimus) Caes(ar)*, and mentions Julian's third consulship of 360; Speidel 1997 and

Conti 2004, p. 187 with n. 435 suggest that the anonymous soldier of AE 1992.1074 (an inscription in hexameters found in Abla in southern Spain; Le Roux 1992) served under Julian in Gaul. See, however, Drew-Bear and Zuckerman 2004, which accept that the soldier served under Julian, but reject the restoration [*Caesar iunxit*] in the first line and propose to read [*domnus iunxit*], which 'permet de dater l'épitaphe après la proclamation impériale [sc. in 360], voire même après la mort de Julien' (p. 427). COMPARISON WITH PRECEDING EMPERORS: Amm.16.1.4, trans. Hamilton, slightly adapted; for Marcus Aurelius as Julian's model, see Ch. 7 n. 5, this volume. BATTLE OF STRASBOURG: Amm. 16.12 is the principal source, cf. Hatt and Schwartz 1963–1964; Woods 1997a; Ratti 2002, Brodka 2009, 54–65. PRIDE: Jul. *Ep. ad Ath.* 279c, trans. Wright, slightly modified. PAMPHLET: Eun. *Fr.* 17 Blockley, cf. Lib. *Or.* 13.25, Lib. *Ep.* 35.6 Foerster (= 38.6 Norman); and see Penella 2009. BRAGGART: Amm. 16.12.67 *irrisive Victorinum . . . nominabant.* HAILED AS AUGUSTUS: Amm. 16.12.64.

13. HELENA: PLRE I, Helena 2, cf. Aujoulat 1983, Wieber-Scariot 1999, 231–238. BABY MURDERED: Amm. 16.10.19. HELENA'S DEATH: In *Or.* 37 Libanius puts an end to his friendship with Polycles (PLRE I, Polycles), because Polycles 'had defamed the emperor's memory by publishing a discourse suggesting that Julian had poisoned his wife Helena' (Malosse 2014, 96); cf. Cribiore 2011. SEXUAL NEEDS MINIMAL: Amm. 16.5.4 (implicitly), 16.5.8, and 25.4.2, Mamert. *Grat.* 13, Lib. *Or.* 18.179, trans. Norman, slightly adapted (explicitly). VIRGINS: Amm. 24.4.27.

14. LETTERS: Jul. *Ep.* 9, 11, 12, 14, cf. Jul. *Or.* 4 Bidez (= 8 Wright), 252d. SECRET RITES: Eun. *VS* 7.3.7; Kaldellis 2005. ELEUSINIAN MYSTERIES: Bremmer 2014, 1–20. EPIPHANY: Amm. 21.2.4–5, trans. Hamilton, adapted.

15. BELLONA: Amm. 21.5.1. INSPECTION OF ENTRAILS AND AUGURAL RITES: Amm. 22.1.1–2. LETTER TO THE ATHENIANS: Jul. *Ep. ad Ath.* 280c–d; for the date of this letter, see Humphries 2012, 77 with n. 10 on p. 88. JULIAN'S 'COMING OUT' (the precise date is disputed): Jul. *Ep.* 26, 28, 29, Amm. 22.5.2, trans. Rolfe. As to the 'decrees' that Amm. mentions, there are some other testimonies: *Chron. Pasch.* s. a. 362, *Art. pass.* 22, Chrys. *Pan. Bab.* 2, 76. In the Theodosian Code, unfortunately, there is not a word about these *decreta*, only an indirect allusion to their content in *CTh* 15.1.3 of June 29, 362, and perhaps in 10.1.8 of February 4, 364 (Bonamente 2009, 48–49), which makes it difficult to decide whether the *decreta* are to be called 'edict(s) of toleration' (Norman ad Lib. *Or.* 12.69; DiMaio 1989), or rather, 'an edict of restoration' (Ensslin 1923, 105; Weis 1933). As to the date of proclamation, *Hist. Aceph.* 3.1 Martin furnishes the terminus ante quam (and not the actual date), February 4, 362. Cf. further Bowersock

1978, 61–62, Den Boeft et al. 1995, 8–9, 53–57, Bringmann 2004, 79, Marcos 2009, 195 with n. 38. ARRIVAL IN CONSTANTINOPLE: Amm. 21.12.3 and 22.2.4.

Chapter 2

1. CONSTANTINE: PLRE I, Constantinus 4; Kienast 1996², 298–303; cf., e.g., Neri 1992, Lenski 2006, Schuller and Wolff 2007, Van Dam 2011, Barnes 2011, Maraval 2011, Bardill 2012, Melloni 2013, Potter 2013, Singor 2014, Lenski 2016. MAXENTIUS: PLRE I, Maxentius 5; Kienast 1996², 291–292; Leppin 2007. DREAM: Lact. *Mort. pers.* 44.5 or VISION: Eus. *VC* 1.28.2 (with Av. Cameron and Hall 1999, 204–206); cf. Drake 2000, 184 ('the real issue is not what [Constantine] actually saw but what [he] and others made of it'), Weiss 2003, Singor 2003, Harris 2005, Heinen 2007; see also Ch. 14 n. 10, this volume. BATTLE OF 'THE MILVIAN BRIDGE': Maxentius was killed at the bridge, but the battle started at Saxa Rubra (Aur. Vict. *Caes.* 40.23), Harris 2005, 489–490; Kuhoff 1991 and the relevant pages of the literature on Constantine just cited; for other celestial cross appearances in the fourth century see Nicholson 2000, 312–316 and J. W. Drijvers 2009.

2. IMPACT OF CONSTANTINE'S CONVERSION: Drake 2006; cf. Av. Cameron 2015, 7: '. . . there was no one moment at which the empire became "Christian." Rather, we must imagine a complex process or processes, unevenly spread and taking far longer than many have supposed in the past.' PAGANS AND CHRISTIANS BEFORE CONSTANTINE: MacMullen 1984, Lane Fox 1986, Hopkins 1999. PERCENTAGE: Hopkins 1998; for other estimates see Stark 1996, 4–13, with the critical remarks of Bremmer 2010, 45–48.

3. TACITUS: Tac. *Ann.* 15.44.4; see the provocative postulate of Shaw 2015. TERTULLIAN: Tert. *Apol.* 40. PERSECUTIONS: De Ste. Croix 1974 and the literature cited in Ch. 7 n. 7, this volume.

4. DECIUS: Rives 1999, Selinger 2002, Bleckmann 2006. DIOCLETIAN: Aubreville 2009 (arguing that the Christians did not provoke the persecution by their behavior, but were chosen as a group of victims because they were 'different').

5. TERTULLIAN: *Apol.* 50.

6. CONSTANTINE'S CHRISTIANITY: Wallraff 2001, 267 ('We can probably assume correctly that he considered himself a Christian, but what he understood by Christianity was quite different from what we understand, and from what even the contemporary theologians understood by Christianity'), Edwards 2006, Wallraff 2013, Rosen 2013. COINS: Van der Vin 2007.

7. DONATISTS: e.g., Tengström 1964, Grasmück 1964, Frend 1971[2], Maier 1987–1989, Girardet 1989, Kaufman 2009, Evers 2012, Perrin 2013.

8. 'ARIAN CONTROVERSY': " "Arianism," as an umbrella term (*Sammelbegriff*) and as a label for particular developments in late-classical Christian theology and doctrine (*Lehrbildung*), has given rise to an abundance of misunderstandings.' Thus wrote Brennecke (Brennecke 2014a, 1) in a short, lucid exposition of the main problems. Cf. further Brennecke 2014b and see, e.g., Hanson 1988; Williams 2002; Löhr 2005, Löhr 2006; Galvao-Sobrinho 2006, Lyman 2008, Clauss 2010, 22–72, Martin 2014b. In modern literature the term *Arians* often denotes only the early followers of Arius, while for later developments *Homoians* is used. I shall use for both categories 'Arians,' placed in inverted commas. Documents with respect to the early phase of the controversy can be found in Opitz 1934–1935 and Brennecke et al. 2007. COUNCIL OF NICAEA: Brennecke 1994, Alberigo 2006.

9. NICENE DECLARATION: Opitz 1935, 51–52, no. 24 (= Brennecke et al. 2007, 109, no. 26). HOMOOUSIOS: Stead 1994. ARIUS' EXILE: Van Nuffelen 2008, 162–167, Barnes 2009.

10. ARIUS AND CONSTANTINE: Norderval 1988, Drake 2014, 46–51. TERMINOLOGY: see the literature cited in n. 8.

11. GREGORY OF NYSSA: *Deit.*, PG 46.557: Ἐὰν περὶ τῶν ὀβολῶν ἐρωτήσῃς, ὁ δέ σοι περὶ γεννητοῦ καὶ ἀγεννήτου ἐφιλοσόφησε·κἂν περὶ τιμήματος ἄρτου πύθοιο, Μείζων ὁ Πατὴρ, ἀποκρίνεται, καὶ ὁ Υἱὸς ὑποχείριος. Εἰ δὲ, Τὸ λουτρὸν ἐπιτήδειόν ἐστιν, εἴποις, ὁ δὲ ἐξ οὐκ ὄντων τὸν Υἱὸν εἶναι διωρίσατο; trans. A. H. M. Jones.

Chapter 3

1. LETTER TO PHOTINUS: Jul. *Ep.* 90 (= 30 Weis = 55 Wright, whose translation I have borrowed or adapted).

2. *AGAINST THE GALILAEANS*: cf. Meredith 1980, Bouffartigue 1992, 379–397, Hoffmann 2004, Hunt 2012, and the next note. PAGAN(ISM): see the Introduction n. 2, this volume.

3. NEW-FANGLED GALILAEAN GOD: Jul. *Ep.* 90 (= 55 Wright = 30 Weis), trans. Wright. THEOLOGIZING FISHERMEN: *ibid.* trans. Wright, adapted. CYRILLUS: Burguière 1985, Riedweg et al. 2016 and 2017, Boulnois et al. 2016. Crawford 2014, 4 n. 10 cites several short summaries of Cyril's life, among them McGuckin 2004, 1–125, and Farag 2007, 11–69; cf. further Davids 1999 and Wessel 2004, 15–73. AGAINST THE GALILAEANS: Demarolle 1986; Klein 1986, 286: 'Man wundert sich heute, wenn man hört, daß dieser aus persönlichem Haß eilends niedergeschriebene Traktat, der kaum eigene Gedanken bringt und sich häufig in Nebensächlichkeiten verliert, bei den Christen eine so starke

Erregung hervorrief'; Flamant et al. 1996, 403; Elm 2012, 300–321 ('Julian's work *Against the Galilaeans* [or *Against the Christians*] occupies a special place among his imperial pronouncements, orations and letters,' p. 300), Boulnois 2008 and Boulnois 2014; the best modern edition is that of Masaracchia 1990; for Julian's (good) knowledge of the Bible see Bouffartigue 1992, 683–684, Rinaldi 1997, 197–215 ('i referimenti alla Bibbia in Giuliano sono circa 180,' p. 210), Cook 2000, 277–334 ('Julian's attacks on gospel traditions indicate a close knowledge of the texts,' p. 289), Ugenti 2012, and Ch. 8 n. 4, this volume.

4. JEWS AND CHRISTIANS: Jul. *C. Gal.* 43a, Fr. 3 Masaracchia and passim. JULIAN'S SYMPATHY FOR JUDAISM: Jul. *C. Gal.* 354b, Fr. 86 Masaracchia ('I revere always the God of Abraham, Isaac and Jacob,' trans. Wright); cf. Jul. *Ep.* 89a (= 20 Wright = 47 Weis), 453d–454a; J. Vogt 1939, Aziza 1978. ANIMAL SACRIFICES: Jul. *C. Gal.* 305b, 305d, 306a–b, 343c–d, 346e–347c, 356c–e, Fr. 71, 72, 83–87 Masaracchia, 1990. CHURCH HISTORIANS: Socr. 3.20.3–4, Soz. 5.22.4, Thdt. *HE* 3.20.1. TEMPLE IN JERUSALEM: Amm. 23.1.2–3, Greg. Naz. *Or.* 5.4, Socr. 3.20.4–15, Soz. 5.22.4–14, Rufin. *HE* 10.38-40, see Den Boeft et al. 1998, 4–11 and cf., e.g., Adler 1893; Brock 1976; Brock 1977; Blanchetière 1980; Lewy 1983, Levenson 1990 and Levenson 2004; J. W. Drijvers 1992a and 2009, 245–248; Penella 1999; Simmons 2000, 1256–1259 (arguing, ingeniously but not convincingly, that a 'motive [sc. for rebuilding the temple] that has never been investigated concerns an oracle, undoubtedly derived from Porphyry's *Philosophia ex oraculis*, and quoted by Augustine in the *De Civitate Dei*' [18.53]); Demandt 2007², 128 n. 92: 'Das Erdbeben . . . ist historisch, es fand am 19. Mai 363 statt'; Elm 2014, 177–179. JESUS' WORDS: Mt. 24:1–2, Mc. 13:1–2, Lc. 21:5–6. NATIONAL DEITY: Jul. *C. Gal.* 100c, 148b–c, Fr. 19, 28 Masaracchia; Sirinelli 1983, 366: 'il a envers les Juifs une attitude double.'

5. JULIAN AND PORPHYRY: Lib. *Or.* 18.178, trans. Norman. Not everyone agrees with Libanius: 'Julian possessed neither the analytical, theological, historical and linguistic expertise of Porphyry,' according to Simmons 2000, 1260, which calls the *Contra Galilaeos* 'a disappointing work, often repetitive (*ibid.*); cf. Klein 1986, 286 (quoted in n. 3). Julian and Porphyry are called 'rabid dogs against Christ' (*rabidi adversum Christum canes*) in the preface of Jerome's *De viris illustribus*. Some recent studies on Porphyry: Bouffartigue 2011 (which argues that the treatises of Julian and Porphyry have less in common than is usually thought; otherwise Simmons 2000, 1257: 'it would be unreasonable to think that he [sc. Porphyry] did not have a significant influence on Julian'), Magny 2014, Simmons 2015 (with on pp. 52–91 a catalogue of all the writers whose works contain information about Porphyry's *Contra Christianos*), Becker 2016; Männlein-Robert 2017.

6. PRAYER TO THE MOTHER OF THE GODS: Jul. *Or.* 8 Rochefort (= 5 Wright) 20, 180b, trans. Wright. Cf. for this hymn Näsström 1986, Bouffartigue 1992, 359–379, Hose 2008, Elm 2012, 118–136, Liebeschuetz 2012; for its date Ugenti 1992, ix–xi, Den Boeft et al. 1995, 153. WORDS OF JESUS: Jn. 14:6.

7. *HYMN TO KING HELIOS:* Jul. *Or.* 11 Lacombrade = 4 Wright; cf. for this *Hymn* Wojaczek 1989, Papathanassiou 1990, Hose 2008, Alt 2011, Mastrocinque 2011, A. Smith 2012, Elm 2012, 286–299; for Julian's debt to Iamblichus (PLRE I, Iamblichus 1) in this oration and in his *Hymn on the Mother of the Gods* see Finamore 1985, 133–144; in *Ep.* 12 Bidez (= 2 Wright = 18 Weis), Julian calls Iamblichus a 'truly godlike man, who ranks next to Pythagoras and Plato,' trans. Wright. Cf. Balty 1974, 267–269 ('La pensée de Jamblique imprègne en effet profondément l'oeuvre de Julien', p. 268). ZEUS, HADES, HELIOS, SERAPIS: Jul. *Or.* 11 (4).10, 136a: Εἷς Ζεύς, εἷς Ἀΐδης, εἷς Ἥλιος ἐστι Σάραπις: 'ein Vers, der nicht zu identifizieren ist' (Hose 2008, 167 with n. 61). Cf. Pseudo Iustinus Martyr, *Cohortatio ad Gentiles* p. 16 Morel Εἷς Ζεύς, εἷς Ἀΐδης, εἷς Ἥλιος εἷς Διόνυσος/Εἷς θεὸς ἐν πάντεσσι, Macr. *Sat.* 1.18.18 and Serv. *Ecl.* 5.66 (*sed constat secundum Porphyrii librum, quem solem appellavit, triplicem esse Apollinis potestatem, et eundem esse Solem apud superos, Liberum patrem in terris, Apollinem apud inferos*). Elm 2012, 293, referring to Conti 2004, pp. 59–64 and no. 34 on pp. 83–84, observes, 'Modern scholars accuse Julian, in his *Hymn to King Helios*, of muddled thinking or at least obtuse sentence structure . . . Inscriptions demonstrate, however, that at least some local nobles grasped well the central message of the emperor's hymn and indeed of his rule when they proclaimed, "One God wins. One Julian, the Augustus. Eternally, you, Augustus Julian"; "Julian, the eternal victor and triumphator, born to benefit the state"; "Soli invicto Aug(usto) sac(rum)"; ex philosophias basileuonta . . . hyph' Hēliou . . . Ioulianon . . . theōtaton autokratora Augouston."' Indeed, especially the inscriptions mentioning Julian in one breath with the words εἷς θεός, found on a series of milestones from the Gerasa (Jerash)-Philadelphia (Amman) road in the province of Arabia (Conti 2004, nos. 3, 5, 7, and 8), and on a marble column in the province of Palaestina Prima (Conti no. 16), are very interesting (cf. Markschies and Hildebrandt in Peterson [1926] 2012, 409 for nos. 7 and 8, and *idem*, 413–414 for no. 16; cf. for no. 16 also Ch. 12 n. 8, this volume). The acclamation εἷς θεός frequently occurs in Syria, Phoenicia, Palestine, Arabia, and Egypt (the classical study is Peterson [1926] 2012; cf. Markschies 2001), and has been regarded as originally Jewish or Samaritan or pagan or Christian or gnostic-Christian (Di Segni 1994). Its meaning in the case of the Julianic inscriptions is disputed. Dussaud 1912, 77 thinks that it proves that Julian received divine honors already during his lifetime. Peterson [1926] 2012, 273 rejects this view, and also argues, rightly in my

opinion, that a connection with Julian's attempt to revive paganism was 'eine unnötige Annahme.' According to Peterson, 'handelt [es] sich vielmehr um eine schon längst übliche Akklamation, mit der man Kaisern und Göttern huldigt' (in the same vein Dietz 2000, 836–838, and Belayche 2010, 161). Balty 1974, 272–275, on the other hand, maintains that the acclamation was certainly connected with Julian's polemic against Christianity (as did already Avi-Yonah 1944, 160); Balty holds the governor of Arabia, Belaeus (PLRE I, Belaeus), responsible for the texts on the milestones. Cf. further Bowersock 2006, 703: 'Is this an example of pagan monotheism, so memorably documented in the volume edited by P. Athanassiadi and M. Frede? [Athanassiadi and Frede 1999; see also Mitchell and Van Nuffelen 2010.] Is Julian himself being addressed as the one God?' Bowersock refers to Nock 1957, the author of which led off his paper with Lib. *Or.* 18.304 [see Ch. 16 n. 6, this volume], and continues, "(Conti) No. 45, from Side, seems to illustrate this point . . . , but nos. 3, 5, 7, and 8 from the Gerasa-Philadelphia road, are more complex.' Bowersock concludes, 'One god, one Julian need not mean that he is the one god, but it rather looks that way.' JULIAN WORSHIPS ALL THE GODS: Lib. *Or.* 17.4, trans. Norman, cf. *Or.* 18.171, and, for a survey of the pagan temples in Antioch in the time of Julian, Saliou 2015b.

8. VARIOUS WAYS OF WORSHIPPING: Jul. *Ep.* 89b, 293a (= 48 Weis = II p. 308 Wright); see for this letter Casella 2002–2003. IMAGES OF THE GODS: *ibid.*, 294b–d; cf. Johnston 2008, 464, citing *Ep.* 89b, 293b–c, Th. Nesselrath 2013, 143–144. PAGAN CHURCH: Jul. *Ep.* 89b, 297a–305d (= 48 Weis = II p. 316–338 Wright), cf. Koch 1927, Koch 1928, Klein 1986, 289 ('Geradezu als sklavische Nachbildung christlicher Formen erweisen sich die Vorschriften über Eigenschaften und Lebensweise eines Priesters'), Nicholson 1994 ('Historians have often stressed the similarities between the priests of Maximinus and those of Julian and the Christian clergy. . . . There is, though, a complete contrast between the religious characteristics required of Maximinus' priests and the holiness expected by Julian and the Christian Church,' pp. 4–5), Mazza 1998, Olszaniec 2000, Scrofani 2005, J. Hahn 2007, Csízy 2010, Elm 2012, 321–324, and Th. Nesselrath 2013, 83–135 ('Es ist nicht einfach, das christliche Klerikerbild mit dem Julians zu vergleichen, da es in christlichen Texten oft mehr um das theologische Konzept des Priestertums an sich geht, als um direkte praktische Handlungsanweisungen, wie Julian seinen Priestern gab,' p. 123).

9. ATHANASIUS: see n. 6 of the Introduction, this volume. IF IN HISTORY and JULIAN: Demandt 2001[3], 104 raises the question, but denies that the progress of Christianity could have been stopped: 'Hätte Julianus Apostata länger gelebt, so hätte er vermutlich das Scheitern seiner heidenfreundlichen Politik erfahren' (p. 142); cf. August. *C. Litt. Petil.* 2.208: *quid, si non in tam longo imperio Constantinus et tam longa felicitate vixisset. . . et quid, si*

non Iulianus tam cito abreptus esset e vita? DECLARATION OF PARIS: infra,
n. 12. CONSTANTIUS' DEATH: *Chron. Min.* I pp. 239–240 Mommsen,
Socr. 2.47.4, Amm. 21.15.3 with Den Boeft et al. 1991, 232–235, and Szidat
1996, 185–189. ALEXANDER THE GREAT: Socr. 3.21.6–7, Fouquet 1981,
194–195, Den Boeft et al. 1991, 112 (ad Amm. 21.8.3), Jul. *Or.* 6 Rochefort
(= *Ep. ad Themist.*) 253a, Amm. 24.4.27 (*Alexandrum imitatus*), Baynes 1912;
Bruhl 1930, 219–220; Wirth 1976, 203–210; Szidat 1988; Bouffartigue 1992
(index), Franco 1997, Lane Fox 1997.

10. DANGER: Momigliano 1986, 293: 'Julian may have been a failure, but he
    was once a real menace.' LIBANIUS: *Or.* 18.121, trans. Norman, adapted.
    GREGORY: see the literature cited in nn. 2–5 of the Introduction, this vol-
    ume, especially Elm 2010 and Elm 2012, 336–377; for the date of Gregory's
    Orations 4 and 5 see Elm 2012, 342–343. CAESARIUS: PLRE I, Caesarius
    2. JULIAN CALLED BY HIS NAME: Greg. *Or.* 5.38. Asmus 1910, 328;
    Gregory was the first to call Julian 'Apostata' (ἀποστάτης): Greg. Naz. *Or.*
    4.1, 18.32, cf. n. 2 of the Introduction, this volume. EPHRAEM: Ephr. *cJul.*
    1.20 (trans. J. M. Lieu); see, for Ephraem, Griffith 1987, Shepardson 2008,
    and Contini 2015, 285–291. CHRYSOSTOM: Chrys. *Jud.* 5.11 (PG 48.900);
    Pan. Juv. 1 (PG 50.573); *Hom. 4.1 in Mt.* (PG 57.41), *Hom. 43.3 in Mt.* 12:
    38–39 (PG 57.460); *Pan. Bab. 1*, 3 (SC 362, 299–300); *Exp. in Ps. 110*, 4–5
    (PG 55.285); Di Santo 2005, 351: 'il Crisostomo intende operare un'autentica
    damnatio memoriae di Giuliano.'

11. JOHN CHRYSOSTOM: *Oppugn.* 2.9 (PG 47. 344), trans. Hunter, adapted;
    Wilken 1983, 29–33. GREGORY: *Or.* 36.5. LAW OF THEODOSIUS:
    CTh 16.7.4, trans. Pharr, cf. *CTh* 16.7.1–3, 16.7.1.5 and see Vincenti 1995.
    EUGENIUS: PLRE I, Eugenius 6; the question 'ob die Erhebung des
    Eugenius in ihrem Kern eine religiöse Auseinandersetzung zwischen Heiden
    und Christen war und ob man in ihr einen letzten Aufstand des Heidentums
    sehen kann' is disputed; see Szidat 1979 (the quotation on p. 489), which
    denies it; cf. Salzman 2010 and for Eugenius in general Szidat 2010, pas-
    sim. RESTITUTION OF TEMPLES: Ambr. *Ep.* 57.6. BEARD: Delbrueck
    1933, Tafel 16, Eug. 1–3, Elmer 1936, 33 ('Der Philosophenbart ist entweder
    lang und zottig oder etwas anliegend und weich'; cf. for the various forms of
    Julian's beard above, n. 4 of the Introduction, this volume), Bellinger et al.
    1964, Bloch 1971, 164 with n. 60; in general for Eugenius' coinage Pearce
    1937, for *imperatores barbati* Franke 1996 (which speaks on p. 76 about
    Eugenius). Note, however, that according to Mattheis 2014, 38 (references
    in n. 92), 'noch bis ins 5. Jh. manche Kaiser auf Münzbildern mit einem Bart
    dargestellt wurden.' BASILICA IN MILAN: Paul. Med. *V. Ambr.* 31.2.

12. JULIAN MADE AUGUSTUS IN PARIS: Amm. 20.4.17–18, with Szidat
    1977, 151–160, and Den Boeft et al. 1987, 91–101; cf. further Müller-
    Seidel 1955, Rosen 1969, Selem 1971, Tumanischvili Bandelli 1980, Buck

1990, 113–114, Elliott 1991, Buck 1993, Kotula 1994a; see for the years in Paris also Casella 2009. EUTROPIUS: 10.15.1; see for Eutropius n. 2 of the Introduction and Ch. 8 n. 8, both in this volume. RAISING ON A SHIELD: Amm. 20.4.17, Lib. *Or.* 13.34, Teitler 2002.

13. JULIAN'S LETTER TO CONSTANTIUS: Amm. 20.8.5–17. CONSTANTIUS' REACTION: Amm. 20.9.2. LETTER OF CONSTANTIUS: Amm. 20.9.4.

14. PROPHETIC SIGNS AND DREAMS: Amm. 21.1.6, cf. Weber 2000, 220. GALLUS: Amm. 21.1.2. FRANKS: Amm. 20.10. EPIPHANY: as is noted by Den Boeft et al. 1991, 30, the early history of this Christian feast is rather complicated; to the references cited can be added Förster 2007.

15. APRIL 361: when exactly Julian left Gaul is nowhere stated, but Szidat 1975 has plausibly argued for the middle of April as the date of Julian's departure; cf. in general the chronological overviews in Szidat 1977, 93–95 and Szidat 1996, 241–243. FROM GAUL TO SIRMIUM: Amm. 21.8.1–21.10.1, with Den Boeft et al. 1991, 105–131, Szidat 1996, 69–98, Fournier 2011, and Kovács 2016, 169–175. TROOPS DIVIDED à la ALEXANDER: Amm. 21.8.3. BOATS: Amm. 21.9.2, Zos. 3.10.2, Lib. *Or.* 13.40. JULIAN IN BONONIA AND SIRMIUM: Amm. 21.9.5–21.10.2. LUCILLIANUS: PLRE I, Lucillianus 3.

16. JULIAN OCCUPIES THE PASS OF SUCCI: Amm. 21.10.2. JULIAN RETREATS TO NAISSUS: 21.10.5. Does Eun. *Fr.* 23.2 Blockley refer to a campaign in these regions? Thus says Blockley 1981 and n. 44 ad loc. (conjecturing Δαρδάνων instead of Ναρδινῶν), but Paschoud 2006, 475 is skeptical. Cf. Ch. 1 n. 12, this volume, re *Sarmaticus*. CONSTANTIUS DECIDES TO DIRECT HIS FORCES AGAINST JULIAN: Amm. 21.13.6–8. CONSTANTIUS' DEATH: above, n. 9.

Chapter 4

1. ARRIVAL IN CONSTANTINOPLE: Ch. 1 n. 15, this volume. ACTIVITIES IN CONSTANTINOPLE: Amm. 22.3.1–13, 22.4.1–7.10, 22.9.1–2, Him. *Or.* 41.8 (see for Himerius, PLRE I, Himerius 2, Barnes 1987); cf. Den Boeft et al. 1995, 17–46, 151–154. 'SECOND ROME': Jul. *Or.* 1, 8c, Socr. 1.16.1, cf. Chantraine 1992. SETTLED SCORES WITH SUPPORTERS OF CONSTANTIUS: for the trials at Chalcedon (Julian himself was not present) see Amm. 22.3 with Den Boeft et al. 1995, 17–35. APPOINTMENT OF CLOSE FRIENDS ON HIGH POSITIONS: Caltabiano 2009; cf. J. Hahn 2011, Elm 2012, 88–143. WRITING AT NIGHT: Amm. 16.5.4–5, Jul. *Ep.* 28 (= 9 Wright = 5 Weis), cf. Teitler 1985, 69; Lib. *Or.* 18.175 (cf. Wiemer 2014, 210).

2. LAWS ISSUED IN CONSTANTINOPLE: They are, in chronological order (cf. Seeck 1919, 209–210): *CTh* 7.4.7 of January, 6, on the issue of military allowances; 8.1.6, concerning the position of *numerarii*, issued on January 17 (trans. Pharr); 2.29.1 of February 1, on venal *suffragium* (cf. Amm. 22.6.5); 9.2.1, about certain rights of senators, dated February 5; 8.5.12 (trans. Pharr), dealing with the *cursus publicus*, received at Syracuse on February 22 (and therefore issued some time before this date; it is sometimes argued that this law was directed against the Christians [quod non], see for discussion Brendel 2013, 229–230); 8.1.7, concerning the position of *numerarii* once again, issued on March 1; 9.42.5 about people who conceal the property of proscribed persons, posted at Rome on March 9 (and therefore to be dated earlier); 10.3.1, concerning the restoration of public landholdings to the municipalities, March 13 (the date is Seeck's; the mss. read *id. Mart.* instead of *III id. Mart.*); 11.16.10, 11.23.2, 12.1.50 (cf. 13.1.4), *CJ* 11.70.1, 11.70.2, all concerned with taxation and/or decurions and all issued on March 13; *CTh* 11.39.5 of March 23, about the trustworthiness of written instruments; 11.19.2, concerning farms belonging to the emperor's patrimony, dated March 28; 12.13.1, about the *aurum coronarium*, issued on April 29 ; 11.12.2, dealing with tax exemptions, April 30, and 13.3.4 about privileges of *archiatri*, issued on May 12. Cf. Wienand 2016.

3. QUIPS AGAINST CONSTANTINE AND HIS SONS: Jul. *Or.* 7, 227c–228c (Jul. *Or.* 7 is a pamphlet against the Cynic Heraclius, written during Julian's stay in Constantinople 361–362: Lib. *Or.* 17.16, 18.157, Eun. *Fr.* 25.3 Blockley, cf. Bouffartigue 1993, R. Smith 1995, 49–90, Döring 1997, Lagacherie 2011, Marcone 2012, Soler 2014, De Vita 2015). THE *CAESARES* (*SYMPOSIUM, OR KRONIA*): R. Smith 2012, 281–283 gives a short, lucid introduction to this work; its date of composition is disputed, some scholars opt for (the winter of) 361–362 at Constantinople, others for 362–363 at Antioch; on this question see Lacombrade 1964, 27–30; Baldwin 1978, 450–451; Bouffartigue 1992, 402–404; Müller 1998, 37–38; Sardiello 2000, vii–ix; R. Smith 2012, 313 n. 1; cf. for this work also Bowersock 1982 and Quiroga Puertas 2017. WORDS OF JESUS: Jul. *Or.* 10 (= *Caesares*), 336a–b. BAPTISM: Mc. 16:16, Act. 2:38, 22:16, cf. Lc. 18:13. BAPTISM OF CONSTANTINE: Eus. *VC* 4.61.2–62.4, cf. Sandnes 2012. JULIAN AND CONSTANTINE: J. Vogt 1955, Sardiello 1993, Amerise 2001, Amerise 2002 and Caltabiano 2017.

4. WOLF'S FRIENDSHIP (λυκοφιλία): Jul. *Ep.* 40 Bidez (= 30 Wright = 10 Weis); for the notion of friendship in Julian's works see Guido 1998 and Schramm 2013, 300–453. PANEGYRICS ON CONSTANTIUS: Jul. *Or.* 1 and 3, cf. for *Or.* 1 Tougher 2012 and Pagliara 2015, 90–97, for *Or.* 3 (= 2 Wright) Curta 1995b, Curta 1997, Drake 2012, Pagliara 2015, 97 ff. LETTER TO THE ATHENIANS: Jul. *Ep. ad Ath.* 270c, trans. Wright; Elm 2012, 75–80, Humphries 2012. NAISSUS: Julian wrote also letters to the

troops in Italy, and to Sparta and Corinth in Greece; Ando 2000, 195–199 (Zos. 3.10.3–4; Zosimus, as Kaegi 1975, 167–168 has pointed out, mistakenly identifies the site where these letters were written with Sirmium instead of Naissus). Amm. 21.10.7 mentions a letter to the Senate of Rome, which was coolly received; when the letter was read in the House, all senators shouted, 'We demand reverence for the man who made you what you are'; Ehling 2001.

5. CONSTANTIUS' LAWS WITH RESPECT TO SACRIFICES AND TEMPLES: *CTh* 16.10.2–6 (he followed his father: Eus. *VC* 2.44, 2.45.1, 4.23, 4.25.1, *CTh* 16.10.2, Lib. *Or.* 1.27, Soz. 3.17.2 with Barnes 1984, Barnes 1989, 322–333, Bradbury 1994; but see Belayche 2005, 352); for Constantine see also Bleckmann 2012 (on animal sacrifices) and Huck 2015 (for Constantine's image as a lawgiver in the church historians); in general for Constantius: Ch. 1 n. 2, this volume. LAWS ABOLISHED: Amm. 22.5.2, with Den Boeft et al. 1995, 53–57. TEMPLORUM RESTAURATOR: see Ch. 6 n. 3, this volume. TEMPLES RESTORED TO THE CITIES: *CTh* 10.3.1, *Hist. Aceph.* 3.1, Lib. *Or.* 13.45, Amm. 25.4.15; Wiemer 1995, 102–107, and Den Boeft et al. 2005, 146–150; cf. also Bransbourg 2009. PRIVILEGES FOR CLERICS: *CTh* 12.1.49, 13.1.1, 16.2.1–15, cf. Dupont 1967. PRIVILEGES ABOLISHED: *CTh* 12.1.50, 13.1.4, Jul. *Ep.* 54 (= 39 Wright = 57 Weis). BISHOPS RECALLED: Jul. *Ep.* 46 (= 15 Wright = 28 Weis), 110 (= 24 Wright = 60 Weis), 398d, 114 (= 41 Wright = 58 Weis), 436a–b, *Hist. Aceph.* 3.2, Athan. *Fest. Ind.* s. a. 361, Socr. 3.1.48, Soz. 5.5.1. ARIANISM: see Ch. 2 n. 8, this volume.

6. AETIUS: Jul. *Ep.* 46 Bidez (= 15 Wright = 28 Weis); see for Aetius Ch. 1 n. 9, this volume. ULTERIOR MOTIVE: Amm. 22.5.4 (according to Bowersock 1978, 71 Amm. is here too cynical), Soz. 5.5.7, *Chron. Pasch.* s. a. 362, Philost. 7.4. Van Nuffelen 2008, 159, Marcos 2009, 195. OTHER CHRISTIANS INVITED: An interesting case of a bishop recalled from exile by Julian is that of Eusebius of Vercellae, a town in northern Italy. He had been exiled by Constantius because of his orthodoxy, and was later venerated as a martyr, although he was only a *confessor* (e.g., CIL 5.6723; further references in PCBE II.1 Eusebius 1). Vallejo Girvés 2007, 1478–1480. Whether Bishop Basil of Caesarea was also invited is disputed: 'Il est . . . peu vraisemblable que le destinataire [of *Ep.* 32 Bidez = 26 Wright = 27 Weis] en ait été Basile de Césarée' (thus wrote Bidez in his introduction to the letter); cf. Marcos 2009, 198 n. 73, J. Hahn 2011, 111, Elm 2012, 57 n. 156 and 466 n. 113. Elm 2012, 57 further mentions as new Christian men invited to court Eunomius and 'a certain Novatus.'

7. ATHANASIUS AND CONSTANTIUS: Barnes 1993, Gwynn 2012; cf. in general for exiled bishops Fournier 2006 and for the different forms of exile Delmaire 2008 ('La nuance entre *exilium, relegatio* et *deportatio* est généralement mal respectée,' p. 115). ATHANASIUS' RETURN FROM

EXILE: *Hist. Aceph.* 3.3–4, Athan. *Fest. Ind.* s. a. 362 (cf. for Athanasius' exile n. 10 below). GEORGE'S LIBRARY: Jul. *Ep.* 106 (= 38 Wright = 38 Weis), 411c and 107 (= 23 Wright = 37 Weis), 378a–c, cf. Volkoff 1980. GEORGE, BISHOP OF ALEXANDRIA: Krumbacher 1911, 304–317, Dummer 1971, Gorce 1984, Caltabiano 1985, Brennecke 1988, 116–119, Aja Sánchez 1991, Brennecke 1997, 234–247, Haas 1997, 280–295 (= Haas 1991, revised), J. Hahn 2004, 66–74. ARIUS: see Ch. 2 nn. 8–10, this volume. TEMPLE OF PATRONESS GODDESS (*Genii templum*): Amm. 22.11.7. MITHRAS: Socr. 3.2.2–10, Soz. 5.7.5–7. SERAPIS: Jul. *Ep.* 60 (= 21 Wright = 53 Weis = Socr. 3.3.4–25).

8. DATE OF CONSTANTIUS' DECEASE: Ch. 3 n. 9, this volume. DEATH OF GEORGE: *Hist. Aceph.* 2.8–10, Amm. 22.11.8–10, Socr. 3.2.1–3, Jul. *Ep.* 60 (= 21 Wright = 53 Weis = Socr. 3.3.4–25), Soz. 5.7.7, Philost. 7.2, cf. the literature cited in n. 7 and Drake 2010.

9. LETTER TO THE ALEXANDRIANS: Jul. *Ep.* 60 (= 21 Wright = 53 Weis = Socr. 3.3.4–25).

10. LUKEWARM RESPONSE: but Marcos 2009, 198: 'Julian severely rebuked the Alexandrians for the crime.' ATHANASIUS EXILED BY JULIAN: Jul. *Ep.* 110 (= 24 Wright = 60 Weis), 111 (= 47 Wright = 61 Weis), 112 (= 46 Wright = 43 Weis), *Hist. Aceph.* 3.5, Athan. *Fest. Ind.* s. a. 363; cf. Seel 1939, Barnes 1993, 158–159, Van Nuffelen 2008, 159 and 170–171, where the author inter alia points to contradictions in Jul. *Ep.* 110 and tentatively suggests that the letter is not authentic ('Il pourrait s'agir d'un faux,' p. 171). GAP BETWEEN PAGANS AND CHRISTIANS: 'The short and turbulent reign of Julian "the Apostate" (360–363), the last pagan emperor, produced a sharp revival of pagan-Christian conflict that temporarily overshadowed the ongoing controversies within the Christian church' (Gaddis 2005, 88–89).

11. NOT A PERSECUTOR: cf. Bowersock 1978, 92: 'Clever and cunning, Julian was now indisputably a persecutor.'

Chapter 5

1. HEALING OF ANTHIMUS' SON: *Mir. Art.* 1; cf. for this work (BHG 173–173c), e.g. Déroche 1993, Crisafulli and Nesbitt 1997, Krueger 2004, 63–70; Efthymiadis and Déroche 2011, 66 ('Humour and comic effects are . . . a hallmark of the collection of miracles of St Artemios for which internal evidence allows a precise dating between 658 and 668, the year in which the Emperor Constans II died; see *mir.* 23 and 41'), Efthymiadis 2014, 111–113. I dealt earlier with Artemius in Teitler 2013. See now for Artemius in hagiographical literature Trovato 2014, 199–221, Busine 2015.

NOTES

2. TEXT OF THE *ARTEMII PASSIO* (BHG 170–171c): Kotter 1988, 185–245 and, partly, Bidez and Winkelmann, 1972², 151–165 (cf. pp. 166–175 for the text of the *martyrium vetus* [BHG 169y–z]). An English translation of the greater part: Vermes 1996 in Lieu and Montserrat, 224–256 (with introduction and notes by Lieu on pp. 210–223 and 256–262, respectively). For Artemius and Julian see the very informative pages of Trovato 2014, cited in n. 1 above. DATE OF THE *ARTEMII PASSIO*: Burgess 2003, 23. PASSIONS ÉPIQUES: Delehaye 1966², 171–226; see, for Father Delehaye, Joassart 2000. CHURCH HISTORIANS CONSULTED: *Art. pass.* praef. and 4, cf. Burgess 2003, 13–17.

3. ARTEMIUS SENATOR: *Art. pass.* 4. PRESENT IN 312: *Art. pass.* 45. CONTRAST CONSTANTINE-JULIAN: Lieu 1996, 218. FRIENDSHIP WITH CONSTANTIUS: *Art. pass.* 9. DUX AEGYPTI: e.g., *P. Oxy.* 7.1103 (cf. PLRE I, Artemius 2 for further references).

4. TEMPLE OF SERAPIS: Jul. *Ep.* 60 (= 21 Wright = 53 Weis), 379a–b (= Socr. *HE* 3.3.4–25) κατέλαβεν ὁ στρατηγὸς τῆς Αἰγύπτου τὸ ἁγιώτατον τοῦ θεοῦ τέμενος, ἀποσυλήσας ἐκεῖθεν εἰκόνας καὶ ἀναθήματα καὶ τὸν ἐν τοῖς ἱεροῖς κόσμον, cf. Thdt. *HE* 3.18.1. ARTEMIUS AND ATHANASIUS: Athan. *Fest. Ind.* s. a. 360, *V. Pach.* 1.137–138. ANTI-ARIAN TENOR: *Art. pass.* 6, 17, 20. TWO ARTEMII: Batiffol 1889, 253–254.

5. ARTEMIUS AND EGYPT: *Art. pass.* 18, 19, 36. RELICS: *Art. pass.* 9, 16–18. ST. ANDREW: Dvornik 1958, especially 227–230. *CHRONICON PASCHALE*: s. a. 357, cf. M. and M. Whitby 1989, 33, with n. 102 for other sources. CONCOCTION: I follow Burgess 2003 against Woods 1991.

6. PLACE WHERE ARTEMIUS DIED: *Art. pass.* 22, *Chron. Pasch.* s. a. 363. AMMIANUS: 22.11.2–3: *tunc et Artemius ex duce Aegypti Alexandrinis urgentibus atrocium criminum mole supplicio capitali mul- tatus est ... cumque tempus interstetisset exiguum, Alexandrini Artemii comperto interitu, quem verebantur, ne cum potestate reversus, id enim mina- tus est, multos laederet ut offensus, iram in Georgium verterunt episcopum.* ANTIOCH: Marasco 1997.

7. DEPARTURE FROM CONSTANTINOPLE: Amm. 22.9.2. VISIT OF PESSINUS: 22.9.5, cf., for the sanctuary of the Mother of the Gods, Verlinde 2015. *HYMN TO THE MOTHER OF THE GODS*: for literature see Ch. 3 n. 6, this volume. IN ANCYRA: Amm. 22.9.8. ARRIVAL IN ANTIOCH: Amm. 22.9.14–15; it is unanimously accepted that Julian arrived in Antioch in July 362, before the 28th of that month (*CTh* 1.16.8, for which cf. CIL 3.459 and Feissel 2000); some scholars go even further and claim to know the exact day on which the emperor marched into the city, that is, on July 18 or 19 (cf., e.g., Flamant et al. 1996, 408; Bringmann 2004, 83; Rosen 2006, 548; H.-G. Nesselrath, 2015, ix n. 9), but this view is untenable, as is shown in Den Boeft et al. 1995, 177–180.

8. SUFFERINGS OF EUGENIUS AND MACARIUS: *Art. pass.* 25–34.
   ARTEMIUS' CAREER AND HIS COMING TO ANTIOCH: *Art. pass.* 35,
   translation (adapted) Vermes 1996, whose translation I also borrow hereafter. Cf. Burgess 2003, 10: 'This entire account of Artemius' career . . . sounds
   like, and with regard to important claims can be proven to be, hagiographic
   exaggeration and fabrication,' contra Woods 1991, which on the basis of this
   passage tries to make Artemius *magister equitum per Orientem.*
9. ARTEMIUS BEFORE JULIAN: *Art. pass.* 35–36. Cf. Zonar. 13.12.44 ὑπ'
   αὐτοῦ καὶ ὁ μέγας Ἀρτέμιος ἐκολάσθη μὲν ὡς χριστιανός, ἐπήνεκτο δὲ αὐτῷ ὁ
   τοῦ Γάλλου φόνος αἰτίαμα.
10. GALLUS: *Art. Pass.* 36, cf. for him Ch.1 n. 9, this volume. ARTEMIUS'
    SUFFERINGS: *Art. pass.* 37 ff. ANAXAGORAS: *Art. pass.* 47. DATE OF
    ARTEMIUS' DEATH: *Art. pass.* 67.
11. THE DEACONESS ARISTE: *Art. pass.* 67.

Chapter 6

1. VIENNA: Amm. 15.8.22. CONSTANTINOPLE: Amm. 22.5.2; trans.
   Hamilton; for measures of Julian's Christian predecessors 'de paganis, sacrificiis et templis' see Ch. 4 n. 5, this volume, and especially *CTh* 16.10. 4 of
   Constantius II: *placuit omnibus locis adque urbibus universis claudi protinus
   templa;* see further Bonamente 2009, Bonamente 2010, Greenwood 2013.
2. LITERARY SOURCES: *Hist. Aceph.* 3.1 Martin, Him. *Or.* 41.8, Lib. *Or.*
   18.126–129, 30.41, Socr. 3.1.48, Soz. 5.3.1 (cf. Arce 1975b, 201, 214), 5.15.4–
   5 (cf. Kristensen 2013, 74), *Art. pass.* 22, Zonar. 13.12.30–34 (cf. Arce
   1975b, 207–208). JURIDICAL SOURCE: *CTh* 15.1.3, if this is a law of
   Julian, as seems likely (but it is disputed; cf. Brendel 2013, 21 and 187–190),
   Marcos 2009, 196 with n. 41. IMPORTANCE OF EPIGRAPHICAL
   SOURCES: Kotula 1994b, Greenwood 2014b ('Generally, scholars studying Julian's religious restoration have not taken adequate account of the epigraphic evidence,' p. 103). INSCRIPTIONS: see n. 8 of the Introduction,
   this volume. INSCRIPTION OF 'ANZ (alas, one can only speculate about
   the condition of this site and others like it in present-day Syria): ILS 9465
   (= Conti 2004, no. 1, cf. Arce 1975b, 209 (which gives as an approximate date
   March 362), Dietz 2000, 817 and Greenwood 2014b, 112–113; the response
   to Julian's decrees was not everywhere so enthusiastic; see Athanassiadi-
   Fowden 1981, 110–11.
3. MA' AYAN BARUKH: AE 1969–1970.631, Eck 2000, and Conti 2004,
   no. 18, cf. Arce 1975b, 211–215 (the author of which thinks that *templorum
   restaurator* 'puede referirse en concreto a la reconstrucción del templo de
   Jerusalem,' p. 215, which does not seem very likely), Dietz 2000, 807–810,

Benoist 2009, 111, and Greenwood 2014b, 110–11; the inscription is also important in regard of other aspects of Julian's reign, cf. Brendel 2013, 179 with literature in nn. 908–910. MINET-EL-HOSN: AE 1907.191 (= Conti 2004, no. 17), cf. Dietz 2000, 808–810. THESSALONIKI: SEG 31 (1981) no. 641 (= Conti 2004, no. 54): Ἐπὶ τοῦ θεοφιλεστάτου καὶ ἀνανεωτοῦ τῶν ἱερῶν ('Die Formel verrät den Versuch, die heidnischen Kulte wiederherzustellen und findet ihre Entsprechung in dem lateinischen *restitutor sacrorum* . . . und *templorum restaurator*,' Conti ad loc.), cf. Dietz 2000, 818–819 and Benoist 2009, 112; for Julian as 'restitutor Romanae religionis' see Olszaniec 1999. SAMOS: Robert 1948, 55–59; cf. PLRE, I, Plutarchus 4 and Chaniotis 1987; PLRE I, Aedesius 4, Arce 1975b, 209.

4. EL MAHDER: ILS 752 (= Conti 2004, no. 167), cf. Greenwood 2014b, 106–108. ANNOUNA: AE 1893.87 (= Conti 2004, no. 176), cf. Greenwood 2014b, 108–109; for other North African inscriptions from the time of Julian, apart from those just mentioned, see Conti 2004, no. 131–187; Salama 1971, 286 n. 27: '. . . par une coïncidence paradoxale, aucune inscription ne fait état de constructions de temples sous Julien.' NOVATIANS: Socr. 2.38.23–24, Soz. 4.20.6; Isele 2010, 91; cf. Soz. 4.20.7–8 and 5.5.10 for a similar event in Cyzicus; H. J. Vogt 1968, 237–238; for the origin of the schism see Curti 1980 and Grattarola 1984; for a critical edition and an English translation of Novatian's *De Trinitate* and a discussion of his christology: Papandrea 2008.

5. MUTUAL HOSTILITY BETWEEN CHRISTIANS: Amm. 22.5.4, trans. Hamilton. JULIAN AND THE DONATIST REQUEST: Opt. 2.16.2, 3.3.18; August. *C. Ep. Parm.* 1.12.19, *Enarr. 2 in Ps.* 36.18, *C. Litt. Petil.* 2.92, 203, 205, 224; August. *Ep.* 93.4.12, *Ep.* 105.2.9, cf. *CTh* 16.5.37 and see Frend 1971², 187–192, Maier 1989, 42–43, and Morgenstern 1993. LEMELLEFENSE: Opt. 2.18.1–2. TIPASA: Opt. 2.18.4–19.4; cf. Buenacasa Pérez 2000, 515, and Shaw 2011, 149–157 (for Tipasa especially 155 n. 21).

6. MARCUS OF ARETHUSA: Greg. Naz. *Or.* 4.88–91, Soz. 5.10.8–14, Thdt. *HE* 3.7.6–10, Halkin 1985 (BHG 2248 and 2250), Trovato 2014, 123–125. CHURCHES INSTEAD OF TEMPLES: Jul. *Or.* 7, 228b–c, cf. Deichmann 1939, Hanson 1978 (Hanson does not mention this case), Greenwood 2013. According to Greg. Naz. *Or.* 4.91 Marcus had helped to rescue Julian during the massacre of Constantinople in 337 (Ch. 1 nn. 1–3, this volume).

7. MATERIAL FOR A TRAGEDY: Thdt. *HE* 3.7.6. WITTY REMARK: Greg. Naz. *Or.* 4.89, Soz. 5.10.12, Thdt. *HE* 3.7.9.

8. LIBANIUS' SECOND LETTER: *Ep.* 819 Foerster (= 103 Norman). LIBANIUS' FIRST LETTER: *Ep.* 763 Foerster (cf. Bradbury 2004, no. 130). LIBANIUS ABOUT MARCUS: *Ep.* 819.6 Foerster, trans. Norman; cf. in general on Libanius' behavior in this case Norman 1983, 160–161; whereas Libanius defends the Christian Orion here, he elsewhere blames Christians for the closing, or worse, of temples and sanctuaries: *Or.*

7.10, 17.7, 18.126, *Ep.* 88.2; cf. for the looting and destruction of temples Amm. 22.4.3, Lib. *Or.* 12.69, 14.63, 18.114, 24.36, and, already for the time of Constantine, e.g., Eus. *VC* 3.54–58 with Av. Cameron and Hall 1999, 301–305; but, as Saradi-Mendelovici 1990 argues, the peak of hostile actions against pagan monuments (for a general account see Deichmann 1954; cf. also Fowden 1978 and Thornton 1986) is not as strongly attested for the time of the Constantinian dynasty as for the end of the fourth century under Theodosius. BELAEUS: PLRE I, Belaeus. During his governorship the religious conflict in Bostra broke out, which is the subject of Jul. *Ep.* 114 (= 41 Wright = 58 Weis); see Ch. 18 n. 3, this volume.

9. LIBANIUS DEFENDS CHRISTIANS: *Ep.* 724.2, 757, 828, 1364.7 Foerster; Marcos 2009, 195. ELEUSIUS: Socr. 3.11.3, Soz. 5.15.4–6; Fowden 1978, 60, Isele 2010, 63 (with n. 168), 92; cf. also above, n. 4.

Chapter 7

1. FAMOUS VISITORS OF TROY: Borgeaud 2009–2010. JULIAN AND PEGASIUS: PCBE III, Pègasios 1, Jul. *Ep.* 79 Bidez (= 19 Wright = 35 Weis); Asmus 1902, Lucassen 1934, Bolton 1968 (about the fact that Pegasius did not hiss to himself [ἐσύριττεν], as Christians often did after they had made the sign of the cross on their foreheads), Armstrong 1984, 13–14 and Schöllgen 2004. SACRIFICING FORBIDDEN: *CTh* 16.10.2, 16.10.4–5, cf. Lib. *Or.* 17.7, 18.23 (for Constantine in this respect Ch. 4 n. 5, this volume). Leppin 1999, 471–472, Bonamente 2010. Differently: Delmaire 2004; cf. further below, n. 4.

2. AURELIA LEULIS: P. Meyer 15 (= Hengstl 1978 no. 62), cf. Lane Fox 1988, 455–456 and in general Selinger 2002. APOSTLES' RESOLUTION: Act. 15:29. JAMES: Act. 15:20, cf. Grimm 1996, 105, 122, 144, 145, 249 n. 17, Piepenbrink 2005, 313–319. IMPORTANCE OF SACRIFICES: Bradbury 1995, Belayche 2001, Saggioro 2002, Belayche 2005; see Aldrete 2014 for some practical aspects of Roman animal sacrifice.

3. LAW OF FEBRUARY 19, 356: *CTh* 16.10.6 (cf. *CTh* 16.10.4, probably also issued in 356: *Volumus etiam cunctos sacrificiis abstinere*). BAN ON SACRIFICES DISREGARDED: Amm. 19.12.12, Lib. *Or.* 1.27, cf. Lib. *Ep.* 1351.3. Bradbury 1995, 344 cites the case of Anatolius, praetorian prefect of Illyricum (357–360; PLRE I, Anatolius 3), who, according to Eun. *VS* 10.6.8, when in Athens 'with great courage offered sacrifices and formally visited all the temples' (trans. Wright). However, Eunapius probably refers to another Anatolius, who also was praetorian prefect of Illyricum, but earlier, in circa 344–347; see, e.g., Norman 1957 and Bradbury 2000. TERTULLUS: Amm. 19.10.4, cf. for him PLRE I, Tertullus 2. For (public) sacrifices after the time of Julian see Salzman 2011.

4. CONSTANTIUS AND HIS SPIES: Sinnigen 1959, Blum 1969, Vogler 1979, 184–210, but see Teitler 1985, 235–237. DETERRENT RATHER THAN PUNITIVE MEASURES: Bradbury 1995, 343; for a discussion of Constantius' policy with respect to paganism see Leppin 1999, which suggests that one should see the emperor's measures in the light of his pursuit of unity within Christianity: 'es war für den Kaiser taktisch klug, seinen Heidenfeindlichkeit unter Beweis zu stellen' (p. 474); cf. also Mattheis 2014, 42. LETTER TO MAXIMUS: Jul. *Ep.* 26 Bidez (= 8 Wright = 21 Weis), 415c (for the date: Den Boeft et al. 1995, 53–54). TWICE A DAY: Jul. *Ep.* 98 Bidez (= 58 Wright = 24 Weis), 401b, cf. Lib. *Or.* 12.79–80 and *Or.* 18.169–170 (where Libanius admits that this was an expensive affair); Th. Nesselrath 2013, 140–143 ('Das Opfer spielte eine hervorragende Rolle in der von Julian entworfenen reichsweiten paganen religiösen Organisation,' p. 140).

5. AMMIANUS QUOTED: 22.12.6, cf. 22.14.3, 25.4.17, Chrys. *Pan. Bab. 1*, 5, Zonar. 13.12.38 (ἑκατόμβας ὅλας). LIBYAN INSCRIPTION: PBSR 23 (1955) 139 no. 22. SACRIFICIAL MEAT ON THE MENU: Amm. 22.12.6, Lib. *Or.* 18.126, cf. MacMullen 1981, 36–42, Megitt 1994, Grimm 1996, 38. LIBANIUS QUOTED: *Or.* 24.35, trans. Norman. JULIAN AND MARCUS AURELIUS: Jul. *Or.* 6 Bidez (= *Ep. ad Themist.*), 253a, Jul. *Caes.* 335c, Amm. 16.1.4 (cf. 22.5.4, 25.4.17), Eutr. 10.16.3. Lacombrade 1967, Hunt 1995, Kelly 2005; cf. in general for Marcus Aurelius as an ideal emperor in Late-Antique thought Stertz 1977. *P. Fay.* 20, in which Marcus Aurelius together with Trajan is respectfully mentioned and which is regarded by some scholars as an edict issued or reissued by Julian (cf., e.g., Schmidt-Hofner 2012, 44, and see the literature cited in Den Boeft et al. 2005, 143, and Brendel 2013, 209–210), should be ascribed to Alexander Severus (so, e.g., Oliver 1978 and Pack 1986, 132–134). LAMPOON: Amm. 25.4.17, trans. Hamilton.

6. TITLE *MISOPOGON*: Amm. 22.14.2, Greg. Naz. *Or.* 5.41, Socr. 3.17.9, Zonar. 13.12.37; this document has been studied by many scholars: Alonso-Núñez 1979, Prato and Micalella 1979, Marcone 1984, Gleason 1986, Prato et al. 1987, Long 1993, Müller 1998, Wiemer 1998, Janka 2008, Quiroga Puertas 2009, Van Hoof and Van Nuffelen 2011, Elm 2012, 327–335, Hawkins 2012, Van Hoof and Van Nuffelen 2013; note that in Antioch not only Julian was ridiculed, but also that altars recently restored by him were crashed over: Jul. *Misop.* 361b. AVERSION TO GAMES: Jiménez Sánchez 2003. BULL ON COINS: Kent 1981, 46–47, cf. Thieler 1962; Gilliard 1964, 138–141; Arce 1972–1974; Szidat 1981; Desnier 1985; Munzi 1996; Vanderspoel 1998; Marco-Simón 1999; Woods 2000; Conton 2004; Tougher 2004; Ehling 2005–2006, López Sánchez 2012, 172–179, Brendel 2016. COINS RIDICULED: Jul. *Misop.* 355d, Socr. 3.17.5, Soz. 5.19.2, Ephr. *cJul.* 1.16–18. TERMS OF ABUSE: Amm. 22.14.3, Greg. Naz. *Or.* 4.77, Chrys. *Pan. Bab. 2*, 103, Zonar. 13.12.35. FATE OF OXEN: Amm. 25.4.17.

7. FINE FOR NOT SACRIFICING: Socr. 3.13.9; REWARD FOR SACRIFICING: Socr. 3.13.2. NO COMPULSION: Lib. *Or.* 18.121–122, Soz. 5.15.8, trans. Hartranft; Ambr. *Ep.* 10.74.17 claims that in the time of Julian someone who had overturned an altar and had disturbed a sacrifice was condemned by a judge and made a martyr, but he is not specific and seems guilty of special pleading in his conflict over the Callinicum affair with the emperor Theodosius. Drake 2011, 209. Scorza Barcellonna 1995, 58 identifies the anonymous man with Aemilianus of Durostorum (for whom see Ch. 16 n. 13, this volume). PAGANS, CANNIBALISM AND INFANTICIDE: Socr. 3.13.11; cf. Chrys. *Pan. Bab.* 2, 4 and *Laz.* 2.2 for the accusation of infanticide by pagans in general; in *Pan. Bab.* 2, 79 Chrysostom accuses among others Julian of this crime, but he adds that the emperor did not dare to do it openly; Rives 1995, 83: 'Thus in the later fourth century C.E. we find human sacrifice attributed to the pagans who rejected Christianity and to the heretics who distorted it' (but Rives does not give references). Martelli 1982, 322 refers to Thdt. *HE.* 3.26 ('un vero e proprio sacrificio di fanciulli), but Theodoret speaks of a woman, not of children; see for Theodoret's story Ch. 16 n. 3, this volume. CHRISTIANS AND CANNIBALISM: cannibalism and incest ('Thyestian meals and Oedipodal conjugations,' Athenag. *Leg.* 3.1) were crimes often imputed to Christians and by orthodox Christians to heretics and Jews; cf., e.g., apart from Rives 1995, Roig Lanzillotta 2007 and Bremmer 2013, both with many references to earlier literature.

8. JULIAN IRRITATED BY SLACKNESS IN OFFERING: Jul. *Ep.* 78 Bidez (= 35 Wright = 11 Weis), 375c, *Misop.* 362a–b. FINANCIAL INCENTIVE: Lib. *Or.* 18.168. TRICK: Greg. Naz. *Or.* 4.82–84, Soz. 5.17.8–12, Thdt. *HE* 3.16.6–17.8. INCENSE OFFERING: Pfister 1914, Müller 1978, Haensch 2004, 528. CHRISTIANIZATION OF THE ARMY SINCE CONSTANTINE: see the literature cited in Ch. 15 n. 2, this volume. SIZE OF JULIAN'S ARMY: Brok 1959, 251–252, Paschoud 1979, 110–111, Den Boeft et al. 1998, 42. ONLY ELITE TROOPS REWARDED: Lenski 2000, 511.

9. GREGORY'S STORY: *Or.* 4.84.

10. SOZOMEN: 5.17.12. THEODORET: *HE* 3.17.5–8, trans. Jackson, adapted (Ch. 13 in his numeration).

11. ROMANUS: Theodoret's Romanus identified with the tribune of that name in Amm. 22.11.2 (who in his turn is supposed to be identical with the *comes Africae* Romanus of Amm. 27.9.1, cf. Den Boeft et al. 1995, 200): Woods, 1995a, 49 n. 80, Woods 1997b, 275–276 and Lenski, 2000, 512. However, Marasco 2004–2005, 151 n. 41: 'L'identificazione del personaggio con il tribuno Romano, mandato in esilio da Giuliano (Amm. 22, 11, 2) è incerta.'

Chapter 8

1. DATE OF DEPARTURE FROM CONSTANTINOPLE: Den Boeft et al. 1995, 154–155. ARRIVAL IN CHALCEDON: Amm. 22.9.3. ENCOUNTER WITH MARIS: Socr. 3.12.1–7, Soz. 5.4.8–9, Zonar. 13.12.27–28; cf. Brennecke 1988, 142–143. 'CITY OF THE BLIND': Hdt. 4.144, Tac. *Ann.* 12.63.1–2, Plin. *Nat.* 5.149. It seems to me that Zonaras is probably right in stating that Julian's altercation with Maris took place in Chalcedon, where Maris was bishop; Lenski 2015, 349 follows Socrates and Sozomen, who situate the incident in Constantinople. Chalcedon was also the place where in 361 some of the leading supporters of Constantius were put on trial (Julian himself was not present): Amm. 22.3 with Den Boeft et al. 1995, 17–35. APOSTASY AND ATHEISM: for apostasy see n. 2 of the Introduction, this volume; for atheism as a crime that pagans, Jews, and Christians imputed to one another Bremmer 2007. IMPORTANCE OF CONSTANTINOPLE: Chantraine 1992, Van Dam 2014. GALILAEAN GOD: Soz. aptly adopts the terminology of Julian himself here, who in all his writings except *Ep.* 114, 437d Bidez (= Wright 41 = 58 Weis), where he cites a Christian bishop, calls the Christians 'Galilaeans'; cf. the literature cited in n. 2 of the Introduction.

2. SOCRATES' COMMENT: 3.12.5–7 Hansen; Drake 2011, 206. ZONARAS AND HIS SOURCES: Bleckmann 1992, 6–15 ('Zusammenfassend ist also festzustellen, daß Zonaras deswegen für die Alterumswissenschaft von Bedeutung ist, weil er antike Quellen durch Exzerpierung handbuchartig aufgearbeitet hat,' p. 15), Karpozēlos 2009, 465–534, Al. Cameron 2011, 659–690, Bleckmann 2015.

3. SCHOOL EDICT: *CTh* 13.3.5 (*dat. XV Kal. Iul.*, i.e., June 17), trans. Pharr. ANCYRA: The place of issue of *CTh* 13.3.5 is not stated in the manuscripts; Bowersock 1978, 85 suggests that it was Constantinople, Klein 1981, 73 n. 4 Antioch, Foss 1977, 39 Ancyra; Ancyra seems the best choice, cf. Wiemer 1995, 108 and McLynn 2014, 124. The bibliography concerning Julian's School Edict is enormous, see, e.g., Henning 1937; Basabe 1951; Hardy 1968; Pricoco 1980 (Pricoco denies that the law was essentially directed against Christian teachers); Klein 1981; Pack 1986, 261–300; Dal Covolo 1988; Banchich 1993; Tedeschi 1996; Saracino 2002; Matthews 2000, 274–277; Germino 2004; Watts 2006, 68–76, Gemeinhardt 2008; Goulet 2008; Saggioro 2008; Stenger 2009, 101–110; Carvalho 2010; Hepperle 2010, 111–117; Scrofani 2010, 66–75; Wedemeyer 2011, 182–194; Elm 2012, 139–143; McLynn 2014; Vössing 2014; Cecconi 2015.

4. 'EXPLANATORY STATEMENT': Jul. *Ep.* 61c Bidez (= 36 Wright = 55 Weis). The connection between this text and *CTh* 13.3.5 is disputed. Some scholars suppose that there must have been a second law, which is now lost,

and that it is this law, not *CTh* 13.3.5, to which *Ep.* 61c is related (e.g., Banchich 1993: 'the two texts are primarily discrete elements within Julian's legislation on education', p. 10). CLASSICAL AUTHORS: Julian's list resembles that of Lib. *Ep.* 1036.4–5, a letter in which Libanius in 392 reproaches Postumianus (PLRE I, Postumianus 3) for having written to him in Latin instead of in Greek, although he knew his Homer, Hesiod, and the rest of the poets, and Demosthenes, Lysias, and the rest of the orators, Herodotus, and Thucydides. GOSPELS: Julian, who had received a Christian education (cf. Ch. 1 n. 6, this volume), was of course familiar with the Gospels (see Ch. 3 n. 3, this volume). For example, in his *Or.* 7 ('To the Cynic Heraclius'), 219 d, he alludes to Mt. 14:25–26, Mc. 6:48–49, Jn. 6:19: '[Heracles] walked on the sea as though it were dry land'; Greenwood 2014b, 140–141, De Vita 2015, 133.

5. CHRISTIANS AND CLASSICAL EDUCATION: Tatian, *Oratio ad Graecos* 1–3, Caesarius of Arles, *Sermones* 99, Basil, *De legendis gentilium libris* 1.27–28 and 4.50–51, August. *Doctr.* 2.71–72, Socr. 3.16 (with H.-G. Nesselrath 1999 and Gelzer 2001). PROHAERESIUS: PLRE I, Proaeresius: Hier. *Chron.* s. a. 362, Eun. *VS* 10.8.1; Jul. *Ep.* 31 Bidez (= 14 Wright = 26 Weis) is addressed to him; Watts 2006, 48–78, Becker 2013, 481–484, McLynn 2014, 131–133. MARIUS VICTORINUS: PLRE I, Victorinus 11: August. *Conf.* 8.5.10, McLynn 2014, 130–131. Hecebolius (PLRE I, Hecebolius 1), a sophist of Constantinople, was of a different character. According to Socr. 3.13.5, he was a Christian under Constantius, a pagan under Julian, and a Christian again after Julian's death; Kinzig 1993. AMMIANUS: 22.10.7 (quoted in n. 5 of the Introduction, this volume), 25.4.20; significant is the fact that Libanius abstains from any comment on the school law; see Wiemer 1995, 108–110.

6. Socr. 3.16.1, 3.16.19, Soz. 5.18.1, Rufin. *HE* 10.33, Thdt. *HE* 3.8.1, Martin 2008, 75 n. 36; cf. also Jo. Ant. *Fr.* 271 Roberto = 204 Mariev καί ποτε Χριστιανοὺς ἐκώλυσεν Ἑλληνικῆς παιδείας μεταλαμβάνειν (for an introduction to Johannes Antiochenus, who wrote his *Historia chronica* early in the seventh century, see Treadgold 2010, 311–329; for Julian in his work see Trovato 2014, 353–360 and Trovato 2015), August. *Civ.* 18.52 *an ipse* [sc. Iulianus] *non est ecclesiam persecutus, qui christianos liberales litteras docere ac discere vetuit?* 'Was not he a persecutor, who forbade the Christians to teach and to be taught the liberal arts?'), and Ambr. *Ep.* 72.4. Basabe 1951, 401–403 takes the words of Socrates, Augustine, and their contemporaries to mean that Julian issued two laws, the first affecting Christian teachers, the second Christian pupils. SPECULATIONS: Thdt. *HE* 3.21. Similar remarks can be found in Hier. *Chron.* s. a. 363, Rufin. 10.37, and Chrys. *Pan. Bab. 2*, 121. Ephr. *cJul.* 3.14 states that before the Persian campaign started Julian had written down and published what 'he would do to the churches' (trans. J. M. Lieu); cf. Colpe 1996, 313: 'man [kann] von einer Christenfeindschaft

bei Julian auf Grund seiner *Handlungen* [italics mine, HCT] pauschal nicht reden.'

7. DECREE OF MARCH 13, 362: *CTh* 12.1.50 and Jul. *Ep.* 54 (= 39 Wright = 57 Weis), cf. *CTh* 12.1.59 and 16.2.7, with Elliott 1978 and Brendel 2013, 127–138; Rapp 2005, 184: 'The imperial legislation confirms that the *curiales* were the largest recruiting ground for the clergy at all levels, from deacon to bishop.' DECREE OF FEBRUARY 12, 363: *CTh* 9.17.5 and Jul. *Ep.* 136b (= 56 Wright = 62 Weis), with, e.g., Geffcken 1914, 75–76, R. Smith 1995, 111–112, De Filippis Cappai 2000, Volp 2002, 254–255, Bringmann 2004, 139–140, and Brendel 2013, 260–265; see also Ch. 10 n. 7, this volume. CHOICE OF PERSONNEL: Haehling 1978, 537–547. JULIAN AND THE CITIES: Soz. 5.3.4, Lib. *Or.* 18.129. The best study of Julian's policy towards the cities is Pack 1986.

8. PHILOSTORGIUS: 7.6, trans. Walford. HIERONYMUS: *In Hab.* 2.3.1002 (cf. *In Zach.* 3.14.476), *Chron.* s. a. 362–363, Ambrosiast. *Comm. II Thess.* 2.7; in general for Julian in Christian Latin authors Caltabiano 1993, in the church historians and other authors Dupont 1979, Penella 1993, Leppin, 1996, 72–90, Krivouchine 1997 (Socrates), Wallraff 1997, 100–104 (Socrates), H.-G. Nesselrath 2001, Urbainczyk 2002, 30–31 ('Theodoret's history is markedly different from the other two [sc. Socr. and Soz.], being much more outspoken in its condemnation of those he considered enemies. The emperor Julian, for instance, is described in the blackest terms, with no redeeming features'), Buck 2003 (Socrates), Van Nuffelen 2004, 364–367, Buck 2006 (Sozomen), Martin 2008 (Theodoret); see for Socrates and Sozomen also the literature cited in n. 2 of the Introduction, this volume. MODERN SCHOLARS: Bowersock 1978, 85 ('he never contemplated any other solution to the religious problem than total elimination') and 92 ('Clever and cunning, Julian was now indisputably a persecutor'); Scicolone 1979, 420 ('Aspetti della persecuzione Giulianea'), Momigliano 1974, 1401 ('Julian's persecution of the Christians'), Bayliss 2004, 15 ('a revival of some persecution against Christians'). N.b. I by no means claim to be the first to reject the idea that Julian was a persecutor; cf., e.g., Jones 1964, 123 ('the edict against Christian professors, which, though unfair . . . hardly amounted to persecution'), Klein 1986, 287; Bouffartigue 1998, Bouffartigue 2004, Bouffartigue 2007, Maraval 1992, 143, J. Hahn 2004, 177, Marcos 2009, Drake 2011, 204 ('Julian himself was too shrewd to play the persecutor'); Penella 1993, 31 admits that 'although the emperor Julian moved in various ways against Christians and the institutional church, his professed policy was that physical violence should not be used against the followers of Christ,' but he also states that Julian 'lapsed into violence against them on occasion.' RUFINUS: *HE* 10.33; cf. Thelamon 1981, 281–284. EUTROPIUS: PLRE I, Eutropius 2, Eck 1972–1973, 330, and Lippold 1974, 271; Bonamente 1977; Bird 1988; Burgess 2001; Rohrbacher 2002, 49–56;

the quoted words: 10.16.3 (*religionis Christianae nimius insectator, perinde tamen, ut cruore abstineret*). Bonamente 1986, 159–164; some manuscripts omit *nimius*; cf. the critical apparatus of Hellegouarc'h 1999 and see, e.g., Irmscher 1955, 362. LIBANIUS: *Or.* 18.121. SOZOMENUS: 5.4.8–9 (cf. 5.4.6–7, 6.6.6). GREGORIUS NAZIANZENUS: Julian not as cruel as some of his predecessors: *Or.* 4.57–58. Kurmann 1988, 196–199 refers for similar passages to *Or.* 4.27, 68, 84, *Or.* 21.32 and *Or.* 42.3; cf. also *Or.* 7.11. On the other hand, '[Gregory] too, as his oration *In Praise of the Maccabees* shows (*Or.* 15), considered Julian a persecutor' (Elm 2012, 180); see in this respect further *Or.* 4.85–86. Marcos 2009, 193–194.

9. THEODORETUS: *HE* 3.15.1; Urbainczyk 2002, 30–31, Martin 2008. JULIAN: *Ep.* 61c Bidez (= 36 Wright = 55 Weis), 424a.

Chapter 9

1. FROM CHALCEDON TO PESSINUS: Amm. 22.9.3–8; Den Boeft et al. 1995, 156–165. See in general for Julian's journey through Asia Minor Bringmann 2017. BASIL: I discussed this martyr earlier in Teitler 1996.

2. SOZOMENUS: 5.11.7–11. Brennecke 1988, 149–150 argues, 'daß Basilius ein Presbyter aus dem Klerus des gleichnamigen Bischofs von Ankyra gewesen sein muß und . . . wie sein gleichnamiger Bischof als Homöusianer anzusehen [ist].'

3. RELATION BETWEEN SOCRATES AND SOZOMEN: Chesnut 1986², 204. *PASSIO BASILII PRESBYTERI*: BHG 242. The editio princeps was published by the Bollandists in Antwerp in 1668: AASS Mart. III, *15–*17 (I have consulted the 1865 Parisian reprint, ed. J. Carnandet, *12–*15), based on codex Vaticanus Graecus 655 (saec. XVI). The first editor, Van Papenbroeck, was apparently unaware of the fact that the manuscript he used was directly copied from another Vatican manuscript, Vaticanus Graecus 1667 (saec. X or XI). Cf. for this Krascheninnikov 1907, vi–ix and Delehaye 1908, 423. Krascheninnikov 23–24 lists the main variants. It also prints for the first time on pp. 1–12 a later version of the *passio*, written by Johannes Hagioelita (BHG 243); see for all this Trovato 2014, 165–169. BOLLANDISTS: AASS Mart. III (1865) 378: 'Conscripta, quantum conjectando assequimur, ab iis qui martyrio ejus praesentes interfuere'; for the history of the Bollandists: Van Ommeslaeghe 1988, Aigrain and Godding 2000, 329–388, Godding et al. 2007. MODERN SCHOLARS: WOODS 1992a, 36 states that 'on the whole the Acta seem a reliable historical source' (Woods is followed by, e.g., Scorza Barcellona 1995, 69–71 and Fatti 2009, 77 n. 117), and argues on p. 37 that the *passio* was 'composed shortly after the death of Basil' and was 'the source of Sozomen's brief notice concerning Basil' rather than the other way around. SCEPSIS: Krascheninnikov 1907, xx: 'Quae tamen coniectura [sc. of the Bollandists] tam leviculo fulta

argumento num recte se habeat, equidem subdubito'; Sauget 1987; Brennecke 1988, 131 n. 88: 'in der historisch allerdings recht problematischen Vita des Presbyters Basilius von Ankyra,' and 149: 'Dieses Martyrium ist ebenfalls bei Sozomenus überliefert, von dem die gesamte hagiographische Tradition abhängig ist.' See further Busine 2019.

4. ALTERCATION: *Basil pass.* 13–14. JULIAN IN ANCYRA: Amm. 22.9.8, cf. n. 1. FLAYING: *Basil. pass.* 15. SOZOMEN, VIOLENCE, AND JULIAN: 5.11.12, 5.17.12, cf. 5.4.6–7, 5.5.1, 5.17.1, 6.6.6; it should be noted, however, that Sozomen in 5.5.5–6 makes Julian responsible for shedding the blood of Christians, though to a much lesser degree than preceding persecutors; cf. Socr. 3.19.2–3.

5. LIBANIUS, EUTROPIUS, JULIAN, RUFINUS, SOCRATES: See Ch. 8 n. 8, this volume. GREGORY OF NAZIANZUS: *Or.* 4.57–58; Bernardi 1983, 164 n. 1 ad 4.57 aptly quotes Tert. *Apol.* 50 *sanguis martyrum, semen christianorum,* 'the blood of the martyrs, seed of the Christians' (often translated as 'the blood of the martyrs is the seed of the church'), to which Gregory implicitly refers.

6. FRUMENTINUS (OR FRUMENTIUS): The manuscript reads Φρου-βέτιμον Κόμητα Κουταρίων (i.e., *comitem scutariorum*) in section 15, but Φρουβεντῖνος in section 19; see further infra, n. 8.

7. MIRACLES: Delehaye 1966[2], 207. TERMS OF ABUSE: *ibid.,* 191–192. INVOKING GOD: *ibid.,* 195. INTERROGATIONS: *ibid.,* 179, 185.

8. LENGTH OF BASIL'S ANSWERS: This was already suspected by the pious Le Nain de Tillemont 1700 (728): 'La longueuer des discours se peut excuser sur ce que le Saint estoit accoutumé à parler. Mais je pense qu'il vaut mieux avouer qu'ils sont de l'auteur des actes.' Delehaye 1966[2], 184: 'Dans les Actes historiques l'interrogatoire est bref et serré; les discours de quelque étendue sont l'exception. Dans les Passions épiques on pourrait dire qu'ils sont la règle'. DIALOGUES AND COMPOSITION: Delehaye 1966[2], 189, 221. TOSSING OF HISTORICAL NAMES: Delehaye 1966[2], 177. Felix (PLRE I, Felix 3, Olszaniec 2013, 168–172) was Julian's *comes sacrarum largitionum*, Pegasius was the priest Julian met in Troy; cf. for him Ch. 7 n. 1, this volume. A governor Saturninus is not known (cf. PLRE I, *!Saturninus!* 4). The name of FRUMENTINUS or Frumentius is not attested anywhere else, either. Woods 1992a, 35 admits this. (The authors of PLRE I stigmatized his name as coming from a source of doubtful reliability: *!Frumentinus!*). Woods also admits that 'there was no such office as *comes scutariorum* properly speaking' (*ibid.,* citing for the *scutarii* and other palace guards, including their command structure, Frank 1969, esp. pp. 47–59), but he continues, "we are not entitled . . . to dismiss Frumentinus as a fictitious character.' Are we not? The occurrence of bogus names and titles in hagiographical sources is a strong indicator of spuriousness, as Delehaye

1966², 177 notes: "Il [i.e., the author of unreliable martyrologies] donne aux juges des noms bizarres ou des titres de fantaisie.' But let us for once leave aside the unreliability of our source. What is Woods's reasoning? Not being able to detect a *comes scutariorum* in the historical sources, he first postulates that a *comes domesticorum* must be meant. Secondly, not being able to find a *comes domesticorum* of the name of Frumentinus, either (we know that Julian's *comes domesticorum* from late 361 until mid-363 was Dagalaifus), he would have us believe that Frumentinus is 'the otherwise unattested forename of the *comes domesticorum* Dagalaifus' (Woods 1992a, 36–37). Although a rather ingenious proposal, this is in my opinion not very convincing (as Woods himself admits, 1997b, 277 n. 27). It would seem that Trovato 2014, 169 n. 18 is of the same opinion, although for the rest the author gives Woods the benefit of the doubt: 'Le identificazioni proposte da Woods non sono in effetti impossibili, tranne, a causa della differenza dei nomi, quelle riguardanti Asclepio e Frumentino.'

9. 'JULIANISATION': Dufourcq 1900, 242.

Chapter 10

1. SCRIPTURES: Mt. 9:20–22 (trans. NASB), cf. Mc. 5:25–34, Lc. 8:43–48.

2. STATUE OF JESUS IN PANEAS: Eus. *HE* 7.17.1–18.4; Philost. 7.3; Soz. 5.21.1–4, cf. *Art. pass.* 57; Jo. Mal. 10.238–239; Greg. Tur. *Mir.* 1.20; *Par.* 48 with Av. Cameron and Herrin 1984, 237–238. Dobschütz 1899, 197–205, *250–*273; Thümmel 1984, 219–222; Dietz 2000, 849; J. F. Wilson 2004, 98–103; Stewart 2007, 32–33; Kristensen 2013, 246–247. In general about the destruction of statues Stewart 1999.

3. MAXIMINUS DAIA: Phot. *Bibl.* 271, p. 505b Bekker. PATRON GODDESS OF CONSTANTINOPLE: *Par.* 38, with Av. Cameron and Herrin 1984, 217–218. NICOMEDIA: *Par.* 47, cf. Soz. 5.17.3–4. LAW OF FEBRUARY 19, 356: *CTh* 16.10.6 (already referred to in Ch. 7 n. 3, this volume).

4. IMAGES OF THE GODS RESTORED: *Hist. Aceph.* 3.1; Lib. *Or.* 18.126; *Chron. Pasch.* s. a. 362; cf. Lib. *Ep.* 710 and 712. EMESA: Thdt. *HE* 3.7.5, cf. *Chron. Pasch.* s. a. 362, Theophan. *Chron.* p. 48 De Boor; Brennecke 1988, 124; Dietz 2000, 848–849. EUSTATHIUS: *Chron. Pasch.* s. a. 362; Brennecke 1988, 124. CYRILLUS: Thdt. *HE* 3.7.2–4; *Chron. Pasch.* s. a. 362, Theophan. *Chron.* p. 47 De Boor; Cazzaniga 1973, 309–310; Dietz 2000, 848; Kristensen 2013, 88.

5. AMACHIUS: before he became governor of Phrygia, Flavius Amachius had governed Sardinia under Constantius II: PLRE I, Amachius. MACEDONIUS, THEODULUS, TATIANUS: Socr. 3.15.1–8 (the quotation in section 8, trans. Zenos), Soz. 5.11.1–3; Cazzaniga 1973, 310–311.

6. DAPHNE: for the distance from Antioch, see Martin 2011, 404–405; APOLLO OF DAPHNE: Amm. 22.13.1 with Den Boeft et al. 1995, 228–230; Brinkerhoff 1970, 33–37 with figs. 41–45, Terrinoni 2018. BRYAXIS: Cedren. p. I, 536 Bekker; Neudecker 1997, 806: 'Die überlieferte Werkliste ergibt eine so lange Schaffenszeit, daß sie bereits in der Antike auf zwei homonyme Künstler aufgeteilt wurde.' DATE: Amm. 22.13.1. ASCLEPIADES: Amm. 22.13.3. PLRE I, Asclepiades 4. BOLT OF LIGHTNING: Chrys. *Pan. Bab. 2*, 94, Thdt. *HE* 3.11.5; for Chrysostom and Julian: Capone 2005, Rist 2005, Di Santo 2005, Torres 2008. ARSON BY CHRISTIANS: Jul. *Misop.* 346b, cf. 361c. GREAT CHURCH: Amm. 22.13.2; Deichmann 1972; its topographical situation is unknown: Saliou 2000, Martin 2011, 415–419, Mayer and Allen 2012, 68–80, Saliou 2014. INVESTIGATION: Amm. 22.13.2, Soz. 5.20.6, Lib. *Ep.* 1376 (Libanius himself served on the commission of investigation); Festugière 1959, 83, J. Hahn 2011, 117 with n. 29, Wiemer 2014, 194.
7. BABYLAS' PREVIOUS HISTORY: Caraffa and Raggi 1962; Lieu 1986, 51–55; Matthews 1989, 439–440. BABYLAS' DEATH: Euseb. *HE* 6.39.4 (Philost. 7.8 dates his death to the reign of Numerianus [283–284]); Boulhol 2004, 106–107, Rist 2005, 870–872. CEMETERY IN ANTIOCH: according to *Art. pass.* 55 Babylas' remains were set down near Antioch ἐν τῷ καλουμένῳ κοιμητηρίῳ, 'a house outside the city which has received many bodies of men from ancient times and of a few who were martyrs for their piety' (trans. Vermes); cf. Franchi de' Cavalieri 1928; Downey 1938; Martin 2011, 405 and above all Mayer and Allen 2012, 85–89. BABYLAS' RELICS AND GALLUS CAESAR: Chrys. *Pan. Bab. 2*, 67, 76; Soz. 5.19.12–13. Rist 2005, 876 ('Dieser Vorgang ist die erste uns aus den Quellen bekannte Translation von Reliquien'); Woods 2005 (arguing that an inscription cited by Jo. Mal. 13.17 refers to a church built by Gallus Caesar for Babylas and not to the Great Church in Antioch completed by Constantius II); Agosti 2005, 23–29; Mayer and Allen 2012, 96–97. TRANSLATIO OF RELICS: Brown 1981, 88–94; Clark 2001; Torres 2008 (pointing inter alia to the difference between the Eastern and the Western part of the Empire, pp. 208 ff.); cf. also Guinot 1995, 336 n. 38, 337 n. 43, and Rist 2005, 878–880. IMPURITY BY ASSOCIATION WITH DEATH: *CTh* 9.17.5, Eun. *VS* 6.11.8, Jul. *Ep.* 136b (= 56 Wright = 62 Weis) with Bidez's commentary, pp. 129–132, and Canetti 2002, 55; Torres 2009; Greenwood 2013, 293 ('We know from inscriptions that pagans believed the presence of dead bodies was polluting and required purification,' with references in n. 38); see also the literature cited in Ch. 8 n. 7, this volume. For Christian burial customs see Rebillard 2003. SILENCE OF APOLLO AND TRANSLATION TO ANOTHER CEMETERY: Jul. *Misop.* 361b, Chrys. *Pan. Bab. 2*, 80–91, Socr. 3.18.1–4, Soz. 5.19.14–19, Thdt. *HE* 3.10.1–3, *Art. pass.* 53–55, Zonar. 13.12.39–41. PSALMS: Socr. 3.18.3–4, Soz. 5.19.18–19, Thdt. *HE* 3.10.3; Ps. 97:7, trans. NASB. PURIFICATION TEMPLE AREA:

Amm. 22.12.8. BABYLAS' NEW RESTING PLACE: Chrys. *Pan. Bab.*
1, 10, Soz. 7.10.5, Evagr. 1.16 (for an introduction to Evagrius Scholasticus
see Treadgold 2010, 299–308); Eltester 1937, 281–283; Lassus 1938, 37–38;
Downey1938,46n.10;MayerandAllen2012,44–48,Shepardson2014,60–91,
Saliou 2015a, 94 with n. 26. See also Ch. 15 n. 1, this volume.
8. RUFINUS: *HE* 10.33 (Julian not a persecutor), *HE* 10.37 (Theodorus). We
find the same story about the praetorian prefect (PLRE I, Secundus 3) in
Greg. Naz. *Or.* 4.91, but there about mediation in the case of persecution
of Bishop Marcus of Arethusa; this is not mentioned by Iara 2015, which
accepts Rufinus' story about Theodorus and Secundus' role in it as historical
('his means of persuasion were extremely cruel: by torturing a Christian he
demonstrated that persecution was no option,' p. 179 n. 58, cf. p. 206); cf.
Olszaniec 2013, 370 with n. 1910. See for Secundus also Ch. 13 n. 2, and Ch.
14 n. 13, both in this volume.
9. THEODORUS IN GREEK CHURCH HISTORIES: Socr. 3.19.1–10, Soz.
5.20.2–4, Thdt. *HE* 3.11.1–3. PUBLIA: Thdt. *HE* 3.19.1–6; Krause 1995,
66–73, esp. 68, Martin 2008, 80. PSALMS: Ps. 135:15, 135:18, 68:1, trans.
NASB.

Chapter 11

1. JULIAN'S UNCLE: PLRE I, Iulianus 12 and Martindale 1974, 249.
COMITES ORIENTIS: Downey 1934 is still unsurpassed. COUNT
JULIANUS IN DAPHNE: Thdt. *HE* 3.11.5. BOLT OF LIGHTNING: cf.
Chrys. *Pan. Bab.* 2, 94.
2. JULIANUS AN APOSTATE, LIKE HIS NEPHEW: *Art. pass.* 23.
PILLARS: Jul. *Ep.* 80 (= 12 Weis = 29 Wright, whose translation is used),
cf. Lib. *Ep.* 695.3 (with Bradbury 2004, 184 n. 15) and Amm. 22.13.2 (with
Den Boeft et al. 1995, 231–232); Marcos 2009, 195. JULIAN ABOUT
HIS UNCLE: Jul. *Misop.* 340a, 365c, 371a. COMES JULIANUS IN THE
GREAT CHURCH: Thdt. *HE* 3.12.1–3; Martin 2008, 78–79.
3. ILLNESS AND DEATH OF *COMES* JULIANUS: Thdt. *HE* 3.13.1–3.
SICKBED OF FORTY DAYS: Philost. 7.10. JULIANUS' DAY OF
DEATH: Barnes 1992a, 6; Den Boeft et al. 1998, 14.
4. GOD'S PUNISHMENT: Philost. 7.10; Greg. Naz. *Or.* 5.2 mentions no
names. MAGGOTS: Chrys. *Pan. Bab.* 2, 92, *Hom in Mt.* 4.1, *Laud. Paul.* 4.6,
Ephr. *cJul.* 4.3, Soz. 5.8.2–3; cf. Lact. *Mort. pers.* 35.3 about the death of the
emperor Galerius (PLRE I, Maximianus 9); Africa 1982, Nardi 1995.
5. SOZOMENUS: 5.7.9–5.8.4; cf. Cassiod. *Hist. tripart.* 6.10.
6. DISCREPANCY ARGUED AWAY: Allard 1910[3], III, 71.
INTERPOLATION: J. Hahn 2004, 176 n. 236: 'Die Sozomenos-Notiz

könnte m.E. zu einem späteren Zeitpunkt in den Text des Kirchenhistorikers eingefügt worden sein.' *THEODORETI PASSIO*: BHL 8074–8076 (cf. Franchi de' Cavalieri 1920, 57–88), BHG 2425 (cf. Halkin 1986, 123). Brennecke 1988, 147 n. 171: 'Über Sozomenus ist das Martyrium des Theodorit in die hagiographische Überlieferung eingegangen.' Trovato 2014, 141–150 ('Il Giuliano della passione di Teodoreto è pertanto uno dei più notevoli dell'agiografia greca, molto differente dall'imperatore privo di individualità che appare in tante passioni epiche,' p. 150).

7. TORTURE: *Thdt. pass.* 3–4, 7. Vergote 1972, 102–121. DAY OF DEATH: Gaiffier 1956, 16; Galuzzi 1969.

8. *COMES* JULIANUS BEFORE JULIAN: *Thdt. pass.* 9. JULIAN'S REACTION: *Thdt. pass* 9–10 (but I stick to section 11 of the Latin version, for I am not able to understand the logic of section 10 in Halkin 1986).

Chapter 12

1. BUSIRIS: Soz. 5.11.4–6.

2. LETTER TO ARISTOXENUS: Jul. *Ep.* 78 Bidez (= 35 Wright = 11 Weis), 375c. 'GENUINE HELLENE': See for the various connotations of the word ἕλλην and its derivations Bouffartigue 1991 and Al. Cameron 1993; there cannot be any doubt that it here means 'pagan.' NAME CAESAREA: according to Soz. given by the emperor Claudius, but see Teja 1980, 1105. JULIAN AND CAESAREA: Soz. 5.4.1–5, Lib. *Or.* 16.14.

3. JULIANS' PUNITIVE MEASURES: Soz. 5.4.1–6; 'would not hesitate to kill those Galilaeans' is my translation of οὐδὲ τὰς κεφαλὰς συγχωρήσει τοὺς Γαλιλαίους ἔχειν; cf. 'until none of the Galilaeans remained in existence' (trans. Hartranft). CLERICS DRAFTED INTO THE ARMY: in Egypt, according to Rufin. *Hist. Mon.* 7.3.2, monks were enlisted during Julian's reign. Whether the clerics mentioned by Sozomen were to serve as real soldiers ('milites armati') or as bureaucrats ('milites inermes,' 'officiales') is disputed. Cf. Greg. *Or.* 18.33–34, and, e.g., Van Dam 2002, 227 n. 11, Métivier 2005, 116–117, Fatti 2009, 72 ff. See in general for Christians and pagans in the army of the fourth century the literature cited in Ch. 15 n. 2, this volume.

4. EUPSYCHIUS: Soz. 5.11.7–8; in the tenth century Arethas of Caesarea (Scripta minora 1, p. 300 Westerink 1968) tells us that Eupsychius was not only just married, but that he was a priest as well. Compernass 1935, 93, 107; Westerink 1972, 200–201; Halkin 1973; Westerink 1983; in general for Eupsychius: Aubert 1963, Burchi 1965, Fatti 2009, passim; Fatti 2011, 125–129. I discussed this martyr earlier in Teitler 2014.

5. EUPSYCHIUS EXECUTED: Rosen 2006, 279: 'Der Kaiser machte Eupsychios den Prozeß und ließ ihn mit einem Teil seiner Helfer hinrichten,

die anderen schickte er in die Verbannung'; in the same vein Fatti 2009, 101 ff. and 2011, 125–129; the position of Buenacasa Pérez 2000, 525 is not clear: he does refer to Soz. 5.4.1–5 (without mentioning Eupsychius), but not to 5.11.7–8 ('los cristianos de Caesarea . . . fueron castigados por Juliano por haber demolido los templos de Zeus y Apolo'). MARTYROLOGIA: *Menologium Basilii* (April 9), *Synaxarium Constantinopolitanum* (April 9), cited by Compernass 1935, 107; cf. Gaiffier 1956, 12 and see for these works Trovato 2014, 298–303 and 283–297, respectively. GREGORY OF NAZIANZUS ON JULIAN AND CAESAREA: *Or.* 4.92, cf. *Or.* 18.33–34; Métivier 2005, 116–117; Fatti 2009, passim; Elm 2012, 357. SILENCE OF GREGORY ABOUT EUPSYCHIUS: an argumentum ex silentio, admittedly, not accepted by Scorza Barcellona 1995, 60 n. 23: 'da questo silenzio non si può ricavare però un argomento contro la storicità del fatto'; Brennecke 1988, 150–152 explains Gregory's silence by supposing that Eupsychius adhered to a Christian denomination that Gregory disliked. PASSIO EUPSYCHII: BHG 2130, Halkin 1984.

6. FEAST OF EUPSYCHIUS: Greg. Naz. *Ep.* 58.7, Basil. *Ep.* 100, 142, 200, 252, cf. 176; Girardi 1990, 159–161, Pouchet 1992, 234–236; for the date Devos 1992, 256–258. DAMAS AND OTHER MARTYRS: Basil. *Ep.* 252 with Pouchet 1992, 413. HYPOTHESIS OF TWO EUPSYCHII: Fatti 2009, 186, 213–220.

7. EUSEBIUS, NESTABUS, AND ZENO: Soz. 5.9.1–10. Aja Sánchez 1999 and Aja Sánchez 2001. SOZOMEN ONLY SOURCE: Sabbah in SC 495 (Sabbah 2005) 130 n. 1 ('confirmé en substance par Théodoret, *H.E.* III, 7, 1') is wrong. The suggestion of Halkin 1966, 337 that the *passio* of Eusebius of Phoenicia (BHG 2131) has something to do with Sozomen's Eusebius ('Ou bien s'agirait-il d'un dédoublement de S. Eusèbe martyrisé à Gaza avec ses frères Nestabe et Zénon sous Julien l'Apostat?') does not seem to me plausible, either. PAGANISM IN GAZA: Downey 1972, 1127; the transition from paganism to Christianity in Gaza in the course of the fifth century is sketched by Van Dam 1985. MAIUMA: apart from the name of a town, also the name of a festival; Belayche 2004, Mattheis 2014, 105–110. RENAMED CONSTANTIA: Eus. *VC* 4.37–38, Socr. 1.18.13, Soz. 2.5.7–8, 5.3.6; Pohlsander 1993, 164. JULIAN AND CONSTANTIA: Soz. 5.3.6–7, cf. 7.28.4.

8. GAZA AND ASCALON: Thdt. *HE* 3.7.1, *Chron. pasch.* s.a. 362. HELIOPOLIS: Greg. Naz. *Or.* 4.86–87, Soz. 5.10.5–7. SOZOMEN'S GRANDFATHER: Soz. 5.15.14–17. Van Nuffelen 2004, 51–53; see for Sozomen also the literature cited in Ch. 8 n. 8, this volume. As to Thdt. *HE* 3.7.1, this text is referred to by Avi-Yonah in support of his view that the people of Ascalon proclaimed their loyalty to Julian in an Εἷς θεός inscription, found in Ascalon, which was published by him (Avi-Yonah 1944, 160–161

no. 1 = Conti 2004, no. 16; cf. Markschies and Hildebrandt in Peterson [1926] 2012, 413). In view of the fact that Theodoret is probably mistaken, the alternative as proposed by Conti p. 69 seems more likely: 'Unklar ist, von wem die Weihung ausging: stammte sie von der Partei, die auch den anti-christlichen Aufstand in Ascalon entfachte [with in n. 43: Thdt. HE, III, 3: Chronicon Paschale, in PG 92, col. 741], oder vom Statthalter?' Cf. also the suggestion mentioned in Belayche 2010, 161 n. 120 (Belayche herself is of another opinion; see Ch. 3 n. 7, this volume): 'One might also imagine that this was the proposition of a Jew who recognised the providence of his own God in the emperor's person; for it dates to the time of Julian's stay in Antioch, in 362–363 [see, however, for the date Di Segni 1994, 104 and Conti 2004, 69, which opt for 361–362], from where the emperor informed the Jews by letter that he wished to see the Temple at Jerusalem rebuilt.'

9. EUSEBIUS, NESTABUS, ZENO, AND NESTOR: Soz. 5.9.1–10, trans. Hartranft, adapted.

10. GREGORY NAZIANZENUS: Greg. Naz. Or. 4.93. SOZOMEN AND ZENO: Soz. 7.28.6 (according to Soz. 7.28.4, Zeno's brother Ajax was also mishandled by pagans).

11. JULIAN AND THE DISTURBANCES IN GAZA: Soz. 5.9.11–13 and already Greg. Naz. Or. 4.93 (cf. Or. 4.86); PLRE I, Cyrillus 1. JULIAN'S LETTER TO THE ALEXANDRIANS: Ch. 4 n. 9.

Chapter 13

1. FROM CAPPADOCIA TO ANTIOCH: Amm. 22.9.13–15, with Den Boeft et al. 1995, 173–181.

2. JULIAN IN ANTIOCH: Marcone 1981, Rosen 1998, J. Hahn 2004, 161–177, Kleinman 2008–2009, Elm 2012, 269–335. JULIAN'S FOURTH CONSULATE: Amm. 23.1.1, with Den Boeft et al. 1998, 1–4; for the consul-ate in Late Antiquity, Bagnall et al. 1987, Cecconi 2007, and Sguaitamatti 2012. FLAVIUS SALLUSTIUS: PLRE I, Sallustius 5 (he is not to be confused with Saturninus Secundus Salutius, PLRE I, Secundus 3); whether Flavius Sallustius or Secundus Salutius should be identified as the author (PLRE I, Sallustius 1) of the Neoplatonic treatise Περὶ θεῶν καὶ κόσμου is disputed; cf., e.g., Rochefort 1956, which opts for Salutius (but calls him Saloustios), Étienne 1963, which prefers Sallustius, and Bowersock 1978, 125 ('Salutius by far the most plau-sible candidate'); cf. Olszaniec 2013, 371–372 with n. 1921. LIBANIUS: Or. 12.4; cf. for this speech Lib. Or. 1.127 and Wiemer 1995, 153–154. Lib. Ep. 1430.2 (cf. Ep. 818.3) makes clear that the philosopher and rhetorician Themistius (PLRE I, Themistius 1) also composed an oration (now lost) in honor of Julian's fourth consulship; for Themistius and Julian's letter to him,

Or. 6 Bidez, 253a–267b, see, e.g., Daly 1980; Barnes and Vanderspoel 1981; Criscuolo 1983; Brauch 1993; Vanderspoel 1995, 115–134; Errington 2000, 873–878; Bouffartigue 2006b; Bringmann 2008a, 92–93; C.P. Jones 2010; Elm 2012, 96–106; Watt 2012; Watt 2013; Swain 2013; Schamp 2014; Chiaradonna 2015; cf. also Marcos 2009, 203 n. 118. *KALENDAE IANUARIAE*: Graf 2012, Mattheis 2014, 98–110. CHRISTIANS AND CHRISTIANIZATION IN ANTIOCH: Festugière 1959, 80–82, Liebeschuetz 1972, 224–228. Sandwell 2007. PHILOSOPHER: IK 12.313a (= Conti 2004, no. 26): *philosophiae principi*, cf. IK 17.1.3021 (= Conti 2004, no. 27), ILS 751 (= Conti 2004, no. 28): *filosofi[ae] magistro*, cf. CIL 3.14201.8 (= Conti 2004, no. 30), ILS 751 n. 2 (= Conti 2004, no. 34): τὸν ἐκ φιλοσοφίας βασιλεύοντα. Bringmann 2008a, 87–90, Benoist 2009, 116. BURIED NEAR TARSUS: Amm. 23.2.5, 25.9.12–13 and 25.10.5 with Den Boeft et al. 2005 ad loc.; according to Philost. 8.1, Julian's burial place in Tarsus was opposite to that of the Tetrarch Maximinus Daia: 'Das ist sicher kein Zufall' (Ehling 2010, 253; cf. Ch. 3 n. 8, this volume); Julian's remains were later removed to Constantinople. Downey 1959; Grierson 1962; DiMaio 1978; Arce 1984b; Arce 1988; Asutay-Effenberger and Effenberger 2006; Woods 2006; Johnson 2008.

3. *MISOPOGON*: see Ch. 7 n. 6, this volume. QUOTATION: Jul. *Misop.* 342b, trans. Wright, adapted. *MISOPOGON* AS WEAPON: Lib. *Or.* 18.198. NO TORTURE, NO EXECUTIONS: Lib. *Or.* 18.195. ENEMIES AND ATTACKS: Lib. *Or.* 16.19; 18.162, 172, 199, 200.

4. PUNITIVE MEASURES ACCORDING TO AMMIANUS: Amm. 22.11.1–2.

5. JULIAN'S CLEMENCY: Amm. 21.12.20 and 22.10.5, with Den Boeft et al. 1991, 179 and Den Boeft 1995, 191, respectively; cf. Brandt 1999, 179 ff. JULIAN'S PUNISHMENTS: e.g., Amm. 24.3.2, with Den Boeft et al. 2002, 73–75.

6. RELEVANT CHAPTERS: *Art. pass.* 25–34, 39; cf. Zonar. 13.12.44.

7. JULIAN'S ARRIVAL IN ANTIOCH: *Art. pass.* 24–25. FIRST ALTERCATION: *Art. pass.* 25–26.

8. EUGENIUS AND JULIAN: *Art. pass.* 27–31.

9. MACARIUS AND JULIAN: *Art. pass.* 32–34. JEREMIAH 10:11, cited in *Art. pass.* 33, trans. NASB.

10. ARTEMIUS' INTERVENTION: *Art. pass.* 35. OASIS IN ARABIA: *Art. pass.* 39. Presumably, Oasis is a corruption of the name Augasis (further unknown), which is found in an older version of Artemius' martyrium, p. 171 Bidez and Winkelmann 1972[2]; there Arabia is not spoken of, Gaiffier 1960, 35–36. Instead of Oasis in Arabia, the Great Oasis in Egypt must be meant, a well-known place of exile: e.g., *Dig.* 48.22.7.5; *CTh* 9.32.1; Socr. 7.34.11; Zos. 5.9.5; Schwartz 1966, Wagner 1987, 117–120, Vallejo Girvés 2002 (esp. p. 692) and Delmaire 2008, 120–121.

11. *PASSIO EUGENII ET MACARII*: BHG 2126, Halkin 1960; Grégoire 1905, 41-50, Trovato 2014, 177–179; there exists a Latin translation: BHL 5103. DATE: Gaiffier 1960, 38: 'antérieure au début du IXᵉ siècle.' BROTHERS: *Eugen. pass.* 3. COURTIER: *ibid.* 4; the man (ὀνόματι Σέλευκον) is identified by Woods 1992b, 873 with PLRE I, Seleucus 1. SNAKES: *Eugen. pass.* 5. NO MARTYR'S DEATH: *ibid.* 6.

12. DINDONA: *Eugen. pass.* 6. DRAGON AND SHOOTING STAR: *Eugen. pass.* 8. WELL: *ibid.* 9. DEATH: *ibid.* 10.

13. DATE: apart from December 20 and February 22 we also come across January 23, February 19, and December 22 as days on which Eugenius and Macarius were venerated; Gaiffier 1960, 33–35.

Chapter 14

1. *EUSIGNII PASSIO*: BHG 638–640 (for the date see Winkelmann 1970, 288); I have used the text of BHG 639 = Devos 1982 (for a Coptic version see Coquin and Lucchesi 1982). In general about the martyr and his passion: Sauget 1965 and Trovato 2014, 222–240. DEATH OF EUSIGNIUS: *Eus. pass.* 12 (the martyrologium Romanum gives Antioch, not Caesarea, as the city where Eusignius died, cf. Gaiffier 1956, 22). HISTORICAL (UN)RELIABILITY: BHG 638–640ᵉ are 'sans valeur' (Gaiffier 1956, 22); cf. J. Hahn 2004, 174 and Trovato 2014, 222 ('una fantasiosa passione') with n. 102, in which among others Klien-Paweletz 2002, 1–161 [non vidi] is cited, which 'analizza e confronta le varie redazioni della passione di Eusignio, ritinendo che sia davvero esisto un sant'Eusignio martire sub Iuliano, e che l'archetipo della passione sia stato scritto tra il 362/3 e il 370, ma non spiega il totale silenzio degle autori tardoantichi sulla vicenda.'

2. LATER GENERATIONS: 'il testo, pur avendo caratteristiche di una passione epica (dibattiti, torture, un segretario verbalizzatore destinato a tramandare gli avvenimenti), presenta notevole originalità' (Trovato 2014, 223). BANNER OF THE CROSS: *Eus. pass.* 9 and 11A. TORTURE: *Eus. pass.* 6; Grig 2002, 327: 'The later martyr acts are infamous for a preponderance of torture.' STENOGRAPHY: *Eus. pass.* 2, cf. *Art. pass.* 2 and in general for stenography and the acts of the martyrs Teitler 2007b, 531–533. EUSTOCHIUS: *Eus. pass.* 4.

3. JULIAN'S PREDECESSOR: *Eus. pass.* 1 (he is here called Constantinus, not Constantius). 113 YEARS: cf. Lefebvre 1944. HELLENE: see Ch. 12 n. 2, this volume.

4. BEGINNING OF INTERROGATION AND DEPARTURE TO CAESAREA: *Eus. pass.* 2–3.

5. INTERROGATION CONTINUED: *Eus. pass.* 5–6. SON OF A WHORE: πορνογέννητος (*Eus. pass.* 6) is a rare word; the author of the

passio puns upon the word πορφυρογέννητος, 'born in the purple.' Trovato 2014, 223–225.

6. CONSTANTIUS CHLORUS, HELENA AND CONSTANTINE: *Eus. pass.* 7–8.

7. CONSTANTINE: Ch. 2 n. 1, this volume. HELENA: PLRE I, Helena 3, cf. J. W. Drijvers 1992b and J. W. Drijvers 2011a, Kienast 1996², 304–305, Leadbetter 1998, Dräger 2010², Georgiou 2013. CONSTANTIUS CHLORUS: PLRE I, Constantius 12, Kienast 1996², 280–282. TETRARCHY: Vollmer 1991. MAXENTIUS: Ch. 2 n. 1, this volume. LICINIUS: PLRE I, Licinius 3, Barnes 1972, 162 and Martindale 1980, 488; cf. further Chantraine 1982 and Kienast 1996², 294–295.

8. WAR AGAINST BYZANTINES: *Eus. pass.* 9. FOUNDATION OF CONSTANTINOPLE: *ibid.* 10. WAR AGAINST BARBARIANS AND CONVERSION: *ibid.* 11–11B.

9. HELENA IN JERUSALEM AND CONSTANTINE IN PERSIA: *Eus. pass.* 11B. EUSIGNIUS' DECAPITATION AND BURIAL: *ibid.* 12.

10. CONSTANTINE AND *LABARUM*: Eus. *VC* 1.30–31 (with Av. Cameron and Hall 1999, 208–212), cf. 2.16, 2.55, 4.21; Socr. 1.2.7; Soz. 1.4.1–4; in general about the *labarum*: e.g., Leclercq 1928; Egger 1960; Lukaszewicz 1990; R.-Alföldi 1998; see also the literature cited in Ch. 2 n. 1, this volume; pictures: Av. Cameron and Hall 1999, 209 fig. 2; R.-Alföldi 1999, 187, fig. 236 and 196, fig. 246. SHOWPIECE: Eus. *VC* 1.31.1–2. GUARD: Eus. *VC* 2.8.1, *CTh* 6.25.1. REPLICAS: Eus. *VC* 1.31.3, cf. Hier. *Ep.* 107.2 *vexilla militum crucis insignia sunt*, but see Al. Cameron 2011, 104–105: 'There is certainly no reason to believe that all the hundreds of traditional devices of the various units were *replaced* by the cross, nor is there any evidence (e.g., in the more than 150 shield devices illustrated in the *Notitia Dignitatum*) that the addition of a cross became general practice. When Jerome cites [in *Ep.* 107.2] as an illustration of the rapid decline of paganism that 'soldiers' standards bear the sign of the Cross,' he is either speaking metaphorically or making a sweeping generalization on the basis of the story about the Milvian Bridge.' JULIAN AND LABARUM: Greg. Naz. *Or.* 4.66, Soz. 5.17.2–4, cf. Greg. Naz. *Or.* 4.80–81 and Tomlin 1998, 26–27.

11. CHRISTIAN SYMBOLS ON COINS OF CONSTANTIUS: RIC 8, 272 no. 252 (Rome), 8, 323 no. 97 (Aquileia), 8, 369 no. 282 (Siscia), 8, 435 no. 72 (Heraclea), 8, 496 no. 84 (Cyzicus); cf. in general W. Hahn 2000; R.-Alföldi 1998. COINS OF IULIANUS CAESAR WITH CONSTANTIUS AND *LABARUM* ON THE REVERSE: RIC 8, 378 nos 387, 388, 389 (Siscia). MEDALLIC BRONZE WITH BUST OF IULIANUS AUGUSTUS AND SHIELD WITH CHRISTOGRAM: RIC 8, 192 no. 204 (Lyons), cf. p. 45 n. 29; Kent 1981, 175–176: 'Somewhere near the start of the reign ... should be placed, if it is authentic, the unique medallic AE 2 REPARATIO

GALLIARUM, with its type of trophy and captives. The obverse legend D N IVLIANVS P F AVG, is unique for Lyons. The facing bust with christogram on shield must belong to a time before Julian's apostasy was announced'; cf. Guidetti 2015, 28 n. 31. Since 1981 three coins of Iulianus Augustus with *labarum* have appeared: Sánchez Vendramini 2013, 124 fig. 2 (Thessaloniki; obv. FL CL IVLIA-NVS P F AVG, rev. VIRTVS-EXERCITVS) and http://www.forumancientcoins.com/board/index.php?topic=41758.0 (consulted on January 13, 2016). *LABARUM* AND JOVIAN: Ehling 1996. *PASSIO SANCTORUM BONOSI ET MAXIMILIANI MILITUM*: BHL 1427; cf. in the first place Woods 1995a (with on p. 27 n. 1 an overview of those scholars 'who have accepted the passion of Bonosus and Maximilianus as a valuable historical source,' on p. 36: 'the passion was not necessarily a complete fiction' and on p. 55, 'an undervalued and neglected source for an important historical period'), but see Den Boeft et al. 2005, 193–194. Sceptical of the historicity also J. Hahn 2004, 173. According to Al. Cameron 2011, 105, 'Woods successfully identified a modest amount of "accurate and detailed information about the personalities and events of the reign of Julian" in the *Passions of Saints Bonosus and Maximilianus*, but the trial and torture scenes are pure fiction, as are the grounds alleged for their trial.'

12. TITLE: *Passio ss. Bonosi et Maximiliani militum, de numero Herculianorum seniorum sub Iuliano imperatore et Iuliano comite eius, sub die XII kalendas Octobres.* HERCULIANI AND IOVIANI: Amm. 22.3.2 (with Den Boeft et al. 1995, 20–21), 25.6.2, cf. *Not. Dign. Occ.* 5.145–146, 7.3–4 and Woods 1995a, 31–32; I do not know what the basis is for the statement in López Sánchez 2012, 176, that 'Bonosus and Maximilianus were the standard-bearers of the *Iovani Cornuti Seniores* and *Iovani Cornuti Iuniores*.' IOVIANUS AND HERCOLIANUS: *Bon. pass.* 11. JULIANUS, *COMES ORIENTIS*: Ch. 11 n. 1, this volume; otherwise Woods 1995b, 61: '[The author of the *Bon. pass*]) mistakenly identified the Julian who presided at the trial of Bonosus and Maximilianus as the *comes Orientis* Julian, the maternal uncle of the emperor Julian, although he was really the *comes Iovianorum et Herculianorum* of the same name' (i.e., PLRE I, Iulianus 13).

13. TORMENTS AND REACTION OF SECUNDUS: *Bon. pass.* 5. SECUNDUS: see Ch. 10 n. 8 and Ch. 13 n. 2, this volume.

14. TORTURE AS PART OF LEGAL PROCEEDINGS: Grodzynski 1984; MacMullen 1986; Angliviel de la Beaumelle 1992; Harries 1999, 122–134; Chauvot 2000. DIVISION BETWEEN CIVIL AND MILITARY JURISDICTION: *CTh* 2.1.2.

15. IMPRISONMENT, UNSLAKED LIME, HORMISDAS: *Bon. pass.* 7-8. HORMISDAS: PLRE I, Hormisdas 2 (it is nowhere else stated than in the *Bon. pass.* that he was a Christian). REACTION OF BYSTANDERS AND SECUNDUS: *Bon. pass.* 10.

16. DEATH OF BONOSUS AND MAXIMILIANUS AND OF *COMES*
JULIANUS: *ibid.* 11-12.
17. DEATH OF HISTORICAL *COMES* JULIANUS: Amm. 23.1.4; cf. Ch. 11
n. 3, this volume. CHRONOLOGICAL PROBLEM: Gaiffier 1956, 6-7;
Sfair 1963, 353; Woods 1995a, 39: 'Several commentators have felt obliged,
therefore, to redate the deaths of Bonosus and Maximilianus to the period
December 362–January 363,' referring to among others Kaegi 1967, 259 and
Gleason 1986, 109; Woods 1995a, 40: 'It [the death of the *comes* Julianus]
was not included as a chronological indicator, and should not be interpreted
as such.' *COMES* JULIANUS, NOT THE EMPEROR, ACCUSED: cf.
Marcos 2009, 197: 'Julian cannot be accused of responsibility for the popular
anti-Christian movements, in which the greatest atrocities were committed,
which were sporadic and of which there is no proof that they were manipu-
lated'; cf. further Marcos 2009, 204.

Chapter 15

1. CHRYSOSTOM'S TWO WORKS ON BABYLAS: the sermon = *Pan.
Bab. 1*, ('homélie') and the earlier work = *Pan. Bab. 2* ('discours'). DATE
OF SERMON: Grillet and Guinot 1990 (SC 362), 279–280: later than
386; date of *Pan. Bab. 2*: Schatkin, Blanc, Grillet 1990 (SC 362): 378 or
379, Shepardson 2009: possibly on Babylas' feast day, January 24, 380; cf.
Shepardson 2013 and Rohmann 2018. INVECTIVE: Guinot 1995, 325–333
(cf. Rist 2005, 868–878 for a somewhat different interpretation). There is
a marked difference between *Pan. Bab. 1* and *Pan. Bab. 2*: 'ce qui frappe à la
lecture du *Discours sur Babylas*, c'est la place marginale qu'y occupe la figure
de Julien' (Célérier 2013, 333), 'en revanche, comme l'ont constaté les édit-
eurs [sc. Grillet and Guinot] . . . Julien constitue le sujet central de l'*Homélie
sur Babylas*' (Célérier 2013, 334). *Pan. Bab. 2* can be seen as part of 'a literary war' (Carruthers 1998, 47) between Chrysostom and Libanius; the latter composed an oration lamenting the events in Daphne, now almost totally
lost, from which Chrysostom liberally quotes, cf. Schatkin et al. in SC 362,
pp. 37–39, Jul. *Ep.* 98 Bidez (= 58 Wright = 24 Weis), 400b and Lib. *Or.* 60
Foerster. CHRYSOSTOM AND JULIAN: see Ch. 10 n. 6, this volume.
2. SERMON ABOUT JUVENTINUS AND MAXIMINUS: Chrys. *Pan.
Juv.*, PG 50.571–578 (BHG 975); Franchi de' Cavalieri 1953. DATE OF
THIS SERMON: Guinot 1995, 331 n. 26. CHRISTIAN SOLDIERS IN
JULIAN'S ARMY: August. *Enarr. in Ps.* 124.7, with Barzano 1991, 90; in
general for Christians and pagans in the army of the fourth century Gabba
1974; Tomlin 1998; Haensch 2004, cf. further n. 7 below. NAMES NOT
MENTIONED: Delehaye 1966[2], 150–152.

3. IMPRISONMENT AND CHARGE OF HIGH TREASON: Chrys. *Pan.*
   Juv., 574, 576. JANUARY 29: Peeters 1924.
4. BODYGUARD: Thdt. *HE* 3.15.4 ἀσπιδηφόροι γὰρ ἦσαν καὶ βασιλέως
   πεζέταιροι, cf. Chrys. *Pan. Juv.*, 571 στρατιωτῶν ξυνωρίς; note that Amm.
   22.11.2 also speaks of a guilty verdict regarding two members of Julian's
   bodyguard, but their names were Romanus and Vincentius, not Juventinus
   and Maximinus, and, as we have seen, they were exiled, not executed.
   Jo. Mal. 13.19 ἀπὸ δὲ τῶν πλησίον αὐτοῦ ('belonging to the emperor's in-
   crowd') δύο κανδιδᾶτοι χριστιανοί; cf. Bouffartigue 2006a, 141; Boulhol
   2004. Brennecke 1988, 145 thinks, because of Malalas' ἀπὸ δὲ τῶν πλησίον
   αὐτοῦ, that the two men were 'Verwandte Julians.' There is a hymn, in a Syriac
   translation (the Greek original is lost), of the sixth-century bishop Severus of
   Antioch (PO 7, fasc. 5, 611–612), which, apart from 'Iuventius and Maximus'
   (sic), mentions another victim, a certain Longinus. See in general for the relation between the different sources Franchi de' Cavalieri 1953. MALALAS:
   according to Jo. Mal. 13.19, the remains of the martyrs were placed ἐν τῷ
   μαρτυρίῳ τῷ λεγομένῳ κοιμητηρίῳ, for which see Ch. 10 n. 7, this volume.
5. CONSPIRACY OF SOLDIERS: Lib. *Or.* 15.43; 16.19; 18.199; in *Or.* 18.199
   Libanius speaks of ten soldiers; in *Ep.* 1120.3 he mentions only eight.
   CONNECTION BETWEEN LIBANIUS' WORDS AND JUVENTINUS
   AND MAXIMINUS: Norman ad Lib. *Or.* 18.199, J. Hahn 2004, 173;
   skeptical in this respect are Bliembach 1976, 124 and Scholl 1994, 142.
   CONSPIRATORS SPARED: Lib. *Or.* 12.85, 15.43, 16.19, *Ep.* 1120.3, cf.
   18.101 and see Malosse 1995a, 329–330; Amm. 25.4.9, trans. Hamilton,
   adapted. JULIAN'S CLEMENCY: Amm. 16.5.12–13, 21.5.12, 21.9.5–10.1,
   22.7.5, 22.10.5, 22.14.4–5; Den Boeft et al. 2005, 132–133. COURT–
   MARTIAL: Jul. *Ep.* 98, 402a Bidez (= 58 Wright = 24 Weis), trans. Wright.
6. DEATH SENTENCES: Amm. 22.11.2.
7. DISTINGUISHED SCHOLAR: Barnes 1998, 53. EXAGGERATION: 'Il
   Giuliano del Crisostomo presenta dei tratti chiaramente caricaturali,' Di
   Santo 2005, 382. It should be noted, however, that Chrysostom is not the
   only author who alleges that Julian forbade Christians to serve in the army
   (or the imperial bodyguard); cf., e.g., Greg. Naz. *Or.* 4.64–65, Rufin. *HE*
   10.33, Thdt. *HE* 3.8.2, Jo. Ant. *Fr.* 271 Roberto = 204 Mariev. But, as Tomlin
   1998 (p. 33) notes, 'authentic military martyrs are hard to find'; cf. Lenski
   2002, 275–276.
8. TASK OF HISTORIAN: Ranke 1874, vii.
9. CHRYSOSTOM'S BIRTH DATE: 344 or 347 (according to Christ et al.
   1924[6], 1457); 349 (Carter 1962, 362; Rist 1998, 1059), 354 (Lietzmann 1916,
   1812; Greenslade and Liebeschuetz 1996, 329). CHRYSOSTOM AND
   THE HISTORY OF ANTIOCH: Soler 2001. CHRYSOSTOM PUPIL OF
   LIBANIUS: Socr. 6.3.1, Soz. 8.2.2; Fabricius 1957; Fabricius 1962, 22 n. 1

and 132; Hunter 1988; Hunter 1989; Wiemer 1995, 214–215 with n. 118. See, however, Malosse 2008, which regards the story that Chrysostom was a pupil of Libanius as fictional, invented by Chrysostom hagiography in the fifth century.

10. Delehaye 1966², 166: 'En lisant les panégyriques des saints Juventin et Maximin, de S. Lucien, de S. Ignace ... on ne se défend pas de l'impression que S. Jean Chrysostome se souvenait d'avoir lu des Actes ou des chroniques.' Franchi de' Cavalieri 1953, 180: 'Ma se il Crisostomo ebbe davvero sotto gli occhi una Passione della ξυνωρὶς στρατιωτῶν ἁγίων, certo non fu quella che intorno alla metà del V secolo connobbe e compendiò Teodoreto.'

Chapter 16

1. AMMIANUS: *abolenda nobis natio molestissima* (23.5.19). LIBANIUS: *Or.* 18.282. OMENS AND DISAPPROVAL: Amm. 23.1.5–7, Den Boeft et al., 1998, 14–19; cf. also Liebeschuetz 1988. SALLUSTIUS: Amm. 23.5.4, PLRE I, Sallustius 5; see for him Ch. 13 n. 2, this volume. THE PERSIAN CAMPAIGN: Fontaine 1977; Bowersock 1978, 106–119; Paschoud 1979, Matthews 1989, 140–179, Den Boeft et al. 1998, Den Boeft et al. 2002, Bringmann 2004, 169–186; Rosen 2006, 345–374, Brodka 2009, 76–105; see further, e.g., Klotz 1916, Brok 1959, Chalmers 1960, Austin 1972, Blockley 1973, Ridley 1973, Arce 1974, Wirth 1978, DiMaio 1981, Kaegi 1981, Klein 1986, 290 ('eine Kette strategischer Fehler'), Benedetti Martig 1990, Fornara 1991, Meulder 1991, Sabbah 1992, Seager 1997, R. Smith 1999, Ivic 2004, Lendon 2005, 290–309, Vannesse 2012.

2. DEPARTURE FROM ANTIOCH AND ROUTE: Amm. 23.2.6, Jul. *Ep.* 98 Bidez (= 58 Wright = 24 Weis) with Cumont 1917 and Den Boeft et al. 1998, xv–xvii. Salway 2012, 143 states the belief that the Εἷς θεός inscriptions on the milestones along the Gerasa-Philadelphia road in the province of Arabia (for which see Ch. 3 n. 7, this volume), 'may reflect investment in the infrastructure of this area as part of the preparations for the Persian campaign of 363,' but this does not seem likely in view of Julian's itinerary, as Balty 1974, 275 with n. 109 on p. 299 argues against J. Germer-Durand. DOMETIUS: Jo. Mal. 13.20, cf. *Chron. Pasch.* s. a. 363; see for the *Acta Graeca S. Dometii martyris* (BHG 560) Peeters 1939; Amore 1964d; Parmentier 1989; Boulhol 2004, 110–111; Bouffartigue 2006a, 142; Trovato 2014, 171–175.

3. ROUTE FROM HIERAPOLIS TO CARRHAE: Den Boeft et al. 1998, xviii. JULIAN IN CARRHAE: Amm. 23.3.1–5. Den Boeft et al. 1998, 36–38. WOMAN SACRIFICED: Thdt. *HE* 3.26 (and in later Byzantine authors, e.g., Theophan. *Chron.* p. 53 De Boor and Cedren. vol. 1, p. 527 Bekker); Theodoret's report was rejected by, e.g., Voltaire (as quoted by Ziegler 1974,

141) and Schwenn 1915, 192–193, but accepted by Massalsky 1941, which further argues that Julian on his way from Gaul eastward in 361 ritually killed a human being in a shrine of Mithras near Fertörakos in Hungary; Vermaseren 1951 rightly declines this view. For literature on (the accusation of) human sacrifices (which was strictly forbidden by Roman law, cf., e.g., *[Paul]. Sent.* 5.23.16) see Ch. 7 n. 7, this volume. For Julian and Mithras see in the first place Gnoli 2009, which on p. 215 approvingly cites Athanassiadi-Fowden 1992, xiv: 'I have over-emphasized [in 1981] Julian's Mithraism and ... I feel that I may have distorted the balance of Julian's religious belief, especially in the imperial years by making him lean too heavily on the cult of Mithra.'

4. RITES FOR THE MOTHER OF THE GODS: Amm. 23.3.7. CERCUSIUM: Amm. 23.5.1. SUPPLIES: Vannesse 2012. AMMIANUS JOINS JULIAN'S ARMY: this can be inferred from the sudden appearance of the first person plural in 23.5.7, where it is said that 'we' reached Zaitha: *profecti exinde* (sc. Cercusium) *Zaithan venimus locum* (this 'we' should be taken in the sense of 'I and the rest of the army'); Fontaine 1977, vol 1, pp. 15–24, esp. 17, Den Boeft et al. 1998, 96. ALONG THE EUPHRATES: Gawlikowski 1990, Lane Fox 1997. OMINOUS INCIDENTS: Amm. 23.5.8 and 23.5.12. Weber 2000, 475: 'In Ammians Darstellung ist der gesamte Perserfeldzug von Vorzeichen unterschiedlichster Art durchsetzt'; cf. also Thelamon 2014.

5. FROM DURA TO CTESIPHON: Den Boeft et al. 2002, xiii–xxiii. CTESIPHON: Austin 1972. JUNE 16, 363: Amm. 24.8.5. JULIAN'S DEATH: n. 2 of the Introduction, this volume.

6. MESSENGER STONED: Zos. 3.34.2, cf. Lib. *Or.* 18.304. LIBANIUS' REACTION: *Ep.* 1424.2, trans. Norman. In Libanius' *Autobiography* he later writes, 'My first impulse was to look for my sword, for life would be harder to bear than any death' (*Or.* 1.135, trans. Norman); cf. further *Ep.* 1422.1–2, 1426.1 and *Or.*17 (*Lament over Julian*). Libanius no doubt was very upset when he heard of Julian's death, but, as Watts 2014, 48–55 argues, 'as time passed and the magnitude of his personal loss sank in, Libanius' response to the death of Julian became ever more dramatic' (p. 49). MUTINY: Amm. 25.10.7. JOVIAN: PLRE I, Iovianus 3; his proclamation as emperor: Amm. 25.5.1–6, with Den Boeft et al., 2005, 169–190. DIVINE HONORS: Lib. *Or.* 18.304, cf. Lib. *Or.* 15.36 (when Julian was still alive: 'At some time or other men will offer sacrifice and prayer to you, and set up altars as they do to Heracles,' trans. Norman, with Nock 1957, 122), Eun. *Fr.* 1 (p. 10, line 97–98 Blockley), Eun. *VS* 7.4.11 (with Becker 2013, 319), Eutr. 10.16.2 *inter divos relatus est*, IK 43.50 (= Conti 2004, no. 45), in which 'das griechische θεός als *divus* aufzufassen ist und die Inschrift somit den einzigen epigraphischen Beleg für die von Libanios bezeugte Verehrung darstellt, die dem nach seinem Tod konsekrierten Kaiser in zahlreichen Städten des Ostens gewidmet wurde' (Bringmann 2008b, 245),

and see Nock 1957, Den Boeft et al. 2005, 114–115, Conti 2009, 124–125; cf. also Ch. 3 n. 7, this volume. LIBANIUS' LAMENT (MONODY): *Or.* 17; for the authors whose works are used by Libanius in composing this *Lament for Julian* see H.-G. Nesselrath 2014, 260–265. JOY IN ANTIOCH: Thdt. *HE* 3.28.1–2, cf. Lib. *Ep.* 1220.2 and *Ep.* 1430.3. MAXIMUS: see Ch. 1 n. 8, this volume. JOY ELSEWHERE: Lib. *Ep.* 1220.2. DAMNATIO MEMORIAE: Julian's name was erased from some inscriptions: CIL 3.7088 (= Conti 2004, no. 28), AE 1990.957 (= Conti 2004, no. 33), SIG³ 906b (= Conti 2004, no. 35), CIL 8.5338 (= Conti 2004, no. 136), ILAlg 1.2100 (= Conti 2004, no. 138), AE 1916.10 (= Conti 2004, no. 170), AE 1987.1075 (= Conti 2004, Incertae no. 15). This has been seen as a form of *damnatio memoriae* by Conti 2009 (p. 79, p. 172) and others, e.g., Ruggeri 1999, 313, 321, but cf. Delmaire 2003, 305: 'on notera que le martelage affecte des empereurs qui n'ont jamais fait l'objet d'une condamnmation officielle, comme Dioclétien, Galère, Julien . . . les chrétiens ont effacé les noms des empereurs persécuteurs (Dioclétien, Maximien, Galère, Daia, Julien),' and Bowersock 2006, 704–705 ('it makes no sense to speak of a *damnatio memoriae* of Julian, but, for reasons of personal interest or ambition, a handful of dedicants who had honored him tried to clear themselves of the taint of association with him,' p. 705). Cf. also Agosti 2015, 231.

7. DIDYMUS: Pall. *H. Laus.* 4.4, Soz. 6.2.6–7, Weber 2000, 481–482. Julian's death was officially announced in Alexandria by the *praefectus Aegypti* Olympus (PLRE I, Olympus 3) on August 19, 363 (*Hist. Aceph.* 4.1); according to Epiphanius in the *Apophtegmata Patrum* (PG 65, 161a–164a), Bishop Athanasius already knew this earlier: 'crows flying around the temple of Serapis in the presence of Athanasius continually cried κρᾶς, κρᾶς; that is in Latin, Athanasius explained, "tomorrow" (*cras*): "tomorrow you shall see the glory of God; just afterwards the death of the emperor Julian was announced,"' trans. Ward; Brown 1982, 85. JULIANUS SABAS: Thdt. *HR* 2.14, *HE* 3.24.1–4. EUGENIUS AND MACARIUS: *Eugen. pass.* 8. BASIL AND MERCURY: Jo. Mal. 13.25, *Chron. Pasch.* s. a. 363; Delehaye 1909, 96 ff.; Baynes 1937, Binon 1937 (Documents), Binon 1937 (Essai), Orlandi 1968, Orlandi and Di Giuseppe Camaioni 1976, Frend 1986, 69–70, Weber 2000, 479–480, Martin 2004, 98–101; Boulhol 2004, 111–115, Teja and Acerbi 2009 (arguing for a Cappadocian origin of the legend), Trovato 2014, 51–273, and the literature cited in n. 3 of the Introduction, this volume; for a similar story: Soz. 6.2.3–5 with Weber 2000, 480–481. Whitby 2000, 206 n. 21 observes, 'long-distance announcements of current events are quite common in miracle collections,' and '[they] usually involve the death of an important personage, e.g. John the Almsgiver (*Life of John* Ch. 46) or the emperor Maurice (Theophylact viii.13.7–14); cf. also Rufus, *Plerophories* 6, 54; *Pratum Spirituale* 57 (Holy Men).' Trovato 2014, 253–254.

8. BASIL BECOMES BISHOP OF CAESAREA: in 370 CE; Campenhausen 1967[4], 93, Rousseau 1994, 2; for Julian's relation with Basil see Elm 2012, 57, 69, 466. *JULIAN ROMANCE*: Nöldeke 1874a and Nöldeke 1874b, Hoffmann 1880 (Syriac text), Gollancz 1928 (English translation), J. W. Drijvers 1999, J. W. Drijvers 2007, and J. W. Drijvers 2011b, Schwartz 2011, Contini 2015, 291–296. GREEK ORIGINAL: Peeters 1921, 78–88, Binon 1937 (Documents), 9–10, Van Esbroeck 1987, 196; otherwise: H. J. W. Drijvers 1994. MERCURY AND JOVIAN: *Julian Romance*, pp. 153–155, 190, 198, 201 Gollancz; cf. Richer 1978, 253–254, Martin 2014a, 318.

9. JULIAN AND EUSEBIUS: *Julian Romance* pp. 10–65 Gollancz; cf. J. W. Drijvers 2007, 6 ff., Schwartz 2011, 571–575.

10. APOLLONIUS AND APOLLONIA: BHL 643, cf. BHL 644 and 645; AASS Febr. II 280–282, nn. 24–33, Amore 1962. APOLLONIA OF ALEXANDRIA: Eus. *HE* 6.41.7, with Bruck 1915 and Gordini and Raggi 1962. APOLLONIUS AND COMMODUS: Eus. *HE* 5.21.2–5 with Brandi 1962.

11. *PASSIO PIMENII*: BHL 6849, 6849a; Delehaye 1936, 259–263 (text), cf. *ibid.* 124–143 (comments), Gordini 1968, Amore 1975, 230–231.

12. MANY THOUSANDS OF CHRISTIANS: *Pass. Pimen.* 2. FLAVIANUS, BENEDICTA, PRISCUS AND PRISCILLIANUS (elsewhere Crispus and Crispinianus): *Pass. Pimen.* 3; Gaiffier 1956, 27 ff., Amore 1964a, 319–320, Stiernon 1965. DAFROSA: *ibid.* 3–4; Amore 1964b, 422–423. DEMETRIA: *ibid.* 3–4; Amore 1964c, 550. BIBIANA (Viviana): *ibid.* 3–4; Donckel 1935 and Donckel 1937, Gaiffier 1956, 27 ff., Gordini and Celletti 1963, Amore 1975, 297–299. JOHANNES AND PAULUS: *ibid.* 3; BHL 3236–3242, Franchi de' Cavalieri 1902 and Franchi de' Cavalieri 1915, Delehaye 1936, 124 ff., Gaiffier 1956, 27 ff., Gaiffier 1957, 43–46, Nulle 1961, 324–327, De Sanctis 1962 and De Sanctis 1965a, Murjanoff 1965, Halkin 1974, Amore 1975, 287–297, Trovato 2014, 241–249. GALLICANUS: BHL 3236–3242; Delehaye 1936, 124 ff., Grégoire and Orgels 1954 and Grégoire and Orgels 1957, Gaiffier 1956, 27 ff., De Sanctis 1965b, Halkin 1974, Mossay and Bundy 1981, Champlin 1982, Rosen 2006, 405–406, Trovato 2014, 245–249. HILARINUS: BHL 3236–3242; Delehaye 1936, 124 ff., De Gaiffier 1948, Amore 1966. HROTSVITHA: Philip 1929, 17–19, Conti and Doria 2005, 17–19, 37–42, 82–88, Rosen 2006, 406. LORENZO DE' MEDICI: Simioni 1914 (text); H.-G. Nesselrath 1992, Murdoch 2003, 209 with n. 13, Pagliara 2010, 19–24. As Curta 1995a, 117 notes, in De' Medici's play *St. Mercury* struck Julian with a sword, not with a lance (for the lance and the sword see nn. 2 and 3 of the Introduction, this volume).

13. MARTINUS: Sulp. Sev. *Mart.* 4., with Burton 2017 ad loc. Barnes 1996, Barnes 2010, 199–228; cf. Trovato 2014, 131–134. VALENTINIAN: Thdt. *HE* 3.16.4. Lenski 2002 against Woods 1995c and Woods 1998. AEMILIANUS: Thdt. *HE*

3.7.5, *Chron. Pasch.* s. a. 363, Hier. *Chron.* s. a. 363, BHG 33; Halkin 1972 and Halkin 1987, Scorza Barcellonna 1995, 58, Atanassov 2012, 338–341 (Atanassov claims that 'recently the last doubts as to the martyrous death of St. Aemilianus have been completely dispersed, thanks to an inscription of the 4th century,' and that 'the newly discovered inscription constitutes an incontestable substantiation of the authenticity of the martyr's death of St. Aemilianus in Durostorum'; in fact, the inscription on an altar for Iuppiter Optimus Maximus, AE 2011.1137, has nothing to do with either Aemilianus or Julian), Trovato 2014, 161–164. CYRIACUS (JUDAS): BHO 233–236, BHG 465, BHL 7023–7025. Drijvers and Drijvers 1997, Trovato 2014, 151–155, Trovato 2018. DOROTHEUS: BHG 2114–2116. Trovato 2014, 135–140. MANUEL, SABEL, ISMAEL: BHG 1023–1024. Trovato 2014, 185–193. TIMOTHEUS: BHG 2460. Trovato 2014, 195–197.

Chapter 17

1. HEAD IN HANDS: Elophius belongs to the more than hundred so-called cephalophorous saints, of whom Dionysius of Paris (alias Saint Denis) is the most famous; Hébert 1913–1914, Saintyves 1929, Delehaye 1934, 135–138, Gessler 1941, Moretus Plantin 1953, Coens 1956, Coens 1963, and Coens 1964.
2. ELOPHIUS' BONES: Widricus, *Vita Gerardi episcopi Tullensis* 5; Hegel 1950. PASSIO SANCTI ELIPHII: BHL 2481, AASS Oct. VII, 16, 812–815. ADAPTATION BY RUPERTUS OF DEUTZ: BHL 2482, PL 170.427–436. EUCHARIUS CUM SUIS: AASS Oct. III, 3, 150–157; IV, 8, 228–233; XII, 27, 223–233.
3. IMPRISONMENT IN GRAND: *Eliph. pass.* 3. CONVERSIONS: *ibid.* 4–5.
4. ALTERCATION: *Eliph. pass.* 6–7. PRAYER GRANTED: *ibid.* 7–8. BURIAL PLACE CHOSEN: *ibid.* 9. ELIPHIUS' DEATH: *ibid.* 10. WALK WITH HEAD IN HANDS: *ibid.* 11. VILLAGE OF SAINT-ÉLOPHE: Bertaux and Valentin 1995, Bertaux 1999.
5. JULIANISATION: Ch. 9 n. 9, this volume.

Chapter 18

1. PRUDENTIUS: *Apoth.* 446–550, with in 454 *perfidus ille Deo, quamvis non perfidus orbi.* Arce 1976, Palla 1998, Klein 2006, Gnilka 2007.
2. LENIN AND MAO: Bowersock 1978, 20. AMMIANUS: 25.4.1 (trans. Hamilton) and passim, cf. Mamert. *Grat.* 21.4, Neri 1984, 4–5, Criscuolo 1996, Den Boeft et al. 2005, 116 ff., Pollmann 2011 and Cacciapaglia 2004.

LIBANIUS: *Or.* 18.281, trans. Norman, adapted, cf. *Or.* 18.121–122 and passim; Casella 2014; for Libanius as an admirer of Euripides see Criscuolo 2014, 234–237.

3. LETTER TO ATARBIUS: Jul. *Ep.* 83, 376c Bidez (= 49 Weis = 37 Wright, whose translation I borrow here and hereafter, with some adaptions). LETTER TO HECEBOLIUS: Jul. *Ep.* 115, 424c (= 40 Wright = 59 Weis). LETTER TO THE CITIZENS OF BOSTRA: Jul. *Ep.* 114, 438b (= 41 Wright = 58 Weis), cf. Soz. 5.15.11–12, Sartre 1985, 105–106, Bringmann 2004, 141–142, Rosen 2006, 306–308; cf. also Jul. *Ep.* 61c, 424a Bidez (= 36 Wright = 55 Weis), cited at the end of Chapter 8, this volume. TOLERANCE: Bouffartigue 1998, Bouffartigue 2004, Bouffartigue 2007, Marcos 2009 ('Julian's ideas about freedom, the voluntary nature of worship and the value of persuasion as the only licit resort in the religious sphere are extraordinary similar to those expressed by Christian apologists during the persecutions,' pp. 200–201, referring to Bouffartigue 2007, 5 ff.); see for a different view Haehling 1994².

4. PAGANS PREFERRED TO CHRISTIANS: Jul. *Ep.* 83, 376c Bidez (= 37 Wright = 49 Weis), trans. Wright. THOUSANDS OF VICTIMS: *Pass. Pimen.* 2.

5. VOLTAIRE (1694–1778): 'Julien' in Voltaire 1786, 182–196; cf. Mervaud 1976, Rosen 2006, 424–425. CAVAFY (1863–1933): 'Julian and the Antiochians,' 'Julian in Nicomedia,' 'Julian Seeing Contempt,' in Cavafy 1992; cf. Rosen 2006, 440–441. IBSEN (1828–1906): *Emperor and Galilean,* Ibsen 1963; cf. Abel 2000, Hoem 2001, Rosen 2006, 438, Faber and Høibraaten 2011. VIDAL (1925–2012): *Julian* (Vidal 1964); cf. Rosen 2006, 454. See in general for Julian's impact on later generations Rosen's excellent ch. 10 (Rosen 2006, 394–462).

BIBLIOGRAPHY

This is not an exhaustive list of scholarship devoted to the emperor Julian. It lists only the publications referred to in the notes.

Abel, D. 'Wisdom! Light! Beauty! A Thematic Analysis of Ibsen's *Emperor and Galilean.*' *Modern Drama* 43 (2000): 78–86.

Acerbi, S. See R. Teja.

Aceto, F. 'Note sull'autenticità dell'*Ep.* 84 di Giuliano imperatore.' *Rivista di Cultura Classica e Medioevale* 50 (2008): 187–206.

Adler, M. 'The Emperor Julian and the Jews.' *Jewish Quarterly Review* 5 (1893): 591–651 (= 'Kaiser Julian und die Juden.' In R. Klein [ed.], *Julian Apostata* [Wege der Forschung 509]. Darmstadt, Germany: 1978, 48–111).

Africa, T. 'Worms and the Death of Kings: A Cautionary Note on Disease and History.' *Classical Antiquity* 1 (1982): 1–17.

Agosti, G. 'Miscellanea epigrafica I. Note letterarie a carmi epigrafici tardoantichi'. *Medioevo Greco* 5 (2005): 1–30.

Agosti, G. '*Paideia* greca e religione in iscrizioni dell'età di Giuliano.' In A. Marcone (ed.), *L'imperatore Giuliano: Realtà storica e rappresentazione* (Studi sul Mondo Antico 3). Milan: 2015, 223–239.

Aigrain, R., and R. Godding. *L'hagiographie: Ses sources—Ses méthodes—Son histoire* (Subsidia Hagiographica 80). Brussels: 2000.

Aja Sánchez, J. R. 'El linchamiento del obispo Jorge y la violencia religiosa tardoromana.' In A. González Blanco, F. J. Fernández Nielo, and J. Remesal Rodríguez (eds.), *Arte, sociedad, economía y religión durante el Bajo Imperio y la Antigüedad Tardía: Homenaje al Professor Dr. D. José Ma. Blázquez Martinez al cumplir 65 años* (Antigüedad y Cristianismo 8). Murcia, Spain: 1991, 111–136.

Aja Sánchez, J. R. 'Gaza, Sozomeno y los mártires cristianos de la época del emperador Juliano.' *Polis* 11 (1999): 7–34.

Aja Sánchez, J. R. 'Obispos y mártires palestinos: El caso de Gaza (s. IV).' *Gerión* 19 (2001): 569–594.

Alberigo, G. 'Concilium Nicaenum I 325.' In G. Alberigo (ed.), *Conciliorum oecumenicorum generaliumque decreta 1: The Oecumenical Councils; From Nicaea I to Nicaea II (325–787).* Turnhout, Belgium: 2006, 1–15.

Aldrete, G. S. 'Hammers, Axes, Bulls, and Blood: Some Practical Aspects of Roman Animal Sacrifice.' *Journal of Roman Studies* 104 (2014): 28–50.

Alföldi, A. 'Some Portraits of Julianus Apostata.' *American Journal of Archaeology* 66 (1972): 403–405 (= 'Einige Porträts des Kaisers Julian Apostata.' In R. Klein [ed.], *Julian Apostata* [Wege der Forschung 509]. Darmstadt, Germany: 1978, 298–304).

Allard, P. *Julien l'Apostat: Flavius Claudius Julianus Apostata*, 3. Paris: 1910³.

Alonso-Núñez, J. M. 'The Emperor Julian's *Misopogon* and the Conflict between Christianity and Paganism.' *Ancient Society* 10 (1979): 311–324.

Alt, K. 'Einige Fragen zu Kaiser Julians Preisrede auf den König Helios.' In N. Almazova et al. (eds.), *Variante Loquella: Alexandro Gavrilov septuagenario.* Saint Petersburg, Russia: 2011, 183–194.

Amerise, M. 'La figura di Costantino nei *Caesares* di Giuliano.' *Rivista Storica dell'Antichità* 31 (2001): 211–219.

Amerise, M. 'La figura di Costantino nei *Caesares* di Giuliano.' *Rivista Storica dell'Antichità:* 32 (2002): 141–149.

Amore, A. 'Apollonia.' In A. Amore et al. (eds.), *Biblioteca Sanctorum* 2, Rome: 1962, 268.

Amore, A. 'Crispo (Crispino), Crispiniano e Benedetta.' In A. Amore et al. (eds.), *Biblioteca Sanctorum* 4. Rome: 1964a, 319–320.

Amore, A. 'Dafrosa.' In A. Amore et al. (eds.), *Biblioteca Sanctorum* 4. Rome: 1964b, 422–423.

Amore, A. 'Demetria.' In A. Amore et al. (eds.), *Biblioteca Sanctorum* 4. Rome: 1964c, 550.

Amore, A. 'Domezio.' In A. Amore et al. (eds.), *Biblioteca Sanctorum* 4. Rome: 1964d, 746.

Amore, A. 'Ilarino.' In A. Amore et al. (eds.), *Biblioteca Sanctorum* 7. Rome: 1966, 712.

Amore, A. *I martiri di Roma.* Rome: 1975.

Ando, C. *Imperial Ideology and Provincial Loyalty in the Roman Empire* (Classics and Contemporary Thought 6). Berkeley: 2000.

Andrei, O. 'Giuliano: Da apostata a l'Apostata (Sul buon uso dell'apostasia).' In A. Marcone (ed.), *L'imperatore Giuliano. Realtà storica e rappresentazione* (Studi sul Mondo Antico 3). Milan: 2015, 252–283.

Andreotti, R. 'L'opera legislativa ed amministrativa dell' imperatore Giuliano.' *Nuova Rivista Storica* 14 (1930): 236–273 (= 'Kaiser Julians Gesetzgebung und Verwaltung.' In R. Klein [ed.], *Julian Apostata* [Wege der Forschung 509]. Darmstadt, Germany: 1978, 130–190).

Angliviel de la Beaumelle, L. 'La torture dans les *Res Gestae* d'Ammien Marcellin.' In M. Cristol et al. (eds.), *Institutions, société et vie politique dans l'empire romain au IVe siècle ap. J.-C.* (Actes de la table ronde autour de l'oeuvre d'André Chastagnol, Paris, 20–21 janvier 1989). Rome: 1992, 91–113.

Arand, T. *Das schmähliche Ende: Der Tod des schlechten Kaisers und seine literarische Gestaltung in der römischen Historiographie* (Prismata 13). Frankfurt: 2001.

Arce, J. J. 'Algunos problemas de la numismática del Emperador Fl. Cl. Iulianus.' *Archivo Español de Arquelogía* 45–47 (1972–1974): 477–496.

Arce, J. J. 'On Festus' Sources for Julian's Persian Expedition.' *Athenaeum* 52 (1974): 340–343.

Arce, J. J. *Estudios sobre las fuentes literarias, epigráficas y numismáticas para la historia del Emperador Fl. Cl. Juliano.* Granada, Spain: 1975a.

Arce, J. J. 'Reconstrucciones de templos paganos en época del emperador Juliano (361–363 d.C.).' *Rivista Storica dell'Antichità* 5 (1975b): 201–215.

Arce, J. J. 'Los versos de Prudencio sobre el emperador Juliano.' *Emerita* 44 (1976): 129–144.

Arce, J. J. *Estudios sobre el emperador Fl. Cl. Juliano (Fuentes literarias: Epigrafía; Numismática)* (Anejos de Archivo Español de Arqueologia 8). Madrid: 1984a.

Arce, J. J. 'La tumba del emperador Juliano.' *Lucentum* 3 (1984b): 181–191.

Arce, J. J. *Funus imperatorum: Los funerales de los emperadores romanos.* Madrid: 1988.

Arina, P. 'La legislazione di Giuliano.' *Atti dell'Accademia di Scienze Morali e Politiche della Società Nazionale di Scienze, Lettere ed Arti di Napoli* 96 (1985): 197–239.

Armstrong, A. H. 'The Way and the Ways: Religious Tolerance and Intolerance in the Fourth Century.' *Vigiliae Christianae* 38 (1984): 1–17.

Arnold, W. H. See M. DiMaio.

Asutay-Effenberger, N., and A. Effenberger. *Die Porphyrsarkophage der oströmischen Kaiser: Versuch einer Bestandserfassung, Zeitbestimmung und Zuordnung.* Wiesbaden, Germany: 2006.

Asmus, R. 'Julians Brief über Pegasius.' *Zeitschrift für Kirchengeschichte* 23 (1902): 479–495.

Asmus, R. 'Vergessene Physiognomonika.' *Philologus* 65 (1906): 410–424.

Asmus, R. 'Die Invektiven des Gregorius von Nazianz im Lichte der Werke des Kaisers Julian.' *Zeitschrift für Kirchengeschichte* 31 (1910): 325–367.

Atanassov, G. 'Christianity along the Lower Danube Limes in the Roman Provinces of *Dacia Ripensis, Moesia Secunda* and *Scythia Minor* (4th–6th C. AD).' In L. Vagalinski, N. Sharankov, and S. Torbatov (eds.), *The Lower Danube Roman Limes (1st–6th C. AD).* Sofia, Bulgaria: 2012, 327–380.

Athanassiadi-Fowden, P. *Julian and Hellenism: An Intellectual Biography.* Oxford: 1981 (repr. 1992 as *Julian, an Intellectual Biography*).

Athanassiadi, P., and M. Frede (eds.). *Pagan Monotheism in Late Antiquity.* Oxford: 1999 (repr. with corrections 2002).

Aubert, R. 'Eupsychius.' In R. Aubert et al. (eds.), *Dictionnaire d'Histoire et de Géographie Ecclésiastiques* 15. Paris: 1963, 1419–1420.

Aubreville, Ph. 'Zur Motivation der tetrarchischen Christenverfolgung.' *Zeitschrift für Antikes Christentum* 13 (2009): 415–429.

Aujoulat, N. 'Eusébie, Hélène et Julien, I: Le témoignage de Julien.' *Byzantion* 53 (1983): 78–103. 'II: Le témoignage des historiens.' *Byzantion* 53 (1983): 421–452.

Austin, N. J. E. 'Julian at Ctesiphon: A Fresh Look at Ammianus' Account.' *Athenaeum* 50 (1972): 301–309.

Austin, N. J. E. 'Autobiography and History: Some Late Roman Historians and Their Veracity.' In B. Croke and A.M. Emmett (eds.), *History and Historians in Late Antiquity.* Sydney, Australia: 1983, 54–65.

Avi-Yonah, M. 'Greek Inscriptions from Ascalon, Jerusalem, Beisān, and Hebron.' *Quarterly of the Department of Antiquities in Palestine* 10 (1944): 160–169.

Azarnoush, M. 'La mort de Julien l'Apostat selon les sources iraniennes.' *Byzantion* 61 (1991): 322–329.

Aziza, C. 'Julien et le Judaïsme.' In R. Braun and J. Richer (eds.), *L'empereur Julien: De l'histoire à la légende (331–1715).* Paris: 1978, 141–158.

Babelon, E. 'L'iconographie monétaire de Julien l'Apostat.' *Revue Numismatique* 7 (1903): 130–163 (repr. in E. Babelon, *Mélanges numismatiques* 4. Paris: 1912, 36–69).

Bagnall, R. S., Al. Cameron, S. R. Schwartz, and K. A. Worp. *Consuls of the Later Roman Empire.* Atlanta: 1987.

Baker-Brian, N., and S. Tougher (eds.). *Emperor and Author: The Writings of Julian the Apostate.* Swansea, UK: 2012.

Baldwin, B. 'The Career of Oribasius.' *Acta Classica* 18 (1975): 85–97 (repr. in B. Baldwin, *Studies on Late Roman and Byzantine History, Literature and Language,* London Studies in Classical Philology 12. Amsterdam: 1984, 157–169).

Baldwin, B. 'The *Caesares* of Julian.' *Klio* 60 (1978): 449–466 (repr. in B. Baldwin, *Studies on Late Roman and Byzantine History, Literature and Language,* London Studies in Classical Philology 12. Amsterdam: 1984, 171–188).

Balty, J. Ch. 'Julien et Apamée: Aspects de la restauration de l'hellénisme et de la politique antichrétienne de l'empereur.' *Dialogues d'Histoire Ancienne* 1 (1974): 267–304.

Banchich, T. M. 'Julian's School Laws: *Cod. Theod.* 13.3.5. and *Ep.* 42.' *Ancient World* 24 (1993): 5–14.

Barceló, P. A. *Roms auswärtige Beziehungen unter der Constantinischen Dynastie (306–363)* (Eichstätter Beiträge 3). Regensburg, Germany: 1981.

Barceló, P. A. 'Caesar Gallus und Constantius II: Ein gescheitertes Experiment?' *Acta Classica* 42 (1999): 23–34.

Barceló, P. A. *Constantius II. und seine Zeit: Die Anfänge des Staatskirchentums*. Stuttgart: 2004.

Barceló, P. A. *Das Römische Reich im religiösen Wandel der Spätantike: Kaiser und Bischöfe im Widerstreit*. Regensburg, Germany: 2013.

Bardill, J. *Constantine, Divine Emperor of the Christian Golden Age*. Cambridge, UK: 2012.

Barnes, T. D. 'Some Persons in the *Historia Augusta'. Phoenix* 26 (1972): 140–182.

Barnes, T. D. 'Imperial Chronology A.D. 337–350.' *Phoenix* 34 (1980): 160–166.

Barnes, T. D., and J. Vanderspoel. 'Julian and Themistius.' *Greek, Roman and Byzantine Studies* 22 (1981): 187–189.

Barnes, T. D. 'Constantine's Prohibition of Pagan Sacrifice.' *American Journal of Philology* 105 (1984): 69–72 (repr. in T. D. Barnes, *From Eusebius to Augustine. Selected Papers 1982–1993* [Variorum Collected Studies Series 438]. Aldershot: 1994 no. IV).

Barnes, T. D. 'Himerius and the Fourth Century.' *Classical Philology* 82 (1987): 206–225 (repr. in T. D. Barnes, *From Eusebius to Augustine. Selected Papers 1982–1993* [Variorum Collected Studies Series 438]. Aldershot: 1994, no. XVI).

Barnes, T. D. 'Christians and Pagans in the Reign of Constantius.' In A. Dihle (ed.), *L'Église et l'empire au IVe siècle* (Fondation Hardt, Entretiens sur l'Antiquité Classique 34). Vandoeuvres and Geneva, Switzerland: 1989, 301–337 (322–337 repr. in T. D. Barnes, *From Eusebius to Augustine. Selected Papers 1982–1993* [Variorum Collected Studies Series 438]. Aldershot: 1994, no. VIII).

Barnes, T. D. 'New Year 363 in Ammianus Marcellinus: Annalistic Technique and Historical Apologetics.' In J. den Boeft, D. den Hengst, and H. C. Teitler (eds.), *Cognitio Gestorum: The Historiographic Art of Ammianus Marcellinus* (Koninklijke Nederlandse Akademie van Wetenschappen. Verhandelingen, Afd. Letterkunde, Nieuwe Reeks 148). Amsterdam: 1992a, 1–8.

Barnes, T. D. 'Hilary of Poitiers on His Exile.' *Vigiliae Christianae* 46 (1992b): 129–140 (repr. in T. D. Barnes, *From Eusebius to Augustine. Selected Papers 1982–1993* [Variorum Collected Studies Series 438]. Aldershot: 1994, no. XVII).

Barnes, T. D. *Athanasius and Constantius: Theology and Politics in the Constantinian Empire*. Cambridge, MA: 1993.

Barnes, T. D. 'The Military Career of Martin of Tours.' *Analecta Bollandiana* 114 (1996): 25–32.

Barnes, T. D. *Ammianus Marcellinus and the Representation of Historical Reality* (Cornell Studies in Classical Philology 56). Ithaca, NY, and London: 1998.

Barnes, T. D. 'The Exile and Recalls of Arius.' *Journal of Theological Studies* 60 (2009): 109–129.

Barnes, T. D. *Early Christian Hagiography and Roman History* (Tria Corda, Jenaer Vorlesungen zu Judentum, Antike und Christentum 5). Tübingen, Germany: 2010 (2016²).

Barnes, T. D. *Constantine: Dynasty, Religion and Power in the Later Roman Empire.* Chichester, UK, and Oxford: 2011.

Barzano, A. 'I cristiani, l'esercito e la guerra.' In M. Sordi (ed.), *L'impero romano-cristiano: Problemi politici, religiosi, culturali* (Cultura & Attualità). Rome: 1991, 77–93.

Basabe, E. 'El cristianismo y los clasicos paganos: Un persecución original de Juliano el Apostata.' *Helmantica* 2 (1951): 385–415.

Batiffol, P. 'Fragmente der Kirchengeschichte des Philostorgius.' *Römische Quartalschrift für christliche Altertumskunde und für Kirchengeschichte* 3 (1889): 252–289.

Bayliss, R. *Provincial Cilicia and the Archaeology of Temple Conversion* (British Archaeological Reports, International Series 1281). Oxford: 2004.

Baynes, N. H. 'Julian the Apostate and Alexander the Great.' In N. H. Baynes, *Byzantine Studies and Other Essays.* London: 1955, 346–347 (= *English Historical Review* 27 [1912] 759–760).

Baynes, N. H. 'The Early Life of Julian the Apostate.' *Journal of Hellenic Studies* 45 (1925): 251–254.

Baynes, N. H. 'The Death of Julian the Apostate in a Christian Legend.' *Journal of Roman Studies* 27 (1937): 22–29 (repr. in N. H. Baynes, *Byzantine Studies and Other Essays.* London: 1955, 271–281).

Becker, M. *Eunapios aus Sardes: Biographien über Philosophen und Sophisten; Einleitung, Übersetzung, Kommentar* (Roma Aeterna 1). Stuttgart: 2013.

Becker, M. *Porphyrios, Contra Christianos: Neue Sammlung der Fragmente, Testimonien und Dubia mit Einleitung, Übersetzung und Anmerkungen* (Texte und Kommentare 52). Berlin: 2016.

Beckwith, C. L. 'The Condemnation and Exile of Hilary of Poitiers at the Synod of Béziers (356 C.E.).' *Journal of Early Christian Studies* 13 (2005): 21–38.

Belayche, N. ' "Partager la table des dieux": L'empereur Julien et les sacrifices.' *Revue de l'Histoire des Religions* 218 (2001): 457–486.

Belayche, N. 'Sacrifice and Theory of Sacrifice during the "Pagan Reaction": Julian the Emperor.' In A. I. Baumgarten (ed.), *Sacrifice in Religious Experience,* Studies in the History of Religions 93. Leiden, The Netherlands, Boston, and Cologne: 2002, 101–126 (= Belayche 2001, trans. F. Lachaud and M. Brain).

Belayche, N. 'Pagan Festivals in Fourth-Century Gaza.' In B. Bitton-Ashkelony and A. Kofsky (eds.), *Christian Gaza in Late Antiquity* (Jerusalem Studies in Religion and Culture 3). Leiden, The Netherlands, 2004: 5–22.

Belayche, N. 'Realia versus *leges*? Les sacrifices de la religion d'état au IVᵉ siècle.' In S. Georgoudi, R. Koch Piettre, and F. Schmidt (eds.), *La cuisine et l'autel: Les sacrifices en questions dans les sociétés de la Méditerranée ancienne* (Bibliothèque de l'École des Hautes Études, Section des Sciences Religieuses 124). Turnhout, Belgium: 2005, 343–370.

Belayche, N., *'Deus deum . . . summorum maximus* (Apuleius): Ritual Expressions of Distinction in the Divine World in the Imperial Period.' In S. Mitchell and P. Van Nuffelen (eds.), *One God: Pagan Monotheism in the Roman Empire.* Cambridge, UK: 2010, 141–166.

Bellinger, A. R., P. Bruun, J. P. C. Kent, and C. H. V. Sutherland. 'Late Roman Gold and Silver Coins at Dumbarton Oaks: Diocletian to Eugenius.' *Dumbarton Oaks Papers* 18 (1964): 161–236.

Benedetti Martig, I. *Studi sulla guerra persiana nell'Orazione funebre per Giuliano di Libanio.* Pubblicazioni della Facoltà di Lettere e Filosofia dell'Università di Pavia, Dipartimento di Scienze dell'Antichità 55. Florence: 1990.

Benoist, S. 'Identité du prince et discours impérial: Le cas de Julien.' *Antiquité Tardive* 17 (2009): 109–117.

Bernardi, J. 'Un réquisitoire: Les invectives contre Julien de Grégoire de Nazianze.' In R. Braun and J. Richer (eds.), *L'empereur Julien: De l'histoire à la légende (331–1715).* Paris: 1978, 89–98.

Bernardi, J. *Grégoire de Nazianze, Discours 4–5, Contre Julien: Introduction, texte critique, traduction et notes* (SC 309). Paris: 1983.

Bertaux, Ch., and J. Valentin. *Soulosse-sous-Saint-Élophe.* Mirecourt, France: 1995.

Bertaux, J.-P. (ed.). *La plaine vosgienne à l'époque gallo-romaine: Soulosse-sous-Saint-Élophe, Liffol-le-Grand, Grand* (Itinéraires du Patrimoine 58). Metz, France: 1999.

Bidez, J. 'L'évolution de la politique de l'empereur Julien en matière religieuse.' *Bulletin de la Classe des Lettres de l'Académie Royale de Belgique* 7 (1914): 406–461.

Bidez, J. 'L'apostasie de Julien.' *Bulletin de l'Association Guillaume Budé*, no. 7 (1925): 9–14.

Bidez, J. *La vie de l'empereur Julien.* Paris: 1930 (cf. J. Bidez, *Julian der Abtrünnige*, Munich: 1940[5]).

Bidez, J., and F. Winkelmann. *Philostorgius Kirchengeschichte, mit dem Leben des Lucian von Antiochien und den Fragmenten eines Arianischen Historiographen* (Die Griechischen Christlichen Schriftsteller der ersten Jahrhunderte). Berlin 1972[2].

Binon, S. *Documents grecs inédits relatifs à S. Mercure de Césarée: Tradition littéraire—Tradition liturgique* (Université de Louvain, Recueil de Travaux Publiés par les Membres des Conférence d'Histoire et de Philologie 2.41). Louvain, Belgium: 1937.

Binon, S. *Essai sur le cycle de Saint Mercure, martyr de Dèce et meurtrier de l'empereur Julien* (Bibliothèque de l'École des Hautes Études, Sciences religieuses 53). Paris: 1937.

Bird, H. W. 'Eutropius: His Life and Career.' *Échos du Monde Classique* 32 (1988): 51–60.

Blanc, C. See M. A. Schatkin.

Blanchetière, F. 'Julien: Philhellène, Philosémite, Antichrétien; L'affaire du Temple de Jérusalem (363).' *Journal of Jewish Studies* 31 (1980): 61–81.

Bleckmann, B. *Die Reichskrise des III. Jahrhunderts in der spätantiken und byzantinischen Geschichtsschreibung: Untersuchungen zu den nachdionischen Quellen der Chronik des Johannes Zonaras* (Quellen und Forschungen zur Antiken Welt 11). Munich: 1992.

Bleckmann, B. 'Gallus, César de l'Orient?' In F. Chausson and É. Wolff (eds.), *Consuetudinis amor: Fragments d'histoire romaine II*ᵉ*–VI*ᵉ *siècles offerts à Jean-Pierre Callu* (Saggi di storia antica 19). Rome: 2003, 45–56.

Bleckmann, B. 'Zu den Motiven der Christenverfolgung des Decius.' In K.-P. Johne, T. Gerhardt, and U. Hartmann (eds.), Deleto paene imperio Romano: *Transformationsprozesse des Römischen Reiches im 3. Jahrhundert und ihre Rezeption in der Neuzeit.* Stuttgart: 2006, 57–71.

Bleckmann, B. 'Vom Tsunami von 365 zum Mimas-Orakel: Ammianus Marcellinus als Zeithistoriker und die spätgriechische Tradition.' In J. den Boeft, J. W. Drijvers, D. den Hengst, and H. C. Teitler (eds.). *Ammianus after Julian: The Reign of Valentinian and Valens in Books 26–31 of the Res Gestae.* (Mnemosyne, Bibliotheca Classica Batava; Monographs on Greek and Roman Language and Literature 289). Leiden, The Netherlands: 2007, 7–31.

Bleckmann, B. 'Einige Vergleiche zwischen Ammian und Philostorg: Gallus, die *imitatio Alexandri* Julians und die Usurpation Prokops.' In D. Meyer (ed.), *Philostorge et l'historiographie de l'Antiquité tardive* (Collegium Beatus Rhenanus 3). Stuttgart: 2011, 79–92.

Bleckmann, B. 'Konstantin und die Kritik des blutigen Opfers.' In G. Bonamente, N. E. Lenski, and R. Lizzi Testa (eds.), *Costantino prima e dopo Costantino = Constantine before and after Constantine* (Atti del Convegno tenuto il 27–30 aprile 2011 a Perugia e Spello; Munera, Studi Storici sulla Tarda Antichità 35). Bari, Italy: 2012, 165–180.

Bleckmann, B. 'Last Pagans, Source Criticism and Historiography of Late Antiquity.' *Millennium* 12 (2015): 103–115.

Bliembach, E. *Libanius, Oratio 18 (Epitaphios: Kommentar (§§ 111–308),* PhD University of Würzburg, Würzburg, Germany: 1976.

Bloch, H. 'Ein neues inschriftliches Zeugnis der letzten Erhebung des Heidentums in Westrom 393/394 n. Chr.' In R. Klein (ed.), *Das frühe Christentum im römischen Staat* (Wege der Forschung 267). Darmstadt, Germany: 1971, 129–186 (translation of 'A New Document of the Last Pagan Revival in the West, 393–394 A.D.' *Harvard Theological Review* 38 [1945]: 199–244).

Blockley, R. C. 'Constantius Gallus and Julian as Caesars of Constantius II.' *Latomus* 31 (1972): 433–468.

Blockley, R. C. 'Festus' Source on Julian's Persian Expedition.' *Classical Philology* 68 (1973): 54–55.

Blockley, R. C. 'Eunapius fr. XIV.7: Julian as an Homeric Hero?' *Liverpool Classical Monthly* 6 (1981): 213–214.

Blum, W. *Curiosi und Regendarii: Untersuchungen zur Geheimen Staatspolizei der Spätantike.* Munich: 1969.

Bolton, C. A. 'The Emperor Julian against "Hissing Christians."' *Harvard Theological Review* 61 (1968): 496–497.

Bonamente, G. 'La biografia di Eutropio "lo storico."' *Annali della Facoltà di Lettere e Filosofia, Università di Macerata* 10 (1977): 159–210.

Bonamente, G. *Giuliano l'Apostata e il 'Breviario' di Eutropio.* Università di Macerata, Pubblicazioni della Facoltà di Lettere e Filosofia 33. Rome: 1986.

Bonamente, G. 'Politica antipagana e sorte dei templi da Costantino a Theodosio II.' In U. Criscuolo and L. De Giovanni (eds.), *Trent'anni di studi sulla Tarda Antichità: bilanci e prospettive* (Atti del Convegno Internazionale Napoli, 21–23 novembre 2007). Naples, Italy: 2009, 25–59.

Bonamente, G. 'Sviluppo e discontinuità nella legislazione antipagana: Da Costantino il Grande ai figli.' In G. Bonamente and R. Lizzi Testa (eds.), *Istituzioni, carismi ed esercizio del potere (IV–VI secolo d.C).* (Atti del convegno svolto a Perugia nel giugno 2008; Munera, Studi Storici sulla Tarda Antichità 31). Bari, Italy: 2010, 61–76.

Borgeaud, Ph. 'Trojan Excursions: A Recurrent Ritual, from Xerxes to Julian.' *History of Religions* 49 (2009–2010): 339–353.

Borries, E. von. 'Iulianos 26/Iulianos (Apostata).' *RE* 10 (1917): 26–91.

Bouffartigue, J. 'Julien ou l'hellénisme décomposé.' In S. Said (ed.), *ΕΛΛΗΝΙΣΜΟΣ: Quelques jalons pour une histoire de l'identité Grecque* (Actes du Colloque de Strasbourg 25–27 octobre 1989; Université des Sciences Humaines de Strasbourg, Travaux du Centre de Recherche sur le Proche-Orient et la Grèce Antiques 11). Leiden, The Netherlands: 1991, 251–266.

Bouffartigue, J. *L'Empereur Julien et la culture de son temps* (Collection des Études Augustiniennes, Série Antiquité 133). Paris: 1992.

Bouffartigue, J. 'Le cynisme dans le cursus philosophique au IVᵉ siècle: Le témoignage de l'Empereur Julien.' In M.-O. Goulet-Cazé and R. Goulet (eds.), *Le cynisme ancien et ses prolongements* (Actes du Colloque International du CNRS, Paris, 22–25 juillet 1991). Paris: 1993, 339–358.

Bouffartigue, J. 'Du prétendu parti païen au prétendu fléau de Dieu: Observations sur l'action antichrétienne de l'empereur Julien.' In *Giuliano imperatore: Le sue idee, i suoi amici, i suoi avversari* (Atti del Convegno Internazionale di Studi, Lecce 10–12 dicembre 1998). *Rudiae* 10 (1998 [2000]): 59–90.

Bouffartigue, J. 'Philosophie et anti-christianisme chez l'empereur Julien.' In M. Narcy and E. Rebillard (eds.), *Hellénisme et christianisme* (Mythes, Imaginaires, Religions 1). Villeneuve d'Ascq, France: 2004, 111–131.

Bouffartigue, J. 'L'authenticité de la *Lettre* 84 de l'empereur Julien.' *Revue de Philologie, de Littérature et d'Histoire Anciennes* 79 (2005): 231–242.

Bouffartigue, J. 'Malalas et l'histoire de l'empereur Julien.' In S. Augusta-Boularot, J. Beaucamp, A.-M. Bernardi, and E. Caire (eds.), *Recherches sur la Chronique de Jean Malalas* II (Centre de Recherche d'Histoire et Civilisation de Byzance, Monographies 24). Paris: 2006a, 137–152.

Bouffartigue, J. 'La lettre de Julien à Thémistios: Histoire d'une fausse manoeuvre et d'un désaccord essentiel.' In Á. González Gálvez and P.-L. Malosse (eds.), *Mélanges A. F. Norman* (Topoi: Orient-Occident, Supplément 7). Paris: 2006b, 113–118.

Bouffartigue, J. 'L'empereur Julien était-il intolérant?' *Revue des Études Augustiniennes et Patristiques* 57 (2007): 1–14.

Bouffartigue, J. 'Porphyre et Julien contre les chrétiens: Intentions, motifs et méthodes de leurs écrits.' In S. Morlet (ed.), *Le traité de Porphyre contre les chrétiens: Un siècle de recherches, nouvelles questions* (Actes du colloque international organisé les 8 et 9 septembre 2009 à l'Université de Paris IV-Sorbonne). Paris 2011: 407–429.

Boulhol, P. 'La geste des saints et l'histoire du monde: À propos des sources hagiographiques de Malalas.' In J. Beaucamp et al. (eds.), *Recherches sur la Chronique de Jean Malalas I* (Actes du Colloque 'La Chronique de Jean Malalas [VIe s. è. Chr.]: Genèse et Transmission,' organisé les 21 et 22 mars 2003 à Aix-en-Provence [Maison Méditerranéenne des Sciences de l'Homme] par l'UMR 6125 'Textes et Documents de la Méditerranée Antique et Médiévale' [Université de Provence-CNRS] (Monographies, Centre de Recherche d'Histoire et Civilisation de Byzance 15). Paris: 2004, 103–116.

Boulnois, M.-O. 'Dieu peut-il être envieux ou jaloux? Un débat sur les attributs divins entre l'empereur Julien et Cyrille d'Alexandrie.' In D. Auger and É. Wolff (eds.), *Culture classique et christianisme: Mélanges offerts à Jean Bouffartigue* (Textes, Histoire et Monuments de l'Antiquité au Moyen Age). Paris: 2008, 11–25.

Boulnois, M.-O. 'Le *Contre les Galiléens* de l'empereur Julien répond-il au *Contre Celse* d'Origène?' In E. Amato (ed.), *ΕΝ ΚΑΛΟΙΣ ΚΟΙΝΟΠΡΑΓΙΑ: Hommages à la mémoire de Pierre-Louis Malosse et Jean Bouffartigue* (Revue des Études Tardo-antiques [RET], Supplément 3). [Nantes, France]: 2014, 103–128.

Boulnois, M.-O. et al., *Cyrille d'Alexandrie, Contre Julien* (vol. 2), *Livres III–V* (SC 582). Paris: 2016.

Bowersock, G. W. 'Gibbon and Julian.' In P. Ducrey (ed.), *Gibbon et Rome à la lumière de l'historiographie moderne*. Université de Lausanne, Publications de la Faculté des Lettres 22. Geneva, Switzerland: 1977, 191–213 (repr. in G. W. Bowersock, *Selected Papers on Late Antiquity* [Munera 16]. Bari, Italy: 2000, 7–27).

Bowersock, G. W. *Julian the Apostate*. London: 1978.

Bowersock, G. W. 'The Emperor Julian on his Predecessors.' *Yale Classical Studies* 27 (1982): 159–172(repr. in G. W. Bowersock, *Selected Papers on Late Antiquity* [Munera 16]. Bari, Italy: 2000, 29–41).

Bowersock, G. W. *Hellenism in Late Antiquity* (Jerome Lectures 18). Ann Arbor, MI: 1990.

Bowersock, G. W. *Martyrdom and Rome* (The Wiles Lectures given at the Queen's University of Belfast). Cambridge, UK, and New York: 1995.

Bowersock, G. W. 'The Epigraphy of the Emperor Julian.' *Journal of Roman Archaeology* 19 (2006): 703–705.

Bradbury, S. 'Constantine and the Problem of Anti-Pagan Legislation in the Fourth Century.' *Classical Philology* 89 (1994): 120–139.

Bradbury, S. 'Julian's Pagan Revival and the Decline of Blood Sacrifice.' *Phoenix* 49 (1995): 331–356.

Bradbury, S. 'A Sophistic Prefect. Anatolius of Berytus in the Letters of Libanius.' *Classical Philology* 95 (2000): 172–186.

Bradbury, S. *Selected Letters of Libanius from the Age of Constantius and Julian* (Translated Texts for Historians 41). Liverpool, UK: 2004.

Brandi, M. V. 'Apollonio.' In A. Amore et al. (eds.), *Biblioteca Sanctorum* 2. Rome: 1962, 276–277.

Brandt, A. *Moralische Werte in den Res gestae des Ammianus Marcellinus* (Hypomnemata 122). Göttingen, Germany: 1999.

Bransbourg, G. 'Julien, l'*immunitas Christi*, les dieux et les cites.' *Antiquité Tardive* 17 (2009): 151–158.

Brauch, Th. L. 'Themistius and the Emperor Julian.' *Byzantion* 63 (1993): 79–115.

Braun, R. 'Julien et le christianisme.' In R. Braun and J. Richer (eds.), *L'empereur Julien: De l'histoire à la légende (331–1715)*. Paris: 1978, 159–188.

Braun, R., and J. Richer (eds.). *L'empereur Julien. De l'histoire à la légende (331–1715)*. Paris: 1978.

Braun, R. See also J. Richer.

Bremmer, J. N. 'Atheism in Antiquity.' In M. Martin (ed.), *The Cambridge Companion to Atheism*. Cambridge, UK: 2007, 11–26.

Bremmer, J. N. *The Rise of Christianity through the Eyes of Gibbon, Harnack and Rodney Stark* (A Valedictory Lecture on the Occasion of His Retirement from the Chair of Religious Studies, in the Faculty of Theology and Religious Studies, Delivered in Abbreviated Form before the University of Groningen on 29 January 2010). Groningen, The Netherlands: 2010.

Bremmer, J. N. 'Early Christian Human Sacrifice between Facta and Fiction.' In À. A. Nagy and F. Prescendi (eds.), *Sacrifices humains: Dossiers, discours, comparaisons* (Actes du colloque tenu à l'Université de Genève, 19–20 mai 2011; Bibliothèque de l'École des Hautes Études, Sciences Religieuses 160). Turnhout, Belgium: 2013, 165–176.

Bremmer, J. N. *Initiation into the Mysteries of the Ancient World* (Münchner Vorlesungen zu Antiken Welten 1). Berlin: 2014.

Brendel, R. *Kaiser Julians Gesetzgebungswerk und Reichsverwaltung* (Studien zur Geschichtsforschung des Altertums 32), Hamburg, Germany: 2017.

Brendel, R. 'Die Münzprägung Kaiser Julians in der neueren Forschung', *Jahrbuch für Numismatik und Geldgeschichte* 66 (2016): 241–266.

Brennecke, H. C. *Studien zur Geschichte der Homöer: Der Osten bis zum Ende der homöischen Reichskirche* (Beiträge zur historischen Theologie 73). Tübingen, Germany: 1988.

Brennecke, H. C. 'Nicäa I. Ökumenische Synode von 325.' *Theologische Realenzyklopädie* 24 (1994): 429–441.

Brennecke, H. C. 'Christliche Quellen des Ammianus Marcellinus?'. *Zeitschrift für Antikes Christentum* 1 (1997): 226–250.

Brennecke, H. C., U. Heil, A. von Stockhausen, and A. Wintjes (eds.). *Athanasius Werke*, III.1: *Dokumente zur Geschichte des Arianischen Streites*; 3. Lieferung, Bis zur Ekthesis Makrostichos. Berlin and New York: 2007.

Brennecke, H. C. 'Introduction: Framing the Historical and Theological Problems.' In G. M. Berndt and R. Steinacher (eds.), *Arianism: Roman Heresy and Barbarian Creed.* Farnham, UK, and Burlington, VT: 2014a, 1–19.

Brennecke, H. C. *'Arianismus': Inszenierungen eines Konstrukts* (Erlanger Universitätsreden 83/2014, 3. Folge). Erlangen, Germany: 2014b.

Bringmann, K. *Kaiser Julian* (Gestalten der Antike). Darmstadt, Germany: 2004.

Bringmann, K. 'Julian, Kaiser und Philosoph.' In C. Schäfer (ed.), *Kaiser Julian 'Apostata' und die philosophische Reaktion gegen das Christentum* (Millennium Studies 21). Berlin and New York: 2008a, 87–104.

Bringmann, K. 'Review of S. Conti, *Die Inschriften Kaiser Julians* (2004).' *Klio* 90 (2008b): 244–245.

Bringmann, K. 'Kaiser Julian auf der Reise durch Kleinasien. Der Reformator des Heidentums wird Zeuge einer sterbenden Religion.' In W. Ameling (ed.), *Die Christianisierung Kleinasiens in der Spätantike* (Asia Minor Studien 87). Bonn, Germany: 2017, 21–32.

Brinkerhoff, D. M. *A Collection of Sculpture in Classical and Early Christian Antioch.* New York: 1970.

Brock, S. P. 'The Rebuilding of the Temple under Julian: A New Source.' *Palestine Exploration Quarterly* 108 (1976): 103–107.

Brock, S. P. 'A Letter Attributed to Cyril of Jerusalem on the Rebuilding of the Temple.' *Bulletin of the School of Oriental and African Studies* 40 (1977): 267–286 (repr. in S. P. Brock, *Syriac Perspectives on Late Antiquity* [Variorum Collected Studies Series 199]. London: 1984, no. X).

Brodka, D. *Ammianus Marcellinus: Studien zum Geschichtsdenken im vierten Jahrhundert n. Chr.* (Electrum 17). Cracow, Poland: 2009.

Brok, M. F. A. *De Perzische expeditie van keizer Julianus volgens Ammianus Marcellinus*. Diss. Leiden University. Groningen, The Netherlands: 1959.

Brown, P. *The Cult of the Saints: Its Rise and Function in Latin Christianity* (Haskell Lectures on History of Religions, New Series 2). Chicago: 1981 (enlarged ed. 2015).

Brown, P. 'The Last Pagan Emperor: Robert Browning's *The Emperor Julian*.' In P. Brown, *Society and the Holy in Late Antiquity*. Berkeley and Los Angeles 1982: 83–102 (originally in *The Times Literary Supplement* of 8 April 1977).

Brown, P. *Power and Persuasion in Late Antiquity: Towards a Christian Empire* (The Curti Lectures. The University of Wisconsin-Madison 1988). Madison: 1992.

Browning, R. *The Emperor Julian*. Berkeley and Los Angeles: 1976.

Bruck, W. *Das Martyrium der heiligen Apollonia und seine Darstellung in der bildenden Kunst* (Kulturgeschichte der Zahnheilkunde in Einzeldarstellungen 2). Berlin: 1915.

Bruhl, A. 'Le souvenir d'Alexandre et les Romains.' *Mélanges d'Archéologie et d'Histoire de l'École Française de Rome* 47 (1930): 202–221.

Bruun, P. *The Roman Imperial Coinage, VII, Constantine and Licinius, A.D. 313–337*. London: 1984².

Buck, D. F. 'Some Distortions in Eunapius' Account of Julian the Apostate.' *Ancient History Bulletin* 4.5 (1990): 113–115.

Buck, D. F. 'Eunapius on Julian's Acclamation as *Augustus*.' *Ancient History Bulletin* 7.2 (1993): 73–80.

Buck, D. F. 'Socrates Scholasticus on Julian the Apostate.' *Byzantion* 73 (2003): 301–318.

Buck, D. F. 'Sozomen on Julian the Apostate.' *Byzantion* 76 (2006): 53–73.

Buenacasa Pérez, C. 'La persecución del emperador Juliano a debate: Los cristianos en la política del último emperador pagano (361–363).' *Cristianesimo nella Storia* 21 (2000): 509–529.

Bundy, D. D. 'The Acts of Saint Gallicanus: A Study of the Structural Relations.' *Byzantion* 57 (1987): 12–31.

Bundy, D. D. See also J. Mossay.

Burchi, P. 'Eupsichio.' In A. Amore et al. (eds.), *Biblioteca Sanctorum* 5. Rome: 1965, 237–238.

Burgess, R. W. 'Eutropius *v.c. magister memoriae*?' *Classical Philology* 96 (2001): 76–81 (= R. W. Burgess, *Chronicles, Consuls, and Coins*. Farnham, UK: 2011, No. VIII).

Burgess, R. W. 'The *Passio S. Artemii*, Philostorgius, and the Dates of the Invention and Translations of the Relics of Sts Andrew and Luke.' *Analecta Bollandiana* 121 (2003): 5–36 (= R. W. Burgess, *Chronicles, Consuls, and Coins*. Farnham, UK: 2011, No. XI).

Burgess, R. W. 'The Summer of Blood. The "Great Massacre" of 337 and the Promotion of the Sons of Constantine.' *Dumbarton Oaks Papers* 62 (2008): 5–51 (= R. W. Burgess, *Chronicles, Consuls, and Coins*. Farnham, UK: 2011, No. X).

Burguière, P., *Cyrille d'Alexandrie, Contre Julien* (vol. 1), *Livres I–II (SC 322)*, Paris: 1985.

Burton, Ph. *Sulpicius Severus' Vita Martini*. Oxford: 2017.

Busine, A. 'Julien et les martyrs d'Antioche. L'exemple du *dux* Artemius.' In S. Ratti (ed.), *Une antiquité tardive noire ou heureuse?* (Actes du colloque international de Besançon, 12 et 13 novembre 2014). Besançon, France: 2015, 119–135.

Busine, A. 'Basil and Basilissa at Ancyra. Local Legends, Hagiography, and Cult'. *Greek, Roman and Byzantine Studies* 59 (2019): 262–286.

Büttner-Wobst, Th. 'Der Tod des Kaisers Julian: Eine Quellenstudie.' *Philologus* 51 (1892): 561–580 (repr. in R. Klein [ed.], *Julian Apostata* [Wege der Forschung 509]. Darmstadt, Germany: 1978, 24–47).

Cabouret, B. 'Libanius' *Letters*.' In L. Van Hoof (ed.), *Libanius: A Critical Introduction*. Cambridge, UK: 2014, 144–159.

Cacciapaglia, A. 'Le *virtutes* di Giuliano imperatore nella testimonianza dei contemporanei.' *Annali della Facoltà di Lettere e Filosofia della Università di Bari* 47 (2004): 111–128.

Caltabiano, M. 'La propaganda di Giuliano nella "Lettera agli Ateniesi."' In M. Sordi (ed.), *Propaganda e persuasione occulta nell'Antichità* (Pubblicazioni della Università Cattolica del Sacro Cuore, Contributi dell'Istituto di Storia Antica 2). Milan: 1974, 123–138.

Caltabiano, M. 'Il comportamento di Giuliano in Gallia verso i suoi funzionari.' *Acme* 32 (1979): 417–442.

Caltabiano, M. 'L'assassinio di Giorgio di Cappadocia (Alessandria, 361 d. C.).' *Quaderni Catanesi di Studi Classici e Medievali* 7 (1985): 17–59.

Caltabiano, M. *L'Epistolario di Giuliano Imperatore: Saggio storico, traduzione, note e testo in appendice* (Koinonia: Collana di Studi e Testi 14). Naples, Italy: 1991.

Caltabiano, M. 'L'imperatore Giuliano negli autori Latini Cristiani del IV secolo.' In *Cristianesimo Latino e cultura Greca sino al sec. IV* (XXI Incontro di studiosi dell'antichità cristiana, Roma, 7–9 maggio 1992; Studia Ephemeridis Augustinianum 42). Rome: 1993, 101–116.

Caltabiano, M. 'Giuliano imperatore nelle *Res Gestae* di Ammiano Marcellino: Tra panegirico e storia.' In *Giuliano imperatore: Le sue idee, i suoi amici, i suoi avversari* (Atti del Convegno Internazionale di Studi, Lecce 10–12 dicembre 1998). *Rudiae* 10 (1998 [2000]): 335–355.

Caltabiano, M. 'La comunità degli Elleni: Cultura e potere alla corte dell'imperatore Giuliano.' *Antiquité Tardive* 17 (2009): 137–149.

Caltabiano, M. 'Giuliano l'Apostata e Costantino. Rottura o continuità?.' In R. Macchioro (ed.), *Costantino a Milano. L'editto e la sua storia (313–2013)* (Fonti e Studi 28). Milan: 2017, 151–164.

Cameron, Al. 'Julian and Hellenism.' *Ancient World* 24.1 (1993): 25–29.

Cameron, Al. *The Last Pagans of Rome*. Oxford and New York: 2011.

Cameron, Al. See also R. S. Bagnall.

Cameron, Av. 'Christian Conversion in Late Antiquity: Some Issues.' In A. Papaconstantinou, N. McLynn, and D. L. Schwartz (eds.), *Conversion in Late Antiquity: Christianity, Islam, and Beyond* (Papers from the Andrew W. Mellon Foundation Sawyer Seminar, University of Oxford, 2009–2010). Farnham, UK, and Burlington, VT: 2015, 3–21.

Cameron, Av., and J. Herrin. *Constantinople in the Early Eighth Century: The Parastaseis Syntomoi Chronikai; Introduction, Translation and Commentary* (Columbia Studies in the Classical Tradition 10). Leiden, The Netherlands: 1984.

Cameron, Av., and S. G. Hall. *Eusebius, Life of Constantine: Introduction, Translation, and Commentary*. Oxford: 1999.

Campenhausen, H. von. *Griechische Kirchenväter*. Stuttgart: 1967⁴.

Canetti, L. *Frammenti di eternità: Corpi e reliquie tra Antichità e Medioevo* (Sacro/Santo, Nuova Serie 6). Rome: 2002.

Capone, A. 'L'imperatore Giuliano negli scritti di Giovanni Crisostomo.' In *Giovanni Crisostomo: Oriente e Occidente tra IV e V secolo* (XXXIII Incontro di Studiosi dell'Antichità Cristiana, Roma, 6–8 maggio 2004; Studia Ephemeridis Augustinianum 93/2). Rome: 2005, 821–831.

Caputo, G. 'Graffiti figurati al teatro di Leptis Magna: Dea Roma e busto di Giuliano l'Apostata.' *Dionisio* 45 (1971–1974): 193–200.

Caraffa, F., and A. M. Raggi. 'Babila.' In A. Amore et al. (eds.), *Biblioteca Sanctorum* 2. Rome: 1962, 679–681.

Carrié, J.-M. 'Julien législateur: Un mélange des genres?' *Antiquité Tardive* 17 (2009): 175–184.

Carruthers, M. *The Craft of Thought: Meditation, Rhetoric, and the Making of Images, 400–1200* (Cambridge Studies in Medieval Literature 34). Cambridge, UK: 1998.

Carter, R. E. 'The Chronology of Saint John Chrysostom's Early Life.' *Traditio* 18 (1962): 357–364.

Carvalho, M. M. de. 'Um caso político-cultural na antiguidade tardia: O imperador Juliano e seu conceito de educação.' *Maringá* 32 (2010): 27–39.

Casella, M. 'Le "colpe" della cultura pagana: Riflessioni sull' *Epistola* 89 b di Giuliano.' *Koinonia* 26–27 (2002–2003): 131–143.

Casella, M. 'Julien: Les années parisiennes.' *Antiquité Tardive* 17 (2009): 91–107.

Casella, M. 'Elogio delle virtù nell'immagine politica di Giuliano in Libanio.' In E. Amato (ed.), *EN ΚΑΛΟΙΣ ΚΟΙΝΟΠΡΑΓΙΑ: Hommages à la mémoire de Pierre-Louis Malosse et Jean Bouffartigue* (*Revue des Études Tardo-antiques* [*RET*], Supplément 3). [Nantes, France]: 2014, 169–195.

Cavafy, C. P. *Collected Poems*. Revised ed. Translated by E. Keeley and Ph. Sherrard, edited by G. Savidis. Princeton, NJ: 1992.

Cazzaniga, I. 'Eco di riti e culti orientali nelle torture di alcuni martiri giulianei di Siria e i frammenti papiracei testé editi del romanzo "Phoenikiká" di Lollianos.' *Vetera Christianorum* 10 (1973): 305–318.

Cecconi, G. A. 'Lineamenti di storia del consolato tardoantico.' In M. David (ed.), *Eburnea diptycha: I dittici d'avorio tra Antichità e Medioevo* (Munera 26). Bari, Italy: 2007, 109–127.

Cecconi, G. A. 'Giuliano, la scuola, i cristiani: Note sul dibattito recente.' In A. Marcone (ed.), *L'imperatore Giuliano: Realtà storica e rappresentazione* (Studi sul Mondo Antico 3). Milan: 2015, 204–222.

Célérier, P. *L'ombre de l'empereur Julien: Le destin des écrits de Julien chez les auteurs païens et chrétiens du IVe au VIe siècle.* Paris: 2013.

Celletti, M.C. See G. D. Gordini.

Cerri, A. 'Il viaggio di Giuliano Cesare nelle Gallie (Dicembre 355).' *Rendiconti/ Istituto Lombardo, Accademia di Scienze e Lettere, Classe di Lettere, Scienze Morali e Storiche* 106 (1972): 567–578.

Chalmers, W. R. 'Eunapius, Ammianus Marcellinus, and Zosimus on Julian's Persian Expedition.' *Classical Quarterly* 10 (1960): 152–160 (= 'Julians Perserzug bei Eunapius, Ammianus Marcellinus und Zosimus.' In R. Klein [ed.], *Julian Apostata* [Wege der Forschung 509]. Darmstadt, Germany: 1978, 270–284).

Champlin, E. 'Saint Gallicanus (consul 317).' *Phoenix* 36 (1982): 71–76.

Chaniotis, A. 'Plutarchos, praeses insularum (Prosopography of the Later Roman Empire I Plutarchus 4).' *Zeitschrift für Papyrologie und Epigraphik* 68 (1987): 227–231.

Chantraine, H. 'Die Erhebung des Licinius zum *Augustus*.' *Hermes* 110 (1982): 477–487.

Chantraine, H. 'Konstantinopel—vom Zweiten Rom zum Neuen Rom.' *Geschichte in Wissenschaft und Unterricht* 43 (1992): 3–15.

Chauvot, A. 'Ammien Marcellin, les clarissimes et la torture au IVe siècle.' In *Romanité et cité chrétienne: Permanences et mutations, intégration et exclusion du Ier au Ve siècle; Mélanges en l'honneur d'Yvette Duval.* Paris: 2000, 65–76.

Chesnut, G. F. *The First Christian Histories: Eusebius, Socrates, Sozomen, Theodoret and Evagrius.* Macon, GA: 1986[2].

Chiaradonna, R. 'La *Lettera a Temistio* di Giuliano Imperatore e il dibatto filosofico nel IV secolo.' In A. Marcone (ed.), *L'imperatore Giuliano: Realtà storica e rappresentazione* (Studi sul Mondo Antico 3). Milan: 2015, 149–171.

Christ, W. von, W. Schmid, and O. Stählin. *Geschichte der griechischen Literatur, II, Die nachklassische Periode der griechischen Literatur, zweite Hälfte, Von 100 bis 530 nach Christus* (Handbuch der Altertumswissenschaft 7.2.2). Munich: 1924[6] (repr. 1961).

Chuvin, P. *Chronique des derniers païens: La disparition du paganisme dans l'Empire romain, du règne de Constantin à celui de Justinien.* Paris: 1991.

Clark, G. 'Translating Relics: Victricius of Rouen and Fourth-Century Debate.' *Early Medieval Europe* 10 (2001): 161–176.

Clauss, M. *Der Kaiser und sein wahrer Gott: Der spätantike Streit um die Natur Christi.* Darmstadt, Germany: 2010.

Coens, M. 'Aux origines de la céphalophorie: Un fragment retrouvé d'une ancienne passion de S. Just, martyr de Beauvais.' *Analecta Bollandiana* 74 (1956): 86–114.

Coens, M. 'Nouvelles recherches sur un thème hagiographique: La céphalophorie.' In M. Coens, *Recueil d'études Bollandiennes* (Subsidia Hagiographica 37). Brussels: 1963, 9–31.

Coens, M. 'La plus ancienne passion de Saint Laurian, martyr céphalophore en Berry.' *Analecta Bollandiana* 82 (1964): 57–86.

Cohen, L. 'Sur l'iconographie de Julien.' In R. Braun and J. Richer (eds.), *L'empereur Julien: De l'histoire à la légende (331–1715).* Paris: 1978, 213–227.

Colpe, C. '*Civilitas Graeca* und *Eupistia Hellenike:* Kennworte zur Religonspolitik des Kaisers Julian.' In G. Schöllgen and C. Scholten (eds.), *Stimuli: Exegese und ihre Hermeneutik in Antike und Christentum; Festschrift für Ernst Dassmann* (Jahrbuch für Antike und Christentum, Ergänzungsband 23). Münster, Germany: 1996, 308–328.

Compernass, J. 'Zwei Schriften des Arethas von Kaisareia gegen die Vertauschung der Bischofssitze.' In S. G. Mercati (ed.), *Studi Bizantini e Neoellenici* 4. Rome: 1935, 87–125.

Conduché, D. 'Ammien Marcellin et la mort de Julien.' *Latomus* 24 (1965): 359–380 (= 'Ammianus Marcellinus und der Tod Julians.' In R. Klein [ed.], *Julian Apostata* [Wege der Forschung 509]. Darmstadt, Germany: 1978, 24–47).

Conti, S. *Die Inschriften Kaiser Julians* (Altertumswissenschaftliches Kolloquium. Interdisziplinäre Studien zur Antike und zu ihrem Nachleben 10). Stuttgart: 2004.

Conti, S., and A. Doria. *Giuliano l'Apostata: Un imperatore romano nella letteratura tedesca del Medioevo* (Quaderni di Hesperides, Serie Testi 6). Trieste, Italy: 2005.

Conti, S. 'Un aspetto della propaganda imperiale tardo-antica: La titolatura di Giuliano nelle fonti letterarie ed epigrafiche.' In U. Criscuolo (ed.), *Forme della cultura nella Tarda Antichità*, II (Atti del VI Convegno dell'Associazione di Studi Tardoantichi, Napoli e S. Maria Capua Vetere, 29 settembre–2 ottobre 2003). *Koinonia* 30–31 (2006–2007): 29–44.

Conti, S. 'Da eroe a dio: La concezione teocratica del potere in Giuliano.' *Antiquité Tardive* 17 (2009): 119–126.

Contini, R. 'Ancora su Giuliano Imperatore nella letteratura siriaca.' In A. Marcone (ed.), *L'imperatore Giuliano: Realtà storica e rappresentazione* (Studi sul Mondo Antico 3). Milan: 2015, 284–305.

Conton, R. 'Il rovescio con il toro nei bronzi di Giuliano.' *Rivista Italiana di Numismatica e Scienze Affini* 105 (2004): 135–147.

Cook, J. G. *The Interpretation of the New Testament in Greco-Roman Paganism* (Studien und Texte zu Antike und Christentum 3). Tübingen, Germany: 2000.

Coppola, G. *La politica religiosa di Giuliano l'Apostata* (Introduzione e note a cura di A. Tedeschi, con una Nota di L. Canfora). Bari, Italy: 2007.

Coquin, R.-G., and E. Lucchesi. 'Une version Copte de la passion de saint Eusignios.' *Analecta Bollandiana* 100 (1982): 185–208.

Crawford, M. R. *Cyril of Alexandria's Trinitarian Theology of Scripture.* Oxford: 2014.

Cribiore, R. 'Defending Julian: Libanius and *Or.* 37.' In O. Lagacherie and P.-L. Malosse (eds.), *Libanios, le premier humaniste: Études en hommage à Bernard Schouler.* Alessandria, Italy: 2011, 167–175.

Crisafulli, V. S., and J. W. Nesbitt. *The Miracles of St. Artemios: A Collection of Miracle Stories by an Anonymous Author of Seventh-century Byzantium* (The Medieval Mediterranean 13). Leiden, The Netherlands, and New York: 1997.

Criscuolo, U. 'Libanio e Giuliano.' *Vichiana* 11 (1982): 70–87.

Criscuolo, U. 'Sull'epistola di Giuliano imperatore al filosofo Temistio.' *Koinonia* 7 (1983): 89–111.

Criscuolo, U. 'Giuliano e l'ellenismo: Conservazione e riforma.' *Orpheus* 7 (1986): 272–292.

Criscuolo, U. 'Gregorio di Nazianzo e Giuliano.' In U. Criscuolo (ed.), *Talariskos: Studi Graeca Antonio Garzya sexagenario a discipulis oblata.* Naples, Italy: 1987, 165–208.

Criscuolo, U. 'Virtutes Iuliani.' In G. Germano (ed.), *Classicità, Medioevo e Umanesimo: Studi in onore di Salvatore Monti* (Pubblicazioni del Dipartimento di Filologia Classica dell'Università degli Studi di Napoli 13). Naples, Italy: 1996, 259–274.

Criscuolo, U. 'Giuliano nell'epitafio di Libanio.' In *Giuliano imperatore: Le sue idee, i suoi amici, i suoi avversari* (Atti del Convegno Internazionale di Studi, Lecce 10–12 dicembre 1998). *Rudiae* 10 (1998 [2000]): 267–291.

Criscuolo, U. 'La religione di Giuliano.' *Mediterraneo Antico* 4 (2001): 365–388.

Criscuolo, U. 'Libanios et les philosophes de Julien: Le cas de Maxime d'Ephèse.' In A. González-Gálvez and P.-L. Malosse (eds.), *Mélanges A. F. Norman* (Topoi: Orient-Occident, Supplément 7). Lyons, France 2006: 103–112.

Criscuolo, U. 'Mimesi tragica in Libanio.' In E. Amato (ed.), *ΕΝ ΚΑΛΟΙΣ ΚΟΙΝΟΠΡΑΓΙΑ: Hommages à la mémoire de Pierre-Louis Malosse et Jean Bouffartigue* (Revue des Études Tardo-antiques [RET], Supplément 3). [Nantes, France]: 2014, 229–242.

Csízy, K. K. 'Chronologische Probleme im Zusammenhang mit der Erziehung des Kaisers Julian.' *Acta Antiqua Academiae Scientiarum Hungaricae* 44 (2004): 109–114.

Csízy, K.K. 'Über die Relation zwischen den Tugenden eines Priesters und eines Herrschers: Die Brieffragmente 89A und 89B von Julian dem Abtrünnigen.' *Acta Antiqua Academiae Scientiarum Hungaricae* 50 (2010): 79–87.

Cumont, F. V. M. 'La marche de l'empereur Julien d'Antioche à l'Euphrate.' In F. V. M. Cumont, *Études Syriennes*, Paris: 1917, 1–33.

Curta, F. 'How to Do with Saints: On the Iconography of St. Mercurius's Legend.' *Revue Roumaine d'Histoire* 34 (1995a): 109–129.

Curta, F. 'Atticism, Homer, Neoplatonism and Fürstenspiegel: Julian's *Second Panegyric* on Constantius.' *Greek, Roman and Byzantine Studies* 36 (1995b) 177–211.

Curta, F. 'Kaiserliche Lobrede und Politisches Programm: Die Dritte Rede des Julianus Caesars.' *Eranos* 95 (1997): 39–56 (repr. in F. Curta, *Text, Context, History, and Archaeology. Studies on Late Antiquity and the Middle Ages* [Florilegium Magistrorum Historiae Archaeologiaeque 6]. Bucarest: 2009, 21–40).

Curta, F. 'Language, ἔθνη, and National Gods: A Note on Julian's Concept of Hellenism.' *Ancient World* 33.1 (2002): 3–19.

Curti, C. 'Lo scisma di Novaziano nell' interpretazione dello storico Socrate.' In *La storiografia ecclesiastica nella tarda antichità* (Atti del Convegno tenuto in Erice 3–8 xii 1978; Scuola Superiore di Archeologia e Civiltà Medievali [3° corso]; C. C. S. 'E. Majorana'). Messina, Italy: 1980, 313–337.

Dal Covolo, E. 'La paideia anticristiana dell' imperatore Giuliano: A proposito dell' editto del 17 giugno 362.' In S. Felici (ed.), *Crescità dell'uomo nella catechesi dei Padri (età postnicena)* (Convegno di Studio e Aggiornamento, Facoltà di Lettere Cristiane e Classiche [Pontificium Institutum Altioris Latinitatis], Rome, 20–21 marzo 1987; Biblioteca di Scienze Religiose 80). Rome: 1988, 73–85.

Daley, B. E. *Gregory of Nazianzus* (The Early Church Fathers). London and New York: 2006.

Daly, L. J. 'In a Borderland: Themistius' Ambivalence toward Julian.' *Byzantinische Zeitschrift* 73 (1980): 1–11.

Davids, A. 'Cyril of Alexandria's First Episcopal Years.' In J. den Boeft and M. L. van Poll-van de Lisdonk (eds.), *The Impact of Scripture in Early Christianity* (Vigiliae Christianae Supplements 44). Leiden, The Netherlands: 1999, 187–201.

De Biasi, L. 'Il ritratto di Giuliano in Ammiano Marcellino 25.4.22.' In I. Lana (ed.), *La storiografia latina del IV secolo D.C.* Turin, Italy: 1990, 192–197.

De Carvalho, M. M. See Carvalho, M. M. de.

De Filippis Cappai, C. 'Sulla statuizione di Giuliano Augusto in materia di sepolcri ed esequie (*Cod. Theod. 9,17,5*).' *Quaderni del Dipartimento de Filologia Linguistica e Tradizione Classica 'Augusto Rostagni'* 14 (2000): 235–239.

De Gaiffier, B. See Gaiffier, B. de.

Deichmann, F. W. 'Frühchristliche Kirchen in antiken Heiligtümern.' *Jahrbuch des Deutschen Archäologischen Instituts* 54 (1939): 105–136.

Deichmann, F. W. 'Christianisierung II (der Monumente).' In Th. Klauser et al. (eds.), *Reallexikon für Antike und Christentum* 2. Stuttgart: 1954, 1228–1241.

Deichmann, F. W. 'Das Oktogon von Antiocheia: Heroon-Martyrion, Palastkirche oder Kathedrale?' *Byzantinische Zeitschrift* 65 (1972): 40–56.

Delbrueck, R. *Spätantike Kaiserporträts von Constantinus Magnus bis zum Ende des Westreichs* (Studien zur spätantiken Kunstgeschichte im Auftrage des Deutschen Archäologischen Instituts 8). Berlin and Leipzig: 1933.

Delehaye, H. 'Bulletin des publications hagiographiques.' *Analecta Bollandiana* 27 (1908): 419–511.

Delehaye, H. *Les Légendes grecques des saints militaires*. Paris: 1909.

Delehaye, H. *Cinq leçons sur la méthode hagiographique* (Subsidia Hagiographica 21), Brussels: 1934 (repr. 1981).

Delehaye, H. *Étude sur le légendier romain: Les saints de Novembre et de Décembre* (Subsidia Hagiographica 23). Brussels: 1936 (repr. 1968).

Delehaye, H. *Les passions des martyrs et les genres littéraires* (Subsidia Hagiographica 13B). Brussels: (1921) 1966².

Delmaire, R. 'La *damnatio memoriae* au Bas-Empire à travers les textes, la législation et les inscriptions.' *Cahiers du Centre Gustave Glotz* 14 (2003): 299–310.

Delmaire, R. 'La législation sur les sacrifices au IVᵉ siècle: Un essai d'interprétation.' *Revue Historique de Droit Français et Étranger* 82 (2004): 319–333.

Delmaire, R. 'Exil, relégation, déportation dans la législation du Bas-Empire.' In Ph. Blaudeau (ed.), *Exil et relégation: Les tribulations du sage et du saint durant l'antiquité romaine et chrétienne (Iᵉʳ–VIᵉ s. ap. J.-C.)* (Actes du colloque organisé par le Centre Jean-Charles Picard, Université de Paris XII–Val de Marne, 17–18 juin 2005). Paris: 2008, 115–132.

Del Tredici, K. L. *Three Historical Problems in the Ancient Sources for the Reign of Constantius II (337–361)*. PhD Fordham University, New York: 1982.

Demandt, A. *Ungeschehene Geschichte: Ein Traktat über die Frage: Was wäre geschehen, wenn . . . ?* Göttingen, Germany: 2005⁴.

Demandt, A. *Die Spätantike: Römische Geschichte von Diocletian bis Justinian 284–565 n. Chr.* (Handbuch der Altertumswissenschaft III.6). Munich: 2007².

Demarolle, J.-M. 'Le *Contre les Galiléens*: Continuité et rupture dans la démarche polémique de l'empereur Julien.' *Ktèma* 11 (1986): 39–47.

De' Medici, L. See Medici, L. de.

Den Boeft, J., D. den Hengst, and H. C. Teitler. *Philological and Historical Commentary on Ammianus Marcellinus XX*. Groningen, The Netherlands: 1987.

Den Boeft, J., D. den Hengst, and H. C. Teitler. *Philological and Historical Commentary on Ammianus Marcellinus XXI*. Groningen, The Netherlands: 1991.

Den Boeft, J., J. W. Drijvers, D. den Hengst, and H. C. Teitler. *Philological and Historical Commentary on Ammianus Marcellinus XXII*. Groningen, The Netherlands: 1995.

Den Boeft, J., J. W. Drijvers, D. den Hengst, and H. C. Teitler. *Philological and Historical Commentary on Ammianus Marcellinus XXIII*. Groningen, The Netherlands: 1998.

Den Boeft, J., J. W. Drijvers, D. den Hengst, and H. C. Teitler. *Philological and Historical Commentary on Ammianus Marcellinus XXIV*. Leiden, The Netherlands: 2002.

Den Boeft, J., J. W. Drijvers, D. den Hengst, and H. C. Teitler. *Philological and Historical Commentary on Ammianus Marcellinus XXV*. Leiden, The Netherlands: 2005.

Den Boeft, J. 'Ammianus Marcellinus' Judgement of Julian's Piety.' In A. Houtman, A. de Jong, and M. Misset-van de Weg (eds.), *Empsychoi Logoi: Religious Innovations in Antiquity; Studies in Honour of Pieter Willem van der Horst*. Leiden, The Netherlands: 2008, 65–79.

Den Boer, W. 'Caesar Flavius Claudius Constantius (Gallus).' *Tijdschrift voor Geschiedenis* 62 (1949): 161–197.

Den Boer, W. 'Two Letters from the *Corpus Iulianeum*.' *Vigiliae Christianae* 16 (1962): 179–197 (repr. in W. den Boer, *Syngrammata. Studies in Graeco-Roman history*. Leiden: 1979, 27–145).

Den Hengst, D. *Ammianus Marcellinus: Julianus, de laatste heidense keizer; Nadagen van een wereldrijk* (vertaald en toegelicht door D. den Hengst). Amsterdam: 2013.

Den Hengst, D. See also J. den Boeft.

Déroche, V. 'Pourquoi écrivait-on des recueils de miracles? L'exemple des miracles de Saint Artémios.' In C. Jolivet-Lévy, M. Kaplan, and J.-P. Sodini (eds.), *Les saints et leur sanctuaire à Byzance: Textes, images et monuments*. Paris: 1993, 95–116.

De Sainte Croix, G. E. M. 'Why Were the Early Christians Persecuted?' *Past and Present* 26 (1963): 6–38 (repr. in M. I. Finley [ed.], *Studies in Ancient Society*. London 1974: 210–262).

De Sanctis, G. *I Santi Giovanni e Paolo martiri Celimontani*. Rome: 1962.

De Sanctis, G. 'Gallicano.' In A. Amore et al. (eds.), *Biblioteca Sanctorum* 6. Rome: 1965a, 12–13.

De Sanctis, G. 'Giovanni e Paolo.' In A. Amore et al. (eds.), *Biblioteca Sanctorum* 6. Rome: 1965b, 1046–1049.

Desnier, J.-L. 'Renaissance taurine.' *Latomus* 44 (1985): 402–409.

De Vita, M. C. 'Giuliano e l'arte della "nobile menzogna" (*Or.* 7, *Contro il Cinico Eraclio*).' In A. Marcone (ed.), *L'imperatore Giuliano: Realtà storica e rappresentazione* (Studi sul Mondo Antico 3). Milan: 2015, 119–148.

Devos, P. 'Une recension nouvelle de la passion Grecque BHG 639 de saint Eusignios.' *Analecta Bollandiana* 100 (1982): 209–228.

Devos, P. 'Aspects de la correspondance de S. Basile de Césarée avec S. Eusèbe de Samosate et avec S. Amphiloque d'Iconium.' *Analecta Bollandiana* 110 (1992): 241–259.

Dietz, K. 'Kaiser Julian in Phönizien.' *Chiron* 30 (2000): 807–855.

Di Giuseppe Camaioni, S. See T. Orlandi.

DiMaio, M. 'The Transfer of the Remains of the Emperor Julian from Tarsus to Constantinople.' *Byzantion* 48 (1978): 43–50.

DiMaio, M. '"*Infaustis ductoribus praeviis*": The Antiochene Connection, Part II.' *Byzantion* 51 (1981): 502–510.

DiMaio, M. 'The Emperor Julian's Edicts of Religious Toleration.' *Ancient World* 20 (1989): 99–109.

DiMaio, M., and W. H. Arnold. '"*Per vim, per caedem, per bellum*": A Study of Murder and Ecclesiastical Politics in the Year 337 A.D.' *Byzantion* 62 (1992): 158–211.

Di Santo, E. 'Giuliano l'Apostata nel pensiero di Giovanni Crisostomo: Imperatore, filosofo, persecutore.' *Augustinianum* 45 (2005): 349–387.

Di Segni, L. 'Εἷς θεός in Palestinian Inscriptions.' *Scripta Classica Israelica* 13 (1994): 94–115.

Dobschütz, E. von. *Christusbilder: Untersuchungen zur christlichen Legende* (Texte und Untersuchungen zur Geschichte der altchristlichen Literatur, Neue Folge 3). Leipzig, Germany: 1899.

Dodds, E. R. 'Theurgy and Its Relationship to Neoplatonism.' *Journal of Roman Studies* 37 (1947): 55–69.

Donckel, E. 'Studien über den Kultus der hl. Bibiana.' *Römische Quartalschrift für christliche Altertumskunde und für Kirchengeschichte* 43 (1935): 23–33.

Donckel, E. 'Der Kultus der hl. Bibiana in Rom.' *Rivista di Archeologia Cristiana* 14 (1937): 125–135.

Doria, A. See S. Conti.

Döring, K. 'Kaiser Julians Plädoyer für den Kynismus.' *Rheinisches Museum für Philologie* 140 (1997): 386–400 (repr. in K. Döring, *Kleine Schriften zur antiken Philosophie und ihrer Nachwirkung* (Philosophie der Antike 31), Stuttgart: 2010, 291–302).

Dorival, G. 'Julien et le christianisme d'après les *Lettres*.' In D. Auger and É. Wolff (eds.), *Culture classique et christianisme: Mélanges offerts à Jean Bouffartigue*

(Textes, Histoire et Monuments de l'Antiquité au Moyen Age). Paris: 2008, 27–41.

Downey, G. 'The Shrines of St. Babylas at Antioch and Daphne.' In R. Stillwell et al. (eds.), *Antioch-on-the-Orontes 2: The Excavations 1933–1936* (Publications of the Committee for the Excavation of Antioch and Its Vicinity). Princeton, NJ: 1938, 45–48.

Downey, G. *A Study of the Comites Orientis and the Consulares Syriae*. PhD Princeton University: 1934.

Downey, G. 'The Tombs of the Byzantine Emperors at the Church of the Holy Apostles in Constantinople.' *Journal of Hellenic Studies* 79 (1959): 27–51.

Downey, G. 'Gaza.' In Th. Klauser et al. (eds.), *Reallexikon für Antike und Christentum* 8. Stuttgart: 1972, 1123–1134.

Dräger, P. *Historie über Herkunft und Jugend Constantins des Grossen und seine Mutter Helena von einem unbekannten Verfasser: Incerti auctoris historia de ortu atque iuventute Constantini Magni eiusque matre Helena*. Trier, Germany: 2010².

Drake, H. A. *Constantine and the Bishops: The Politics of Intolerance* (Ancient Society and History). Baltimore: 2000.

Drake, H. A. 'The Impact of Constantine on Christianity.' In N. E. Lenski (ed.), *The Cambridge Companion to the Age of Constantine*. Cambridge, UK: 2006, 111–136.

Drake, H. A. 'The Curious Case of George and the Camel.' In D. Luckensmeyer and P. Allen (eds.), *Studies of Religion and Politics in the Early Christan Centuries* (Early Christian Studies 13). Strathfield, Australia: 2010, 173–193.

Drake, H. A. 'Intolerance, Religious Violence, and Political Legitimacy in Late Antiquity.' *Journal of the American Academy of Religion* 79 (2011): 193–235.

Drake, H. A. '"But I Digress . . .": Rhetoric and Propaganda in Julian's Second Oration to Constantius.' In N. Baker-Brian and S. Tougher (eds.), *Emperor and Author: The Writings of Julian the Apostate*. Swansea, UK: 2012, 35–46.

Drake, H. A. 'Nicaea to Tyre (325–335): The Bumpy Road to a Christian Empire.' *Antiquité Tardive* 22 (2014): 43–52.

Drew-Bear, Th., and C. Zuckerman. '*Gradatim cuncta decora*: Les officiers sortis du rang sous les successeurs de Constantin.' In Y. Le Bohec and C. Wolff, *L'armée romaine de Dioclétien à Valentinien Ier* (Actes du Congrès de Lyon, 12–14 septembre 2002; Université Jean Moulin-Lyon 3, Collection du Centre d'Études Romaines et Gallo-Romaines, N.S. 26). Lyon and Paris: 2004, 419–430.

Drijvers, H. J. W. 'The Syriac Romance of Julian: Its Function, Place of Origin and Original Language.' In R. Lavenant (ed.), *VI Symposium Syriacum 1992* (Orientalia Christiana Analecta 247). Rome: 1994, 201–214.

Drijvers, H. J. W., and J. W. Drijvers. *The Finding of the True Cross: The Judas Kyriakos Legend in Syriac; Introduction, Text and Translation.* Leuven, Belgium: 1997.

Drijvers, J. W. 'Ammianus Marcellinus 23.1.2–3: The Rebuilding of the Temple in Jerusalem.' In J. den Boeft, D. den Hengst, and H. C. Teitler (eds.), *Cognitio Gestorum: The Historiographic Art of Ammianus Marcellinus* (Koninklijke Nederlandse Akademie van Wetenschappen: Verhandelingen, Afdeling Letterkunde, Nieuwe Reeks 148). Amsterdam: 1992a, 19–26.

Drijvers, J. W. *Helena Augusta: The Mother of Constantine the Great and the Legend of Her Finding of the True Cross* (Brill's Studies in Intellectual History 27). Leiden, The Netherlands: 1992b.

Drijvers, J. W. 'The Syriac Julian Romance: Aspects of the Jewish-Christian Controversy in Late Antiquity.' In H. L. J. Vanstiphout (ed.), *All Those Nations . . . : Cultural Encounters within and with the Near East; Studies presented to Han Drijvers at the Occasion of His Sixty-fifth Birthday by Colleagues and Students.* Groningen, The Netherlands: 1999, 31–42.

Drijvers, J. W. 'Julian the Apostate and the City of Rome: Pagan-Christian Polemics in the Syriac Julian Romance.' In W. J. van Bekkum, J. W. Drijvers, and A. C. Klugkist (eds.), *Syriac Polemics: Studies in Honour of Gerrit Jan Reinink* (Orientalia Lovaniensia Analecta 170). Leuven, Belgium: 2007, 1–20.

Drijvers, J. W. 'The Power of the Cross: Celestial Cross Appearances in the Fourth Century.' In A. Cain and N. E. Lenski (eds.), *The Power of Religion in Late Antiquity* (Selected Papers from the Seventh Biennial Shifting Frontiers in Late Antiquity Conference, University of Colorado, Boulder, March 22–25, 2007). Farnham, UK, and Burlington, VT: 2009, 237–248.

Drijvers, J. W. 'Helena Augusta, the Cross and the Myth: Some New Reflections.' *Millennium* 8 (2011a): 125–174.

Drijvers, J. W. 'Religious Conflict in the Syriac *Julian Romance.*' In P. Brown and R. Lizzi Testa (eds.), *Pagans and Christians in the Roman Empire, the Breaking of a Dialogue (4th–6th Century A.D.)* (Proceedings of the International Conference at the Monastery of Bose, October 2008: Christianity and History. Series of the John XXIII Foundation for Religious Studies in Bologna 9). Berlin: 2011b, 131–162.

Drijvers, J. W. See also J. den Boeft.

Dufourcq, A. *Étude sur les Gesta martyrum romains.* Paris: 1900.

Dummer, J. 'Fl. Artemius Dux Aegypti.' *Archiv für Papyrusforschung und verwandte Gebiete 21* (1971): 121–144 (repr. In J. Dummer, [ed.] M. Vielberg, *Philologia sacra et profana: Ausgewählte Beiträge zur Antike und zu ihrer Wirkungsgeschichte.* Wiesbaden and Stuttgart: 2006, 172–199).

Dupont, C. 'Les privilèges des clercs sous Constantin.' *Revue d'Histoire Ecclésiastique* 62 (1967): 729–752.

Dupont, C. 'La politique de Julien à l'égard du christianisme dans les sources littéraires des IVᵉ et Vᵉ siècles après Jésus-Christ.' In *Atti dell'Accademia Romanistica Costantiniana* (3° Convegno Internazionale, Perugia-Trevi-Gualdo Tadino, 28 settembre–1° ottobre 1977). Perugia, Italy: 1979, 197–218.

Dussaud, R. *Les monuments Palestiniens et Judaïques (Moab, Judée, Philistie, Samarie, Galilée)*. Paris: 1912.

Dvornik, F. *The Idea of Apostolicity in Byzantium and the Legend of the Apostle Andrew* (Dumbarton Oaks Studies 4). Cambridge, MA: 1958.

Eck, W. 'Review of The *Prosopography of the Later Roman Empire: Vol. I: A.D. 260–395.' Zephyrus* 23 (1972–1973): 325–336.

Eck, W. 'Zur Neulesung der Iulian-Inschrift von Ma'ayan Barukh.' *Chiron* 30 (2000): 857–859.

Edwards, M. 'The Beginnings of Christianization.' In N. E. Lenski (ed.), *The Cambridge Companion to the Age of Constantine*. Cambridge, UK: 2006, 137–158.

Effenberger, A. See N. Asutay-Effenberger.

Efthymiadis, S., and V. Déroche. 'Greek Hagiography in Late Antiquity (Fourth–Seventh Centuries).' In S. Efthymiadis (ed.), *The Ashgate Research Companion to Byzantine Hagiography, I, Periods and Places*. Farnham, UK, and Burlington, VT: 2011, 35–94.

Efthymiadis, S. 'Collections of Miracles (Fifth–Fifteenth Centuries).' In S. Efthymiadis (ed.), *The Ashgate Research Companion to Byzantine Hagiography, II, Genres and Contexts*. Farnham, UK, and Burlington, VT: 2014, 103–142.

Egger, R. *Das Labarum. Die Kaiserstandarte der Spätantike* (Österreichische Akademie der Wissenschaften, philosophisch-historische Klasse, Sitzungsberichte 234. Band 1: Abhandlung). Vienna: 1960 (repr. in R. Egger, *Römische Antike und frühes Christentum. Ausgewählte Schriften von Rudolf Egger zur Vollendung seines 80. Lebensjahres*. Klagenfurt: 1963, 325–344).

Ehling, K. 'Der Ausgang des Perserfeldzuges in der Münzpropaganda des Jovian.' *Klio* 78 (1996): 186–191.

Ehling, K. 'Kaiser Julian, der Senat und die Stadt Rom.' *Zeitschrift für Epigraphik und Papyrologie* 137 (2001): 292–296.

Ehling, K. '"Wer wird jetzt noch an Schicksalserforschung und Horoskop glauben?" (Ephraim d. Syrer 4, 26): Bemerkungen zu Julians Stiermünzen und dem Geburtsdatum des Kaisers.' *Jahrbuch für Numismatik und Geldgeschichte* 55–56 (2005–2006): 111–132.

Ehling, K. 'Der Tetrarch Maximinus Daia, sein Grab bei Tarsos und Kaiser Julian.' *Historia* 59 (2010): 252–255.

Eitrem, S. 'Kaiser Julian als Briefschreiber.' *Symbolae Osloenses* 33 (1957): 111–126.

Elliott, T. G. 'The Tax Exemptions Granted to Clerics by Constantine and Constantius II.' *Phoenix* 32 (1978): 326–336.

Elliott, T. G. 'Eunapius' Account of Julian the Apostate.' *Ancient History Bulletin* 5.3 (1991): 88.

Elm, S. 'Gregory of Nazianzus's *Life of Julian* revisited (*Or.* 4 and 5): The Art of Governance by Invective.' In S. McGill, C. Sogno, and E. Watts (eds.), *From the Tetrarchs to the Theodosians: Later Roman History and Culture, 284–450 CE* (Yale Classical Studies 34). Cambridge, UK: 2010, 171–182.

Elm, S. *Sons of Hellenism, Fathers of the Church: Emperor Julian, Gregory of Nazianzus, and the Vision of Rome* (Transformation of the Classical Heritage 49). Berkeley: 2012.

Elm, S. 'Church—Festival—Temple: Reimagining Civic Topography in Late Antiquity.' In C. Rapp and H. A. Drake (eds.), *The City in the Classical and Post-Classical World.* Cambridge, UK: 2014, 167–182.

Elmer, G. 'Eugenius: Eine historisch-numismatische Studie.' *Numismatische Zeitschrift* 69 (1936): 29–51.

Eltester, W. 'Die Kirchen Antiochias im IV. Jahrhundert.' *Zeitschrift für die Neutestamentliche Wissenschaft* 36 (1937): 251–286.

Ensslin, W. 'Kaiser Julians Gesetzgebungswerk und Reichsverwaltung.' *Klio* 18 (1923): 104–199.

Errington, R. M. 'Themistius and His Emperors.' *Chiron* 30 (2000): 861–904.

Étienne, R. 'Flavius Sallustius et Secundus Salutius.' *Revue des Études Anciennes* 65 (1963): 104–113.

Evans, E. C. *Physiognomics in the Ancient World* (Transactions of the American Philosophical Society 59.5). Philadelphia: 1969.

Evers, A. 'Augustine on the Church (against the Donatists).' In M. Vessey (ed.), *A Companion to Augustine.* Chichester, UK: 2012, 375–385.

Faber, R., and H. Høibraaten (eds.). *Ibsens 'Kaiser und Galiläer': Quellen—Interpretationen—Rezeptionen.* Würzburg, Germany: 2011.

Fabricius, C. 'Vier Libaniusstellen bei Johannes Chrysostomus.' *Symbolae Osloenses* 33 (1957): 135–136.

Fabricius, C. *Zu den Jugendschriften des Johannes Chrysostomos: Untersuchungen zum Klassizismus des vierten Jahrhunderts.* PhD Lund University, Lund, Sweden: 1962.

Farag, L. M. *St. Cyril of Alexandria, a New Testament Exegete: His Commentary on the Gospel of John* (Gorgias Dissertations 29). Piscataway, NJ: 2007.

Faro, S. 'Oribasio medico, *quaestor* di Giuliano l'Apostata.' In *Studi in onore di Cesare Sanfilippo,* VII (Università di Catania, Pubblicazioni della Facoltà di Giurisprudenza 94). Milan: 1987, 261–268.

Fatti, F. *Giuliano a Cesarea: La politica ecclesiastica del principe Apostata* (Studi e Testi Tardoantichi 10). Rome: 2009.

Fatti, F. 'Il principe, la Tyche, i cristiani: Giuliano a Cesarea.' In P. Brown and R. Lizzi Testa (eds.), *Pagans and Christians in the Roman Empire, the Breaking of a Dialogue (4th–6th Century A.D.)* (Proceedings of the International Conference at the Monastery of Bose, October 2008; Christianity and

History. Series of the John XXIII Foundation for Religious Studies in Bologna 9). Berlin: 2011, 121–129.

Feissel, D. 'Une constitution de l'empereur Julien: Entre texte épigraphique et codification (*CIL* III, 459 et *CTh* I, 16, 8).' In E. Lévy (ed.), *La codification des lois dans l'Antiquité* (Actes du Colloque de Strasbourg, 27–29 novembre 1997; Université Marc Bloch de Strasbourg, Travaux du Centre de Recherche sur le Proche-Orient et la Grèce Antiques 16). Paris: 2000, 315–337 (repr. in D. Feissel, *Documents, Droit, Diplomatique de l'Empire Romain Tardif* [Bilans de Recherche 7]. Paris: 2010, 205–222).

Felgentreu, F. 'Zur Datierung der 18. Rede des Libanios.' *Klio* 86 (2004): 206–217.

Festugière, A. J. 'Julien à Macellum.' *Journal of Roman Studies* 47 (1957): 53–58 (= 'Julian in Macellum.' In R. Klein [ed.], *Julian Apostata* [Wege der Forschung 509]. Darmstadt, Germany: 1978, 241–255).

Festugière, A. J. *Antioche païenne et chrétienne: Libanius, Chrysostome et les moines de Syrie* (Bibliothèque des Écoles Françaises d'Athènes et de Rome 194). Paris: 1959.

Finamore, J. F. *Iamblichus and the Theory of the Vehicle of the Soul.* Chico, CA: 1985.

Fittschen, K. 'Privatporträts hadrianischer Zeit.' In J. Bouzek and I. Ondřejová (eds.), *Roman Portraits: Artistic and Literary.* Mainz, Germany: 1997, 32–36.

Flamant, J., Ch. Piétri, and G. Gottlieb. 'Julian Apostata (361–363) und der Versuch einer altgläubigen Restauration.' In Ch. Piétri and L. Piétri (eds.), *Das Entstehen der einen Christenheit (250–430)* (Die Geschichte des Christentums. Religion, Politik, Kultur, Deutsche Ausgabe, ed. N. Brox et al., 2). Freiburg, Germany: 1996, 396–413.

Fleck, T. *Die Portraits Julianus Apostatas* (Antiquitates, Archäologische Forschungsergebnisse 44). Hamburg: 2008.

Flower, R. *Emperors and Bishops in Late Roman Invective.* Cambridge, UK: 2013.

Fontaine, J. *Ammien Marcellin, Histoire, Tome IV (Livres XXIII–XXV):* *Introduction, Texte, Traduction, Notes* (Collection des Universités de France), 2 vols. Paris: 1977.

Fontaine, J. 'Le Julien d'Ammien Marcellin.' In R. Braun and J. Richer (eds.), *L'empereur Julien: De l'histoire à la légende (331–1715).* Paris 1978, 31–65.

Fornara, C. W. 'Julian's Persian Expedition in Ammianus and Zosimus.' *Journal of Hellenic Studies* 111 (1991): 1–15.

Förster, H. *Die Anfänge von Weihnachten und Epiphanias: Eine Anfrage an die Entstehunghypothesen* (Studien und Texte zu Antike und Christentum 46). Tübingen, Germany: 2007.

Forum Ancient Coins. Classical Numismatics Discussion. 'Topic: Julian II, Virtus Exercitus – New Reverse Type?' http://www.forumancientcoins.com/board/index.php?topic=41758.0 (consulted on January 13, 2016).

Foss, C. 'Late Antique and Byzantine Ankara.' *Dumbarton Oaks Papers* 31 (1977): 27–87.

Fouquet, C. 'L'hellénisme de l'empereur Julien.' *Bulletin de l'Association Guillaume Budé*, no. 2 (1981): 192–202.

Fournier, E. 'Exiled Bishops in the Christian Empire: Victims of Imperial Violence?' In H. A. Drake (ed.), *Violence in Late Antiquity: Perceptions and Practices* (Papers Presented at the Fifth Biennial Conference on Shifting Frontiers in Late Antiquity, Held at the University of California, Santa Barbara, in March 20–23, 2003). Aldershot, UK: 2006, 157–166.

Fournier, E. 'The *Adventus* of Julian at Sirmium: The Literary Construction of Historical Reality in Ammianus Marcellinus.' In R. Frakes, E. DePalma Digeser, and J. Stephens (eds.), *The Rhetoric of Power in Late Antiquity: Religion and Politics in Byzantium, Europe and the Early Islamic World* (Library of Classical Studies 2). London and New York: 2010, 13–45.

Fowden, G. 'Bishops and Temples in the Eastern Roman Empire AD 320–435.' *Journal of Theological Studies* 29 (1978): 53–78.

Frakes, R. M. 'The Dynasty of Constantine down to 363.' In N. E. Lenski (ed.), *The Cambridge Companion to the Age of Constantine*. Cambridge, UK: 2006 (2011²), 91–107.

Franchi de' Cavalieri, P. 'Di una probabile fonte della leggenda dei SS. Giovanni e Paolo.' In P. Franchi de' Cavalieri, *Nuove Note agiografiche* (Studi e Testi 9). Rome: 1902, 53–65.

Franchi de' Cavalieri, P. 'Del testo della *Passio SS. Iohannis et Pauli*.' In P. Franchi de' Cavalieri, *Note agiografiche 5* (Studi e Testi 27). Rome 1915, 41–62.

Franchi de' Cavalieri, P. 'S. Teodoreto di Antiochia.' In P. Franchi de' Cavalieri, *Note agiografiche 6* (Studi e Testi 33). Rome: 1920, 57–101.

Franchi de' Cavalieri, P. 'Il κοιμητήριον di Antiochia.' In P. Franchi de' Cavalieri, *Note agiografiche 7* (Studi e Testi 49). Rome: 1928, 146–153.

Franchi de' Cavalieri, P. 'I SS. Gioventino e Massimino.' In P. Franchi de' Cavalieri, *Note agiografiche 9* (Studi e Testi 175). Vatican City: 1953, 167–200.

Franco, C. 'L'immagine di Alessandro in Giuliano Imperatore.' *Studi Classici e Orientali* 46 (1997): 637–658.

Frank, R. I. *Scholae Palatinae: The Palace Guards of the Later Roman Empire* (Papers and Monographs of the American Academy in Rome 23). Rome: 1969.

Franke, P. R. '*Imperator barbatus*: Zur Geschichte der Barttracht in der Antike.' In V. Dotterweich and P. Barceló (eds.), *Contra quis ferat arma deos? Vier Augsburger Vorträge zur Religionsgeschichte der römischen Kaiserzeit: Zum 60. Geburtstag von Gunther Gottlieb*. Munich: 1996, 55–77.

Frend, W. H. C. *The Donatist Church: A Movement of Protest in Roman North Africa*. Oxford: 1971².

Frend, W. H. C. 'Fragments of an Acta Martyrum from Q'asr Ibrim.' *Jahrbuch für Antike und Christentum* 29 (1986): 66–70.

Gabba, E. 'I Cristiani nell'esercito romano del quarto secolo d.C.' In E. Gabba, *Per la storia dell'esercito romano in età imperiale* (Il Mondo Antico 3). Bologna, Italy: 1974, 75–109.

Gaddis, M. *There Is No Crime for Those Who Have Christ: Religious Violence in the Christian Roman Empire* (Transformation of the Classical Heritage 39). Berkeley, Los Angeles, and London: 2005.

Gärtner, H. 'Kaiser Julians letzter Tag: Anmerkungen zur Darstellung Ammians (Res gestae 25, 3)'. In P. Neukam (ed.), *Neue Perspektiven* (Klassische Sprachen und Literatur 23), Munich: 1989, 65–95.

Gaiffier, B. de. 'Les avatars de S. Hilarinus.' *Analecta Bollandiana* 66 (1948): 276–277.

Gaiffier, B. de. '"Sub Iuliano Apostata" dans le Martyrologe Romain.' *Analecta Bollandiana* 74 (1956): 5–49.

Gaiffier, B. de. 'Palatins et eunuques dans quelques documents hagiographiques.' *Analecta Bollandiana* 75 (1957): 17–46.

Gaiffier, B. de. 'Les martyrs Eugène et Macaire morts en exil en Maurétanie.' *Analecta Bollandiana* 78 (1960): 24–40.

Gawlikowski, M. 'La route de l'Euphrate d'Isidore à Julien.' In P.-L. Gatier, B. Helly, and J.-P. Rey-Coquais (eds.), *Géographie historique au Proche-Orient (Syrie, Phénicie, Arabie, grecques, romaines, byzantines)* (Actes de la Table Ronde de Valbonne, 16–18 septembre 1985; Notes et Monographies Techniques du CRA 23). Paris: 1990, 77–98.

Galuzzi, A. 'Teodoreto.' In A. Amore et al. (eds.), *Biblioteca Sanctorum* 12. Rome: 1969, 228.

Galvao-Sobrinho, C. R. 'Embodied Theologies: Christian Identity and Violence in Alexandria in the Early Arian Controversy.' In H. A. Drake (ed.), *Violence in Late Antiquity: Perceptions and Practices* (Papers Presented at the Fifth Biennial Conference on Shifting Frontiers in Late Antiquity, Held at the University of California, Santa Barbara, in March 20–23, 2003). Aldershot, UK: 2006, 321–331.

García Ruiz, M. P. 'Eusebia vista por Amiano: Un retrato entre líneas.' *Cuadernos de Filología Clásica: Estudios Latinos* 28 (2008): 49–64.

García Ruiz, M. P. 'The "Marcellus Case" and the Loyalty of Julian: "Latent Aguments" and Cultural Otherness in Ammianus' *Res Gestae*.' In M. P. García Ruiz and A. J. Quiroga Puertas (eds.), *Praising the Otherness: Linguistic and Cultural Alterity in the Roman Empire; Historiography and Panegyrics* (Talanta 45). Amsterdam: 2013 (2014), 81–96.

Gauthier, N. 'L'expérience religieuse de Julien dit l'Apostat.' *Augustinianum* 27 (1987): 227–235.

Geffcken, J. *Kaiser Julianus* (Das Erbe der Alten 8). Leipzig, Germany: 1914.

Gelzer, Th. 'Zum Hintergrund der hohen Schätzung der paganen Bildung bei Sokrates von Konstantinopel.' In B. Bäbler and H.-G. Nesselrath (eds.), *Die Welt des Sokrates von Konstantinopel: Studien zu Politik, Religion und Kultur im späten 4. und frühen 5. Jh. n. Chr. zu Ehren von Christoph Schäublin.* Munich and Leipzig: 2001, 111–124.

Gemeinhardt, P. 'Dürfen Christen Lehrer sein? Anspruch und Wirklichkeit im christlichen Bildungsdiskurs der Spätantike.' *Jahrbuch für Antike und Christentum* 51 (2008): 25–43.

Georgiou, A. 'Helena: The Subversive Persona of an Ideal Christian Empress in Early Byzantium.' *Journal of Early Christian Studies* 21 (2013): 597–624.

Germino, E. *Scuola e Cultura nella legislazione di Giuliano l'Apostata* (Pubblicazioni della Facoltà di Giurisprudenza della seconda Università di Napoli 27). Naples, Italy: 2004.

Germino, E. 'La legislazione dell'imperatore Giuliano: Primi appunti per una palingenesi.' *Antiquité Tardive* 17 (2009): 159–174.

Gessler, J. 'De HH. Cefaloforen: Een onderzoek naar den oorsprong van deze legende en het ontstaan der cefaloforenbeelden.' *Belgisch Tijdschrift voor Oudheidkunde en Kunstgeschiedenis/Revue Belge d'Archéologie et d'Histoire de l'Art* 11 (1941): 193–212.

Gibbon, E. *The History of the Decline and Fall of the Roman Empire*, ed. D. Womersley. 3 vols. Harmondsworth, UK: 1994 (repr. 1995).

Giebel, M. *Kaiser Julian Apostata: Die Wiederkehr der alten Götter.* Düsseldorf, Germany, and Zurich, Switzerland: 2002.

Gilliard, F. D. 'Notes on the Coinage of Julian the Apostate.' *Journal of Roman Studies* 54 (1964): 135–141.

Gilliard, F. D. 'The Birth-Date of Julian the Apostate.' *California Studies in Classical Antiquity* 4 (1971): 147–151 (= 'Das Geburtsdatum von Julian Apostata.' In R. Klein [ed.], *Julian Apostata* [Wege der Forschung 509]. Darmstadt, Germany: 1978, 448–454).

Girardet, K. M. 'Die Petition der Donatisten an Kaiser Konstantin (Frühjahr 313)—historische Voraussetzungen und Folgen.' *Chiron* 19 (1989): 185–206.

Girardi, M. *Basilio di Cesarea e il culto dei martiri nel IV secolo: Scrittura e tradizione* (Vetera Christianorum Quaderni 21). Bari, Italy: 1990.

Girotti, B. 'Sull'aborto e la sterilità di Eusebia e Costanzo: Riflessioni a partire da Ammiano, 16.10.18–19.' In V. Neri and B. Girotti (eds.), *La famiglia tardoantica: Società, diritto, religione.* Milan: 2016, 171–188.

Gleason, M. W. 'Festive Satire: Julian's *Misopogon* and the New Year at Antioch.' *Journal of Roman Studies* 76 (1986): 106–119.

Gnilka, Chr. 'Julian bei Prudentius (Zu Prud. *apoth.* 449–54).' In Chr. Gnilka, *Philologische Streifzüge durch die römische Dichtung.* Basel, Switzerland: 2007, 412–415.

Gnoli, T. 'Giuliano e Mitra.' *Antiquité Tardive* 17 (2009): 215–234.

Godding, R., et al. (eds.). *Bollandistes, saints et légendes: Quatre siècles de recherche.* Brussels: 2007.

Godding, R. See also R. Aigrain.

Gollancz, H. *Julian the Apostate, Now Translated for the First Time from the Syriac Original (the Only Known Ms. in the British Museum, Edited by Hoffmann of Kiel)*. Oxford: 1928.

Gorce, D. 'Georges de Cappadocie.' In R. Aubert et al. (eds.), *Dictionnaire d'Histoire et de Géographie Ecclésiastiques* 20. Paris: 1984, 602–610.

Gordini, G. D., and A. M. Raggi. 'Apollonia di Alessandria.' In A. Amore et al. (eds.), *Biblioteca Sanctorum* 2. Rome: 1962, 258–275.

Gordini, G. D., and M. C. Celletti. 'Bibiana (Vibiana, Viviana).' In A. Amore et al. (eds.), *Biblioteca Sanctorum* 3. Rome: 1963, 177–181.

Gordini, G. D. 'Pimenio.' In A. Amore et al. (eds.), *Biblioteca Sanctorum* 10. Rome: 1968, 871–873.

Gottlieb, G. See J. Flamant.

Goulet, R. 'Réflexions sur la loi scolaire de l'empereur Julien.' In H. Hugonnard-Roche (ed.), *L'enseignement supérieure dans les mondes antiques et médiévaux: Aspects institutionnels, juridiques et pédagogiques* (Colloque international de l'Institut des Traditions Textuelles, Paris, 7–8 octobre 2005; Textes et traditions 16). Paris: 2008, 175–200.

Graf, F. 'Fights about Festivals: Libanius and John Chrysostom on the *Kalendae Ianuariae* in Antioch.' *Archiv für Religionsgeschichte* 13 (2012): 175–186.

Grasmück, E. L. *Coercitio: Staat und Kirche im Donatistenstreit* (Bonner Historische Forschungen 22). Bonn, Germany: 1964.

Grattarola, P. 'Gli scismi di Felicissimo e di Novaziano.' *Rivista di Storia della Chiesa in Italia* 38 (1984): 367–390.

Greenslade, S. L., and J. H. W. G. Liebeschuetz. 'Chrysostom, John.' *Oxford Classical Dictionary*³ (1996): 329.

Greenwood, D. N. 'Pollution Wars: Consecration and Desecration from Constantine to Julian.' *Studia Patristica* 62 (2013): 289–296.

Greenwood, D. N. 'Crafting Divine *personae* in Julian's *Oration* 7.' *Classical Philology* 109 (2014a): 140–149.

Greenwood, D. N. 'Five Latin Inscriptions from Julian's Pagan Restoration.' *Bulletin of the Institute of Classical Studies of the University of London* 57.2 (2014b): 101–119.

Grégoire, H. *Saints jumeaux et dieux cavaliers: Étude hagiographique* (Bibliothèque Hagiographique Orientale 9). Paris: 1905.

Grégoire, H., and P. Orgels, 'S. Gallicanus, consul et martyr dans la passion des SS. Jean et Paul, et sa vision "constantinienne" du Crucifié.' *Byzantion* 24 (1954): 579–605.

Grégoire, H., and P. Orgels. 'Saint Gallicanus et saint Hilarinus.' *Silloge Bizantina in onore di Silvio Giuseppe Mercati* (Studi Bizantini e Neoellenici 9). Rome: 1957, 171–175.

Grierson, Ph. 'The Tombs and Obits of the Byzantine Emperors (337–1042): With an Additional Note by Cyril Mango and Ihor Ševčenko.' *Dumbarton Oaks Papers* 16 (1962): 1–63.

Griffith, S. H. 'Ephraem the Syrian's Hymns *Against Julian:* Meditations on History and Imperial Power.' *Vigiliae Christianae* 41 (1987): 238–266.

Grig, L. 'Torture and Truth in Late Antique Martyrology.' *Early Medieval Europe* 11 (2002): 321–336.

Grig, L. *Making Martyrs in Late Antiquity.* London: 2004.

Grillet, B. and J.-N. Guinot. *Homélie sur Babylas. Introduction, texte critique, traduction et notes* (SC 362). Paris: 1990.

Grillet, B. See also M. A. Schatkin.

Grimm, V. E. *From Feasting to Fasting, the Evolution of a Sin: Attitudes to Food in Late Antiquity.* London and New York: 1996.

Grodzynski, D. 'Tortures mortelles et catégories sociales: Les *summa supplicia* dans le droit romain aux IIIe et IVe siècles.' In *Du châtiment dans la cité: Supplices corporels et peine de mort dans le monde antique* (Collections de l'École Française de Rome 79). Rome: 1984, 361–403.

Guidetti, F. 'I ritratti dell'imperatore Giuliano.' In A. Marcone (ed.), *L'imperatore Giuliano: Realtà storica e rappresentazione* (Studi sul Mondo Antico 3). Milan: 2015, 12–49.

Guido, R. 'La nozione di φιλία in Giuliano imperatore.' In *Giuliano imperatore: Le sue idee, i suoi amici, i suoi avversari* (Atti del Convegno Internazionale di Studi, Lecce 10–12 dicembre 1998). *Rudiae* 10 (1998 [2000]) 113–144.

Guinot, J.-N. 'L'Homélie sur Babylas de Jean Chrysostome: La victoire du martyr sur l'hellénisme.' In *La narrativa cristiana antiqua: Codici narrativi, strutture formali, schemi retorici* (XXIII Incontro di Studiosi dell'Antichità Cristiana, Roma, 5–7 maggio 1994; Studia Ephemeridis Augustinianum 50). Rome 1995, 323–341.

Guinot, J.-N. See also B. Grillet.

Guzmán Armario, F. J. 'Las figuras de Cornelio Galo y el César Galo en las Res Gestae de Amiano Marcelino (XVII 4, 5).' *Aevum* 78 (2004): 137–145.

Gwynn, D. M. *Athanasius of Alexandria: Bishop, Theologian, Ascetic, Father.* Oxford and New York: 2012.

Haas, C. J. 'The Alexandrian Riots of 356 and George of Cappadocia.' *Greek, Roman and Byzantine Studies* 32 (1991): 281–301.

Haas, C. J. *Alexandria in Late Antiquity: Topography and Social Conflict.* Baltimore and London: 1997.

Hadjinicolaou, A. 'Macellum, lieu d'exil de l'empereur Julien.' *Byzantion* 21 (1951): 15–22.

Haehling, R. von. 'Die Fiktion vom toleranten Iulian oder Vom Fehlen einer heidnischen Alternative in der nachkonstantinischen Ära.' In H. R.

Seeliger (ed.), *Kriminalisierung des Christentums? Karlheinz Deschners Kirchengeschichte auf dem Prüfstand.* Freiburg, Germany: 1994², 174–184.

Haehling, R. von. *Die Religionszugehörigkei der hohen Amtsträger des Römischen Reiches seit Constantins I. Alleinherrschaft bis zum Ende der theodosianischen Dynastie (324-450 bzw. 455 n. Chr.)* (Antiquitas III 23). Bonn, Germany: 1978.

Haensch, R. 'La christianisation de l'armée romaine.' In Y. Le Bohec and C. Wolff (eds.), *L'armée romaine de Dioclétien à Valentinien Ier* (Actes du Congrès de Lyon, 12–14 septembre 2002; Université Jean Moulin-Lyon 3, Collection du Centre d'Études Romaines et Gallo-Romaines, N.S. 26). Lyon and Paris: 2004, 525–531.

Hahn, I. 'Der ideologische Kampf um den Tod Julians des Abtrünnigen.' *Klio* 38 (1960): 225–232.

Hahn, J. *Gewalt und religiöser Konflikt: Studien zu den Auseinandersetzungen zwischen Christen, Heiden und Juden im Osten des Römischen Reiches (von Konstantin bis Theodosius II.)* (Klio, Beiträge zur Alten Geschichte, Beihefte, Neue Folge 8). Berlin: 2004.

Hahn, J. 'Kaiser Julians Konzept eines Philosophenpriestertums: Idee und Scheitern einer Vision.' In J. Hahn and M. Vielberg (eds.), *Formen und Funktionen von Leitbildern* (Kongress Jena 2003; Altertumswissen-schaftliches Kolloquium 17). Stuttgart: 2007, 147–161.

Hahn, J. 'Julian and His Partisans: Supporters or Critics?' In P. Brown and R. Lizzi Testa (eds.), *Pagans and Christians in the Roman Empire, the Breaking of a Dialogue (4th-6th Century A.D.)* (Proceedings of the International Conference at the Monastery of Bose, October 2008; Christianity and History. Series of the John XXIII Foundation for Religious Studies in Bologna 9). Berlin 2011: 109–120.

Hahn, W., 'Die Zeichen des Menschensohnes am Himmel—zu den Anfängen der Kreuzdarstellung im römischen Münzbild des 4. Jahrhunderts, insbesondere auf dem *Labarum.*' In: B. Kluge and B. Weisser (eds.), *XII. Internationaler Numismatischer Kongress Berlin 1997: Akten—Proceedings—Actes* II. Berlin: 2000, 772–779.

Halkin, F. 'La passion grecque des saints Eugène et Macaire.' *Analecta Bollandiana* 78 (1960): 41–52 (repr. in F. Halkin, *Martyrs grecs IIe–VIIIe s.* (Variorum Collected Studies Series 30). London: 1974, no. V)..

Halkin, F. 'Eusèbe martyr en Phénicie.' *Analecta Bollandiana* 84 (1966): 335–342 (repr. in F. Halkin, *Martyrs grecs IIe–VIIIe s.* (Variorum Collected Studies Series 30). London: 1974, no. XV).

Halkin, F. 'Saint Émilien de Durostorum: Martyr sous Julien.' *Analecta Bollandiana* 90 (1972): 27–35 (repr. in F. Halkin, *Martyrs grecs IIe–VIIIe s.* (Variorum Collected Studies Series 30). London: 1974, no. XXII).

BIBLIOGRAPHY

Halkin, F. 'Aréthas de Césarée et le martyr saint Eupsychius.' *Analecta Bollandiana* 91 (1973): 414.

Halkin, F. 'La passion grecque des saints Gallican, Jean et Paul (BHG 2191).' *Analecta Bollandiana* 92 (1974): 265–286.

Halkin, F. 'La Passion inédite de Saint Eupsychius.' *Le Muséon* 97 (1984): 197–206.

Halkin, F. 'La passion de S. Marc d'Aréthuse, BHG 2248.' *Analecta Bollandiana* 103 (1985): 217–229.

Halkin, F. 'La passion grecque de saint Théodoret d'Antioche.' In *Hagiologie byzantine: Textes inédits publiés en grec et traduits en français* (Subsidia Hagiographica 71). Brussels: 1986, 123–151.

Halkin, F. 'Les recensions de la Passion de Saint Émilien.' In J. Dummer (ed.), *Texte und Textkritik: Eine Aufsatzsammlung* (Texte und Untersuchungen zur Geschichte der altchristlichen Literatur 133). Berlin: 1987, 223–229.

Hall, S. G. See Av. Cameron.

Hamilton, W. *Ammianus Marcellinus, The Later Roman Empire (A.D. 354–378)*, selected and translated by W. Hamilton with an introduction and notes by A. Wallace-Hadrill. Harmondsworth, UK: 1986.

Hanson, R. P. C. 'The Transformation of Pagan Temples into Churches in the Early Christian Centuries.' *Journal of Semitic Studies* 23 (1978): 257–267.

Hanson, R. P. C. *The Search for the Christian Doctrine of God: The Arian Controversy 318–381.* Edinburgh: 1988.

Hardy, B. C. 'The Emperor Julian and His School Law.' *Church History* 37 (1968): 131–143 (= 'Kaiser Julian und das Schulgesetz.' In R. Klein [ed.], *Julian Apostata* [Wege der Forschung 509]. Darmstadt, Germany: 1978, 387–408).

Harries, J. *Law and Empire in Late Antiquity.* Cambridge, UK: 1999.

Harries, J. 'Julian the Lawgiver.' In N. Baker-Brian and S. Tougher (eds.), *Emperor and Author: The Writings of Julian the Apostate.* Swansea, UK: 2012, 121–136.

Harris, W. V. 'Constantine's Dream.' *Klio* 87 (2005): 488–494.

Hatt, J. J., and J. Schwartz. 'Le champ de bataille de Oberhausbergen.' *Bulletin de la Faculté des Lettres de Strasbourg* 42 (1963–1964): 427–434 (= 'Das Schlachtfeld von Oberhausbergen (357 n. Chr.).' In R. Klein [ed.], *Julian Apostata* [Wege der Forschung 509]. Darmstadt, Germany: 1978, 318–330).

Hawkins, T. 'Jester for a Day, Master for a Year: Julian's *Misopogon* and the Kalends of 363 CE.' *Archiv für Religionsgeschichte* 13 (2012): 161–173.

Head, C. *The Emperor Julian.* Boston: 1976.

Hébert, M. 'Les martyrs céphalophores, Euchaire, Élophe et Libaire.' *Revue de l'Université de Bruxelles* 19 (1913–1914): 301–326.

Hegel, E. 'Die Eliphius-Reliquien: Translationen zwischen Lothringen und den Rheinischen Landen in alter und neuer Zeit.' *Archiv für Mittelrheinische Kirchengeschichte* 2 (1950): 283–290.

Heinen, H. 'Der Sieg des Kreuzes: Von der Kreuzesvision Konstantins zur Entdeckung des Kreuzes.' *Trierer Theologische Zeitschrift* 3 (2007): 221–237.

Heintze, H. von. 'Nordsyrische Elfenbeinstatuetten: Zu den Bildnissen des Kaisers Julian.' In O. Feld and U. Peschlow (eds.), *Studien zur spätantiken und byzantinischen Kunst Friedrich Wilhelm Deichmann gewidmet*, III. Bonn: 1986, 31–41.

Hellegouarc'h, J. *Eutrope, Abrégé de l'histoire romaine* (Collection des Universités de France). Paris: 1999.

Henck, N. 'From Macellum to Milan: The Movements of Julian the Apostate from A.D. 348 to 355.' *Kodai* 10 (1999–2000): 105–116.

Hengstl, J. *Griechische Papyri aus Ägypten als Zeugnisse des öffentlichen und privaten Lebens*. Munich: 1978.

Henning, C. J. *De eerste schoolstrijd tussen Kerk en Staat onder Julianus den Afvallige*. PhD University of Nijmegen, Nijmegen 1937.

Hepperle, U. *Hellenismos bei Flavius Claudius Iulianus und der Konsolidierungsprozess des Christentums im Osten des Römischen Reiches*. PhD University of Tübingen, Tübingen: 2010.

Herrin, J. See Av. Cameron.

Hoem, G. '*Emperor and Galilean:* The Problem Child of Literary Scholars.' In P. Bjørby and A. Aarseth (eds.), *Proceedings: IX International Ibsen Conference, Bergen, 5–10 June 2000*, Øvre Ervik, Norway: 2001, 309–314.

Hoffmann, J. G. E. *Iulianos der Abtruennige: Syrische Erzählungen*. Leiden, The Netherlands: 1880.

Hoffmann, R. J. *Julian's Against the Galileans, Edited and Translated*. New York: 2004.

Hollaender, J. See P. Rothenhöfer.

Hopkins, K. 'Christian Number and Its Implications.' *Journal of Early Christian Studies* 6 (1998): 185–226.

Hopkins, K. *A World Full of Gods: The Strange Triumph of Christianity*. London: 1999.

Hose, M. 'Konstruktion von Autorität: Julians Hymnen.' In C. Schäfer (ed.), *Kaiser Julian 'Apostata' und die philosophische Reaktion gegen das Christentum* (Millennium Studies 21). Berlin and New York 2008: 157–175.

Huart, P. 'Julien et l'hellénisme: Idées morales et politiques.' In R. Braun and J. Richer (eds.), *L'empereur Julien: De l'histoire à la légende (331–1715)*. Paris: 1978, 99–123.

Huck, O. 'Constantin, "législateur chrétien": Aux origines d'un topos de l'histoire ecclésiastique.' In Ph. Blaudeau and P. Van Nuffelen (eds.), *L'historiographie tardo-antique et la transmission des savoirs* (Millennium Studies 55). Berlin: 2015, 283–317.

Humphries, M. 'The Tyrant's Mask? Images of Good and Bad Rule in Julian's *Letter to the Athenians*.' In N. Baker-Brian and S. Tougher (eds.), *Emperor and Author: The Writings of Julian the Apostate*. Swansea, UK: 2012, 75–90.

Hunt, E. D. 'Julian and Marcus Aurelius.' In D. Innes et al., *Ethics and Rhetoric. Classical Essays for Donald Russell on his seventy-fifth Birthday*. Oxford: 1995, 287–298.

Hunt, E. D. 'The Successors of Constantine.' In Av. Cameron and P. D. Garnsey (eds.), *The Cambridge Ancient History*, XIII: *The Late Empire, A.D. 337–425*. Cambridge, UK: 1998a, 1–43.

Hunt, E. D. 'Julian.' In Av. Cameron and P. D. Garnsey (eds.), *The Cambridge Ancient History*, XIII: *The Late Empire, A.D. 337–425*. Cambridge, UK: 1998b, 44–77.

Hunt, E. D. 'The Christian Context of Julian's *Against the Galilaeans*.' In N. Baker-Brian and S. Tougher (eds.), *Emperor and Author: The Writings of Julian the Apostate*. Swansea, UK: 2012, 251–261.

Hunter, D. G. 'Borrowings from Libanius in the *Comparatio regis et monachi* of St. John Chrysostom.' *Journal of Theological Studies* 39 (1988): 525–531.

Hunter, D. G. 'Libanius and St. John Chrysostom: New Thoughts on an Old Problem.' *Studia Patristica* 22 (1989): 129–135.

Huttner, U. 'Sterben wie ein Philosoph: Zur Inszenierung des Todes in der Antike.' In M. Zimmermann (ed.), *Extreme Formen von Gewalt in Bild und Text des Altertums* (Münchner Studien zur Alten Welt 5). Munich: 2009, 295–320.

Iara, K. 'Senatorial Aristocracy: How Individual Is Individual Religion?' In É. Rebillard and J. Rüpke (eds.), *Group Identity and Religious Individuality in Late Antiquity*. Washington, DC: 2015, 165–214.

Ibsen, H. 'Emperor and Galilean.' In J. W. McFarlane and G. Orton (eds. and trans.), *The Oxford Ibsen* IV. London: 1963.

Irmscher, J. 'Review of Δ. N. Τριβόλης, *Eutropius historicus καὶ οἱ Ἕλληνες μεταφρασταὶ τοῦ Breviarium ab urbe condita*, Athens: 1941.' *Byzantinoslavica* 16 (1955): 361–365.

Isele, B. *Kampf um Kirchen: Religiöse Gewalt, heiliger Raum und christliche Topographie in Alexandria und Konstantinopel (4.Jh.)* (Jahrbuch für Antike und Christentum, Ergänzungsband, Kleine Reihe 4). Münster, Germany: 2010.

Ivic, N. 'Neutralizing Contingency: Ammianus Marcellinus as a Participant in Julian's Persian Campaign, 363 A.D.' *Arcadia* 39 (2004): 322–332.

James, L. 'Is There an Empress in the Text? Julian's *Speech of Thanks* to Eusebia.' In N. Baker-Brian and S. Tougher (eds.), *Emperor and Author: The Writings of Julian the Apostate*. Swansea, UK: 2012, 47–59.

Janka, M. 'Quod philosophus fuit, satura facta est: Julians *Misopogon* zwischen Gattungskonvention und Sitz im Leben.' In C. Schäfer (ed.), *Kaiser Julian 'Apostata' und die philosophische Reaktion gegen das Christentum* (Millennium Studies 21). Berlin and New York: 2008, 177–206.

Jiménez Sánchez, J. A. 'El emperador Juliano y su relación con los juegos Romanos.' *Polis* 15 (2003): 105–127.

Joassart, B. *Hippolyte Delehaye: Hagiographie critique et modernisme* (Subsidia Hagiographica 81). Brussels: 2000.

Johnson, M. J. 'Observations on the Burial of the Emperor Julian in Constantinople.' *Byzantion* 78 (2008): 254–260.

Johnston, S. I. 'Animating Statues: A Case Study in Ritual.' *Arethusa* 41 (2008): 445–477.

Jonas, R. 'A Newly Discovered Portrait of the Emperor Julian.' *American Journal of Archaeology* 50 (1946): 277–282.

Jonas, R. 'Titus (Flavius Vespasian) and (Flavius Claudius) Julian: Two Gem Portraits from the Jerusalem Area.' *Palestine Exploration Quarterly* 103 (1971): 9–12.

Jones, A. H. M. *The Later Roman Empire 284–602: A Social Economic and Administrative Survey.* 2 vols. Oxford: 1964 (repr. 1986).

Jones, C. P. 'Themistius after the Death of Julian.' *Historia* 59 (2010): 501–506.

Just, P. *Imperator et episcopus: Zum Verhältnis von Staatsgewalt und christlicher Kirche zwischen dem 1. Konzil von Nicaea (325) und dem 1. Konzil von Konstantinopel (381)* (Potsdamer Altertumswissenschaftliche Beiträge 8). Stuttgart: 2003.

Kaegi, W. E. 'Domestic Military Problems of Julian the Apostate.' *Byzantinische Forschungen* 2 (1967): 247–264 (repr. in W. E. Kaegi, *Army, Society and Religion in Byzantium* (Variorum Collected Studies Series 162). London: 1982, no. II).

Kaegi, W. E. 'The Emperor Julian at Naissus.' *Antiquité Classique* 44 (1975): 161–171 (repr. in W. E. Kaegi, *Army, Society and Religion in Byzantium* (Variorum Collected Studies Series 162). London: 1982, no. III).

Kaegi, W. E. 'Constantine's and Julian's Strategies of Strategic Surprise against the Persians.' *Athenaeum* 59 (1981): 209–213 (repr. in W. E. Kaegi, *Army, Society and Religion in Byzantium* (Variorum Collected Studies Series 162). London: 1982, no. IV).

Kaldellis, A. 'Julian, the Hierophant of Eleusis, and the Abolition of Constantius' Tyranny.' *Classical Quarterly* 55 (2005): 652–655.

Karpozēlos, A. Βυζαντινοὶ Ἱστορικοὶ καὶ Χρονογράφοι, vol. 3. Athens, Greece: 2009.

Karpp, H. 'Christennamen.' In Th. Klauser et al. (eds.), *Reallexikon für Antike und Christentum* 2 Stuttgart: 1954, 1114–1138.

Kaufman, P. I. 'Donatism Revisited: Moderates and Militants in Late Antique North Africa.' *Journal of Late Antiquity* 2 (2009): 131–142.

Kelly, G. 'Constantius II, Julian, and the Example of Marcus Aurelius (Ammianus Marcellinus XXI, 16, 11–12).' *Latomus* 64 (2005): 409–416.

Kelly, G. *Ammianus Marcellinus: The Allusive Historian* (Cambridge Classical Studies). Cambridge, UK: 2008.

Kelly, G. 'Ammianus Marcellinus: Tacitus' Heir and Gibbon's Guide.' In A. Feldherr (ed.), *The Cambridge Companion to the Roman Historians*. Cambridge, UK: 2009, 348–361.

Kent, J. P. C. 'An Introduction to the Coinage of Julian the Apostate (A.D. 360–363).' *Numismatic Chronicle* 19 (1959): 109–117 (= 'Eine Einführung in die Münzprägung des Julian Apostata [360–363].' In R. Klein [ed.], *Julian Apostata* [Wege der Forschung 509]. Darmstadt, Germany: 1978, 256–269).

Kent, J. P. C. *The Roman Imperial Coinage*, VIII: *The Family of Constantine I, A.D. 337–364*. London: 1981.

Kienast, D. *Römische Kaisertabelle: Grundzüge einer römischen Kaiserchronologie*. Darmstadt, Germany: 1996^2 (2017^6).

Kinzig, W. '"Trample upon me . . .": The Sophists Asterius and Hecebolius; Turncoats in the Fourth Century A.D.' In L. R. Wickham and C. P. Bammel (eds.), *Christian Faith and Greek Philosophy in Late Antiquity: Essays in Tribute to George Christopher Stead in Celebration of his Eightieth Birthday, 9th April 1993* (Vigiliae Christianae Supplements 19). Leiden, The Netherlands: 1993, 92–111.

Klein, R. *Constantius II. und die christliche Kirche* (Impulse der Forschung 26). Darmstadt, Germany: 1977.

Klein, R. (ed.). *Julian Apostata* (Wege der Forschung 509). Darmstadt, Germany: 1978.

Klein, R. 'Die Kämpfe um die Nachfolge nach dem Tode Constantins des Großen.' *Byzantinische Forschungen* 6 (1979): 101–150 (repr. in R. von Haehling [ed.], R. Klein, *Roma versa per aevum. Ausgewählte Schriften zur heidnischen und christlichen Spätantike* [Spudasmata 74]. Hildesheim, Germany: 1999, 1–49).

Klein, R. 'Kaiser Julians Rhetoren- und Unterrichtsgesetz.' *Römische Quartalschrift für christliche Altertumskunde und für Kirchengeschichte* 76 (1981): 73–94 (repr. in R. von Haehling [ed.], R. Klein, *Roma versa per aevum. Ausgewählte Schriften zur heidnischen und christlichen Spätantike* [Spudasmata 74]. Hildesheim, Germany: 1999, 128–155).

Klein, R. 'Julian Apostata: Ein Lebensbild.' *Gymnasium* 93 (1986): 273–292.

Klein, R. 'Der Julianexkurs bei Prudentius, *apotheosis* 449–502: Struktur und Bedeutung.' *Studia Patristica* 43 (2006): 401–408.

Kleinman, B. 'The Crisis at Antioch under Julian the Apostate.' *Hirundo* 7 (2008–2009): 67–76.

Klien-Paweletz, E. *Das Martyrium des heiligen Eusignios unter Kaiser Iulianos* (*Cod. Vind. hist. gr. 45, f 54–59v* (Diplomarbeit [. . .] an der Geistes- und Kulturwissenschaftlichen Fakultät der Universität Wien). Vienna: 2002.

Klotz, A. 'Die Quellen Ammians in der Darstellung von Julians Perserzug.' *Rheinisches Museum für Philologie* 71 (1916): 461–506.

Koch, W. 'Kaiser Julian der Abtrünnige: Seine Jugend und Kriegsthaten bis zum Tode des Kaisers Constantius (331–361); Eine Quellenuntersuchung.' In

A. Fleckeisen (ed.), *Jahrbücher für classische Philologie Supplementband 25*. Leipzig: 1899, 329–488.

Koch, W. 'Keizer Julianus' afval van het Christendom.' *Nederlandsch Archief voor Kerkgeschiedenis* 19 (1926): 161–186.

Koch, W. 'Comment l'empereur Julien tâcha de fonder une église païenne.' *Revue Belge de Philologie et d'Histoire* 6 (1927): 123–146.

Koch, W. 'Comment l'empereur Julien tâcha de fonder une église païenne.' Part 2. *Revue Belge de Philologie et d'Histoire* 7 (1928): 49–82, 511–550, 1362–1385.

Koch, W. 'Sur le sens de quelques mots et expressions chez Julien.' *Revue Belge de Philologie et d'Histoire* 7 (1928): 539–550.

Kotter, B. *Die Schriften des Johannes von Damaskos V: Opera homiletica et hagiographica* (Patristische Texte und Studien 29). Berlin and New York: 1988.

Kotula, T. '*Provincialis et miles*: Le soulèvement de Julien à Paris et l'Occident romaine.' In Y. Le Bohec (ed.), *L'Afrique, la Gaule, la religion à l'époque romain* (Mélanges à la mémoire de Marcel Le Glay; Collection Latomus 226). Brussels: 1994a, 473–484.

Kotula, T. 'Julien Auguste et l'aristocratie municipale d'Afrique: Réflexions méthodologiques.' *Antiquités Africaines* 30 (1994b): 271–279.

Kovács, P. 'Kaiser Julian in Pannonien, über Pannonien.' In Á. Szabó (ed.), *From Polites to Magos: Studia György Németh sexagenario dedicata* (Hungarian Polis Studies 22), Budapest and Debrecen, Hungary: 2016, 169–187.

Krascheninnikov, M. *Ioannis Hagioelitae de passione sancti Basilii presbyteri Ancyrani narratio* (Acta et Commentationes Imp. Universitatis Jurievensis [olim Dorpatensis]). Yerevan, Armenia: 1907.

Krause, J.-U. *Witwen und Waisen im Römischen Reich, 4: Witwen und Waisen im frühen Christentum* (Heidelberger Althistorische Beiträge und Epigraphische Studien 19). Stuttgart: 1995.

Kristensen, T. M. *Making and Breaking the Gods: Christian Responses to Pagan Sculpture in Late Antiquity* (Aarhus Studies in Mediterranean Antiquity 12). Aarhus, Denmark: 2013.

Krivouchine, I. 'L'empereur païen vu par l'historien ecclésiastique: Julien l'Apostat de Socrate.' *Jahrbuch der Österreichischen Byzantinistik* 47 (1997): 13–24.

Krueger, D. *Writing and Holiness: The Practice of Authorship in the Early Christian East*. Philadelphia: 2004.

Krumbacher, K. *Der heilige Georg in der griechischen Literatur* (Abhandlungen der Königlich Bayerischen Akademie der Wissenschaften, Philosophisch-Philologische und Historische Klasse 25,3). Munich: 1911.

Kuhoff, W. 'Ein Mythos in der römischen Geschichte: Der Sieg Konstantins des Großen über Maxentius.' *Chiron* 21 (1991): 127–174.

Kurmann, A. *Gregor von Nazianz, Oratio 4, Gegen Julian: Ein Kommentar* (Schweizerische Beiträge zur Altertumswissenschaft 19). Basel, Switzerland: 1988.

Lach, R. ' "Was seine Schritte vorwärts lenkte oder drängte": Das Rätsel Julian Apostata bei Edward Gibbon und Felix Dahn.' In C.-F. Berghahn and T. Kinzel (eds.), *Edward Gibbon im deutschen Sprachraum: Bausteine einer Rezeptionsgeschichte* (Germanisch-Romanische Monatsschrift, Beiheft 66). Heidelberg: 2015, 343–358.

Lacombrade, Chr. *L'empereur Julien: Oeuvres complètes, II.2, Discours de Julien empereur, Les Césars, Sur Hélios-Roi, Le Misopogon*. Paris: 1964.

Lacombrade, Chr. 'L'Empereur Julien émule de Marc Aurèle.' *Pallas* 14 (1967): 9–22.

Laconi, S. *Costanzo II: Ritratto di un imperatore eretico*. Rome: 2004.

Lagacherie, O. 'Libanios et Ammien Marcellin: Les moyens de l'héroïsation de l'empereur Julien; Étude comparée du discours 1, 132–133 (*Bios*) de Libanios et de l'*Histoire* XXV, 3, 1–9 d'Ammien Marcellin.' *Revue des Études Grecques* 115 (2002): 792–802.

Lagacherie, O. 'L'art de la parole: pratique et pouvoir du discours. Pouvoir et éloquence à la fin de l'Antiquité: le discours contre Héracleios Le Cynique de l'empereur Julien'. *Vita Latina* 183/184 (2011): 193–204.

Lane Fox, R. *Pagans and Christians*. London: 1986 (repr. Harmondsworth, UK: 1988).

Lane Fox, R. 'The Itinarary of Alexander: Constantius to Julian.' *Classical Quarterly* 47 (1997): 239–252.

Lassus, J. 'L'église cruciforme: Antioch-Kaoussié 12-F.' In R. Stillwell et al. (eds.), *Antioch-on-the-Orontes, 2: The Excavations 1933–1936* (Publications of the Committee for the Excavation of Antioch and its Vicinity). Princeton, NJ: 1938, 5–44.

Leadbetter, B. 'The Illegitimacy of Constantine and the Birth of the Tetrarchy.' In S. N. C. Lieu and D. Montserrat (eds.), *Constantine: History, Historiography, and Legend*. London: 1998, 74–85.

Leclercq, H. 'Labarum.' In F. Cabrol and H. Leclercq (eds.), *Dictionnaire d'Archéologie Chrétienne et de Liturgie* 8.1. Paris: 1928, 927–962.

Leedom, J. W. 'Constantius II: Three Revisions.' *Byzantion* 48 (1978): 132–145.

Lefebvre, G. 'L'âge de 110 ans et la vieillesse chez les Égyptiens.' *Comptes rendus de l'Académie des Inscriptions et Belles-Lettres* (1944): 106–119.

Le Nain de Tillemont, S. *Mémoires pour servir à l'histoire ecclésiastique des six premiers siècles*, VII. Paris: 1700.

Lendon, J. E. *Soldiers and Ghosts: A History of Battle in Classical Antiquity*. New Haven, CT: 2005.

Lenski, N. E. 'The Election of Jovian and the Role of the Late Imperial Guards.' *Klio* 82 (2000): 492–515.

Lenski, N. E. 'Were Valentinian, Valens and Jovian Confessors before Julian the Apostate?' *Zeitschrift für Antikes Christentum* 6 (2002): 253–276.

Lenski, N. E. 'The Reign of Constantine.' In N. E. Lenski (ed.), *The Cambridge Companion to the Age of Constantine*. Cambridge, UK: 2006 (2012²)>, 59–90.

Lenski, N. E. 'Constantine and the Tyche of Constantinople.' In J. Wienand (ed.), *Contested Monarchy: Integrating the Roman Empire in the Fourth Century AD*. Oxford: 2015, 330–352.

Lenski, N. E. *Constantine and the Cities. Imperial Authority and Civic Politics*. Philadelphia: 2016.

Leppin, H. *Von Constantin dem Großen zu Theodosius II.: Das christliche Kaisertum bei den Kirchenhistorikern Socrates, Sozomenus und Theodoret* (Hypomnemata 110). Göttingen, Germany: 1996.

Leppin, H. 'Constantius II. und das Heidentum.' *Athenaeum* 87 (1999): 457–480.

Leppin, H. 'Zum Wandel des spätantiken Heidentums.' *Millennium* 1 (2004): 59–81.

Leppin, H. 'Das Bild des Gallus bei Philostorg: Überlegungen zur Traditionsgeschichte.' In D. Meyer (ed.), *Philostorge et l'historiographie de l'Antiquité tardive* (Collegium Beatus Rhenanus 3). Stuttgart: 2011, 185–202.

Leppin, H., and H. Ziemssen. *Maxentius: Der letzte Kaiser in Rom*. Mainz, Germany: 2007.

Le Roux, P. 'Domesticus et poète: Le cursus versifié d'Abla (Almeria).' In M. Christol et al. (eds.), *Institutions, société et vie politique dans l'empire romain au IVᵉ siècle ap. J.-C.* (Actes de la table ronde autour de l'oeuvre d'André Chastagnol, Paris 20–21 janvier 1989; Collection de l'École Française de Rome 159). Paris: 1992, 265–275.

Levenson, D. B. 'Julian's Attempt to Rebuild the Temple: An Inventory of Ancient and Medieval Sources.' In H. W. Attridge, J. J. Collins, and Th. H. Tobin (eds.), *Of Scribes and Scrolls: Studies on the Hebrew Bible, Intertestamental Judaism, and Christian Origins Presented to John Strugnell on the Occasion of His Sixtieth Birthday*. Lanham, MD, New York, and London: 1990, 261–279.

Levenson, D. B. 'The Ancient and Medieval Sources for the Emperor Julian's Attempt to Rebuild the Jerusalem Temple.' *Journal for the Study of Judaism* 35 (2004): 409–460.

Lévêque, P. 'De nouveaux portraits de l'empereur Julien.' *Latomus* 22 (1963): 74–84 (= 'Neue Porträts des Kaisers Julian.' In R. Klein [ed.], *Julian Apostata* [Wege der Forschung 509]. Darmstadt, Germany: 1978, 305–317).

Lewy, Y. 'Julian the Apostate and the Building of the Temple.' *Jerusalem Cathedra* 3 (1983): 70–96.

Liebeschuetz, J. H. W. G. *Antioch: City and Imperial Administration in the Later Roman Empire*. Oxford: 1972.

Liebeschuetz, J. H. W. G. 'Ammianus, Julian and Divination.' In M. Wissemann (ed.), *Roma Renascens: Beiträge zur Spätantike und Rezeptionsgeschichte; Ilona*

Opelt von ihren Freunden und Schülern zum 9.7.1988 in Verehrung gewidmet. Frankfurt: 1988, 198–213 (also in J. H. W. G. Liebeschuetz, *From Diocletian to the Arab Conquest. Change in the Late Roman Empire*. Aldershot: 1990 [repr. 1996] no. III).

Liebeschuetz, J. H. W. G. 'Julian's Hymn to the Mother of the Gods: The Revival and Justification of Traditional Religion.' In N. Baker-Brian and S. Tougher (eds.), *Emperor and Author: The Writings of Julian the Apostate*. Swansea, UK: 2012, 213–227 (repr. in J. H. W. G. Liebeschuetz, *East and West in Late Antiquity: Invasion, Settlement, Ethnogenesis and Conflicts of Religion* [Impact of Empire 20]. Leiden, The Netherlands: 2015, 325–340).

Liebeschuetz, J. H. W. G. See also S. L. Greenslade.

Lietzmann, H. 'Ioannes 55.' In G. Wissowa, W. Kroll et al. (eds.), *Paulys Real-Encyclopädie der classischen Altertumswissenschaft* 9. Stuttgart: 1916, 1811–1828.

Lieu, S. N. C. (ed.). *The Emperor Julian: Panegyric and Polemic* (Translated Texts for Historians, Greek Series 1). Liverpool, UK: 1986 (1989²).

Lieu, S. N. C. 'From Villain to Saint and Martyr: The Life and After-Life of Flavius Artemius, *Dux Aegypti*.' *Byzantine and Modern Greek Studies* 20 (1996): 56–76.

Lippold, A. 'Review of *The Prosopography of the Later Roman Empire: Vol. 1: A. D. 260–395*.' *Gnomon* 46 (1974): 268-273.

Lippold, A. 'Iulianus I (Kaiser).' In Th. Klauser et al. (eds.), *Reallexikon für Antike und Christentum* 19. Stuttgart: 2001, 442–483.

Löhr, W. 'Arius Reconsidered.' *Zeitschrift für Antikes Christentum* 9 (2005): 524–560.

Löhr, W. 'Arius Reconsidered.' *Zeitschrift für Antikes Christentum* 10 (2006) 121–157.

Long, J. F. 'Structures of Irony in Julian's *Misopogon*.' *Ancient World* 24 (1993): 15–23.

López Sánchez, F. 'Julian and His Coinage: A Very Constantinian Prince.' In N. Baker-Brian and S. Tougher (eds.), *Emperor and Author: The Writings of Julian the Apostate*. Swansea, UK: 2012, 159–182.

Lucassen, L. H. 'Een merkwaardige brief van Julianus Apostata.' *Hermeneus* 6 (1934): 15–18.

Lucchesi, E. See R.-G. Coquin.

Luchner, K. ' "Grund, Fundament, Mauerwerk, Dach?"—Julians φιλοσοφία im Netzwerk seiner Briefe.' In C. Schäfer (ed.), *Kaiser Julian 'Apostata' und die philosophische Reaktion gegen das Christentum* (Millennium Studies 21). Berlin and New York: 2008, 221–252.

Lucien-Brun, X. 'Constance II et le massacre des princes.' *Bulletin de l'Association Guillaume Budé* no. 37 (1973): 585–602.

Luck, G. 'Theurgy and Forms of Worship in Neoplatonism.' In J. Neusner, E. S. Frerichs, and P. V. McCracken Flesher (eds.), *Religion, Science, and Magic in Concert and Conflict.* New York and Oxford: 1989, 185–225.

Lugaresi, L. 'Giuliano Imperatore e Gregorio di Nazianzo: Contiguità culturale e contrapposizione ideologica nel confronto tra ellenismo e cristianesimo.' In *Giuliano imperatore: Le sue idee, i suoi amici, i suoi avversari* (Atti del Convegno Internazionale di Studi, Lecce 10–12 dicembre 1998). *Rudiae* 10 (1998 [2000]): 293–334.

Lukaszewicz, A. 'À propos du symbolisme impérial romain au IVe siècle: Quelques remarques sur le christogramme.' *Historia* 39 (1990): 504–506.

Lunn-Rockliffe, S. 'Diabolical Motivations: The Devil in Ecclesiastical Histories from Eusebius to Evagrius.' In G. Greatrex and H. Elton (eds.), *Shifting Genres in Late Antiquity.* Farnham, UK, and Burlington, VT: 2015, 119–131.

Lyman, R. J. 'Arius and Arians.' In D. G. Harvey and S. A. Hunter (eds.). *The Oxford Handbook of Early Christian Studies.* Oxford: 2008, 237–257.

MacMullen, R. *Paganism in the Roman Empire.* New Haven, CT, and London: 1981.

MacMullen, R. *Christianizing the Roman Empire (A.D. 100–400).* New Haven, CT: 1984.

MacMullen, R. 'Judicial Savagery in the Roman Empire.' *Chiron* 16 (1986): 147–166.

Magny, A. *Porphyry in Fragments: Reception of an Anti-Christian Text in Late Antiquity* (Ashgate Studies in Philosophy and Theology in Late Antiquity). Farnham, UK, and Burlington, VT: 2014.

Maier, J.-L. *Le dossier du Donatisme: Archiv für die Ausgabe der griechischen christlichen Schriftsteller der ersten Jahrhunderte. I: Des origines à la mort de Constance II (303–361).* (Texte und Untersuchungen zur Geschichte der altchristlichen Literatur 134). Berlin: 1987.

Maier, J.-L. *Le dossier du Donatisme: Archiv für die Ausgabe der griechischen christlichen Schriftsteller der ersten Jahrhunderte. II. De Julien l'Apostat à Saint Jean Damascène (361–750)* (Texte und Untersuchungen zur Geschichte der altchristlichen Literatur 135). Berlin: 1989.

Malosse, P.-L. 'Rhétorique et psychologie antiques: Éloge des vertus et critiques obliques dans le portrait de l'Empereur Julien par Libanios.' *Ktèma* 20 (1995a): 319–338.

Malosse, P.-L. 'Les alternances de l'amitié: Julien et Libanios (349–363 et au-delà).' *Revue de Philologie, de Littérature et d'Histoire Anciennes* 69 (1995b): 249–262.

Malosse, P.-L. 'Vie et mort de l'empereur Julien, par Libanios.' *Quaderni di Storia* 24, no. 48 (1998): 43–68.

Malosse, P.-L. 'Enquête sur les relations entre Julien et Gallus.' *Klio* 86 (2004): 185–196.

Malosse, P.-L. 'Les bagues de l'Empereur Julien: La mise en pratique de la rhétorique épistolaire dans la correspondance personnelle d'un empereur.' *Rhetorica* 25.2 (2007): 183–203.

Malosse, P.-L. 'Jean Chrysostome a-t-il été l'élève de Libanios?' *Phoenix* 62 (2008): 273–280.

Malosse, P.-L. 'Actualité et perspectives de la recherche sur Libanios.' In U. Criscuolo and L. De Giovanni (eds.), *Trent'anni di studi sulla Tarda Antichità: Bilanci e prospettive*. Naples, Italy: 2009, 229–244.

Malosse, P.-L. 'Galileans or Gallus? (Julian's Letter to Aetius).' *Classical Quarterly* 60 (2010): 607–609.

Malosse, P.-L. 'Philostorge, Libanios et Julien: Divergences et convergences.' In D. Meyer (ed.), *Philostorge et l'historiographie de l'Antiquité tardive* (Collegium Beatus Rhenanus 3). Stuttgart 2011, 203–220.

Malosse, P.-L. 'Libanius' Orations.' In L. Van Hoof (ed.), *Libanius: A Critical Introduction*. Cambridge, UK: 2014, 81–106.

Männlein-Robert, I. (ed.), *Die Christen als Bedrohung? Text, Kontext und Wirkung von Porphyrios' "Contra Christianos"* (Roma Aeterna 5), Stuttgart, Germany: 2017.

Marasco, G. 'L'imperatore Giuliano e l'esecuzione di Fl. Artemio, *dux Aegypti*.' *Prometheus* 23 (1997): 59–78.

Marasco, G. 'Storiografia locale e prospettiva universale nella *Storia ecclesiastica* di Teodoreto di Cirro.' *Koinonia* 28–29 (2004–2005): 145–167.

Maraval, P. *Les persécutions des chrétiens durant les quatre premiers siècles* (Bibliothèque d'Histoire du Christianisme 30). Tournai, Belgium: 1992.

Maraval, P. *Constantin le Grand: Empereur romain, empereur chrétien, 306–337*. Paris: 2011.

Maraval, P. *Les fils de Constantin: Constantin II (337–340), Constance II (337–361), Constant (337–350)*. Paris: 2013.

Marcone, A. 'Il conflitto tra l'imperatore Giuliano e gli Antiocheni.' *Atene e Roma* 26 (1981): 142–152.

Marcone, A. 'Un panegirico rovesciato: Pluralità di modelli e contaminazione letteraria nel *Misopogon* giulianeo.' *Revue des Études Augustiniennes* 30 (1984): 226–239 (repr. in A. Marcone, *Di Tarda Antichità: Scritti scelti* [Studi Udinesi sul Mondo Antico 6]. Florence: 2008, 15–28).

Marcone, A. *Giuliano l'Apostata*. Teramo, Italy: 1994.

Marcone, A. 'The Forging of an Hellenic Orthodoxy: Julian's Speeches against the Cynics.' In N. Baker-Brian and S. Tougher (eds.), *Emperor and Author: The Writings of Julian the Apostate*. Swansea, UK: 2012, 239–250.

Marcone, A. (ed.). *L'imperatore Giuliano: Realtà storica e rappresentazione* (Studi sul Mondo Antico 3). Milan: 2015.

Marco Simón, F. 'Ambivalencia icónica y persuasión ideológica: Las monedas de Juliano con representación del toro.' *Athenaeum* 87 (1999): 201–214; cf.

F. Marco Simon, 'On Bulls and Stars. Sacrifice and Allegoric Pluralism in Julian's Times.' In A. Mastrocinque, C. Giuffrè Scibona (eds.), *Demeter, Isis, Vesta, and Cybele. Studies in Greek and Roman Religion in Honour of Giulia Sfameni Gasparro* (Potsdamer Altertumswissenschaftliche Beiträge 36), Stuttgart: 2012, 221–236.

Martelli, F. 'Il sacrificio dei fanciulli nella letteratura greca et latina.' In F. Vattoni (ed.), *Atti del Settimana Sangue e Antropologia Biblica nella Patristica (Roma, 23–28 novembre 1981)*, I (Centro Studi Sanguis Christi 2.1). Rome: [1982], 247–323.

Marcos, M. ' "He Forced with Gentleness": Emperor Julian's Attitude to Religious Coercion.' *Antiquité Tardive* 17 (2009): 191–204.

Markschies, C. 'Heis Theos? Religionsgeschichte und Christentum bei Erik Peterson.' In B. Nichtweis (ed.), *Vom Ende der Zeit: Geschichtstheologie und Eschatologie bei Erik Peterson* (Symposium Mainz: Religion-Geschichte-Gesellschaft 16). Münster, Germany: 2001, 38–74.

Martin, A. 'L'histoire ecclésiastique intéresse-t-elle Malalas?' In J. Beaucamp et al. (eds.), *Recherches sur la Chronique de Jean Malalas I* (Actes du Colloque 'La Chronique de Jean Malalas [VIe s. è. Chr.]: Genèse et Transmission'; organisé les 21 et 22 mars 2003 à Aix-en-Provence [Maison Méditerranéenne des Sciences de l'Homme] par l'UMR 6125 'Textes et Documents de la Méditerranée Antique et Médiévale' [Université de Provence-CNRS]; Monographies, Centre de Recherche d'Histoire et Civilisation de Byzance 15). Paris: 2004, 83–102.

Martin, A. 'Théodoret et la tradition chrétienne contre l'empereur Julien.' In D. Auger and É. Wolff (eds.), *Culture classique et christianisme: Mélanges offerts à Jean Bouffartigue* (Textes, Histoire et Monuments de l'Antiquité au Moyen Age). Paris: 2008, 71–82.

Martin, A. 'Des sources pour la topographie d'Antioche: Les *Histoires Ecclésiastiques* de la première moitié du Vᵉ siècle.' *Topoi* 17 (2011): 403–420.

Martin, A. 'La mort de l'empereur Julien: Un document iconographique éthiopien.' In E. Amato, V. Fauvinet-Ranson, and B. Pouderon (eds.), *ΕΝ ΚΑΛΟΙΣ ΚΟΙΝΟΠΡΑΓΙΑ: Hommages à la mémoire de Pierre-Louis Malosse et Jean Bouffartigue* (RET Supplement 3; Textes pour l'Histoire de l'Antiquité Tardive). [Nantes, France]: 2014a, 313–330.

Martin, A. 'La réception du concile de Nicée et son impact sur l'évolution des courants théologiques en Orient (325–381).' *Antiquité Tardive* 22 (2014b): 35–42.

Martindale, J. R. 'Prosopography of the Later Roman Empire: Addenda et Corrigenda to Volume I.' *Historia* 23 (1974): 246–252.

Martindale, J.R. 'Prosopography of the Later Roman Empire: Addenda et Corrigenda to Volume I.' *Historia* 29 (1980): 474–497.

Masaracchia, E. *Giuliano Imperatore: Contra Galilaeos; Introduzione, testo critico e traduzione* (Testi e Commenti 9). Rome: 1990.

Massalsky, N. 'Sacrifizio umano offerto dall'imperatore Giuliano in Ungheria.' *Bullettino del Museo dell'Impero Romano* 12 (1941): 159–166 (= 'Das Menschenopfer des Kaisers Julianus in Ungarn.' *Forschungen und Fortschritte* 17 [1941]: 239–240).

Mastrocinque, A. *Giuliano l'Apostata, Discorso su Helios re* (Studia Classica et Mediaevalia 5). Nordhausen, Germany: 2011.

Mattheis, M. *Der Kampf ums Ritual: Diskurs und Praxis traditioneller Rituale in der Spätantike* (Reihe Geschichte 4). Duisburg, Germany: 2014.

Matthews, J. F. *The Roman Empire of Ammianus*. London: 1989 (repr. Ann Arbor: 2007).

Matthews, J. F. 'Gibbon and the Later Roman Empire: Causes and Circumstances.' In R. McKitterick and R. Quinault (eds.), *Edward Gibbon and Empire*. Cambridge, UK: 1997, 12–33.

Matthews, J. F. *Laying Down the Law: A Study of the Theodosian Code*. New Haven, CT, and London: 2000.

Mayer, W., and P. Allen. *The Churches of Syrian Antioch (300–638 CE)* (Late Antique History and Religion 5). Leuven, Belgium: 2012.

Mazza, M. 'Giuliano o dell'utopia religiosa: Il tentativo di fondare una chiesa pagana?' In *Giuliano imperatore: Le sue idee, i suoi amici, i suoi avversari* (Atti del Convegno Internazionale di Studi, Lecce 10–12 dicembre 1998). *Rudiae* 10 (1998 [2000]): 19–42 (repr. in M. Mazza, *Tra Roma e Costantinopoli. Ellenismo, Oriente, Cristianesimo nella Tarda Antichità, Saggi Scelti* (Testi e Studi di Storia Antica 23). Catania, Italy: 2009, 217–244).

McGuckin, J. A. *St. Gregory of Nazianzus: An Intellectual Biography*. Crestwood, NY: 2001.

McGuckin, J. A. *St. Cyril of Alexandria: The Christological Controversy; Its History, Theology, and Texts*. Crestwood, NY: 2004.

McLynn, N. 'Julian and the Christian Professors.' In C. Harrison, C. Humfress, and I. Sandwell (eds.), *Being Christian in Late Antiquity: Festschrift for Gillian Clark*. Oxford: 2014, 120–136.

Medici, L. de'. *La rappresentazione di San Giovanni e Paolo*. In A. Simioni (ed.), *Lorenzo de' Medici il Magnifico, Opere*, Vol. II. Bari, Italy: 1914, 71–114.

Meggitt, J. J. 'Meat Consumption and Social Conflict in Corinth.' *Journal of Theological Studies* 45 (1994): 137–141.

Melloni, A. (ed.). *Costantino I. Enciclopedia Costantiniana sulla figura e l'immagine dell'imperatore del cosidetto editto di Milano, 313–2013*. 3 vols. [Rome]: 2013.

Meredith, A. 'Porphyry and Julian against the Christians.' In H. Temporini and W. Haase (eds.), *Aufstieg und Niedergang der Römischen Welt (ANRW): Geschichte und Kultur Roms in der neueren Forschung* 23.2. Berlin: 1980, 1119–1149.

Mervaud, Chr. 'Julien l'Apostat dans la correspondance de Voltaire et de Frédéric II.' *Revue d'Histoire Littéraire de la France* 76 (1976): 724–743.

Métivier, S. *La Cappadoce (IVᵉ–VIᵉ siècle): Une histoire provinciale de l'Empire romain d'Orient* (Byzantina Sorbonensia 22). Paris: 2005.

Meulder, M. 'Julien l'Apostat contre les Parthes: Un guerrier impie.' *Byzantion* 61 (1991): 458–495.

Mimouni, S. C. 'Qui sont les *Galiléens* dans la littérature chrétienne ancienne?' *Proche-Orient Chrétien* 49 (1999): 53–67.

Mitchell, S., and P. Van Nuffelen (eds.). *One God: Pagan Monotheism in the Roman Empire*. Cambridge, UK: 2010.

Molac, Ph. 'L'image de Julien l'Apostat chez saint Grégoire de Nazianze.' *Bulletin de Littérature Ecclésiastique* 102 (2001): 39–48.

Momigliano, A. 'The Lonely Historian Ammianus Marcellinus.' *Annali della Scuola Normale Superiore di Pisa* 4 (1974): 1393–1407 (repr. in A. Momigliano, *Sesto Contributo alla Storia degli Studi Classici e del Mondo Antico*, vol. 1 [Storia e Letteratura 149]. Rome: 1980, 143–157).

Momigliano, A. 'The Disadvantages of Monotheism for a Universal State.' *Classical Philology* 81 (1986): 285–297 (repr. in: A. Momigliano, *Ottavo Contributo alla Storia degli Studi Classici e del Mondo Antico* [Storia e Letteratura 169], Rome: [1987] 2006, 313–328).

Moreschini, C. 'L'opera e la personalità dell'imperatore Giuliano nelle due "Invectivae" di Gregorio Nazianzeno.' In *Forma Futuri: Studi in onore del cardinale Michele Pellegrino*. Torino, Italy: 1975, 416–430.

Moretus Plantin, H. *Les passions de S. Lucien et leurs dérivés céphalophoriques*. Namur, Belgium: 1953.

Morgenstern, F. 'Die Kaisergesetze gegen die Donatisten in Nordafrika (Mitte 4. Jh. bis 429).' *Zeitschrift der Savigny-Stiftung für Rechtsgeschichte (Romanistische Abteilung)* 110 (1993): 103–123.

Mossay, J., and D. D. Bundy. '1. Gallican.' In R. Aubert et al. (eds.), *Dictionnaire d'Histoire et de Géographie Ecclésiastique* 19. Paris: 1981, 843–845.

Mudd, M. M. See A. Novikov.

Müller, F. L. *Die beiden Satiren des Kaisers Julianus Apostata (Symposion oder Caesares und Antiochikos oder Misopogon): Griechisch und Deutsch, mit Einleitung, Anmerkungen und Index* (Palingenesia 66). Stuttgart: 1998.

Müller-Seidel, I. 'Die Usurpation Julians des Abtrünnigen im Lichte seiner Germanenpolitik.' *Historische Zeitschrift* 180 (1955): 225–244.

Müller, W. W. 'Weihrauch.' In G. Wissowa, W. Kroll et al. (eds.), *Paulys Real-Encyclopädie der classischen Altertumswissenschaft, Supplementband* 15. Stuttgart: 1978, 700–777.

Munzi, M. 'Considerazioni sulla riforma monetaria dell'imperatore Giuliano.' *Annali dell'Istituto Italiano di Numismatica* 43 (1996): 295–306.

Murdoch, A. *The Last Pagan: Julian the Apostate and the Death of the Ancient World*. Stroud, UK: 2003 (repr. Rochester, VT: 2008).

Murjanoff, M. 'Zur Überlieferung der *Passio SS. Iohannis et Pauli.'* *Analecta Bollandiana* 83 (1965): 361–364.

Nardi, C. 'La figura del "verme" nella *Narratio* del Crisostomo (*Adv. oppugn. vit. mon.* I, 1–2).' In *La narrativa cristiana antiqua: Codici narrativi, strutture formali, schemi retorici* (XXIII Incontro di Studiosi dell'Antichità Cristiana, Roma, 5–7 maggio 1994; Studia Ephemeridis Augustinianum 50). Rome: 1995, 301–322.

Näsström, B.-M. *O Mother of the Gods and Men. Some Aspects of the Religious Thoughts in Emperor Julian's Discourse on the Mother of the Gods.* PhD University of Gothenburg. Gothenburg, Sweden: 1986.

Neri, V. *Costanzo, Giuliano e l'ideale del* Civilis Princeps *nelle Storie di Ammiano Marcellino* (Studi Bizantini e Slavi 1). Rome: 1984.

Neri, V. *Medius Princeps: Storia e immagine di Costantino nella storiografia latina pagana.* Bologna, Italy: 1992.

Nesbitt, J. W. See V. S. Crisafulli.

Nesselrath, H.-G. 'Zur Wiederentdeckung von Julian Apostata in der Renaissance: Lorenzo de' Medici und Ammianus Marcellinus.' *Antike und Abendland* 28 (1992): 133–144.

Nesselrath, H.-G. 'Die Christen und die heidnische Bildung: Das Beispiel des Sokrates Scholastikos (*hist. eccl.* 3,16).' In J. Dummer and M. Vielberg (eds.), *Leitbilder der Spätantike—Eliten und Leitbilder* (Altertumswissenschaftliches Kolloquium 1). Stuttgart: 1999, 79–100.

Nesselrath, H.-G. 'Kaiserlicher Held und Christenfeind: Julian Apostata im Urteil des späteren 4. und des 5. Jahrhunderts.' In B. Bäbler and H.-G. Nesselrath (eds.), *Die Welt des Sokrates von Konstantinopel: Studien zu Politik, Religion und Kultur im späten 4. und frühen 5. Jh. n. Chr. zu Ehren von Christoph Schäublin.* Munich and Leipzig: 2001, 15–43.

Nesselrath, H.-G. *Libanios: Zeuge einer schwindenden Welt* (Standorte in Antike und Christentum 4). Stuttgart: 2012.

Nesselrath, H.-G. 'Libanius and the Literary Tradition.' In L. Van Hoof (ed.), *Libanius: A Critical Introduction.* Cambridge, UK: 2014, 241–267.

Nesselrath, H.-G. (ed.). *Iulianus Augustus Opera* (Bibliotheca Scriptorum Graecorum et Romanorum Teubneriana 2018). Berlin: 2015.

Nesselrath, Th. *Kaiser Julian und die Repaganisierung des Reiches: Konzept und Vorbilder* (Jahrbuch für Antike und Christentum. Ergänzungsbände, Kleine Reihe 9), Münster, Germany: 2013.

Neudecker, R. 'Bryaxis.' *Der Neue Pauly* 2 (1997): 806.

Neumann, K. J. 'Das Geburtsjahr Kaiser Iulians.' *Philologus* 50 (1891): 761–762.

Nicholson, O. 'The "Pagan Churches" of Maximinus Daia and Julian the Apostate.' *Journal of Ecclesiastical History* 45 (1994): 1–10.

Nicholson, O. 'Constantine's Vision of the Cross.' *Vigiliae Christianae* 53 (2000): 309–323.

Nock, A. D. 'Deification and Julian.' *Journal of Roman Studies* 47 (1957): 115–123 (repr. in A. D. Nock, *Essays on Religion and the Ancient World*, Z. Steward [ed.], Oxford: 1972, II, 833–846).

Nöldeke, Th. 'Über den syrischen Roman von Kaiser Julian.' *Zeitschrift der Deutschen Morgenländischen Gesellschaft* 28 (1874a): 263–292.

Nöldeke, Th. 'Ein zweiter syrischer Julianusroman.' *Zeitschrift der Deutschen Morgenländischen Gesellschaft* 28 (1874b): 660–674.

Norderval, O. 'The Emperor Constantine and Arius: Unity in the Church and Unity in the Empire.' *Studia Theologica* 42 (1988): 113–150.

Norman, A. F. 'The Illyrian Prefecture of Anatolius.' *Rheinisches Museum für Philologie* 100 (1957): 253–259.

Norman, A. F. 'Libanius: The Teacher in an Age of Violence.' In G. Fatouros and T. Krischer (eds.), *Libanios* (Wege der Forschung 621). Darmstadt, Germany: 1983, 150–169.

Novikov, A., and M. M. Mudd. 'Reconsidering the Role of Constantius II in the "Massacre of the Princes." ' *Byzantinoslavica* 57 (1996): 26–32.

Nulle, S. H. 'Julian redivivus.' *Centennial Review* 5 (1961): 320–338.

Oikonomides, A. N. 'Ancient Inscriptions Recording the Restoration of Greco-Roman Shrines by the Emperor Flavius Claudius Julianus (361–363 A.D.).' *Ancient World* 15 (1987): 37–42.

Oliver, J. H. 'On the Edict of Severus Alexander (*P. Fayum* 20).' *American Journal of Philology* 99 (1978): 474–485.

Olivetti, A. 'Sulle stragi di Costantinopoli succedute alla morte di Costantino il Grande.' *Rivista di Filologia Classica* 43 (1915): 67–79.

Olszaniec, S. ' "Restitutor Romanae religionis": Kaiser Julian als Erneuerer der heidnischen Bräuche.' *Eos* 86 (1999): 77–102.

Olszaniec, S. 'Julian Apostata und seine Reform der heidnischen Priesterschaft.' *Eos* 87 (2000): 217–241.

Olszaniec, S. *Prosopographical Studies on the Court Elite in the Roman Empire (4th Century AD)*. Toruń, Poland: 2013.

Opitz, H.-G. *Urkunden zur Geschichte des arianischen Streites 318–328* (Athanasius Werke 3.1.1). Berlin and Leipzig, Germany: 1934.

Opitz, H.-G. *Urkunden zur Geschichte des arianischen Streites 318–328* (Athanasius Werke 3.1.2). Berlin and Leipzig, Germany: 1935.

Orgels, P. See H. Grégoire.

Orlandi, T. 'La leggenda di san Mercurio e l'uccisione di Giuliano l'Apostata.' *Studi Copti* 4 (1968): 89–145.

Orlandi, T., and S. Di Giuseppe Camaioni. *Passione e miracoli di S. Mercurio* (Testi e Documenti per lo Studio dell'Antichità 54). Milan: 1976.

Pack, E. *Städte und Steuern in der Politik Julians: Untersuchungen zu den Quellen eines Kaiserbildes* (Collection Latomus 194). Brussels: 1986.

Pagliara, A. *Per la storia della fortuna dell'imperatore Giuliano tra Umanesimo ed età barocca*. Rome: 2010.

Pagliara, A. 'Giuliano Cesare panegirista di Costanzo II.' In A. Marcone (ed.), *L'imperatore Giuliano: Realtà storica e rappresentazione* (Studi sul Mondo Antico 3). Milan: 2015, 87–118.

Palla, R. '*Perfidus ille Deo, quamvis non perfidus orbi.*' In *Giuliano imperatore: Le sue idee, i suoi amici, i suoi avversari* (Atti del Convegno Internazionale di Studi, Lecce 10–12 dicembre 1998). *Rudiae* 10 (1998 [2000]): 359–371.

Papandrea, J. L. *The Trinitarian Theology of Novatian of Rome: A Study in Third-Century Orthodoxy*. Lewiston, NY: 2008.

Papathanassiou, M. 'Astronomie, Astrologie und Physik in der Rede Kaiser Julians auf König Helios.' *Klio* 72 (1990): 498–507.

Parmentier, M. F. G. 'Non-medical Ways of Healing in Eastern Christendom: The Case of St. Dometios.' In A. A. R. Bastiaensen, A. Hilhorst, and C. H. Kneepkens (eds.), *Fructus centesimus: Mélanges offerts à Gerard J. M. Bartelink à l'occasion de son soixante-cinquième anniversaire* (Instrumenta Patristica 19). Steenbrugge, Belgium: 1989, 279–296.

Paschoud, F. *Zosime, Histoire Nouvelle* II.1 *(Livre III)*. Paris: 1979.

Paschoud, F. '"Se non è vero, è ben trovato": Tradition littéraire et verité historique chez Ammien Marcellin.' *Chiron* 19 (1989): 37–54.

Paschoud, F. 'Valentinien travesti, ou: De la malignité d'Ammien.' In J. den Boeft, D. den Hengst, and H. C. Teitler (eds.), *Cognitio Gestorum: The Historiographic Art of Ammianus Marcellinus* (Koninklijke Nederlandse Akademie van Wetenschappen: Verhandelingen, Afd. Letterkunde, Nieuwe Reeks 148). Amsterdam: 1992, 67–84.

Paschoud, F. *Eunape, Olympiodore, Zosime: Scripta Minora. Recueil d'articles, avec addenda, corrigenda, mise à jour et* indices. Bari, Italy: 2006.

Pearce, J. W. E. 'Eugenius and His Eastern Colleagues.' *Numismatic Chronicle* 17, no. 65 (1937): 1–27.

Peeters, P. 'Un miracle de SS. Serge et Théodore et la Vie de S. Basile, dans Fauste de Byzance.' *Analecta Bollandiana* 39 (1921): 65–88.

Peeters, P. 'La date de la fête des SS. Juventin et Maximin.' *Analecta Bollandiana* 42 (1924): 77–82.

Peeters, P. 'S. Dometios le martyr et S. Dometios le médecin.' *Analecta Bollandiana* 57 (1939): 72–104.

Pellizzari, A. 'Testimonianze di un'amicizia: Il carteggio fra Libanio e Giuliano.' In A. Marcone (ed.), *L'imperatore Giuliano: Realtà storica e rappresentazione* (Studi sul Mondo Antico 3). Milan: 2015, 63–86.

Penella, R. J. 'Julian the Persecutor in Fifth-Century Church Historians.' *Ancient World* 24 (1993): 31–43.

Penella, R. J. 'Emperor Julian, the Temple of Jerusalem and the God of the Jews.' *Koinonia* 23 (1999): 15–31.

Penella, R. J. 'Emperor Julian's Gallic Commentary.' *New England Classical Journal* 36 (2009): 253–258.

Pergami, F. *La legislazione di Valentiniano e Valente (364–375)* (Materiali per una Palingenesi delle Costituzioni Tardo-imperiali, Serie Seconda 4). Milan: 1993.

Perrin, M.-Y. 'Costantino e la crisi donatista.' In A. Melloni (ed.), *Costantino I: Enciclopedia Costantiniana sulla figura e l'immagine dell'imperatore del cosidetto editto di Milano, 313–2013*. [Rome]: 2013, I, 275–284.

Peterson, E. *Heis Theos: Epigraphische, formgeschichtliche und religionsgeschichtliche Untersuchungen zur antiken "Ein-Gott"-Akklamationen* (Nachdruck der Ausgabe von Erik Peterson 1926 mit Ergänzungen und Kommentaren von C. Markschies, H. Hildebrandt, B. Nichtweiß et al.; Erik Peterson, Ausgewählte Schriften 8). Würzburg, Germany: 2012.

Petit, P. 'L'empereur Julien vu par le sophiste Libanios.' In R. Braun and J. Richer (eds.), *L'empereur Julien: De l'histoire à la légende (331–1715)*. Paris: 1978, 67–87.

Pfeil, P. 'Der Tod des Julian Apostata: Ein oft besprochenes Rätsel.' In L. Popko, N. Quenouille, and M. Rücker (eds.), *Von Sklaven, Pächtern und Politikern: Beiträge zum Alltag in Ägypten, Griechenland und Rom; Δουλικὰ ἔργα zu Ehren von Reinhold Scholl* (Archiv für Papyrusforschung und verwandte Gebiete, Beiheft 33). Berlin and Boston: 2012, 75–83.

Pfister, F. 'Rauchopfer.' In G. Wissowa, W. Kroll et al. (eds.), *Paulys Real-Encyclopädie der classischen Altertumswissenschaft* 1A. Stuttgart: 1914, 267–286.

Pharr, C. *The Theodosian Code and Novels and the Sirmondian Constitutions: A Translation with Commentary, Glossary, and Bibliography*. New York: 1952.

Philip, K. *Julianus Apostata in der deutschen Literatur* (Stoff- und Motivgeschichte der deutschen Literatur 3). Berlin and Leipzig: 1929.

Piepenbrink, K. *Christliche Identität und Assimilation in der Spätantike: Probleme des Christseins in der Reflexion der Zeitgenossen* (Studien zur Alten Geschichte 3). Frankfurt: 2005.

Piétri, Ch. 'La politique de Constance II: Un premier "césaropapisme" ou l'*imitatio Constantini*?' In A. Dihle (ed.), *L'église et l'empire au IVe siècle* (Fondation Hardt, Entretiens sur l'Antiquité Classique 34). Vandoeuvres and Geneva, Switzerland: 1989, 113–172.

Piétri, Ch. See also J. Flamant.

Pohlsander, H. A. 'Constantia.' *Ancient Society* 24 (1993): 151–167.

Pollmann, K. 'Virtue, Vice, and History in Ammianus Marcellinus' Obituaries on the Emperors Julian and Valentinian I.' In B. R. Suchla (ed.), *Von Homer bis Landino: Beiträge zur Antike und Spätantike sowie deren Rezeptions- und*

Wirkungsgeschichte (Festgabe für Antonie Wlosok zum 80. Geburtstag). Berlin: 2011, 355–384.

Potter, D. S. *Constantine the Emperor.* Oxford: 2013.

Pouchet, R. *Basile le Grand et son univers d'amis d'après sa correspondance: Une stratégie de communion* (Studia Ephemeridis Augustinianum 36). Rome: 1992.

Prato, C., and D. Micalella. *Giuliano Imperatore, Misopogon: Edizione critica, traduzione e commento* (Testi e Commenti 5). Rome: 1979.

Prato, C., J. Fontaine, and A. Marcone. *Giuliano Imperatore. Alla madre degli dei e altri discorsi.* Introduzione di J. Fontaine, testo critico a cura di C. Prato, traduzione e commento di A. Marcone. Vicenza, Italy: 1987.

Prato, C., and D. Micalella. *Giuliano Imperatore, Contro i Cinici ignoranti: Edizione critica, traduzione e commento* (Studi e Testi Latini e Greci 4). Lecce, Italy: 1988.

Pricoco, S. 'L'editto di Giuliano sui maestri (*CTh.* 13, 3, 5).' *Orpheus* N.S. 1 (1980): 348–370.

Prieur, J.-M. 'Aèce selon l' "Histoire ecclésiastique" de Philostorge.' *Revue d'Histoire et de Philosophie Religieuses* 85 (2005): 529–552.

Quiroga Puertas, A. J. 'Julian's *Misopogon* and the Subversion of Rhetoric.' *Antiquité Tardive* 17 (2009): 127–135.

Quiroga Puertas, A. J. 'In Heaven unlike on Earth. Rhetorical Strategies in Julian's *Caesars.*' In A.J. Quiroga Puertas (ed.), *Rhetorical Strategies in Late Antique Literature. Images, Metatexts and Interpretation.* Leiden 2017: 90–103.

Radinger, C. 'Das Geburtsdatum des Kaisers Iulian Apostata.' *Philologus* 50 (1891): 761.

Raggi, A. M. See F. Caraffa and G. D. Gordini.

R. (Radnoti)-Alföldi, M. 'Das *labarum* auf römischen Münzen.' in U. Peter (ed.), *Stefanos nomismatikos: E. Schönert-Geiss zum 65. Geburtstag.* Berlin: 1998 (repr. In M. R. [Radnoti]-Alföldi, *Gloria Romanorum: Schriften zur Spätantike, zum 75. Geburtstag der Verfasserin am 6. Juni 2001,* H. Bellen and H.-M. von Kaenel [eds.] [Historia Einzelschriften 153], Stuttgart: 2001, 270–287).

R. (Radnoti)-Alföldi, M. *Bild und Bildersprache der Römischen Kaiser: Beispiele und Analysen* (Kulturgeschichte der Antiken Welt 81). Mainz, Germany: 1999.

Ramos, P. *La véritable histoire de Julien* (Textes réunis et présentés). Paris: 2012.

Ranke, L. von. *Sämtliche Werke* 33–34. Leipzig, Germany: 1874.

Rapp, C. *Holy Bishops in Late Antiquity: The Nature of Christian Leadership in an Age of Transition* (The Transformation of the Classical Heritage 37). Berkeley: 2005.

Ratti, S. 'Le récit de la bataille de Strasbourg par Ammien Marcellin: Un modèle Livien?' In M. Pivot (ed.), *Regards sur le Monde Antique: Hommages à Guy Sabbah.* Lyon, France: 2002, 257–264 (repr. in S. Ratti, *Antiquus error: Les ultimes feux de la résistance païenne; Scripta varia augmentés de cinq études inédites* [Bibliothèque de l'Antiquité Tardive 14], Turnhout, Belgium: 2010, 167–171).

Rebenich, S., and H.-U. Wiemer (eds.), A Companion to Julian the Apostate (Brill's Companions to the Byzantine World 5), Leiden and Boston 2020.

Rebillard, É. *Religion et sépulture: L'Église, les vivants et les morts dans l'Antiquité tardive* (Civilisations et Sociétés 115). Paris: 2003.

Remus, H. 'The End of "Paganism"?' *Studies in Religion* 33 (2004): 191–208.

Renucci, P. *Les idées politiques et le gouvernement de l'empereur Julien* (Collection Latomus 259). Brussels: 2000.

RIC 7. See P. Bruun.

RIC 8. See J. P. C. Kent.

Richer, J. 'Les romans syriaques (VIᵉ et VIIᵉ siècles).' In R. Braun and J. Richer (eds.), *L'empereur Julien: De l'histoire à la légende (331–1715)*. Paris: 1978, 233–268.

Richer, J., and R. Braun (eds.). *L'empereur Julien: De l'histoire à la légende, II; De la légende au mythe (de Voltaire à nos jours)*. Paris: 1981.

Richer, J. See also R. Braun.

Richter, Th. '26. Juni 363 n. Chr. Zum Todestag des Kaisers Julian.' *Antike Welt* 29 (1998): 261–262.

Richtsteig, E. 'Einige Daten aus dem Leben Kaiser Julians.' *Philologische Wochenschrift* 51 (1931): 428–432.

Ridley, R. T. 'Notes on Julian's Persian Expedition.' *Historia* 22 (1973): 317–330.

Riedweg, Chr. 'Mit Stoa und Platon gegen die Christen: Philosophische Argumentationsstrukturen in Julians *Contra Galilaeos*.' In Th. Fuhrer and M. Erler (eds.), *Zur Rezeption der hellenistischen Philosophie in der Spätantike* (Akten der 1. Tagung der Karl-und-Gertrud-Abel-Stiftung vom 22.–25. September 1997 in Trier: Philosophie der Antike 7). Stuttgart: 1999, 55–81.

Riedweg, Chr. et al., *Kyrill von Alexandrien: Gegen Julian* (vol. 1): *Buch 1–5* (Die Griechischen Christlichen Schriftsteller der ersten Jahrhunderte NF 20). Berlin: 2016; (vol. 2): *Buch 6–10 und Fragmente* (Die Griechischen Christlichen Schriftsteller der ersten Jahrhunderte NF 21). Berlin: 2017.

Rinaldi, G. *La Bibbia dei pagani, I, Quadro storico* (La Bibbia nella Storia 19). Bologna, Italy: 1997.

Rist, J. 'Iohannes Chrysostomos.' *Der Neue Pauly* 5 (1998): 1059–1060.

Rist, J. 'Chrysostomus, Libanius und Kaiser Julian: Überlegungen zu Inhalt und Umfeld der Schrift *De sancto Babyla, contra Iulianum et Gentiles* (CPG 4348).' In *Giovanni Crisostomo: Oriente e Occidente tra IV e V secolo* (XXXIII Incontro di Studiosi dell'Antichità Cristiana, Roma, 6–8 maggio 2004; Studia Ephemeridis Augustinianum 93/2). Rome 2005: 863–882.

Rives, J. B. 'Human Sacrifice among Pagans and Christians.' *Journal of Roman Studies* 85 (1995): 65–85.

Rives, J. B. 'The Decree of Decius and the Religion of Empire.' *Journal of Roman Studies* 89 (1999): 135–154.

Robert, L. *Hellenica. Recueil d'épigraphie, de numismatique et d'antiquités grecques,* IV. *Épigrammes du Bas-Empire.* Paris: 1948.

Rochefort, G. 'Le Περὶ θεῶν καὶ κόσμου de Saloustios et l'influence de l'empereur Julien.' *Revue des Études Grecques* 69 (1956): 50–66.

Rochefort G. 'Les lectures latines de l'empereur Julien.' *Revue des Études Grecques* 75 (1962): xxii-xxiii (cf. *Revue des Études Latines* 40 [1962]: 41–42).

Rochette, B. 'À propos du bilinguisme de l'empereur Julien: Un réexamen.' *Latomus* 69 (2010): 456–478.

Rode, F. *Geschichte der Reaction Kaiser Julians gegen die christliche Kirche.* Jena, Germany: 1877.

Rohmann, D. 'Das Martyrion des Babylas und die polemischen Schriften des Johannes Chrysostomos.' *Vigiliae Christianae* 72 (2018): 206–224.

Rohrbacher, D. *The Historians of Late Antiquity.* London: 2002.

Roig Lanzillotta, L. 'The Early Christians and Human Sacrifice.' In J. N. Bremmer (ed.), *The Strange World of Human Sacrifice* (Studies in the History and Anthropology of Religion 1). Leuven, Belgium: 2007, 81–102.

Rosen, K. 'Beobachtungen zur Erhebung Julians, 360–361 n. Chr.' *Acta Classica* 12 (1969): 121–149 (repr. in R. Klein [ed.], *Julian Apostata* [Wege der Forschung 509]. Darmstadt, Germany: 1978, 409–447).

Rosen, K. 'Kaiser Julian auf dem Weg von Christentum zum Heidentum.' *Jahrbuch für Antike und Christentum* 40 (1997): 126–146.

Rosen, K. 'Julian in Antiochien oder Wie eine Theorie in der Praxis scheitert.' In W. Schuller (ed.), *Politische Theorie und Praxis im Altertum.* Darmstadt, Germany: 1998, 217–230.

Rosen, K. *Julian. Kaiser, Gott und Christenhasser.* Stuttgart: 2006.

Rosen, K. *Konstantin der Große: Kaiser zwischen Machtpolitik und Religion.* Stuttgart: 2013.

Ross, A. J. *Ammianus' Julian: Narrative and Genre in the* Res Gestae (Oxford Classical Monographs). Oxford: 2016.

Rothenhöfer, P., and J. Hollaender. 'Eine Inschrift Kaiser Julians aus der Germania secunda.' *Bonner Jahrbücher* 212 (2012): 153–160.

Rousseau, Ph. *Basil of Caesarea* (The Transformation of the Classical Heritage 20). Berkeley and Los Angeles: 1994.

Royo Martínez, M. del Mar. 'El emperador Juliano II y el programa iconográfico de sus monedas.' *Documenta et Instrumenta* 7 (2009): 161–186.

Ruggeri, A. 'Tradizione e innovazione nell'epigrafia di Giuliano.' *Rivista Storica dell'Antichità* 29 (1999): 313–325.

Sabbah, G. *La méthode d'Ammien Marcellin: Recherches sur la construction du discours historique dans les* Res Gestae (Collection d'Études Anciennes). Paris: 1978.

Sabbah, G. 'Ammien Marcellin 24, 7: L'incendie de la flotte; Histoire et tragédie.' In L. Holtz and J. C. Fredouille (eds.), *De Tertullien aux Mozarabes: Mélanges offerts à Jacques Fontaine à l'occasion de son 70ᵉ anniversaire par ses élèves, amis et collègues*, I. Paris: 1992, 627–642.

Sabbah, G. 'Figures de médecins autour de l'empereur Julien.' In A. Garcea, M.-K. Lhommé, and D. Vallat (eds.), *Polyphonia Romana: Hommages à Frédérique Biville* (Spudasmata 155.2). Hildesheim, Germany: 2013, 689–711.

Saggioro, A. 'Il sacrificio pagano nella reazione al cristianesimo: Giuliano e Macrobio.' In E. Lupieri (ed.), *I cristiani e il sacrificio pagano e biblico* (Annali di Storia dell'Esegesi 19.1). Bologna, Italy: 2002, 237–254.

Saggioro, A. 'Giuliano imperatore e l'*edictum de professoribus*: Integrazione e senso della storia.' In N. Spineto (ed.), *La religione come fattore di integrazione: Modelli di convivenza e di scambio religioso nel mondo antico* (Atti del IV Convegno Internazionale del Gruppo di Ricerca Italo-Spagnolo di Storia delle Religioni, Università degli Studi di Torino, 29–30 settembre 2006; Biblioteca di Studi Storico-Religiosi 2). Alessandria, Italy: 2008, 161–188.

Saintyves, P. 'Les saints céphalophores: Étude de folklore hagiographique.' *Revue de l'Histoire des Religions* 99 (1929): 158–231.

Salama, P. 'Une couronne solaire de l'Empereur Julien.' In *Acta of the Fifth International Congress of Greek and Latin Epigraphy, Cambridge 1967*. Oxford: 1971, 279–286 (repr. in P. Salama, *Promenades d'antiquités africaines: Scripta varia*. Paris: 2005, 191–200).

Saliou, C. 'À propos de la ταυριανὴ πύλη: Remarques sur la localisation présumée de la Grande Église d'Antioche de Syrie.' *Syria* 77 (2000): 217–226.

Saliou, C. 'À Antioche sur l'Oronte, l'église de Constantin entre histoire et mémoire.' *Antiquité Tardive* 22 (2014): 125–136.

Saliou, C. 'Parole et religion à Antioche au IVe siècle: Une approche spatiale.' *Studi e Materiali di Storia delle Religioni* 81 (2015a): 90–104.

Saliou, C. 'Les lieux du polythéisme dans l'espace urbain et le paysage mémoriel d'Antioche-sur-l'Oronte, de Libanios à Malalas (IVᵉ–VIᵉ s.).' In A. Busine (ed.), *Religious Practices and Christianization of the Late Antique City (4th–7th cent.)* (Religions in the Graeco-Roman World 182). Leiden, The Netherlands: 2015b, 38–70.

Salway, B. 'Words and Deeds: Julian in the Epigraphic Record.' In N. Baker-Brian and S. Tougher (eds.), *Emperor and Author: The Writings of Julian the Apostate*. Swansea, UK: 2012, 137–157.

Salzman, M. R. 'Ambrose and the Usurpation of Arbogastes and Eugenius: Reflections on Pagan-Christian Conflict Narratives.' *Journal of Early Christian Studies* 18 (2010): 191–223.

Salzman, M. R. 'The End of Public Sacrifice: Changing Definitions of Sacrifice in Post-Constantinian Rome and Italy.' In J. Wright Knust and Z. Várhelyi (eds.), *Ancient Mediterranean Sacrifice*. Oxford: 2011, 167–184.

Sánchez Vendramini, D. N. 'Sobre una nueva moneda de Juliano y la fecha de su conversón definitiva al paganismo.' *OMNI, Revue Internationale de Numismatique* 7.12 (2013): 121–126.

Sandnes, K. O. 'Christian Baptism as Seen by Outsiders: Julian the Apostate as an Example.' *Vigiliae Christianae* 66 (2012): 503–526.

Sandwell, I. *Religious Identity in Late Antiquity: Greeks, Jews and Christians in Antioch.* Cambridge, UK: 2007.

Sanz, R. 'Julian Apostata in Kleinasien.' *Mitteilungen des Deutschen Archäologischen Instituts (Abteilung Istanbul)* 43 (1993): 455–462.

Saracino, S. 'La politica culturale dell'imperatore Giuliano attraverso il *Cod. Th.* XIII 3, 5 e l'*Ep.* 61.' *Aevum* 76 (2002): 123–141.

Saradi-Mendelovici, H. 'Christian Attitudes toward Pagan Monuments in Late Antiquity and Their Legacy in Later Byzantine Centuries.' *Dumbarton Oaks Papers* 44 (1990): 47–61.

Sardiello, R. 'La raffigurazione di Costantino nei *Cesari* di Giuliano Imperatore (335 B).' *Rudiae* 5 (1993): 137–147.

Sardiello, R. *Giuliano Imperatore, Simposio, i Cesari: Edizione critica, traduzione e commento* (Testi e Studi 12). Galatina, Italy: 2000.

Sargenti, M. 'Aspetti e problemi dell'opera legislativa dell'imperatore Giuliano.' In *Atti dell'Accademia Romanistica Costantiniana* (3° Convegno Internazionale, Perugia-Trevi-Gualdo Tadino, 28 settembre–1° ottobre 1977). Perugia, Italy: 1979, 323–381 (repr. in M. Sargenti, *Studi sul diritto del tardo impero* (Pubblicazioni della Università di Pavia 47). Padua, Italy: 1986, 177–237.

Sartre, M. *Bostra, des origines à l'Islam* (Institut Français d'Archéologie du Proche-Orient, Bibliothèque Archéologique et Historique 117). Paris: 1985.

Sauget, J.-M. 'Eusinio.' In A. Amore et al. (eds.), *Biblioteca Sanctorum* 5. Rome: 1965, 278–279.

Sauget, J.-M. 'Basilio.' In A. Amore et al. (eds.), *Biblioteca Sanctorum* 14, *Prima Appendice*, Rome: 1987, 143.

Schäfer, Chr. (ed.). *Kaiser Julian 'Apostata' und die philosophische Reaktion gegen das Christentum* (Millennium Studies 21). Berlin and New York: 2008.

Schamp, J. 'Thémistios, l'étranger préfet de Julien.' In E. Amato, V. Fauvinet-Ranson, B. Pouderon (eds.), *EN KAΛΟΙΣ KOINOΠPAΓIA: Hommages à la mémoire de Pierre-Louis Malosse et Jean Bouffartigue* (RET Supplement 3; Textes pour l'Histoire de l'Antiquité Tardive). [Nantes, France]: 2014, 421–474.

Schatkin, M.A., C. Blanc, and B. Grillet. *Jean Chrysostome, Discours sur Babylas. Introduction, texte critique, traduction et notes* (SC 362). Paris: 1990.

Scheda, G. 'Die Todesstunde Kaiser Julians.' *Historia* 15 (1966): 380–384 (repr. in R. Klein [ed.], *Julian Apostata* [Wege der Forschung 509]. Darmstadt, Germany: 1978, 381–386).

Schemmel, F. 'Die Schulzeit des Kaisers Julian.' *Philologus* 82 (1927): 455–466.

Schmidt-Hofner, S. 'Trajan und die symbolische Kommunikation bei kaiserlichen Rombesuchen in der Spätantike.' In R. Behrwald and Chr. Witschel (eds.), *Rom in der Spätantike: Historische Erinnerung im städtischen Raum* (Heidelberger Althistorische Beiträge und Epigraphische Studien 51), Stuttgart: 2012, 33–59.

Schmitz, D. 'Schimpfwörter in den Invektiven des Gregor von Nazianz gegen Kaiser Julian.' *Glotta* 71 (1993): 189–202.

Scholl, R. *Historische Beiträge zu den julianischen Reden des Libanios* (Palingenesia 48). Stuttgart: 1994.

Schöllgen, G. 'Pegasios Apostata: Zum Verständnis von "Apostasie" in der 2. Hälfte des 4. Jahrhunderts.' *Jahrbuch für Antike und Christentum* 47 (2004): 58–80.

Schramm, M. *Freundschaft im Neuplatonismus: Politisches Denken und Sozialphilosophie von Plotin bis Kaiser Julian* (Beiträge zur Altertumskunde 319). Berlin: 2013.

Schuller, F., and H. Wolff (eds.). *Konstantin der Große: Kaiser einer Epochenwende* (Vorträge der 'Historische Woche' der Katholischen Akademie in Bayern vom 21. bis 24. Februar in München). Lindenberg, Germany: 2007.

Schwartz, D. L. 'Religious Violence and Eschatology in the Syriac Julian Romance.' *Journal of Early Christian Studies* 19 (2011): 565–587.

Schwartz, J. 'In *Oasin relegare*.' In R. Chevallier (ed.), *Mélanges d'Archéologie et d'Histoire offerts à André Piganiol*, III. Paris: 1966, 1481–1488.

Schwartz, J. See also J. J. Hatt.

Schwartz, S. R. See R. S. Bagnall.

Schwenn, F. *Die Menschenopfer bei den Griechen und Römern*, PhD University of Rostock (Religionsgeschichtliche Versuche und Vorarbeiten 15.3). Gießen: 1915.

Scicolone, S. 'Aspetti della persecuzione giulianea.' *Rivista di Storia della Chiesa in Italia* 33 (1979): 420–434.

Scicolone, S. 'Le accezioni dell'appellativo "Galilei" in Giuliano.' *Aevum* 56 (1982): 71–80.

Scorza Barcellona, F. 'Martiri e confessori dell' età di Giuliano l'Apostata: Dalla storia alla leggenda.' In F. Ela Consolino (ed.), *Pagani e cristiani da Giuliano l'Apostata al Sacco di Roma* (Atti del Convegno Internazionale di Studi, Rende, 12/13 novembre 1993). Soveria Mannelli and Messina, Italy: 1995, 53–83.

Scrofani, G. 'Ὡς ἀρχιερέα: La "chiesa pagana" di Giuliano nel contesto della politica religiosa imperiale di III e IV secolo.' *Studi Classici e Orientali* 51 (2005): 195–215.

Scrofani, G. *La religione impure: La riforma di Giuliano imperatore* (Studi biblici 163). Brescia, Italy: 2010.

Seager, R. 'Perceptions of Eastern Frontier Policy in Ammianus, Libanius, and Julian.' *Classical Quarterly* 47 (1997): 253–268.

Seeck, O. 'Zur Chronologie und Quellenkritik des Ammianus Marcellinus.' *Hermes* 41 (1906): 481–539.

Seeck, O. *Regesten der Kaiser und Päpste für die Jahre 311 bis 476 n. Chr. Vorarbeit zu einer Prosopographie der christlichen Kaiserzeit.* Stuttgart: 1919 (repr. 1964).

Seel, O. 'Die Verbannung des Athanasius durch Julian (Zur Chronologie und Interpretation von Jul. *epist.* 6, 26 und 51).' *Klio* 32 (1939): 175–188.

Selem, A. 'L'atteggiamento storiografico di Ammiano nei confronti di Giuliano dalla proclamazione di Parigi alla morte di Costanzo.' *Athenaeum* 49 (1971): 89–110.

Selem, A. 'Ammiano e la morte di Giuliano (25.3.3–11).' *Rendiconti dell'Istituto Lombardo* (Classe di Lettere, Scienze Morali e Storiche) 107 (1973): 1119–1135.

Selinger, R. *The Mid-Third Century Persecutions of Decius and Valerian.* Frankfurt: 2002.

Sfair, P. 'Bonoso e Massimiliano.' In A. Amore et al. (eds.), *Biblioteca Sanctorum* 3. Rome: 1963, 352–353.

Sguaitamatti, L. *Der spätantike Konsulat* (Paradosis 53). Fribourg, Switzerland: 2012.

Shaw, B.D. *Sacred Violence: African Christians and Sectarian Hatred in the Age of Augustine.* Cambridge, UK: 2011.

Shaw, B. D. 'The Myth of the Neronian Persecution.' *Journal of Roman Studies* 105 (2015): 73-100.

Shepardson, C. *Anti-Judaism and Christian Orthodoxy: Ephrem's Hymns in Fourth-Century Syria* (Patristic Monographs Series 20). Washington, DC: 2008.

Shepardson, C. 'Rewriting Julian's Legacy: John Chrysostom's *On Babylas* and Libanius' *Oration* 24.' *Journal of Late Antiquity* 2 (2009): 99–115.

Shepardson, C. 'Apollo's Charred Remains: Making Meaning in Fourth-Century Antioch.' *Studia Patristica* 62 (2013): 297–302.

Shepardson, C. *Controlling Contested Places: Late Antique Antioch and the Spatial Politics of Religious Controversy.* Berkeley: 2014.

Simmons, M. B. 'Julian the Apostate.' In P. F. Esler (ed.), *The Early Christian World*, II. London: 2000, 1251–1272.

Simmons, M. B. *Universal Salvation in Late Antiquity: Porphyry of Tyre and the Pagan-Christian Debate* (Oxford Studies in Late Antiquity). Oxford and New York: 2015.

Simioni, A. See L. de' Medici (Medici, L. de').

Singor, H. W. 'The *labarum*, Shield Blazons, and Constantine's *caeleste signum*.' In L. de Blois et al. (eds.), *The Representation and Perception of Roman Imperial Power* (Proceedings of the Third Workshop of the International Network Impact of Empire [Roman Empire c. 200 B.C.–A.D. 476] Netherlands Institute in Rome, March 20-23, 2002; Impact of Empire 3). Amsterdam: 2003, 481–500.

Singor, H. W. *Constantijn en de christelijke revolutie in het Romeinse Rijk.* Amsterdam: 2014.

Sinnigen, W. G. 'Two Branches of the Late Roman Secret Service.' *American Journal of Philology* 80 (1959): 238–254.

Sirinelli, J. 'Julien et l'histoire de l'humanité.' In *Mélanges Édouard Delebecque.* Aix-en-Provence, France: 1983, 361–377.

Smith, A. 'Julian's *Hymn to King Helios*: The Economical Use of Complex Neoplatonic Concepts.' In N. Baker-Brian and S. Tougher (eds.), *Emperor and Author: The Writings of Julian the Apostate.* Swansea, UK: 2012, 229–237.

Smith, R. *Julian's Gods: Religion and Philosophy in the Thought and Action of Julian the Apostate.* London and New York: 1995.

Smith, R. 'Telling Tales: Ammianus' Narrative of the Persian Expedition of Julian.' In J. W. Drijvers and E. D. Hunt (eds.), *The Late Roman World and Its Historian. Interpreting Ammianus Marcellinus.* London and New York: 1999, 89–104.

Smith, R. 'The *Caesars* of Julian the Apostate in Translation and Reception, 1580–ca. 1800.' In N. Baker-Brian and S. Tougher (eds.), *Emperor and Author: The Writings of Julian the Apostate.* Swansea, UK: 2012, 281–321.

Smith, R. R. R. 'A Portrait Monument for Julian and Theodosius at Aphrodisias.' In C. Reusser (ed.), *Griechenland in der Kaiserzeit: Neue Funde und Forschungen zu Skulptur, Architektur und Topographie* (Kolloquium zum sechzigsten Geburtstag von Prof. Dietrich Willer, Bern, 12.–13. Juni 1998). Bern, Switzerland: 2001, 125–136.

Soler, E. 'L'utilisation de l'histoire de l'Église d'Antioche au IVᵉ siècle par Jean Chrysostome, dans les débuts de sa predication.' In B. Pouderon and Y.-M. Duval (eds.), *L'historiographie de l'Église des premiers siècles* (Théologie Historique 114). Paris: 2001, 499–509.

Soler, E. ' "Le songe de Julien": Mythes et révélation théurgique au IVᵉ siècle apr. J.-C.' In E. Amato (ed.), *ΕΝ ΚΑΛΟΙΣ ΚΟΙΝΟΠΡΑΓΙΑ: Hommages à la mémoire de Pierre-Louis Malosse et Jean Bouffartigue* (Revue des Études Tardo-antiques [RET], Supplément 3). [Nantes, France]: 2014, 475–496.

Somville, P. 'Portrait physique de l'empereur Julien.' *L'Antiquité Classique* 72 (2003): 161–166.

Speidel, M. P. 'A Spanish Guardsman of Emperor Julian.' *Madrider Mitteilungen/Deutsches Archäologisches Institut, Abteilung Madrid* 38 (1997): 295–299.

Spinelli, M. *Il pagano di Dio: Giuliano l'Apostata l'imperatore maleditto* (Caminantes. Collana di Studi Interreligiosi 6). Ariccia, Italy: 2015.

Stark, R. *The Rise of Christianity: A Sociologist Reconsiders History.* Princeton, NJ: 1996.

Stead, G. C. 'Homousios.' In Th. Klauser et al. (eds.), *Reallexikon für Antike und Christentum* 16. Stuttgart: 1994, 364–433.

Stenger, J. 'Gattungsmischung, Gattungsevokation und Gattungszitat: Julians *Brief an die Athener* als Beispiel.' *Würzburger Jahrbücher für die Altertumswissenschaft* 30 (2006): 153–179.

Stenger, J. *Hellenische Identität in der Spätantike: Pagane Autoren und ihr Unbehagen an der eigenen Zeit* (Untersuchungen zur antiken Literatur und Geschichte 97). Berlin and New York: 2009.

Stertz, S. A. 'Marcus Aurelius as an Ideal Emperor in Late-Antique Thought.' *Classical World* 70 (1977): 433–439.

Stewart, P. 'The Destruction of Statues in Late Antiquity.' In R. Miles (ed.), *Constructing Identities in Late Antiquity.* London: 1999, 159–189.

Stewart, P. 'Continuity and Tradition in Late Antique Perceptions of Portrait Statuary.' In F. Alto Bauer and Chr. Witschel (eds.), *Statuen in der Spätantike* (Spätantike, frühes Christentum, Byzanz, Reihe B, Studien und Perspektiven 23). Wiesbaden, Germany: 2007, 27–42.

Stiernon, D. 'Flaviano.' In A. Amore et al. (eds.), *Biblioteca Sanctorum* 5. Rome: 1965, 880–884.

Stöcklin-Kaldewey, S. *Kaiser Julians Gottesverehrung im Kontext der Spätantike* (Studien und Texte zu Antike und Christentum 86). Tübingen, Germany: 2014.

Straub, J. 'Die Himmelfahrt des Julianus Apostata.' *Gymnasium* 69 (1962): 310–326 (repr. in J. A. Straub, *Regeneratio imperii I. Aufsätze über Roms Kaisertum und Reich im Spiegel der heidnischen und christlichen Publizistik.* Darmstadt, Germany: 1972, 159–177 and in A. Wlosok (ed.), *Römischer Kaiserkult* [Wege der Forschung 372]. Darmstadt, Germany: 1978, 528–550).

Swain, S. (ed.). *Seeing the Face, Seeing the Soul: Polemon's Physiognomy from Classical Antiquity to Medieval Islam.* Oxford: 2007.

Swain, S. *Themistius, Julian, and Greek Political Theory under Rome: Texts, Translations, and Studies of Four Key Works.* Cambridge, UK: 2013.

Szidat, J. 'Zur Ankunft Iulians in Sirmium 361 n. Chr. auf seinem Zug gegen Constantius II.' *Historia* 24 (1975): 375–378.

Szidat, J. *Historischer Kommentar zu Ammianus Marcellinus Buch XX–XXI. Teil I: Die Erhebung Iulians* (Historia Einzelschriften 31). Wiesbaden, Germany: 1977.

Szidat, J. *Historischer Kommentar zu Ammianus Marcellinus Buch XX–XXI. Teil II: Die Verhandlungsphase* (Historia Einzelschriften 38). Wiesbaden, Germany: 1981.

Szidat, J. *Historischer Kommentar zu Ammianus Marcellinus Buch XX–XXI. Teil III: Die Konfrontation* (Historia Einzelschriften 89). Stuttgart: 1996.

Szidat, J. 'Die Usurpation des Eugenius.' *Historia* 28 (1979): 487–508.

Szidat, J. 'Zur Wirkung und Aufnahme der Münzpropaganda (Iul. *Misop.* 355 d).' *Museum Helveticum* 38 (1981): 22–33.

Szidat, J. 'Alexandrum imitatus (Amm. 24,4,27): Die Beziehung Iulians zu Alexander in der Sicht Ammians.' In W. Will and J. Heinrichs (eds.), Festschrift für Gerhard Wirth zum 60. Geburtstag. Amsterdam: 1988, 1023–1035.

Szidat, J. 'Ammian und die historische Realität.' In J. den Boeft, D. den Hengst, and H. C. Teitler (eds.), Cognitio Gestorum: The Historiographic Art of Ammianus Marcellinus (Koninklijke Nederlandse Akademie van Wetenschappen: Verhandelingen, Afd. Letterkunde, Nieuwe Reeks 148). Amsterdam: 1992, 107–116.

Szidat, J. 'Die Usurpation Iulians: Ein Sonderfall?' In F. Paschoud and J. Szidat (eds.), Usurpationen in der Spätantike (Akten des Kolloquiums 'Staatsstreich und Staatlichkeit,' 6.–10. März 1996, Solothurn/Bern; Historia Einzelschriften 111). Stuttgart: 1997, 63–70.

Szidat, J. Usurpator tanti nominis: Kaiser und Usurpator in der Spätantike (337–476 n. Chr.) (Historia Einzelschriften 210). Stuttgart: 2010.

Szidat, J. 'Gaul and the Roman Emperors of the Fourth Century.' In J. Wienand (ed.), Contested Monarchy: Integrating the Roman Empire in the Fourth Century AD. Oxford: 2015, 119–134.

Taisne, A. M. 'Ammien Marcellin, successeur de Tacite dans la description de la mort de Julien (H., XXV, i–v).' In R. Chevallier and R. Poignault (eds.), Présence de Tacite: Hommage au professeur G. Radke. Tours, France: 1992, 243–256.

Tanaseanu-Döbler, I. Konversion zur Philosophie in der Spätantike: Kaiser Julian und Synesios von Kyrene (Potsdamer Altertumswissenschaftliche Beiträge 23). Stuttgart: 2008.

Tanaseanu-Döbler, I. Theurgy in Late Antiquity: The Invention of a Ritual Tradition (Beiträge zur Europäischen Religionsgeschichte 1). Göttingen, Germany: 2013.

Tantillo, I. L'imperatore Giuliano. Rome and Bari, Italy: 2001.

Tantillo, I. 'I costumi epigrafici: Scritture, monumenti, pratiche.' In I. Tantillo and F. Bigi (eds.), Leptis Magna: Una città e le sue iscrizioni in epoca tardoromana (Edizioni dell'Università degli Studi di Cassino: Collana Scientifica 27). Cassino, Italy: 2010, 173–203.

Tedeschi, A. 'Sul divieto di insegnamento per i maestri cristiani (Giuliano, ep. 61c Bidez).' Annali della Facoltà di Lettere e Filosofia della Università di Bari 39 (1996): 17–36.

Teitler, H. C. Notarii and Exceptores: An Inquiry into Role and Significance of Shorthand Writers in the Imperial and Ecclesiastical Bureaucracy of the Roman Empire (from the Early Principate to c. 450 A.D.) (Dutch Monographs on Ancient History and Archaeology 1). Amsterdam: 1985.

Teitler, H. C. 'History and Hagiography: The Passio of Basil of Ancyra as a Historical Source.' Vigiliae Christianae 50 (1996): 73–80.

Teitler, H. C. 'Julian's Death-bed and Literary Convention.' In C. Kroon and D. den Hengst (eds.), Ultima aetas. Time, Tense and Transience in the Ancient World: Studies in Honour of Jan den Boeft. Amsterdam: 2000, 71–81.

Teitler, H. C. 'Raising on a Shield: Origin and Afterlife of a Coronation Ceremony.' *International Journal of the Classical Tradition* 8 (2002): 501–521.

Teitler, H. C. 'Ammianus on Valentinian: Some Observations.' In J. den Boeft, J. W. Drijvers, D. den Hengst, and H. C. Teitler (eds.), *Ammianus after Julian: The Reign of Valentinian and Valens in Books 26–31 of the* Res Gestae (Mnemosyne, Bibliotheca Classica Batava, Monographs on Greek and Roman Language and Literature 289). Leiden, The Netherlands: 2007a, 53–70.

Teitler, H.C. 'Kurzschrift.' In Th. Klauser et al. (eds.), *Reallexikon für Antike und Christentum* 22. Stuttgart 2007b, 518–545.

Teitler, H. C. 'Ammianus, Libanius, Chrysostomus, and the Martyrs of Antioch.' *Vigiliae Christianae* 67 (2013): 263–288.

Teitler, H. C. 'Avenging Julian: Violence against Christians during the Years 361–363.' In A. C. Geljon and R. Roukema (eds.), *Violence in Ancient Christianity: Victims and Perpetrators* (Supplements to Vigiliae Christianae). Leiden, The Netherlands: 2014, 76–89.

Teitler, H. C. See also J. den Boeft.

Teja, R. 'Die römische Provinz Kappadokien in der Prinzipatszeit.' In H. Temporini and W. Haase (eds.), *Aufstieg und Niedergang der Römischen Welt (ANRW: Geschichte und Kultur Roms in der neueren Forschung* 2.7.2). Berlin: 1980, 1083–1124.

Teja, R., and S. Acerbi. 'Una nota sobre San Mercurio el Capadocio y la muerte de Juliano.' *Antiquité Tardive* 17 (2009): 185–190.

Tengström, E. *Donatisten und Katholiken: Soziale, wirtschaftliche und politische Aspekte einer nordafrikanischen Kirchenspaltung.* Stockholm: 1964.

Terrinoni, A. 'L'incendio del tempio di Apollo a Daphne in Ammiano Marcellino: funzione testuale e ascendenze storiografiche di Res Gestae, 22, 13.' *Bollettino di Studi Latini* 48 (2018): 455–470.

Thelamon, F. *Paiens et chrétiens au IVe siècle: L'apport de l' "Histoire ecclesiastique" de Rufin d'Aquilée.* Paris: 1981.

Thelamon, F. 'Échecs et vaines entreprises de Julien par manque de discernement des volontés divines.' In E. Amato (ed.), *ΕΝ ΚΑΛΟΙΣ ΚΟΙΝΟΠΡΑΓΙΑ: Hommages à la mémoire de Pierre-Louis Malosse et Jean Bouffartigue* (Revue des Études Tardo-antiques [RET], Supplément 3). [Nantes, France]: 2014, 525–544.

Thieler, H. 'Der Stier auf den Gross-Kupfermünzen des Julianus Apostata.' *Numismatische Zeitschrift* 27 (1962): 49–54.

Thomas, P. 'La papauté de Julien l'Apostat.' *Annuaire de l'Institut de Philologie et d'Histoire Orientales* 2 (1934): 953.

Thompson, E. A. 'Ammianus' Account of Gallus Caesar.' *American Journal of Philology* 44 (1943): 302–315.

Thompson, E. A. 'The Emperor Julian's Knowledge of Latin.' *Classical Review* 58 (1944): 49–51 ; cf. 'Julian's Knowledge of Latin.' *Classical Review* 64 (1950) 51–53.

Thompson, E. A. *The Historical Work of Ammianus Marcellinus.* Cambridge, UK: 1947 (repr. Groningen, The Netherlands: 1969).

Thornton, T. C. G. 'The Destruction of Idols: Sinful or Meritorious?' *Journal of Theological Studies* 37 (1986): 121–129.

Thümmel, H. G. 'Eusebios' Brief an Kaiserin Konstantia.' *Klio* 66 (1984): 210–222.

Tomlin, R. S. O. 'Christianity and the Late Roman Army.' In S. N. C. Lieu and D. Montserrat (eds.), *Constantine: History, Historiography and Legend.* London: 1998, 21–51.

Torres, J. 'Actitudes de intolerancia político-religiosa: El emperador Juliano y el obispo Juan Crisóstomo en conflicto.' In M. Marcos and R. Teja (eds.), *Tolerancia e intolerancia religiosa en el Mediterráneo antiguo: Temas y problemas* (Bandue 2). Madrid: 2008, 101–121.

Torres, J. 'Emperor Julian and the Veneration of Relics.' *Antiquité Tardive* 17 (2009): 205–214.

Tougher, S. F. 'The Advocacy of an Empress: Julian and Eusebia.' *Ancient World* 48 (1998a): 595–599.

Tougher, S. F. 'In Praise of an Empress: Julian's *Speech of Thanks* to Eusebia.' In Mary Whitby (ed.), *The Propaganda of Power: The Role of Panegyric in Late Antiquity* (Mnemosyne Supplement 183). Leiden, The Netherlands: 1998b, 105–123.

Tougher, S. F. 'Ammianus Marcellinus on the Empress Eusebia: A Split Personality?' *Greece and Rome* 47 (2000): 94–101.

Tougher, S. F. 'Julian's Bull Coinage: Kent Revisited.' *Classical Quarterly* 54 (2004): 327–330.

Tougher, S. F. *Julian the Apostate* (Debates and Documents in Ancient History). Edinburgh: 2007.

Tougher, S. F. 'Reading between the Lines: Julian's *First Panegyric* on Constantius II.' In N. Baker-Brian and S. Tougher (eds.), *Emperor and Author: The Writings of Julian the Apostate.* Swansea, UK: 2012, 19–34.

Traenkle, H. 'Der Caesar Gallus bei Ammian.' *Museum Helveticum* 33 (1976): 162–179.

Trapp, M. 'The Emperor's Shadow: Julian in His Correspondence.' In N. Baker-Brian and S. Tougher (eds.), *Emperor and Author: The Writings of Julian the Apostate.* Swansea, UK: 2012, 105–120.

Treadgold, W. *The Early Byzantine Historians.* New York: 2010.

Trovato, S. *Antieroe dai molti volti: Giuliano l'Apostata nel Medioevo bizantino* (Libri e Biblioteche 34). Udine, Italy: 2014.

Trovato, S. 'Giuliano l'Apostata in Giovanni Antiocheno.' In A. Marcone (ed.), *L'imperatore Giuliano: Realtà storica e rappresentazione* (Studi sul Mondo Antico 3). Milan: 2015, 306–324.

Trovato, S. *"Molti fedeli di Cristo morirono tra terribili pene". Bibliografia agiografica giulianea con edizione della Passio Cyriaci BHG 465b* (Libri e Bibliotheche 40). Udine, Italy: 2018.

Tumanischivili Bandelli, C. 'Sulla usurpazione di Giuliano l'Apostata.' In *Atti del II seminario romanistico Gardesano* (Promosso dall'Istituto Milanese di diritto romano e storia dei diritti antichi, 12–14 giugno 1978). Milan: 1980, 441–465.

Ugenti, V. *Giuliano Imperatore: Alla madre degli dei* (Testi e Studi 6). Galatina, Italy: 1992.

Ugenti, V. 'Julien et la Bible: Lexique et stratégies interprétatives.' In A. Capone (ed.), *Lessico, argomentazioni e strutture retoriche nella polemica di età cristiana (III–V sec.)* (Recherches sur les rhétoriques religieuses 16). Turnhout, Belgium: 2012, 241–251.

Urbainczyk, Th. *Theodoret of Cyrrhus: The Bishop and the Holy Man.* Ann Arbor: 2002.

Valentin, J. See Ch. Bertaux.

Vallejo Girvés, M. '¿Locus Horribilis? El destierro en el Gran Oasis egipcio durante la Antigüedad Tardía.' *L'Africa Romana* 15 (2002): 691–697.

Vallejo Girvés, M. 'Exilios y exiliados a partir de la epigrafía: Un caso peculiar de movilidad geográfica.' In M. Mayer, G. Baratta, and A. Guzmán Almagro (eds.), *XII Congressus Internationalis Epigraphiae Graecae et Latinae: Provinciae Imperii Romani inscriptionibus descriptae* II (Barcelona, 3–8 Septembris 2003; Monografies de la Secció Històrico-Arqueológico 10). Barcelona: 2007, 1477–1482.

Van Dam, R. 'From Paganism to Christianity at Late Antique Gaza.' *Viator* 16 (1985): 1–20.

Van Dam, R. *Kingdom of Snow: Roman Rule and Greek Culture in Cappadocia.* Philadelphia: 2002.

Van Dam, R. *Remembering Constantine at the Milvian Bridge.* Cambridge, UK, and New York: 2011.

Van Dam, R. '"Constantine's Beautiful City": The Symbolic Value of Constantinople.' *Antiquité Tardive* 22 (2014): 83–94.

Vanderspoel, J. *Themistius and the Imperial Court: Oratory, Civic Duty, and Paideia from Constantius to Theodosius.* Ann Arbor: 1995.

Vanderspoel, J. 'Julian and the Mithraic Bull.' *Ancient History Bulletin* 12 (1998): 113–119.

Vanderspoel, J. See also T. D. Barnes.

Van der Vin, J. P. A. 'Het geld van Constantijn.' *Hermeneus* 79 (2007): 89–94.

Van Esbroeck, M. 'Le soi-disant roman de Julien l'Apostat.' In H. J. W. Drijvers et al. (eds.), *IV Symposium Syriacum 1984: Literary Genres in Syriac Literature* (Orientalia Christiana Analecta 229). Rome: 1987, 191–202.

Van Hoof, L., and P. Van Nuffelen. 'Monarchy and Mass Communication: Antioch A.D. 362/3 Revisited.' *Journal of Roman Studies* 101 (2011): 166–184.

Van Hoof, L., and P. Van Nuffelen. ' "No Stories for Old Men": Damophilus of Bithynia and Plutarch in Julian's *Misopogon*.' In A. J. Quiroga Puertas (ed.), *The Purpose of Rhetoric in Late Antiquity: From Performance to Exegesis* (Studien und Texte zu Antike und Christentum 72). Tübingen, Germany: 2013, 209–222.

Van Hoof, L. 'Libanius' *Life* and Life.' In L. Van Hoof (ed.), *Libanius: A Critical Introduction*. Cambridge, UK: 2014, 7–38.

Vannesse, M. 'Ammianus Marcellinus on Julian's Persian Expedition (363 A.D.): A Note on the Supply Chain.' In C. Deroux (ed.), *Studies in Latin Literature and Roman History* XVI (Collection Latomus 338). Brussels: 2012, 639–645.

Van Nuffelen, P. 'Deux fausses lettres de Julien l'Apostat (la lettre aux Juifs, *Ep.* 51 [Wright], et la lettre à Arsacius, *Ep.* 84 [Bidez]).' *Vigiliae Christianae* 56 (2002): 131–150.

Van Nuffelen, P. *Un héritage de paix et de piété: Étude sur les histoires ecclésiastiques de Socrate et de Sozomène* (Orientalia Lovaniensia Analecta 142). Leuven, Belgium: 2004.

Van Nuffelen, P. 'Earthquakes in A.D. 363–368 and the Date of Libanius, *Oratio* 18.' *Classical Quarterly* 56 (2006): 657–661.

Van Nuffelen, P. 'Arius, Athanase et les autres: Dimensions juridiques et politiques du retour d'exil au IVe siècle.' In Ph. Blaudeau (ed.), *Exil et relegation: Les tribulations du sage et du saint durant l'antiquité romaine et chrétienne (Ier–VIe s. ap. J.-C.)* (Actes du colloque organisé par le Centre Jean-Charles Picard, Université de Paris XII-Val de Marne, 17–18 juin 2005). Paris: 2008, 147–175.

Van Nuffelen, P. See also S. Mitchell and L. Van Hoof.

Van Ommeslaeghe, F. 'De Bollandisten en hun bijdrage tot de oud-christelijke studiën van 1838 tot heden.' In A. Hilhorst (ed.), *De heiligenverering in de eerste eeuwen van het Christendom*. Nijmegen, The Netherlands: 1988, 114–129.

Varner, E. R. 'Roman Authority, Imperial Authoriality, and Julian's Artistic Program.' In N. Baker-Brian and S. Tougher (eds.), *Emperor and Author: The Writings of Julian the Apostate*. Swansea, UK: 2012, 183–211.

Vatsend, K. *Die Rede Julians auf Kaiserin Eusebia: Abfassungszeit, Gattungszugehörigkeit, panegyrische Topoi und Vergleiche, Zweck* (Series of Dissertations submitted to the Faculty of Arts, University of Oslo 74). Oslo, Norway: 2000.

Vergote, J. 'Folterwerkzeuge.' In Th. Klauser et al. (eds.), *Reallexikon für Antike und Christentum* 8. Stuttgart: 1972, 112–141.

Verlinde, A. 'The Pessinuntine Sanctuary of the Mother of the Gods in Light of the Excavated Roman Temple: Fact, Fiction and Feasibility.' *Latomus* 74 (2015): 30–72.

Vermaseren, M. J. 'Keizer Julianus en een mensenoffer.' *Hermeneus* 22 (1951): 70–72.

Vermes, M. '[John the Monk], *Artemii passio* (The Ordeal of Artemius, BHG 170–71c, CPG 8082).' In S. N. C. Lieu and D. Montserrat (eds.), *From Constantine to Julian: Pagan and Byzantine Views; A Source History*. London and New York: 1996, 224–256 (with notes by S. N. C. Lieu, 256–262).

Vidal, G. *Julian*. New York: 1964 (repr. 2003).

Vincenti, U. 'La legislazione contra gli apostati data a Concordia nell'anno 391 (*CTh* 16.7.4–5).' *Studia et Documenta Historiae et Iuris* 61 (1995): 399–412.

Vogler, C. *Constance II et l'administration impériale* (Groupe de Recherche d'Histoire Romaine de l'Université des Sciences Humaines de Strasbourg, Études et Travaux 3). Strasbourg, France: 1979.

Vogt, H. J. *Coetus sanctorum: Der Kirchenbegriff des Novatian und die Geschichte seiner Sonderkirche* (Theophaneia: Beiträge zur Religions- und Kirchengeschichte des Altertums 20). Bonn, Germany: 1968.

Vogt, J. *Kaiser Julian und das Judentum: Studien zum Weltanschauungskampf der Spätantike* (Morgenland 30). Leipzig, Germany: 1939.

Vogt, J. 'Kaiser Julian über seinen Oheim Constantin den Grossen.' *Historia* 4 (1955): 339–352 (repr. in R. Klein [ed.], *Julian Apostata* [Wege der Forschung 509]. Darmstadt, Germany: 1978, 222–240) (repr. in K. Christ and F. Taeger (eds.), *Orbis. Ausgewählte Schriften zur Geschichte des Altertums. Zum 65. Geburtstag von Joseph Vogt*. Freiburg, Germany: 1960, 289–304).

Volkoff, O. V. 'Un empereur romain d'Orient bibliophile.' *Les Études Classiques* 48 (1980): 127–139.

Vollmer, D. 'Tetrarchie: Bemerkungen zum Gebrauch eines antiken und modernen Begriffes.' *Hermes* 119 (1991): 435–449.

Volp, U. *Tod und Ritual in den christlichen Gemeinden der Antike* (Supplements to Vigiliae Christianae 65). Leiden, The Netherlands: 2002.

Voltaire [François-Marie Arouet]. 'Julien.' In Voltaire (ed.), *Dictionnaire Philosophique* 5 (Oeuvres complètes de Voltaire 41). Gotha, Germany: 1786, 182–196.

Von Borries, E. See Borries, E. von.

Von Campenhausen, H. See Campenhausen, H. von.

Von Christ, W. See Christ, W. von.

Von Dobschütz, E. See Dobschütz, E. von.

Von Haehling, R. See Haehling, R. von.

Von Ranke, L. See Ranke, L. von.

Vössing, K. 'Bildung und Charakterbildung in Julians Schulgesetzgebung.' In V. Iliescu et al. (eds.), *Graecia, Roma, Barbaricum: In memoriam Vasile Lica.* Galați, Romania: 2014, 329–340.

Wagner, G. *Les Oasis d'Égypte à l'époque grecque, romaine et byzantine d'après les documents grecs (Recherches de papyrologie et d'épigraphie grecques)* (Bibliothèque d'Étude, Institut Français d'Archéologie Orientale 100). Cairo, Egypt: 1987.

Wallace-Hadrill, A. See W. Hamilton.

Wallraff, M. *Der Kirchenhistoriker Sokrates: Untersuchungen zu Geschichtsdarstellung, Methode und Person* (Forschungen zur Kirchen- und Dogmengeschichte 68). Göttingen, Germany: 1997.

Wallraff, M. 'Constantine's Devotion to the Sun after 324.' *Studia Patristica* 34 (2001): 256–269.

Wallraff, M. *Sonnenkönig der Spätantike: Die Religionspolitik Konstantins des Großen.* Freiburg, Germany: 2013.

Ward, B. *The Wisdom of the Desert Fathers: Systematic Sayings from the Anonymous Series of the Apophtegmata Patrum* (Fairacres Publication 48), Oxford: 1995[3].

Watt, J. W. 'Julian's Letter to Themistius—and Themistius' Response?' In N. Baker-Brian and S. Tougher (eds.), *Emperor and Author: The Writings of Julian the Apostate.* Swansea, UK: 2012, 91–103.

Watt, J. W. 'Themistius and Julian: Their Association in Syriac and Arabic Tradition.' In A. J. Quiroga Puertas (ed.), *The Purpose of Rhetoric in Late Antiquity: From Performance to Exegesis* (Studien und Texte zu Antike und Christentum 72). Tübingen, Germany: 2013, 161–176.

Watts, E. J. *City and School in Late Antique Athens and Alexandria* (The Transformation of the Classical Heritage 41). Berkeley and Los Angeles: 2006.

Watts, E. J. 'The Historical Context: The Rhetoric of Suffering in Libanius' *Monodies, Letters* and *Autobiography*.' In L. Van Hoof (ed.), *Libanius: A Critical Introduction.* Cambridge, UK: 2014, 39–58.

Weber, G. *Kaiser, Träume und Visionen in Prinzipat und Spätantike* (Historia Einzelschriften 143). Stuttgart: 2000.

Wedemeyer, H. *Die Religionspolitik des Kaisers Julian: Ein inklusiver Monotheismus in der Spätantike?* PhD University of Bayreuth: 2011 (CD-ROM).

Weis, B. K. *Das Restitutions-Edict Kaiser Julians.* PhD University of Heidelberg. Heidelberg: 1933.

Weiss, P. 'The Vision of Constantine.' *Journal of Roman Archaeology* 16 (2003): 237–259.

Weisweiler, J. 'Unreliable Witness: Failings of the Narrative in Ammianus Marcellinus.' In L. Van Hoof and P. Van Nuffelen (eds.), *Literature and Society in the Fourth Century A.D. Performing Paideia, Constructing the Present, Presenting the Self* (Mnemosyne Supplement 373). Leiden, The Netherlands: 2015, 103–133.

Wessel, S. *Cyril of Alexandria and the Nestorian Controversy: The Making of a Saint and of a Heretic.* New York: 2004.

Westerink, L. G. *Arethae archiepiscopi Caesariensis Scripta minora* (Bibliotheca Scriptorum Graecorum et Romanorum Teubneriana). Berlin: 1968.

Westerink, L. G. 'Marginalia by Arethas in Moscow Greek MS 231.' *Byzantion* 42 (1972): 196–244.

Westerink, L. G. 'The Two Faces of St. Eupsychius.' *Harvard Ukrainian Studies* 7 (1983): 666–679.

Whitby, M. *The Ecclesiastical History of Evagrius Scholasticus* (Translated Texts for Historians 33). Liverpool, UK: 2000.

Whitby, M., and M. Whitby, *Chronicon Paschale 284–628 AD*, translated with notes and introduction (Translated Texts for Historians 7). Liverpool, UK: 1989.

Wieber-Scariot, A. 'Im Zentrum der Macht: Zur Rolle der Kaiserin an spätantiken Kaiserhöfen am Beispiel der Eusebia in den *Res gestae* des Ammianus Marcellinus.' In A. Winterling (ed.), *Comitatus: Beiträge zur Erforschung des spätantiken Kaiserhofes*. Berlin: 1998, 103–131.

Wieber-Scariot, A. *Zwischen Polemik und Panegyrik: Frauen des Kaiserhauses und Herrscherinnen des Osten in den* Res gestae *des Ammianus Marcellinus* (Bochumer Altertumswissenschaftliches Colloquium 41). Trier, Germany: 1999.

Wieber-Scariot, A. 'Eine Kaiserin von Gewicht? Julians Rede auf Eusebia zwischen Geschlechtsspezifik, höfischer Repräsentation und Matronage.' In A. Kolb (ed.), *Herrschaftsstrukturen und Herrschaftspraxis, 2: Augustae; machtbewusste Frauen am römischen Kaiserhof?* (Akten der Tagung in Zürich, 18.–20.9.2008). Berlin: 2010, 253–275.

Wiemer, H.-U. *Libanios und Julian: Studien zum Verhältnis von Rhetorik und Politik im vierten Jahrhundert n. Chr.* (Vestigia, Beiträge zur alten Geschichte 46). Munich: 1995.

Wiemer, H.-U. 'War der 13. Brief des Libanios an den späteren Kaiser Julian gerichtet?' *Rheinisches Museum für Philologie* 139 (1996): 83–95.

Wiemer, H.-U. 'Ein Kaiser verspottet sich selbst: Literarische Form und historische Bedeutung von Kaiser Julians *Misopogon*.' In P. Kneissl and V. Losemann (eds.), *Imperium romanum: Studien zur Geschichte und Rezeption; Festschrift für Karl Christ zum 75. Geburtstag*. Stuttgart: 1998, 733–755.

Wiemer, H.-U. 'Emperors and Empire in Libanius.' In L. Van Hoof (ed.), *Libanius: A Critical Introduction*. Cambridge, UK: 2014, 187–219.

Wienand, J. 'The Law's Avenger. Emperor Julian in Constantinople.' In H. Börm, M. Mattheis, J. Wienand (eds.), *Civil War in Ancient Greece and Rome. Contexts of Disintegration and Reintegration* (Heidelberger Althistorische Beiträge und Epigraphische Studien 58). Stuttgart, Germany: 2016, 347–366.

Wilken, R. L. *John Chrysostom and the Jews: Rhetoric and Reality in the Late 4th Century* (The Transformation of the Classical Heritage 4). Berkeley: 1983.

Williams, D. M. 'A Reassessment of the Early Career and Exile of Hilary of Poitiers.' *Journal of Ecclesiastical History* 42 (1991): 202–217.

Williams, R. *Arius: Heresy and Tradition.* Grand Rapids, MI: 2002.

Wilson, J. F. *Caesarea Philippi: Banias, the Lost City of Pan.* London and New York: 2004.

Wilson, S. G. *Leaving the Fold: Apostates and Defectors in Antiquity.* Minneapolis: 2004.

Winkelmann, F. 'Die Überlieferung der *passio Eusignii* (BHG Nr. 638–640e).' *Philologus* 114 (1970): 276–288.

Winkelmann, F. See also J. Bidez.

Wintjes, J. *Das Leben des Libanius* (Historische Studien der Universität Würzburg 2). Rahden, Germany: 2005.

Wirth, G. 'Alexander und Rom.' In E. Badian (ed.), *Alexandre le Grand: Image et Réalité* (Fondation Hardt, Entretiens sur l'Antiquité Classique 22). Vandoeuvres and Geneva 1976: 181–210.

Wirth, G. 'Julians Perserkrieg. Kriterien einer Katastrophe.' In R. Klein (ed.), *Julian Apostata* (Wege der Forschung 509). Darmstadt, Germany: 1978, 455–507.

Wojaczek, G. 'Die Heliosweihe des Kaisers Julian: Ein initiatorischer Text des Neuplatonismus.' In P. Neukam (ed.), *Neue Perspektiven* (Klassische Sprachen und Literaturen 23). Munich: 1989, 177–212.

Wolff, H. See F. Schuller.

Womersley, D. *Gibbon and the 'Watchmen of the Holy City': The Historian and His Reputation, 1776–1815.* Oxford: 2002.

Woods, D. 'The Date of the Translation of the Relics of SS. Luke and Andrew to Constantinople.' *Vigiliae Christianae* 45 (1991): 286–292.

Woods, D. 'The Martyrdom of the Priest Basil of Ancyra.' *Vigiliae Christianae* 46 (1992a): 31–39.

Woods, D. 'Some Hagiographical Addenda to PLRE.' *Latomus* 51 (1992b): 872–873.

Woods, D. 'Ammianus Marcellinus and the Deaths of Bonosus and Maximilianus.' *Hagiographica* 2 (1995a): 25–55.

Woods, D. 'Julian, Arbogastes, and the *Signa* of the Ioviani and Herculiani.' *Journal of Roman Military Equipment Studies* 6 (1995b): 61–68.

Woods, D. 'A Note Concerning the Early Career of Valentinian I.' *Ancient Society* 26 (1995c): 273–288.

Woods, D. '"On the Standard-Bearers" at Strasbourg: Libanius, *Or.* 18.58–66.' *Mnemosyne* 50 (1997a): 479–480.

Woods, D. 'Ammianus and Some *Tribuni Scholarum Palatinarum* c. A.D. 353–64.' *Classical Quarterly* 47 (1997b): 269–291.

Woods, D. 'Valens, Valentinian I, and the *Ioviani Cornuti*.' In C. Deroux (ed.), *Studies in Latin Literature and Roman History* IX (Collection Latomus 244). Brussels: 1998, 462–486.

Woods, D. 'Julian, Gallienus and the Solar Bull.' *American Journal of Numismatics* 12 (2000): 157–169.

Woods, D. 'Malalas, "Constantius," and a Church-Inscription from Antioch.' *Vigiliae Christianae* 59 (2005): 54–62.

Woods, D. 'On the Alleged Reburial of Julian the Apostate in Constantinople.' *Byzantion* 76 (2006): 364–371.

Woods, D. 'Julian, Arles, and the Eagle.' *Journal of Late Antiquity* 7 (2014): 49–64.

Woods, D. 'Gregory of Nazianzus on the Death of Julian the Apostate (*Or.* 5.13).' *Mnemosyne* 68 (2015): 297–303.

Worp, K. A. See R. S. Bagnall.

Wright, D. F. 'The Baptism(s) of Julian the Apostate.' *Studia Patristica* 39 (2006): 145–150.

Ziegler, R. J. *Julian the Apostate: A Study of His Reputation from the Renaissance to Gibbon.* PhD University of Rochester. Rochester, NY: 1971.

Ziegler, R. J. 'Edward Gibbon and Julian the Apostate.' *Papers on Language and Literature* 10 (1974): 136–149.

Ziemssen, H. See H. Leppin.

Zuckerman, C. See Th. Drew-Bear.

INDEX

Page numbers in italics refer to illustrations.